W9-CLB-249

# Education at War

# Education at War

## THE FIGHT FOR STUDENTS OF COLOR
## IN AMERICA'S PUBLIC SCHOOLS

ARSHAD IMTIAZ ALI
AND TRACY LACHICA BUENAVISTA

*Editors*

FORDHAM UNIVERSITY PRESS

*New York 2018*

Fordham University Press has no responsibility for the
persistence or accuracy of URLs for external or third-party
Internet websites referred to in this publication and does not
guarantee that any content on such websites is, or will
remain, accurate or appropriate.

Fordham University Press also publishes its books in a
variety of electronic formats. Some content that appears in
print may not be available in electronic books.

Visit us online at www.fordhampress.com.

Library of Congress Cataloging-in-Publication Data
available online at https://catalog.loc.gov.

Printed in the United States of America
20 19 18    5 4 3 2 1
First edition

*for Dr. Ather Ali and his beloved family*

# CONTENTS

This project has been a long time coming. We began *Education at War* toward the end of the Obama administration and submitted the book manuscript before the election of President Trump and his subsequent appointment of Education Secretary DeVos, a billionaire with a clear anti–public education agenda. Although the transition from a "postracial" presidential administration to one that has fueled the resurgence of public white supremacist allegiances has in some ways shaped the message of the book, in other ways this transition has had little impact. The latter is due to how we understand the foundation of education to be inherently violent to the communities from which we come. The current political shift makes this point more readily apparent. Admittedly, we both possess a level of pessimism in the ability of state-sanctioned education to address the despair typically imposed onto people who look like us. But we also have hope that our communities can create spaces of learning that seek to guide its members through processes of humanization often absent in schools and universities.

Our lack of faith in state-sponsored education is informed by our complex relationship with education. For coeditor Tracy Lachica Buenavista, American education coupled with militarized violence was *the* tool that achieved social, political, and economic control of the Philippines, a process of colonization that continues to shape the "labor brokering" (Rodriguez 2010) and immigration of Filipinos to the United States and other parts of the globe. And for coeditor Arshad Imtiaz Ali, a British colonial educational and political system in India left a legacy of ethnic and religious conflict, violence, and bifurcation that continues seventy years after the British formally left India. Including and beyond particular national histories in South and Southeast Asia, we have seen the past generation of life in the United States defined by what the government deems both "high-intensity" wars (Afghanistan and Iraq) and seemingly less intensive wars (Somalia, Pakistan, Yemen, among a host of other nations). Such knowledge and experiences fuel many of our frustrating interactions with colleagues who espouse U.S.-centric social justice agendas while simultaneously perpetuating educational solutions that enact war globally. In other words, sometimes social justice projects are grounded in neoliberal agendas that sacrifice Third World peoples for the financial security of U.S. communities of color.

The initial goal of our project was to challenge the political sanitization of Martin Luther King Jr., in order to demonstrate how a reliance on the state to address the deleterious living conditions experienced by communities of color that U.S. policies and practices created historically has been an unreliable strategy for structural transformation. In short, we know that the state would never produce the opportunity for equitable and dignified living conditions for People of Color in the United States, unless forced (for example, through critical social movements). In his antiwar speech "Beyond Vietnam"—which shapes our Introduction and our conceptualization of the book—King puts forth his doubts regarding the government's ability to eliminate the materialism, militarism, and racism that built the nation. This message and King's increasing radicality has typically been overlooked and ignored.

We believe the liberal characterization of King obscures the radical transformation he deemed necessary to uplift communities of color, a phenomenon we see repeated in education. Over the past decade we have often lamented our disconnection and estrangement from education scholars who turned to critical multiculturalism as a goal and solution for educational inequality in the United States. Such work tends to end with the desire for equitable representation and participation in state agendas rather than for a fundamental challenge to the structure of U.S. empire. Often, even critical race theorists in education limit their area of concern to those within the United States, those with citizenship, or those who are "respectable" immigrants and who evoke liberal notions of citizenry. In building a social justice agenda that does not critique U.S. militarism and carcerality, educational activists and scholars deem U.S. life more sanctified than life outside of—and before—the United States. We resist.

In the fall of 2016, the United States elected Donald Trump as president. The election result was a shock to both of us; we believed the project of neoliberal multiculturalism had become nearly hegemonic politically, at least on a national level. This election was instructive. Within weeks we saw President Trump sign executive orders for a "Muslim Ban," to punish sanctuary cities, to build a border wall with Mexico, and to eliminate federal LGBTQI protections—and the list continues to grow. For example, national policy actors have proposed the idea of a Muslim registry despite liberal politicians, grassroots activists, and survivors warning us against the atrocity of Japanese-American internment. Further, in the first six months of her tenure, Education Secretary DeVos has pushed an anti–public education and pro–charter school agenda under the guise of "school choice"; rescinded federal policy documents that outline the rights of students with disabilities, the ability for transgender students to use restrooms in accordance with their gender identity, and how institutions should handle sexual assault cases; and proposed massive cuts to federal student loans and Pell grants for higher education—all which disproportionately impact students of color. The belief that the state was moving toward a neoliberal multicultural agenda has been shattered.

## Our Relationship to Our Work

Trump's directives have emboldened the surveillance, detention, and deportation actions against undocumented immigrants of color, and schools, universities, and the communities in which educational institutions are located have become strategic sites for these policing practices. For example, in Queens, New York, federal immigration officers were denied entry to an elementary school when they attempted to question a fourth-grade immigrant student. In Los Angeles, well-publicized accounts tell of parents being detained as they drop off their children at school. Further, with the 2017 Trump administration's elimination of the Deferred Action for Childhood Arrivals (DACA) program, young people previously protected by the Obama-era executive order are now in fact targeted for deportation. These moments are particularly poignant because they shatter assumptions of educational sites as sanctuaries for students and families.

In an instance close to home, Buenavista was part of an organized effort to prevent U.S. Customs and Border Protection (USCBP) from conducting recruitment activities during two campus career fairs that were scheduled to occur adjacent to the university's resource center for undocumented students. Students, faculty, and staff expressed outrage regarding the idea that an organization committed to the exclusion of undocumented immigrants was not only allowed on campus but also immediately next to a designated safe space. However, university administrators sanctioned USCBP participation, citing potential career opportunities for students and ambiguous policies that prevented them from denying access to any federal agency at public institutions. Further, they called on campus police to serve as USCBP "escorts" in response to faculty inquiries about undocumented student safety.

During the first career fair event, student activists held up signs that read "Don't Recruit Students to Deport Other Students" and "Undocumented and Afraid"; faculty and staff allies declared "Militarization Kills" and "Faculty for Students: Faculty against Deportations." Further, the activists obtained a career fair map that showed that one out of four recruiting organizations were city, county, and federal policing agencies. Student and ally protests were ultimately successful in the early exit of USCBP agents and the cancellation of a second scheduled visit, but their efforts were met with hostility. University representatives questioned student and faculty presence at a campus career fair, and campus police physically shielded armed USCBP recruiters from peaceful protesters, many of whom were undocumented students who understood the potentially serious ramifications of their actions. They, like the majority of their community, were subject to being pushed out and excluded from education and surveilled simply for being.

Similarly, we are in a political moment when just walking with a Muslim body can be read as a threat to domestic safety. Ali is not only a scholar who researches issues related to Muslim youth and communities but is actively a member of, and participant in, these communities. Although he has not faced the same persecution as many of the young people he works with—being arrested, imprisoned, or detained by policing agencies for multiple days—doing teach-ins, workshops, building curricula, and addressing anti-Muslim discrimination now feel as though they are radical acts. Not only are progressive and leftist Muslim activists violently critiqued, but expressing a Muslim makes one a perpetual target of white violence and extremism, given this "domestic front" of the "War on Terror."

As the notion of combating radicalism has become the parlance for discussing Muslim youth and communities, young Muslims are rarely seen as having an existence outside the realm of the political—they cannot be young adults simply trying to understand themselves and define their future. Muslim communities are targeted because of how white supremacy sees Muslims—their fears of Muslim bodies are written on those very young people they survey and spy upon. In reality, Muslim communities are diverse, multiracial, and hold myriad political beliefs. Just like other marginalized communities, Muslim communities maintain elements of anti-Black, anti-immigrant, and other forms of bigotry. Over the course of the 2016 election cycle and the eventual election of Trump, Muslim communities have come together with one another as well as with a broader network of communities of color and targeted communities throughout the United States. Although not all Muslims share the critiques of white supremacy, militarism, and racism, they are for the most part concerned and on some level deeply afraid for their future domestically. In these moments, we hope solidarities can be forged and new modes of organizing and connectedness emerge.

### *Significance of Schools as Both Carceral Spaces and Sites of Resistance*

We detail such moments because they embody the war being waged against students of color. They challenge public discourse regarding the innocence of education and show that schools and universities are carceral spaces in which resistance to dehumanization is deemed punitive practice. The well-being of the most vulnerable students is overlooked in favor of the potential—and not even guaranteed—labor opportunities for their peers. Moreover, the labor opportunities provided to students at institutions that enroll first-generation, low-income students of color frequently involve the surveillance and policing of their community members who have been pipelined out of education.

These examples are indicative of the experiences detailed in this book, which is intended as a call for education and ethnic studies scholars to explore the intersections of our work to help frame and shape a conversation regarding the vestiges of war that shape the lives of youth of color, all of this from the perspectives of education practitioners and scholars who have personal histories with global war via (settler) colonialism, immigration, and subsequent disenfranchisement in the United States. We have curated a collection of essays that centralize a racialized critique of militarism and neoliberalism in education. The authors do this through the examination of antiwar projects across the K–20 education continuum. Further, the chapters are from educators who are from and/or work directly with the communities often pathologized in what Eve Tuck (2009, 409) called "damage-centered" educational discourse, which "document[s] peoples' pain and brokenness to hold those in power accountable for their oppression" while simultaneously treating communities and their members as one-dimensional and without agency. The authors do not just frame the conditions faced by our communities as state mediated but also as collectively resisted. By no means do we intend this project to be exhaustive or define these experiences as the most worthy. Rather, we believe that each chapter provides lessons from particular places while also being instructive to all of us who struggle, live, and love with young people for a radically different future.

Although it is beyond the scope of this Preface to narrate the complex histories of the book's contributors, inherent to their participation was an intention to build a community of scholars committed to a vision of social justice in education that was not grounded in the liberalism and respectability politics that often characterize such work. This project served to provide a figurative and literal space for authors to present ideas we have each been told are not marketable, popular, or significant. In cultivating this text, we hope to have contributed to building a community of educators, activists, teachers, and scholars who work across communities for spaces and places where we, and the young people with whom we work, might exhale a bit more deeply and breathe slightly more free.

We also hope that through our project we can affirm and better facilitate the conversation that needs to be had between educational studies and ethnic studies scholars. Often educational discourse that is community based and action oriented is lauded by educators who remind us that translating research into practice is fundamental in the transformation of society. We agree that attention to such work is warranted but also acknowledge that many of the scholars who conduct this work are trained and/or located in ethnic studies. We are largely influenced by such projects because they represent the ability to conduct research that is simultaneously theoretically, personally, politically, and pedagogically grounded. As education scholars who conduct critical ethnic studies work, we consider our book to be a part of a burgeoning area of scholarship within education and also an explicit example of how the fields of education and ethnic studies directly intersect.

REFERENCES

Rodriguez, R. 2010. *Migrants for export: How the Philippine state brokers labor to the world.* Minneapolis: University of Minnesota Press.
Tuck, E. 2009. Suspending damage: A letter to communities. *Harvard Educational Review* 79 (3): 409–427.

# EDUCATION AT WAR

# Toward an Antiwar Pedagogy: Challenging Materialism, Militarism, and Racism in Education

## *Arshad Imtiaz Ali and Tracy Lachica Buenavista*

> *Our only hope today lies in our ability to recapture the revolutionary spirit and go out into a sometimes hostile world declaring eternal hostility to poverty, racism, and militarism.*
>
> —MARTIN LUTHER KING JR., "Beyond Vietnam"

On April 5, 1968, Dr. Martin Luther King Jr. was assassinated. Before his death, King was increasingly targeted for his radical politics, and a year before his murder, he called for a fundamental shift in the way we understood American politics, delivering the antiwar speech "Beyond Vietnam: A Time to Break Silence" in New York City at the Riverside Church (West and King 2015). At the time, the United States was allied with South Vietnam in a war against North Vietnam and its communist allies, framing its intervention as a mechanism to protect democracy worldwide. With unprecedented film and photographic documentation and coverage by news media, Americans were bombarded with visual images of war's destruction and atrocities, including individuals victimized by napalm bombs, Agent Orange, and other forms of genocidal violence. Widely disseminated images of warfare were coupled with the stories of soldiers who were physically and psychologically wounded as well as of those unable to return. From 1955 to 1975, more than 2.5 million Americans were deployed throughout Southeast Asia—three hundred thousand were wounded, and sixty thousand died (Espiritu 2014, Ybarra 2004). Altogether, Vietnamese and other Southeast Asian military personnel and civilians suffered more than three million deaths. The protracted war campaign, subsequent loss of life, and the fervent antiwar movement in the United States served as the context in which King spoke.

In "Beyond Vietnam," King highlighted the contradictions of the state: While this supposed defense of democracy raged on thousands of miles away, social protests for racial equity, political representation, and an economic livelihood for its most disenfranchised communities spread across the United States. At the time, King's antiwar speech was considered controversial, given his position as a leader in the civil rights movement (McKnight 1998, West and King 2015). His stance against the war directly challenged the same government responsible for the development and implementation of the new civil rights policies that affected so many of his supporters. Although President Lyndon B. Johnson passed important institutional symbols of political progress—the Civil Rights Act (1964) and the Voting Rights Act (1965)—such efforts obscured the material realities that still characterized the daily lives of People of Color. People of Color were systematically excluded from pursuing viable educational and employment opportunities, and their existence was perpetually dehumanized. In combination with the military draft and other forms of institutional racism, social, political, and economic conditions encouraged the enlistment in the military of low-income Americans, many of whom were positioned as fodder for war (Graham 2003, Mariscal 1999, Westheider 1997, Ybarra 2004).

King questioned the American investment in war abroad but simultaneous divestment in the domestic issues that continued to affect People of Color disproportionately. King did not simply offer a critique of the Vietnam War; he problematized the basic morality of American empire, linked the violent assault on bodies of color in the United States to the genocidal intentions of war overseas, and highlighted the mutual relationship of People of Color to what he called the "triplets" of racism, poverty, and militarism globally. He was not the first to make this critique; Malik Shabazz (Malcolm X), among a number of other radical leaders and activists, had advocated an anti-imperialist politics years earlier (Joseph 2007). Nonetheless, King's social and political position as a Nobel Peace Prize winner (1964) and an internationally recognized civil rights leader made his open condemnation of American materialism, racism, and militarism a particularly important moment.

Today, King's critique of American empire lingers as a footnote in comparison to the contemporary depiction of him as the rejuvenator of a great American project (West and King 2015). King's liberal political lessons are often recounted to validate abstract notions of social progress. For example, the election of the first Black American president, Barack Hussein Obama, in 2008 and then again in 2012 is often juxtaposed with King's delivery of his 1963 "I Have a Dream" speech in the nation's capital. Comparing King's speeches, "I Have a Dream" touts a message that takes the nation to task for unfulfilled promises of racial equity; four years later, "Beyond Vietnam" calls for a shift away from imperialist American ideology. The radical message of the latter is considered far less often, despite the persistence of foundational concerns espoused by King and countless other actors for human rights a generation ago. The erasure of King's radicality is further exemplified with his memorialization on the National Mall in Washington, D.C. King's facade sits along with Lincoln and Jefferson and the obelisk dedicated to George Washington. Yet King never held political office and, on the contrary, was deemed a concrete and material threat to domestic security by the FBI, which attempted to "neutralize" and "discredit" him (Garrow 1981; Senate Select Committee 1976, 180). Today, he would be labeled a terrorist. Through the enshrinement and absorption of King into the national consciousness, King's assassination is rewritten as a messianic sacrifice of self for the nation. King is celebrated as a savior of liberal politics locally, nationally, and globally and his character reconstructed from enemy to hero of the state.

King's liberal characterization coincides with the reimagination of the United States as a nation predicated upon social progress. Abstract liberalism, or the idea that individual choice and not structural inequity dictates life outcomes, characterizes American democracy and obscures the dire living conditions to which people are subjected (Bonilla-Silva 2017). Rather, global poverty rates have exponentially increased, social and economic support for the nation's poorest continues to diminish, and the wealth gap between whites and People of Color in the United States continues to increase (Greenstone et al. 2013).

Communities attempting to maintain clean water and protect sacred land in the Dakotas have been attacked with "military-style counterterrorism measures" (Brown 2017). The physical and ideological attack upon NoDAPL activists illuminated the contemporary context of the United States: Any challenges to capital accumulation are responded to by state policing agencies. Similarly, advocating for the seemingly simple goal of recognizing the sanctity of Black life via safety from extrajudicial killings is controversial and considered "radical." Black lives are perpetually dehumanized and disregarded (Dumas and Ross 2016), and mass incarceration remains a mechanism for social control (Alexander 2012, Davis

2003). Black Lives Matter activists are regularly targeted by the surveillance matrix (Joseph 2015).

Hate-group membership and the number of hate crimes have risen,
and communities of color are regularly targeted and victimized culturally, legally, and physically (Southern Poverty Law Center 2015). Immigrant lives are shaped by American carcerality and a homeland security
state (Buenavista 2018, Gonzales 2014). For example, state-sponsored
efforts to build a wall along the U.S.-Mexico border are coupled with
increased funding for the detention and deportation of undocumented
immigrants of color (Miller and Nevins 2017), and fervent anti-Muslim
policies such as the Muslim travel ban and proposed Muslim registry
have transitioned from a perceived impossibility to a frightening reality
(Ali 2017). The United States continues to engage in military invasions for
economic goals, and the growth of the American war project has manifested in the legal justifications for the indefinite imprisonment and murder of citizens and noncitizens without trial, through the utilization of
tools such as drone strikes (Cole 2009). These realities counter the narrative
of progress that is often championed and shapes the context on which this
book is grounded.

## Overview of This Anthology

In *Education at War*, we privilege King's antiwar message from fifty years
ago to frame our understanding of the ways that materialism, militarism,
and racism have not diminished but continue to permeate all facets of American society, particularly within education. We argue that these phenomena constitute a modern-day war: the accumulation of state-sanctioned
policies and actions that heap violence and death onto communities deemed
as threats to U.S. empire. As educators, we understand public education in
the United States as a casualty of war in that the state's divestment in schools,
teachers, and students is directly correlated with the prioritized spending
on national security and defense, or what we consider foreign and domestic policing efforts. Our view is informed by our position as children of
immigrants whose families' labor has been brokered to the United States
and by our direct work with students who are from the communities affected by war and its vestiges. In this context, our position as educators
necessitates a critical analysis of the American culture of war as it shapes
our work—and our ability to carry out our work.

We also find King's analysis useful as critical ethnic studies scholars
who locate ourselves in the field of education. Our work addresses the mili-

tarization of immigration and the simultaneous surveillance and policing of students of color, topics not traditionally tackled in educational discourse. Further, as education is often framed as a civil rights issue and a strategy for the middle-class ascendancy of historically marginalized peoples, we question the assumption of education as a neoliberal tool. Similarly, in *Black Star, Crescent Moon* Sohail Daulatazai (2012) notes that the project of U.S. civil rights intimately relates to the goals of U.S. empire and argues that we are misguided to advocate for domestic civil rights without simultaneously recognizing their global consequences. Aligned with his critique, we assert the need to extend and broaden education discourse to consider better the inextricable link between war, the militarization of education, and mass incarceration and to call attention to the legacy of American imperialism that has long shaped the marginalization of People of Color.

Our concerns are aligned with the work of several scholars who have already noted the ways in which a culture of war is represented through institutional policies and practices within American education (Chatterjee and Maira 2014, Lutz 2006, Nguyen 2016, Saltman and Gabbard 2011). In particular, Kenneth Saltman and David Gabbard (2011) were among the first to address comprehensively the relationship between militarized schooling and the global expansion of markets, and they organized a collection of work that tackled issues such as how corporations shape schooling and education reform, the predatory practice of military recruitment, and the proliferation of programs such as the Junior Reserve Officers Training Corps (JROTC) in K–12 schools. Originally published in 2003, the 2011 edition better considers the social, economic, and political landscape of education in the United States post-9/11 and after the election of President Obama. In both editions, Saltman and Gabbard offer an acute critique of neoliberalism in education.

Such research tends to focus on militarization and education in a domestic context and its deleterious impact on disenfranchised communities. Further, in this work the militarization of education is often examined as an issue of civil rights—an underlying concern is the lack of choice and access to more viable labor opportunities for youth. While we understand the need to examine the material conditions afflicting poor and working communities, these communities are the ones we call our own, and we attempt to reframe educational projects beyond the ability of students to participate as citizens or economic contributors in a system of capitalism, focusing more on disrupting the assumption that education should be used as an economic project of the state. We begin this process of disruption by going beyond equating militarism with war only, and we seek to address explicitly the material vestiges of war that shape the lives of students of color uniquely, including understanding systematic practices of surveillance and incarceration as neocolonial mechanisms of control. We believe that this shift in focus will move us toward an analysis that connects education reform with domestic critiques of white supremacy and war and the global ramifications of state-sanctioned violence, conditions that shape both the presence and experiences of students of color from low-income backgrounds and/or countries.

In what follows, we introduce readers to King's conception of the triplets of materialism, militarism, and racism, which we elucidate by contextualizing King's words within the contemporary moment. We have framed our Introduction in this manner to present each chapter as contributing to our conceptualization of each triplet in research and practice. We envision the potential and possibility of what we call an antiwar pedagogy, a framework informed by the triplets of war and that scholars and practitioners can use to inform their work. We address the question: *How do we develop a pedagogy that is global in perspective yet built upon local contexts and experiences of youth of color in the United States?*

In the last years of King's life, his analysis of American racial violence grew through his engagement with Northern and urban destitution in the United States. He recognized that poverty, urban decay, local violence, and draconian policing were deeply intertwined. He began seeing that the interests of neoliberal economies and governance valued only bodies that were economically productive and that produced capital; both domestically and abroad, poor bodies and bodies of color were useful only in their ability to generate American wealth and disposable when they failed to be "productive." We find King's analytic methods foundational to an antiwar pedagogical project. As educators, we focus not only on the vestiges of war but also on how individuals and communities have developed and enacted an antiwar pedagogy—educational practices and analyses in which spaces of learning are defined and organized to respond to the material and psychological violence of materialism, racism, and militarism.

## The Triplets of War

When machines and computers, profit motives and property rights are considered more important than people, the giant triplets of racism, materialism, and militarism are incapable of being conquered.

MARTIN LUTHER KING JR., "Beyond Vietnam"

Racism, materialism, and militarism—the triplets of war—are not simply assemblages of violence; they are the historic structures that bore and bear the American ontology of war. Thus, in this sense, we understand war to include any process that promotes dehumanization. Ruth Wilson Gilmore (1999, 178) elaborates:

> Indeed, from the genocidal wars against Native Americans to the totalitarian chattel slavery perpetuated in Africans, to colonial expansion, to the obliteration of radical anti-racist and anti-capitalist movements, the annals of U.S. history document a normatively aggressive crisis-driven state. Its modus operandi for solving crises has been the relentless identification, coercive control, and violent elimination of foreign and domestic enemies.

Racist beliefs that indigenous peoples of the Americas were not fully human, the militarism of genocide, and the materialism of empire fueled an expansion that murdered millions. The project of Manifest Destiny, the logic that guided the U.S. invasion of the Philippines in the late 1800s and the Vietnam War, also characterizes the contemporary wars in the Middle East and South Asia. Taken together, we argue that war is the organizing principle of American society. In turn, we ask: How can we understand American education to reflect this organization of war? We believe an analysis based at the intersection of racism, militarism, and materialism will provide a more robust platform to examine the ways young peoples' lives are shaped by the specter of war.

Next, we outline each triplet and discuss the relevance of each to education. We begin with materialism, which we interpret as neoliberalism to set a larger context for the subsequent discussions of militarism and racism. To guide readers through these discussions, we detail the individual chapter contributions. It is important to note that while many authors address more than one triplet in their chapters, we intentionally highlight chapters only once to show how the triplets could manifest in education.

## MATERIALISM

> There is at the outset a very obvious and almost facile connection between the war in Vietnam and the struggle I, and others, have been waging in America. A few years ago there was a shining moment in that struggle. It seemed as if there was a real promise of hope for the poor—both black and white—through the poverty program. There were experiments, hopes, new beginnings. Then came the buildup in

Vietnam, and I watched this program broken and eviscerated, as if it were some idle political plaything of a society gone mad on war, and I knew that America would never invest the necessary funds or energies in rehabilitation of its poor so long as adventures like Vietnam continued to draw men and skills and money like some demonic destructive suction tube. So, I was increasingly compelled to see the war as an enemy of the poor and to attack it as such.

MARTIN LUTHER KING JR., "Beyond Vietnam"

By the spring of 1967, the War on Poverty programs that were intended "not only to relieve the symptom of poverty, but to cure it and, above all, to prevent it" (Johnson 1964) had produced only incremental results, if that. At their inception, these programs—the Economic Opportunity Act (1964), the Food Stamp Act (1964), the Elementary and Secondary School Act (1965), and the Social Security Act (1965)—were seen by optimistic civil rights activists as potential reforms to U.S. social structure in the service of the poor. At their best, these programs provided a small safety net, but they were far from addressing the root causes of U.S. poverty. King realized that these programs would not spark a radical shift in the economic priorities and realities of poor and working people and People of Color in the United States. Furthermore, King promoted an internationalist perspective in order to build a broader understanding of American suffering. King realized that issues of racial violence were intimately tied to the ravages of what he defined as materialism. In the months after this speech, King began to develop the multiracial Poor People's Campaign for antipoverty programs that included housing, employment, and financial support for the millions living below the poverty line (McKnight 1998, West and King 2015).

## Materialism as profit motives and property rights

According to King, materialism encompassed a social world in which "profit motives and property rights are considered more important than people." Although King was deeply critical of communism throughout his life, this critical stance should not be read as a tacit approval of American capitalism. Rather, King's political philosophy might be best summarized in the words of the community activist and philosopher Grace Lee Boggs (2011, 91), who recalled that by 1967 King realized that "we had come to the end of the protest phase of the civil rights revolution and entered into a new phase that requires structural changes in the system to eliminate poverty and unemployment and close the gap between rich and poor in this country and around the world." Although King was assassinated in 1968, before he fully articulated his developing philosophy, Boggs reminds us that his notions of the Beloved Community—one directed by drastically different conceptions of citizenship, politics, work, and life—continue to inform the work of radical activists globally.

King was deeply aware that a society organized around and privileging the expansion of markets over the thriving of human life would produce a society corrupt at its core. "A nation that continues year after year to spend more money on military defense than on programs of social uplift is approaching spiritual death." In "Beyond Vietnam," King recognized that war was most deadly to the poor, for it was the poor who fought and were killed, both as imperialists *and* as those being invaded. Thus, when King used the term "materialism" as one of the triplets to describe American war society, he offered a critique of an economic system that elevated profit motives and global consumption as a priori values above human life. Through such an assertion, King was providing an early analysis of the contemporary neoliberal state. Thus, we operationalize King's notion of materialism through an analysis of neoliberalism.

Neoliberalism is an ideology that opposes stringent government intervention and promotes a free-market economy (Giroux 2014, Harvey 2007). Central to neoliberalism is the belief that government intervention stagnates economic growth, and neoliberal policies are often characterized by a combination of weak government regulation and increased privatization. As such, this system emphasizes individualism, choice, and universalism and downplays structural inequities created and maintained by such a system. King's criticism of the neoliberal state can be seen through his vision of the civil rights movement shifting toward the needs of poor people nationally and globally. While King argued for "a radical redistribution of economic and political power," he also critiqued the structure of capitalism and how monetized social organization increasingly structured human interaction. In today's schools and universities, moreover, we see the most explicit manifestations of King's materialism in the development and implementation of neoliberal policies in contemporary educational contexts.

In "Beyond Vietnam," King urged, "We must rapidly begin the shift from a 'thing-oriented' society to a 'person-oriented' society . . . machines and computers, profit motives and property rights are considered more important than people." Fifty years after King discussed the notion of a "thing-oriented" society, we see that not only does capital accumulation have higher value than human life but also that human life itself is a mediated economic commodity. As Wendy Brown (2015) aptly reminds us, neoliberal educational reforms that have monetized all forms of human interactions are no more apparent than within the K–16 schooling apparatus. The practice of learning is not seen as educational or valuable unless it is economically motivated to produce material outcomes for the expansion of markets.

Neoliberalism and education

Over the past thirty years, neoliberal policies have plagued educational reform in multiple ways, including the decreased government spending on, and the increased privatization of, education (Apple 2001, Au and Ferrare 2015, Lipman 2011). The result: high-stakes schooling, public schools shut down or taken over, a proliferation of charter schools, the dismantling of teachers' unions and the right to organize, and the normalization of corporate partnerships with schools (Buras 2015, Pierce 2013, Stovall 2013). Such conditions have widened the chasm between under-resourced schools and those that are economically affluent, which has made it more difficult for students attending the former to access quality education. We believe that materialism, or neoliberalism, is central to understanding war, empire, and carcerality within a critical race analysis of education. Specifically, in this volume we ask readers to interrogate what we understand to be the purpose of education in the context of the global political economy and how schools serve as sites for consumption and for the preparation of laborers.

We begin the book with Yousef K. Baker's essay "Three Fronts in the Neoliberal Global War: Detroit, Baghdad, and Public Higher Education," in which three case studies of market-driven policies in various geographical contexts lay out the major factors that constitute neoliberal global capitalism. Baker aptly depicts how neoliberalism is not simply an economic policy but serves as an epistemic structuring of the state as primarily a financial entity in which all aspects of human life are mediated in the service of capital. He explains how policies, including those for education reform, often prioritize the economic interests of a transnational capitalist class over popular classes and achieve policy reform via nondemocratic means. The implications include the increasing shift of higher education away from a public site, one meant for the development of students to address the diverse needs of society, to a privatized site intended to train and prepare students to serve the economic needs of the market and become servile political subjects. Baker's ability to connect neoliberalism in various contexts provides readers with a primer on the relevancy of the political economy in shaping and understanding local educational concerns and struggles.

While making the connection between education and neoliberalism is less of a focus among educators, teachers have attempted to better engage their students with larger global issues, albeit through the consumption of uncritical texts. One such example is in the teaching of global citizenship education. In Chapter 2, "Kony 2012 as Citizenship Education: A Grassroots Revolution or a Strategy of Warfare?" Chandni Desai provides an experiential account of the preparation of teachers to facilitate global citizenship education in K–12 classrooms as well as the tensions that arise in the process. American schools and universities increasingly practice global-citizenship education, that is, the use of educational spaces to provide curricular and pedagogical support and resources that prepare students to engage in global issues. Through an antiracist, anti-imperialist, and feminist framework, Desai conducts a discourse analysis of the curricular tools used by teachers to teach about the issue of child soldiers in Uganda and argues that they promote a discourse of development and subsequently animate a pedagogy of war that echoes imperialist and neocolonial discourse. As such, she warns that global-citizenship education has the potential to encompass indoctrination processes that facilitate overly simplistic and deficit-based understandings of complex global issues and support military intervention. She offers educators a practical framework to engage critically in global-citizenship education within the classroom.

## The role of schools in neoliberal discourse

Baker's and Desai's work are informed by the material impact of war abroad, and similarly, in Chapter 3, "Reflections on the Perpetual War: School Closings, Public Housing, Law Enforcement, and the Future of Black Life," David Stovall depicts the materiality of neoliberal warfare on Black communities, lives, and families in the United States. In considering the intersections of race, place, neoliberalism, and empire, educational scholars often use the metaphor of war to discuss the challenges of classroom life. Beyond this figurative language, Stovall provides a powerful narrative that follows his own journey through Woodlawn and the Chicago public schools to argue that the primary politics that structure the lives of Black and Brown communities are containment, elimination, and erasure. "The realities of housing, education, and law enforcement, paired with gun violence, create an instance where these communities have the greatest potential to become collective open-air cages for people to exterminate one another in." In the midst of this, Stovall reminds us that community members and youth in Chicago—and around the country and world— continually envision and act to create a new world that includes them and all of us in its future.

Stovall's examination of neoliberalism's effects on communities of color is further contextualized by Clayton Pierce in Chapter 4, "Caste Education in Neoliberal Society: Branding ADHD and Value-Added Students through the Tactics of 'Population Racism.'" Informed by W. E. B. Du Bois's concept of caste education, Pierce takes a historical-materialist approach to examine the utilization of value-added metrics and psychotropic drugs associated with ADHD as "neoliberal caste tools" to maintain educational disparities within high-stakes and underperforming schools. He contends that current educational-reform initiatives often enact "biopolitical strategies" that simultaneously focus on the control and regulation of marginalized communities, enable capitalist accumulation of wealth among an elite class, and maintain a racial structure of white supremacy in the United States. Pierce offers readers an example of how centering questions around the dialectical relationship between racism and capitalism in education can guide our understanding of the factors that shape the deleterious schooling outcomes for low-income students of color and role of schools in the reproduction of social, political, and economic inequities.

Taken together, the chapter authors encourage us, as educators, to engage in critical discussions of neoliberalism to ground our understanding of local educational concerns and struggles in the context of the global political economy. Through these essays, we see both the violence and erasure of Black lives—and the possibility that radically different futurities are tied to land, space, and place. Although they do not disregard the classroom as a place of change, none of these authors, nor the other authors in this collection, expect radical alternatives to manifest *only* through thinking about classroom life. Our futures within the racist, capitalist, neoliberal state must rely on control of their land, economies, and schools for our self-determination and futures.

With neoliberalism as a contemporary frame to understand King's warning against materialism, it is important to note that we also recognize that King ardently disavowed communism. King argues an intersectional analysis of American empire in this speech, yet he still calls upon the project of American liberalism as his foundation. We differ from King in this regard—we find an important link in building historic and contemporary political and intellectual communities and alliances based upon overlapping and aligned goals. As King discusses materialism, particularly how the manifestation of profit has superseded the value of human lives, his analysis that the poor and People of Color are most devalued in the United States and abroad segues to the precise focus of this anthology.

## MILITARISM

> A true revolution of values will lay hand on the world order and say of war, "This way of settling differences is not just." This business of burning human beings with napalm, of filling our nation's homes with orphans and widows, of injecting poisonous drugs of hate into the veins of peoples normally humane, of sending men home from dark and bloody battlefields physically handicapped and psychologically deranged, cannot be reconciled with wisdom, justice, and love.
> A nation that continues year after year to spend more money on military defense than on programs of social uplift is approaching spiritual death.
> MARTIN LUTHER KING JR., "Beyond Vietnam"

Global war relies heavily on the normalization of militarism—which we understand as the policies and practices that reflect and promote the use of organized state aggression to quell social and political conflict—in the name of national security and economic growth. King warned against American militarism in global practice (for example, the Vietnam War) and its subsequent implications, namely, the funneling of resources to military defense and away from the development and support for domestic social programs. King made his assertions regarding American militarism in 1967, a time during which federal defense spending transitioned from being "periodically expanded" to becoming a *"permanent* warfare apparatus" characteristic of the modern U.S. state (Gilmore 1999, 176). Thus, it makes sense that in the context of the permanency of war that is the United States, militarism and materialism are interconnected phenomena, in that each directly enables the other to grow; state-sanctioned aggressions against indigenous peoples and abroad have been the mechanism for the U.S. accumulation of capital.

Whereas the aggressions of a militaristic U.S. state played out in international arenas such as the Vietnam War, today the consequences of militarism are just as apparent domestically. Although touted as an all-volunteer force, the military is engaged in a "poverty draft" that targets People of Color from low-income backgrounds (Ledesma 2017, Mariscal 2007). In the United States, we are subject to a militarized police state in which police officers receive international training in warfare tactics to address social dissent, police entities serve as beneficiaries of a military weapons surplus, and military technology is used to surveil and criminalize residents (Amar 2010). Further, militarization shapes education and is pervasively represented by the recruitment and support of formerly enlisted officers to pursue second careers as public school teachers, ubiquitous military recruiters and federal and local policies that grant open access to schools and school children, and militarized curriculums that include the nationwide implementation of Junior Reserve Officer Training Corps for students to fulfill physical education and other academic requirements (Saltman and Gabbard 2011). These examples highlight the way in which militarism organizes educational sites.

Often schools are organized to normalize a militarized police state and serve as secondary locations for police personnel. In K–12 education, police are stationed as "educational resource officers" whose supposed intent is to protect students and school staff from outside disturbances. Instead, teachers and administrators more often rely on these resource officers to control truancy, discipline students perceived as disruptive, and apprehend students engaged in criminalized behavior (for example, drug use). Schools enlist "zero-tolerance policies," which teach young people that schools are not sites to learn how to be adults in a democratic society but rather sites of punishment for socially constructed infractions (Galaviz, Palafox, Meiners, and Quinn 2011; Lipman 2004). In exploring militarism in education, we call on educators to pay attention to the intimate relationship between education and social control, in both domestic and global contexts.

Militarization of education

The militarization of education and the dearth of education spending are inherently coupled. For example, in the past decade, funding for and research on science, technology, engineering, and mathematics (STEM) education has pervaded educational discourse. The neoliberal context that facilitates the defunding and privatization of education coincides with the swelling war budget and economy, which in turn has led to phenomena such as diversity and equity work advancing STEM-related agendas that have a high potential to benefit materially from military-sponsored funding. While much of the concern surrounds access to STEM education and enhanced career opportunities for students of color, such diversity and STEM work is devoid of any historical analysis that links the STEM agenda to the production of war technologies.

Chapter 5 warns educators of the ahistoricism that often characterizes diversity and STEM work. In "Toward What Ends? A Critical Analysis of Militarism, Equity, and STEM Education," Shirin Vossoughi and Sepehr Vakil place diversity and STEM research in dialogue with the historical and contemporary relationship of STEM to corporate and military interests. In particular, they ask educators to interrogate the implications of not knowing or considering the human costs associated with the STEM curriculum, which is historically grounded in the building of American empire, particularly via militarized violence. Vossoughi and Vakil's research inspires educators to think about how providing material opportunities for students of color often has ramifications for communities of color who are targeted domestically and globally in the name of national security.

Similarly, the convergence of militarism and neoliberal diversity initiatives in education serves as the foundation of enhanced military presence within schools. The normalization of militarism within K–12 education is captured by Suzie Abajian in Chapter 6, "A Day at the Fair: Marketing Militarism to Students of Color in Elementary Schools." Abajian presents an interpretive account of a career fair held at an elementary school located in Los Angeles, California. In this case study, military recruiters have expanded their presence beyond high schools, colleges, and universities to elementary and middle schools. Specifically, Abajian draws on ethnographic data to depict how instructional and schooling practices promote the military and characterize military participation as viable career options for a student body primarily composed of low-income students of color. Her work reveals the intimate access that military recruiters have to young students of color and K–12 public schools, the early exposure of students to military culture, and the reality of schools as militarized spaces.

Heather L. Horsley further examines the pervasiveness of militarism in education in Chapter 7, "The Paradoxical Implications of Developing Youth in a Chicago Public Military Academy." Through a qualitative study of the Chicago Public Military Academy (PMA), Horsley analyzes the militarization of education through the implementation of military-themed public schools in low-income urban areas of the city. Touted as a tool to increase educational opportunities for some of the city's most vulnerable youth, students articulate how these schools helped them develop meaningful relationships with teachers and peers as well as feel a strong sense of belonging, trust, autonomy, and initiative. At the same time, however, students were unable to understand such notions outside of a militarized context, and embedded in the culture of Chicago PMA was the lesson that military service is a contingency plan to higher education.

To complement the chapters that show how militarism plagues American education, we also focus on community-based efforts against militarized schools and for self-determination. In Chapter 8, "Raza Communities Organizing against a Culture of War: Lessons from the Education Not Arms Coalition (ENAC) Campaign," Miguel Zavala continues the examination of schools as sites of intensified militarization. Grounding his analysis in the context of disparate high-school graduation rates for Latinx students, Zavala explores the role of schools in facilitating the military recruitment of Latinx students and the justification of racialized targeting as a military strategy to address enlistment gaps. Beyond documenting the heavy militarization of schools, Zavala focuses on a grassroots counter-recruitment movement, the Education Not Arms Coalition (ENAC), which took place in San Diego, California, a historic U.S. military space. Among the ENAC demands were the elimination of weapons training on school sites, parental consent prior to JROTC enrollment, and disclosure to parents when JROTC courses did not fulfill college admissions requirements. Drawing from ethnographic observations and interviews with ENAC participants, Zavala explains the relationship between the neoliberal privatization of schools and the increased reliance on military-sponsored curriculums and resources by underserved schools and communities. Furthermore, he also offers a detailed case study of community-based, antimilitary efforts within a school context.

What these essays demonstrate—as well as what this book as a whole attempts to show—is that the context of militarism has profoundly shaped the ability of schools to sustain themselves in light of neoliberal divestment from social programs and services, in this case, public education. Like King, the chapter authors allude to the misguided business of war, critique the state's funneling of resources to defense spending, and warn of divestment's potential impact on humanity. Beyond the portrayal of the diverse ways that militarism infiltrates American education, the authors also echo King's sentiment that an ideological shift from a reliance on structural violence as a solution to social, political, and economic issues constitutes revolution. As such, we hope that educators are able specifically to address macro and micro manifestations of militarism in the educational lives of youth of color with whom they work as well as recognize and engage the ever-present neoliberal and racial realities in schools.

## Racism

> Perhaps the more tragic recognition of reality took place when it
> became clear to me that the war was doing more than devastating the
> hopes of the poor at home. It was sending their sons and their brothers
> and their husbands to fight and to die in extraordinarily high propor-
> tions relative to the rest of the population. We were taking the black
> young men who had been crippled by our society and sending them
> eight thousand miles away to guarantee liberties in Southeast Asia
> which they had not found in southwest Georgia and East Harlem.
>
> MARTIN LUTHER KING JR., "Beyond Vietnam"

In 1967, when King delivered this speech, there was no clear end in sight to
the Vietnam War. The federal government's war on poverty showed few
signs of addressing the central problems of economic and racial violence,
oppression, and structural inequities. Coupled with scarce economic opportunities for the poor and People of Color, U.S. military conscription accounted for the overrepresentation of disenfranchised people in the U.S.
armed forces. The pattern of People of Color positioned as war fodder was
an explicit example used by King to highlight racism in the United States
during the Vietnam War. Racism can generally be understood as the
actions, attitudes, and institutional policies and practices that subordinate People of Color and simultaneously maintain white hegemony, or the
material and ideological advantages exclusive to those racialized as white
(Omi and Winant 2014). American racism is distinctly anti-Black and in a
global context is symptomatic of colonialism (Dumas 2016, Silva 2007). For
example, while Black Americans and other People of Color were deployed
to—and died—in Vietnam at rates disproportionate to their white counterparts, their social positions as devalued bodies in the United States is what
precisely pipelined them into the military (Foner 1999). Thus, racism is
not merely an abstraction regarding racial superiority of one group over
another but is a central tenet of white supremacy that materialized in higher
mortality rates for Blacks and other People of Color in the service of U.S.
empire.

King's critique of racism in "Beyond Vietnam" diverges from the position of many contemporary U.S. civil rights leaders. Fundamentally, he
shifts his analysis from a domestic racial perspective to one of global
racism:

> We are called to speak for the weak, for the voiceless, for the victims
> of our nation and for those it calls "enemy," for no document from
> human hands can make these humans any less our brothers.

King's shift was not simply a rhetorical maneuver; he recognized that the plight of poor and Black Americans was intertwined with the conditions of People of Color and the poor globally. Freedom was not a national goal held within the bounds of the U.S. political entity. Rather, King begins to synthesize an analysis of U.S. foreign and domestic policy as two sides of the same coin. As a testament to his developing internationalist position, King stated that the U.S. invasion of Vietnam was due to Western— namely American—racism, which viewed the Vietnamese as "not ready for democracy."

Returning to King's discussion of the overrepresentation of soldiers of color in the U.S. military, this phenomenon cannot be divorced from the lack of educational and economic opportunities that have plagued communities of color since the inception of the United States. King delivered this speech, moreover, just thirteen years after the U.S. Supreme Court's *Brown v. Board of Education* decision, which made de jure segregation illegal. Yet by 1967, only a small portion of the nation's schools had been formally "desegregated." Now, more than fifty years later, educational researchers have found that public schools are more intensely segregated than they were at the time of the *Brown* decision (Orfield and Lee 2004). Beyond formal school segregation, multiple generations of education scholars have now provided uncontestable evidence about the unequal educational resources in poor communities and communities of color (Darling-Hammond 2010, Lucas 1999, Oakes 2008, Wells et al. 2005). Likewise, scholars have contributed overwhelming evidence of the ways that American schooling isolates, targets, and erases the lives, histories, and experiences of students of color in terms of epistemology, social structures, and culture (Calderón 2014, Spring 2012). Before or after *Brown*, U.S. public education has never been designed to provide equal educational and economic opportunities for all residents of the United States. In short, schooling continues to be a white supremacist project.

Racism in schooling

While critiques of neoliberalism often fail to recognize the differentiated manifestations of capital on racialized bodies in the United States, we explore how the dialectical relationship between racism and capitalism in education guides our understanding of the factors that shape the adverse schooling outcomes for low-income students of color and the role of schools in the reproduction of social, political, and economic inequities. For example, scholars have provided compelling evidence that depicts how the prison-industrial complex shapes the educational experiences of students of color and facilitates the school-to-prison pipeline (Noguera 2003, Nolan 2011). The prison-industrial complex reflects the relationship between government and private interests that rely on the proliferation of U.S. prisons for the accumulation of capital, under the false pretenses of domestic safety and prisoner rehabilitation. This disproportionately targets People of Color (Davis 2003, Gilmore 2007). In particular, researchers have discussed the direct and indirect ways that students of color are overdisciplined in schools, which often result in tracking students into the prison system (Skiba, Nardo, and Peterson 2002; Winn 2011).

Characteristic of the prison-industrial complex is the normalization of punishment and incarceration even beyond carceral sites. Expanding on the carcerality and education discourse, in Chapter 9, "Schools as Carceral Sites: A Unidirectional War against Girls of Color," Connie Wun argues that schools are not only starting points in the school-to-prison pipeline but that they are in and of themselves complex spaces that enact the surveillance, criminalization, and punishment of students of color. An in-depth analysis of ethnographic data at a school in northern California led Wun to outline how young Black girls and other girls of color are subjected to a pattern of referrals, suspensions, and arrests within school sites and how such discipline practices represent what she deems a "unidirectional war" on gendered bodies of color. Wun's research shows the school-sanctioned assault on students of color and in doing so calls for educators to reconsider how we engage with young people, the function of schools, and the carceral character that undergirds our schooling system.

The idea of schools at carceral sites can be historically contextualized through the examination of moments during which education was explicitly used to commit state-sanctioned violence against students. In Chapter 10, "Pedagogies of Resistance: Filipina/o 'Gestures of Rebellion' against the Inheritance of American Schooling," Allyson Tintiangco-Cubales and Edward R. Curammeng bring to light the central way that American curricular and schooling practices were mechanisms for control in the Philippines and explain how the educational disparities plaguing Filipino students in the United States represent contemporary vestiges of American colonialism. In addition to exposing readers to an underexamined historical phenomenon, Tintiangco-Cubales and Curammeng offer a case study of Pin@y Educational Partnerships (PEP), a San Francisco–based ethnic studies education program that pipelines U.S. Filipino students and other students of color into education and other social service careers. Through PEP, they specifically demonstrate the tenets of what they call "pedagogies of resistance": the ways that educators, students, and community members engage in exercises that promote self-determination via education.

Similar to Tintiangco-Cubales and Curammeng, Maryam Griffin addresses the colonial realities for many young People of Color in the United States and on the periphery of the U.S. empire. In Chapter 11, "Of Boxes and Pen: Forged and Forging Racial Categories at a Wartime U.S. University," Griffin captures the complexity of a student activist movement to change the ways that Southwest Asians and North Africans (SWANA) are racially categorized by the University of California. She highlights the contours of naming and claiming one's identity in the context of war as she demonstrates how students engaged in a creative challenge to, and intervention in, the U.S. racial regime. By closely examining a college student political campaign, Griffin demonstrates how students exposed the fiction of racial naturalism as a forgery and worked to correct its errors by intervening in the process of social construction. Griffin shows us how SWANA students challenged racist nativism as they were aware of, and explicitly highlighted, the global nature of the domestic U.S. racial regime. She provides an important lesson for educators regarding student activism and the ways that wartime provides a unique lens to deconstruct complex processes of racialization.

Processes of racialization reflect the multiple forms of violence whites employ to maintain their social, political, and economic positions. This is none the more apparent among communities whose existence in the United States is defined by colonialism. In Chapter 12, "War and Occupation," Dolores Calderón offers a first-person, embodied account of a life marked by the violence of the U.S.-Mexico border and the impact of occupation on indigenous education. Calderón traces how the colonial occupation of indigenous land and bodies is ongoing. Occupation is not history but rather an active and enacted project—an "open wound"—that does not heal. Calderón discusses settler identity as continually enacted not only ideologically but with material signs and actions in the world, including waving the flag of U.S. slavery and through the daily violence not at, but of, the U.S.-Mexico border. Throughout this landed examination of race, Calderón explicates how the particularities of colonialities inscribe and enact violence, and she calls on educators to consider how such a position affects the lives of students of (and not on) the border.

We want to make the point that there are diverse ways that racism shapes education and several mechanisms of racialized social control. As students are differently racialized, they also experience racism differently. Further, we include chapters that offer a glimpse of how political and geographical tensions can nuance how racism operates. In doing so, we believe King's message regarding the intersection between domestic and global struggles for People of Color becomes more apparent. King was clear about the need to recognize the contradictions between racially oppressed Americans not only bearing the burden of a war agenda overseas but the subsequent figurative and literal loss of life they suffered as a result. However, beyond highlighting the contemporary relevance of King's critique of the racialized violence directed at young people, we focus on racism in education to offer pedagogical examples of how students do not simply accept the narratives written onto their bodies.

## Toward an Antiwar Pedagogy

> A true revolution of values will soon look uneasily on the glaring contrast of poverty and wealth. With righteous indignation, it will look across the seas and see individual capitalists of the West investing huge sums of money in Asia, Africa, and South America, only to take the profits out with no concern for the social betterment of the countries, and say, "This is not just." It will look at our alliance with the landed gentry of South America and say, "This is not just." The Western arrogance of feeling that it has everything to teach others and nothing to learn from them is not just.
>
> MARTIN LUTHER KING JR., "Beyond Vietnam"

In an era of post–Cold War transnational capitalism, post-9/11 militarism, and postracial racism, we draw from the work of King to propose a clear articulation of the intersections of materialism, militarism, and racism with education. We contend that the contemporary specter of war is a central way that King's triplets manifest in education. The chapters of this book explore how educators can embrace a revolution of ideas that considers the relationship between education and war and how they can explicitly enact a critique of war in their research and practice. Education is situated within the global political economy that has facilitated exponential growth in the prison- and military-industrial complex and simultaneous divestment in schools, teachers, and students within the United States. Ultimately, such phenomena unevenly and detrimentally affect students of color. In response, we draw upon and explicate King's triplets of war as a protointersectional analysis as one way to imagine a pedagogy that places human life, and not capital accumulation, at its center.

## FIRSTHAND PERSPECTIVES AND EXPERIENTIAL KNOWLEDGE

Our reading of King is informed by our roles as educators, specifically as scholars of color whose presence in the United States is constantly questioned despite directly resulting from American imperialism abroad. As both of us are children of global economic and political displacement, our lives and identities never existed simply as hyphenated Americans. Rather, we both grew up in homes and communities where migration was not a phenomenon to be studied but part of the fabric of our daily lives. Extended family members and play cousins were often in transit, searching for a home across oceans. Conversations about global politics were not about what was happening *over there* but rather localized through understanding what family and community members were experiencing. Far from being relegated to scholarly debates, displacement, structural adjustment programs, and low-intensity warfare were materialized in migration stories and newly arriving (or departing) family members. Learning politics in this context was not developed through scholarly passion or a collegiate opening but instead at the center of everyday conversations. Consequently, our experiential knowledge raises the question: How can we envision a pedagogy in which the lives and histories not only of U.S. communities of color but marginalized communities globally are valued as fully human? By drawing direct connections among the seemingly disparate areas of race, class, militarism, and schooling, our engagement with King informs our antiwar approach to teaching, learning, and educational scholarship.

Throughout this book we offer analysis of multiple manifestations of war in the lives of youth of color in the United States. In this Introduction, we attempt to frame these conversations as a pedagogical example of what we call an antiwar pedagogy—a way of teaching and learning that responds to the gross violence of neoliberalism, militarism, and racism in American society and schools. An antiwar pedagogy links global projects of U.S. imperialism and capitalism with domestic projects of racialized policing in and out of schools, the defunding of education, and the elimination of local jobs. War is not a metaphor. Rather, war is the salient material context from which U.S. empire enacts violence and dehumanization on bodies of color, domestically and abroad.

## THE BELOVED COMMUNITY: AN UNFINISHED PROJECT

We draw upon King's notion of the Beloved Community to imagine an antiwar pedagogy that places human life, not capital accumulation, at its center. King described the Beloved Community as a society that is not geographically bound and in which poverty, militarism, and racism do not mediate people's lives but that is global and in which all humans engage with one another as though they are sisters and brothers. Grace Lee Boggs (2011, 51) describes such a community:

> Our challenge, as we enter the third millennium, is to deepen the commonalities and the bonds between these tens of millions, while at the same time continuing to address the issues within our local communities by two-sided struggles that not only say "No" to the existing power structure but also empower our constituencies to embrace the power within each of us to create the world anew.

Beyond a critique of the contemporary United States, the strength of King's radical shift was his unfinished work of envisioning a Beloved Community. This vision of engaging in local action while still recognizing a broader global context has been taken up in formal and informal ways by educators, activists, youth workers, parents, and young people—some of whom explicitly draw on King's words and others who have never heard his name.

King's idea of a Beloved Community helps us envision an antiwar pedagogy that places the pillars of neoliberalism, militarism, and racism as the center of analysis of American society in order to build locally a network of support that acknowledges and acts against oppression. In other words, our social analysis must be embedded within local knowledge production and in the context of teaching and learning in the lives of the young and elderly. An antiwar pedagogy recognizes the relationship among psychic and material violence, micro and macro racism, and the global and intersectional nature of the triplets. We frame this text around King's speech because King viewed neoliberalism as orienting society toward capital over humans; in turn, militarism oriented society toward taking the things it wanted in the service of neoliberalism. Likewise, while being the targets of overseas wars, People of Color were the fodder in wars of capital accumulation. Thus, the intersections King pointed toward were not relegated to the individual experiences of people. Rather, his protointersectionality exemplified an analysis of systemic violence that left poor and communities of color under-resourced, starting a mile-long race from a mile behind. Kimberlé Crenshaw (1991) has referred to this inequality as a "structural intersectionality" at micro and macro levels, spanning the slight acts of individual racism that we refer to today as microaggressions, the use of slurs and physical intimidation against individuals, unequal housing, and uneven schooling and financial practices.

## Structural Intersectionality and Education in the United States

In many ways, King's conceptualization of the triplets mirrors the contemporary concept of intersectionality (Crenshaw 1993), but we do not contend that his ideas were nascent iterations of the theory. Although much scholarship in educational studies has taken up representational intersectionality (Crenshaw 1993), that is, how stereotypes and narratives of particular forms of oppression mediate a student's experience in and out of school, structural intersectionality must be central in an analysis of education's function in the United States. As opposed to focusing on representational intersectionality primarily to address personal experiences of race, gender, class, sexuality, religion, and ability (among forms of social otherness), which has the potential to further inscribe neoliberal multiculturalist epistemologies by erasing structural power relations, a structural analysis provides the means to understand how multiple forms of oppression and power function to oppress individuals and communities.

Although we do not see intersectionality and an antiwar pedagogy as synonymous, they are complementary. While drawing upon a structural analysis of U.S. law, the project of intersectionality does not develop out of a Third World context of warfare. An antiwar pedagogy utilizes a structural intersectional analysis of the triplets of neoliberalism, militarism, and racism in order to address the epistemology of war that dictates the education of U.S. youth of color. In the most clear sense, we are not interested in a pedagogical project that advocates for, or works toward, a multicultural U.S. empire and war machine. At its core, an antiwar pedagogy is antiempire. We see an unthinkable and unrecoverable violence in pedagogical projects built upon the U.S. exceptionalist ideology that values U.S. life more than the lives of people throughout the world.

We take this moment to remember Dr. King's radical life, fifty years after it was cut short, and have curated a collection of remarkable essays reflecting on the context of war for youth of color. Indeed, this is not a unique moment in this nation. The United States has enacted an unending international war on "terrorism" this century; last century, it was a war on "communism." Both wars resulted in millions of deaths of the world's poor. Domestically, the United States has waged a continual and unending war on native peoples and on enslaved Africans and their descendants. The United States has continually been in a state of war since its establishment; it has dropped bombs on more than thirty nations since the end of World War II (Chomsky 2004). For poor communities and communities of color in the United States, we have always been in a state of crisis. Today is no different. Our hope and our work are for a tomorrow that will be. We find it apropos to end with the words of a radical Dr. King:

> These are the times for real choices and not false ones. We are at the moment when our lives must be placed on the line if our nation is to survive its own folly. Every man of humane convictions must decide on the protest that best suits his convictions, but we must all protest.

## REFERENCES

Alexander, M. 2012. *The new Jim Crow: Mass incarceration in the age of colorblindness.* New York: The New Press.

Ali, A. 2017. The impossibility of Muslim citizenship. *Diaspora, Indigenous, and Minority Education.* doi:10.1080/15595692.2017.1325355.

Amar, P. 2010. New racial missions of policing: Comparative studies of state authority, urban governance, and security technology in the twenty-first century. *Ethnic and Racial Studies* 33 (4): 575–592.

Apple, M. W. 2001. *Educating the "right" way: Markets, standards, god, and inequality.* New York: RoutledgeFalmer.

Au, W., and J. J. Ferrare. 2015. *Mapping corporate education reform: Power and policy networks in the neoliberal state.* New York: Routledge.

Boggs, G. L. 2011. *The next American revolution: Sustainable activism for the twenty-first century.* Berkeley: University of California Press.

Bonilla-Silva, E. 2017. *Racism without racists: Color-blind racism and the persistence of racial inequality in America.* 5th ed. Lanham, Md.: Rowman & Littlefield.

Brown, A. 2017. Leaked documents reveal counterterrorism tactics used at Standing Rock to "defeat pipeline insurgencies." *The Intercept*, May 27. https://theintercept.com/2017/05/27/leaked-documents-reveal-security-firms-counterterrorism-tactics-at-standing-rock-to-defeat-pipeline-insurgencies/

Brown, W. 2015. *Undoing the demos: Neoliberalism's stealth revolution.* New York: Zone.

Buenavista, T. L. 2018. Model (undocumented) minorities and "illegal" immigrants: Centering Asian Americans and U.S. carcerality in undocumented student discourse. *Race, Ethnicity, and Education*, 21 (1): 78–91. doi:10.1080/13613324.2016.1248823.

Buras, K. L. 2015. *Charter schools, race, and urban space: Where the market meets grassroots resistance.* New York: Routledge.

Calderón, D. 2014. Uncovering settler grammars in curriculum. *Educational Studies* 50 (4): 313–338.

Chatterjee, P., and S. Maira. 2014. *The imperial university: Academic repression and scholarly dissent.* Minneapolis: University of Minnesota Press.

Chomsky, N. 2004. *Hegemony or survival: America's quest for global dominance.*
New York: Holt.

Cole, D. 2009. *Torture memos: Rationalizing the unthinkable.* New York: The
New Press.

Crenshaw, K. 1993. Mapping the margins: Intersectionality, identity
politics, and the violence against women of color. *Stanford Law Review*
43:1241–1299.

Darling-Hammond, L. 2010. *The flat world and education: How America's
commitment to equity will determine our future.* New York: Teachers
College Press.

Daulatzai, S. 2012. *Black star, crescent moon: The Muslim international and Black
freedom beyond America.* Minneapolis: University of Minnesota Press.

Davis, A. Y. 2003. *Are prisons obsolete?* New York: Seven Stories.

Dumas, M. J. 2016. Against the dark: Antiblackness in educational policy
and discourse. *Theory into Practice* 55 (1): 11–19.

Dumas, M. J., and k. m. ross. 2016. "Be real Black for me": Imagining
BlackCrit in education. *Urban Education* 51 (4): 415–442.

Espiritu, Y. L. 2014. *Body counts: The Vietnam War and militarized refuge(es).*
Oakland: University of California Press.

Foner, E. 1999. *The story of American freedom.* New York: Norton.

Galaviz, B., J. Palafox, E. R. Meiners, and T. Quinn. 2011. The militarization and the privatization of public schools. *Berkeley Review of Education* 2
(1): 27–45.

Garrow, D. 1981. *The FBI and Martin Luther King Jr.: From "solo" to Mem-
phis.* New York: Norton.

Gilmore, R. W. 1999. Globalisation and U.S. prison growth: From military
Keynesianism to post-Keynesian militarism. *Race & Class* 40 (2–3): 171–188.

———. 2007. *Golden gulag: Prisons, surplus, crisis, and opposition in globalizing
California.* Berkeley: University of California Press.

Giroux, H. A. 2014. *Neoliberalism's war on higher education.* Chicago:
Haymarket.

Gonzales, A. 2014. *Reform without justice: Latino migrant politics and the
homeland security state.* New York: Oxford University Press.

Graham, H. 2003. *The brothers' Vietnam War: Black power, manhood, and the
military experience.* Gainesville: University of Florida Press.

Harvey, D. 2007. *A brief history of neoliberalism.* New York: Oxford University
Press.

Johnson, L. B. 1964. State of the Union address. January 8. http://www.lbjlib
.utexas.edu/johnson/archives.hom/speeches.hom/640108.asp.

Joseph, G. 2015. Feds regularly monitored Black Lives Matter since Ferguson.
*The Intercept,* July 24. https://theintercept.com/2015/07/24/documents

-show-department-homeland-security-monitoring-black-lives-matter
-since-ferguson/.

Joseph, P. 2007. *Waiting 'til the midnight hour: A narrative history of Black power in America.* New York: Holt.

Ledesma, M. C. 2017. Leadership as mission critical: Latina/os, the military, and affirmative action in higher education. *Journal of Hispanic Education* 16 (2): 123–143.

Leonardo, Z. 2007. The war on schools: NCLB, nation creation, and the educational construction of whiteness. *Race, Ethnicity, and Education* 10 (3): 261–278.

Lipman, P. 2004. Education accountability and the repression of democracy post-9/11. *Journal for Critical Education Policy Studies* 2 (1).

———. 2011. *The new political economy of urban education: Neoliberalism, race, and the right to the city.* New York: Routledge.

Lucas, S. 1999. *Tracking inequality: Stratification and mobility in American high schools.* New York: Teachers College Press.

Lutz, C. 2006. Making war at home in the United States: Militarization and the current crisis. In *The anthropology of the state,* ed. A. Sharma and A. Gupta, 291–309. Malden, Mass.: Wiley-Blackwell.

Mariscal, G. 1999. *Aztlan and Viet Nam: Chicano and Chicana experiences of the war.* Berkeley: University of California Press.

Mariscal, J. 2007. The poverty draft: Do military recruiters disproportionately target communities of color and the poor? *Sojourners* 36 (6): 32–35.

McKnight, G. D. 1998. *The last crusade: Martin Luther King Jr., the FBI, and the Poor People's Campaign.* Boulder, Colo.: Westview.

Miller, T., and J. Nevins. 2017. Beyond Trump's big, beautiful wall. *NACLA Report on the Americas* 49 (2): 145–151. doi:10.1080/10714839.2017.1331805.

Nguyen, N. 2016. *A curriculum of fear: Homeland security in U.S. public schools.* Minneapolis: Minnesota University Press.

Noguera, P. A. 2003. Schools, prisons, and social implications of punishment: Rethinking disciplinary practices. *Theory into Practice* 42 (4): 341–350.

Nolan, K. 2011. *Police in the hallways: Discipline in an urban high school.* Minneapolis: Minnesota University Press.

Oakes, J. 2008. Keeping track: Structuring equality and inequality in an era of accountability. *Teachers College Record* 110 (3): 700–712.

Omi, M., and H. Winant. 2014. *Racial formation in the United States: From the 1960s to the 1990s.* 3rd ed. New York: Routledge.

Orfield, G., and C. Lee. "Brown" at 50: King's dream or "Plessy's" nightmare? http://files.eric.ed.gov/fulltext/ED489168.pdf.

Pierce, C. 2013. *Education in the age of biocapitalism: Optimizing educational life for a flat world.* New York: Palgrave Macmillan.

Saltman, K. J., and D. A. Gabbard, eds. 2011. *Education as enforcement: The militarization and corporatization of schools*. New York: Routledge.

Senate Select Committee. 1976. *Book III: Supplementary detailed staff reports*. 94th Cong., 2d sess., S. Rep. 94-755.

Silva, D. F. 2007. *Towards a global idea of race*. Minneapolis: Minnesota University Press.

Skiba, R., R. S. Michael, A. C. Nardo, and R. Peterson. 2002. The color of discipline: Sources of racial and gender disproportionality in school punishment. *Urban Review* 34:317–342.

Southern Poverty Law Center. 2015. Hate map. https://www.splcenter.org/hate-map.

Spring, J. 2012. *Deculturalization and the struggle for equality: A brief history of the education of dominated cultures in the United States*. Columbus, Ohio: McGraw-Hill.

Stovall, D. 2013. Against the politics of desperation: Educational justice, critical race theory, and Chicago school reform. *Journal of Critical Education Studies* 54 (1): 33–43.

Wells, A. S., J. J. Holme, A. J. Revilla, and A. K. Atanda. 2005. How society failed school desegregation policy: Looking past the schools to understand them. *Review of Research in Education* 28:47–100.

West, C., and M. L. King Jr. 2015. *The radical King*. Boston: Beacon.

Westheider, J. E. 1997. *Fighting on two fronts: African Americans and the Vietnam War*. New York: New York University Press.

Winn, M. T. 2011. *Girl time: Literacy, justice, and the school-to-prison pipeline*. New York: Teachers College Press.

Ybarra, L. 2004. *Vietnam veteranos: Chicanos recall the war*. Austin: University of Texas Press.

# Three Fronts in the Neoliberal Global War: Detroit, Baghdad, and Public Higher Education

*Yousef K. Baker*

War in the twenty-first century is not an exceptional state. It is built into everyday profit extraction and political control. In this war, geography has stopped being a barrier that separates or distinguishes. The effects of today's war are never far. What goes on "over there" is part of the same structure operating "over here." We see the same processes that have transformed Baghdad and Detroit working within the U.S. educational system. Like the rest of the public realm, education is being enclosed and forced to become a space where money can be extracted. After years of defunding and divestment, low educational performances are blamed on the very idea of public education (Newfield 2016, 3–7). Policy makers urge a business solution, one of efficiency, cost cutting, and bottom lines (Newfield 2016, 20–24). Using the catchphrases of "more with less," "data-driven strategies," and "student outcomes," quality education is reduced to numbers on a spreadsheet and sold as accountability. All the while, the purpose of education is redefined as a way to channel people into the workforce. After all, within neoliberal global capitalism, we are all just servants of this thing called the market (Brown 2015, 30–35). The educational system trains us to serve that all-encompassing purpose.

Today, with few exceptions, the entire world is governed by and integrated within one type of economic system—capitalism. Capitalist economic relations have also come to dictate social relations and much of international politics (Robinson 2006). Today's capitalism is a specific type of capitalism, different from previous iterations such as competitive capitalism, monopoly capitalism, or welfare capitalism (Magdoff 1982). This new form of capitalism, what I refer to as neoliberal global capitalism, emerged in the 1970s and is now the dominant political economic paradigm.

Neoliberal global capitalism is conditioned by war. Just as a parasite's relationship to its host is predicated on constant struggle, so does the dialectic of capitalism and the masses of people under it. But as capitalism tries always to extend its exploitation, the exploited resist. This friction erupts in wars of many kinds, undertaken to impose endless extractions of resources and to repress any resistance thereto. In other words, Baghdad and Detroit are both battlefronts. So is the higher education system in California. While in some fronts the weapons are guns, tanks, and jets, in others they are drones and separation walls, in others they are police and SWAT teams, and yet in other places they are banks, ATMs, and utility bills. While the mechanism of suppression and the degree of brutality vary, do not let that get you twisted. Regardless of the tactics, the strategies are analogous, with the same goals implemented by similar actors.[1]

My purpose here is to describe some of this war's main features and to provide some signposts that we can use to identify its effects throughout our lives. Through a discussion of events in Baghdad, Detroit, and the higher education system in California, I highlight four features of neoliberal global capitalism. The first is the prioritization of the interests, needs, and desires of global investors, the transnational capitalist class (TCC), over popular classes (Robinson 2004, Sklair 2001).[2] Second, this prioritization occurs through undemocratic means, albeit with legal cover. Third, these undemocratic means are institutionalized through a separation of the political from the economic. Fourth, these measures continually push for the elimination of the final remnants of the public realm and force it under the power of the market. I will then demonstrate how these characteristics of "over there" are playing out in the seemingly mundane higher education policies in California, that is, "over here."

## What Is Neoliberal Global Capitalism?

The period between 1960 and 1980 inaugurated a reorganization of the global economy. This reorganization was partially an attempt to strike a blow against what by the late 1960s and early 1970s was arguably a global insurgency, an "international intifada" (Midnight Notes Collective 1992, viii) simultaneously brewing across the world. This was an intifada waged by colonized people across the world, by the "Muslim Third World" (Daulatzai 2012), Black radicals in the United States, leftist guerillas in the Americas, native peoples in settler-colonial societies, and exiled peoples across the planet. Vijay Prashad (2007) named the upsurge of these movements across the world the "Third World Project," a movement demanding sovereignty, self-determination, peace, and a rebalancing of the colonial global economy. This project sent shock waves throughout the colonial capitals. Henry Kissinger famously threatened Third World leaders in 1976: "The United States, better than almost any other nation, could survive a period of economic warfare" (Gelvin 2012, 201).

In response, a brutal political, economic, cultural, and military campaign followed, one that relegated Third World demands to dreams and resulted in the emergence of neoliberal global capitalism. From an economic viewpoint, this new epoch is defined by a transnationalization of production and the emergence of an integrated transnational global economy, spearheaded by the maturation in certain places and emergence in others of transnationally oriented elite formations, the transnational capitalist class (Robinson 2004, Sklair 2001).

Transnationalization of production refers to assembly lines—previously contained within a nation-state's borders—going global. New economic practices emerged: Products are now made all over the world, with component parts produced in different places; shipped across continents to assembly plants; and sold everywhere (Dicken 2007). Companies extended beyond the confines of the nation-state and gave rise to the transnational corporation (TNC).[3]

Neoliberalism modified the rules of the game. Capitalism structured by neoliberal logic subverts the state and its citizens to the needs of the market. The goal is to have a marketplace with no boundaries, spanning the entire world (Strange 1996, 3–8; Robinson 2014, 77–82). Neoliberalism rejects the idea of collective rights and holds that the state's only responsibility is to individual citizens, ensuring their personal rights and guaranteeing their right to enter the market to fulfill their needs there. A neoliberal state's primary function is to protect the market, guarantee property rights, and be the investor of first and last resort (Gill 1998, 23–24; Robinson 2004, 30–37). Within a neoliberal logic, the market is understood as operating like nature, with its own rhythms and whims that must not be meddled with. Hence government aid to poor people is seen as creating "artificial" demand because in "reality" poor people should not generate any demand, since they do not have access to money.[4]

Neoliberalism stands in contrast to embedded liberalism, or what is popularly known as New Deal economics (Krugman 2008), which governed U.S. policy from after the Second World War up to the 1970s. This policy promoted free trade globally but internally pursued Keynesian economic policies such as full employment, social welfare programs, and industrial expansion (Harvey 2005, 10–12; Ruggie 1982). Neoliberalism, on the other hand, sees such safety nets as unwelcome interventions into the market and consequently tries to eliminate the public realm and transfer all of social life to private enterprise. Privatization commodifies social relations that were not open to profit-making mechanisms, a process we have witnessed in education: More and more of the educational pipeline has become a business where someone makes money in return for providing some sort of schooling (Giroux 2014, 12–20; Hursh 2016, 3, 8–12). Perhaps most shocking is the privatization of things never previously considered commodities, including air and water. Cap-and-trade policies, a favorite of liberals in mainstream American politics, are examples of this (Adler 2000, Anderson and Leal 2015, Anderson and Libecap 2014).

Perhaps the most powerful ideological feature of neoliberalism is how those of us living under it internalize its rationality. Neoliberal ideology has turned business and economic relations into a metaphor for how we see ourselves and how we ought to live our lives. The protagonist of this era is the entrepreneur; his are the qualities to emulate.[5] If our normative vision of the world is one where all aspects of life, including the social and familial, are to be subsumed and subordinated to the market, then it follows that the qualities deemed virtuous are those of the capitalists—the principal actors in the marketplace. And who is an entrepreneur but a budding capitalist, the quintessential bootstrapper? Neoliberalism as a metaphor tells us to live our everyday lives with nothing but the profit motive as our guide (Brown 2011, 23–24).

So far, what I have described is still an abstraction. What does the war state of neoliberal global capitalism actually look like on the ground?

### Baghdad

Bombing Baghdad seems to have become a rite of passage for American administrations since Ronald Reagan. The 2003 invasion that began with "shock and awe" was outrageous in its ability to eclipse in its horror and magnitude the severity of the 1991 American bombings, which according to the United Nations sent Iraq to a "pre-industrial age" (Boutros-Ghali and the United Nations 1996, 187). The 2003 invasion leveled Iraq's institutions and infrastructure once again,[6] rolling out the red carpet for neoliberalism.

Neoliberalism was imposed on Iraq and codified in law by the signature of one man appointed in Washington, D.C., Lewis Paul Bremer III, appointed by President Bush as the head of the Coalition Provisional Authority (CPA) from May 2003 to June 2004. The CPA put in place laws and agreements with international financial and governing institutions that legally opened Iraq to transnational businesses without prejudice and without favoring businesses from countries that had actually led the invasion. Since most of these laws that relate to the economy remain in place today, perhaps Bremer will be remembered as the most consequential ruler of Iraq after Saddam Hussein. Indeed, for all the noise around "democracy promotion," a foreigner hired in the United States and with no connection to Iraq or its people signed Iraq's new state into law.

## Legislating Neoliberalism

Through Orders 18, 56, and 94, the CPA legislated an open and deregulated financial market by decreeing a set of banking laws and the establishment of a new Central Bank of Iraq (CBI). The CBI law repeatedly asserted the independence of the CBI from "any person or entity, including government entities" (Article 2.2 of Order 56, 2004).

Order 18 gave the CBI the right not to inform the Ministry of Finance— or any other government entity—of loans it was giving out or of its broader activities (Order 18, 2003). Although the rationale given was that economic institutions needed to be buffered from political ambitions and interference in order to make sound decisions, in practice this separation masked the class interests that determine economic policies. The law also gave the bank the power to "conduct transactions in foreign assets and manage all official foreign reserves of the state" (Article 27 of Order 56, 2004). Since decision making over state reserves was given to the CBI, the bank could make decisions of great political consequence with no accountability to the political branches of the state, elected authorities, or the public. This could potentially allow pivotal governmental functions to remain strictly in the hands of a technocratic cadre ideologically allied with the TCC. This would enable them to control the very policies important to them without regard to social consequences.

This strategy of making economic institutions autonomous from political ones fundamentally shifts who the sovereign is away from the citizenry and toward the mobile investor or the TCC. It prioritizes one global class of people over local popular classes. Since those who make the decisions are not subject to elections or public scrutiny, it constrains popular movements from being able to seek redress or implement change economically. Moreover, this structural organization advances neoliberalism's ideological position that the economy is not a terrain of political struggle but instead an objective science to be managed by experts in the field.

## NEOLIBERALISM UNDER THE GUISE OF DEVELOPMENT

Neoliberalism under the guise of "development" was used to transform Iraq's economy. "Development" programs operated to promote neoliberalism. These policies deployed the language of "transparency," institutional "best practices," "rights," "modern standards," "competition," and others to give the illusion of impartiality and mask their ideological allegiances (Brown 2015, 135–142).

Neoliberalism masquerading as "development" can be seen in the inclusion of neoliberal governance in laws. Here the Iraqi constitution is instructive. The American occupation implemented a transitional constitution until a permanent constitution was written. The American administration heavily interfered in the writing of the permanent constitution (Iman 2005, Morrow, 2005), which can be tracked by comparing earlier published drafts.[7] In this transition you see a shift from a state providing for the collective needs of the citizenry to a state that only guarantees the rights of citizens to have those needs met. This shift from collective rights to individual rights is part of the neoliberal ideology, which holds individuals as the paramount actors in society.

In the early drafts of the Iraqi constitution, the state was responsible for providing work for everyone or wages for those without work or those who are not able-bodied. In the permanent constitution, however, the state guarantees the right of people to work and regulates capital-labor relations (Article 22 of June 30 draft of Iraq's constitution). The same shift occurs in the language regarding education and health care. In the early draft, the state is tasked with "fighting illiteracy" and providing "citizens with the right of free education" (Article 6 of the June 30 draft of Iraq's constitution). The state was also responsible for providing health care. The permanent constitution, however, absolves the state of these responsibilities: Education becomes a "right guaranteed by the state" (Article 34 of the permanent constitution of Iraq), and health care is a "right" for every Iraqi. In all these cases, the state merely is a guarantor of rights to different services, not the provider of those services. The services become potential arenas for private sector profit making.

In Iraq, neoliberalism was imposed from the top down, from D.C. to Baghdad and onto the rest of Iraq. Military invasion and war were the crucial catalysts for complete economic restructuring. From bombs to pens, the U.S. war on Iraq obliterated the public realm and converted it into a field of unprecedented profit-making possibilities. Macroeconomic decision making was separated from political accountability in relatively autonomous governmental institutions. New cadres of politicians, bureaucrats, and civil society leaders were trained in neoliberal ideology. The goal was to open Iraq to global investors, to the TCC. Their needs, above those of other classes, were of the utmost importance.

## *Detroit*

Burned structures, abandoned homes, boarded-up buildings, broken windows, deserted lots, and dilapidated infrastructure are common scenes on the streets of Detroit. The similarities with Baghdad are eerie, and although Detroit was not bombed like Baghdad, it was victimized by a different kind of war. Detroit was a major metropolis and a standard bearer of American industry. It was the hub of the American automobile industry and the site where Henry Ford's River Rouge plant revolutionized the assembly line. But that is all just part of the American nostalgia for a rosy past. Nostalgia becomes the gimmick upon which "revitalization" projects are built, in the hopes of bringing in money (Barrionuevo 2016), while many others are dispossessed (Sheehan 2015). Today, Detroit is an example of the devastation of neoliberal global capitalism even in the world's richest country. It is the place where water is being shut off to residents and where the United Nations is being called in because no local, regional, or federal authorities seem to care. How did Detroit get here?

One of the defining features of neoliberal global capitalism is the transnationalization of production; that is, manufacturers move around the world looking for cheap wages, lax labor and environmental laws, and government incentives (otherwise known as handouts, if the recipients were ordinary people). As a result, industrialized countries saw manufacturing plants close down and relocate, in what became known as the process of deindustrialization. Cities known for their industrial production—for example, Detroit in the United States and Manchester in England—faded from their respective national scenes. New York and London, housing the financial industry and accounting, legal, and PR businesses servicing large transnational corporations, became the emblematic cities of this new economy (Sassen 2001).

## DEINDUSTRIALIZATION AND SUBURBANIZATION

Neoliberal global capitalism sped up deindustrialization in Detroit, a process that had begun in the 1940s and 1950s. In the 1940s, the United Auto Workers received guarantees for increased wages and benefits from automakers by relinquishing to the companies the "right to control investment decisions and conditions inside their plants" (Boyle 2001, 111). This paved the way for automakers to move their factories elsewhere. In his 1996 book *The Origins of the Urban Crisis*, Thomas Sugrue demonstrates that this deindustrialization trend began after the Second World War. He describes industrial production among manufacturers:

> . . . automated production and relocated plants in suburban and rural areas, and increasingly in the low-wage labor markets of underdeveloped regions like the American South and the Caribbean. The restructuring of the economy proceeded with the full support and encouragement of the American government. Federal highway construction and military spending facilitated and fueled industrial growth in nonurban areas. (Sugrue 2005, 6)

Detroit lost 134,000 industrial jobs between 1947 and 1963 (Boyle 2001, 114), a trend that continued at the same time that the Black population across the United States was migrating to the urban North (Sugrue 2005, 7). Through legal and extralegal means, including brute violence, Sugrue shows how white Detroiters attempted to keep the Black population away from all-white neighborhoods and suburbs. This segregation ensured that just as Black people were attempting to benefit from the political victories of the civil rights movement in the 1960s and integrate into the New Deal economy, jobs began to leave, and, as the economy began to transform, social wages diminished (Prashad 2005, 192). The 1960s and 1970s ushered in the era of neoliberalism, which sped up deindustrialization exponentially, opening up new places throughout the world for firms to set up shop. Between 1969 and 1973, Detroit lost 19 percent of its jobs, a pattern that would continue. The city shed 5 percent of its jobs annually between 1972 and 1992 (Boyle 2001, 120–121).

The combined effects of deindustrialization and suburbanization devastated Detroit's economy, which has not yet been able to recover. Detroit lost 20 percent of its population from 1970 to 1980, a further 7.5 percent in the following decade, and a further 25 percent of its population from 2000 to 2010 (Bomey and Gallagher 2013). Part of this "white flight" was structured by policies such as redlining, in which banks declined loans to Black and Brown people in certain neighborhoods, segregating cities and barring Black and Brown people from building wealth. This drained cities like Detroit of a significant tax base, as property taxes from the new suburbs funded new counties of mostly richer and whiter people, who allocated their tax revenue to services limited to those counties alone (Shapiro 2004, 140–147).

To counteract this loss of revenue, consecutive city administrations raised taxes on utilities, income, and property. Richer and predominately white suburbs hoarded their money in wealthier cities such as Bloomfield Hills and Birmingham in Oakland County (Linebaugh 2009). For these residents, this was an attempt to divest from the city of Detroit, where they felt their taxes had been going to subsidize poor and Black families. Thomas Shapiro has described this process as creating a "privatized notion of citizenship at the expense of solutions that work for all. It creates artificial demand and artificial sources of profit, such as when people pay larger amounts for suburban homes, private schools, gated communities, car alarms, home security systems, and private police services because they feel threatened by city life" (Shapiro 2004, 202). Like in Iraq, Detroit was initially attacked with the destruction of its industries and then further devastated through policies that prioritized the ambitions of the TCC over the needs of people.

Detroit tried to reverse the deindustrializing trend, with little success. In 1990, it financed the construction of Chrysler's Jefferson North Assembly by selling $130 million in bonds, which only added to the city's rising debts (Bomey and Gallagher 2013). In the early 2000s, Detroit found itself in an untenable position: Its debt was accruing interest, with no relief in sight. It turned to the same actors holding much of its debt already—the financial industry.

In 2005, the financial industry helped Detroit's mayor Kwame Kilpatrick put off and reduce debt payments through complex financial products. In a deal that was touted to save the city $277 million a year, the city sold pension bonds. It also bought credit swaps on those bonds to lock in interest rates at a relatively low 6 percent; it also purchased insurance on those bonds. In 2008, as the stock market rapidly lost value and interest rates declined, the city was left on the hook for more money than it had. It had to scramble to renegotiate with its creditors, the swap holders, and the financial insurers. Detroit pledged future revenues from its casinos to its creditors. Credit-rating firms downgraded the city's credit, which meant it had to pay more interest on new loans it took out (Bomey and Gallagher 2013). Today, this financial gimmick accounts for close to one-fifth of the city's debts. It was a cycle of loans to pay back interest on previous loans, all of which was music to creditors' ears.

Creditors were banking on the state or the federal government to back Detroit if it could not repay its loans. In July 2013, Detroit ran out of money. Unlike the major car manufacturers headquartered in the city, no one in the White House or in Congress was willing to come to the city's aid, and Detroit subsequently had to file for bankruptcy (Calmes 2013). Enter the Bremer of Detroit.

## Efforts to Reduce Debt

On March 14, 2013, Michigan's governor Rick Snyder appointed Kevyn Orr the "emergency manager" of Detroit. An experienced bankruptcy lawyer, Orr was given extraordinary powers to oversee the city's finances and make unilateral decisions without the approval of city government. Orr responded to residents calling him a dictator by saying that he would be a "benevolent one" (Finley 2013). As an unaccountable decision maker akin to Bremer, Orr imposed austerity measures on the city. He hired his former law firm Jones Day to help him negotiate with creditors and stakeholders (Guillen 2013b). Orr was the unaccountable technocrat charged with turning the city around.

Neoliberal regimes put both creditors' and investors' needs above all else. In turn, this leaves commitments made to the public vulnerable. In Detroit, Orr sidestepped the city's contractual obligations to its former employees: Pensions were cut dramatically, and union contracts were voided. In addition, Orr renegotiated a deal to restructure the city's debts so that financial firms received a much more favorable deal than residents (Chiaramonte 2013, Guillen 2013a).

When it comes to austerity, nothing is off the table. Under Orr's leadership, in March 2014, the Detroit Water and Sewerage Department (DWSD) threatened to shut off services to more than 150,000 customers who were behind on their water payments. DWSD sent 44,000 warnings in April of that year, and 3,000 people had their water shut off. Left to fend for themselves, different groups in Detroit—the Detroit People's Water Board, Food and Water Watch, Blue Planet Project, Michigan welfare rights organizations, and others—asked the United Nations to intervene and put pressure on the city to turn the water back on for its citizens (Abbey-Lambertz 2014). These organizations argued that DWSD's water rates were higher than the national average, with the city looking to increase the rates even further.

On the same day the organizations reached out to the United Nations, the DWSD issued a press statement arguing that increases in water bills were due to unpaid water bills. This tactic was another way of saying that people were getting something for nothing. DWSD claimed that a very small number of customers were affected by the water shutoffs and that people were beginning to pay their accounts in full. The UN special rapporteurs on adequate housing, extreme poverty and human rights, and on the human right to safe drinking water and sanitation "expressed concern" regarding water shutoffs in Detroit. Catarina de Albuquerque, the rapporteur for water, explained "disconnections due to non-payment are only permissible if it can be shown that the resident is able to pay but is not paying. In other words, when there is genuine inability to pay, human rights simply forbids disconnections" (UNHCR 2014).

Facing a fierce pushback from residents, DWSD had to hold off on further water shutoffs (DWSD 2014b). Orr did, however, move forward with a plan to decentralize water governance. DWSD leased its water lines to Oakland, Wayne, and Macomb counties (DWSD 2014a). Giving management and control to these wealthier counties further disconnected richer populations from poorer ones. Another added assurance to the richer and whiter suburban residents was that their taxes would only provide services to themselves and not poorer residents. This is the new neoliberal social contract, whereby if you want access to services and economic benefits of citizenship, you must be able to pay for them.

The Detroit water crisis was overshadowed in the American consciousness by the tragedy in Flint, where water with dangerous levels of lead was piped to people's homes, causing an unknown number of illnesses (Tanner 2016). The emergency manager of Flint, with the approval of State Treasurer Andy Dillon, rerouted the city's water source for the first time since 1967 to the Flint River to save money (Dixon 2016). This happened just a month after the DWSD shut off services in Detroit. Flint's water crisis is no different structurally than Detroit's. Flint suffered a similarly precipitous economic decline as Detroit; General Motors, once the city's major employer, left the city. Although GM received government aid, no one came to Flint's rescue, even as its unemployment rate climbed to 27.3 percent in 2009 (Highsmith 2015, 5).

For a city with a 55.6 percent Black population—the historian Andrew Highsmith (2015, 5) describes Flint as a "hypersegregated postindustrial metropolis"—the water crisis was also a racialized one, much like Detroit. Flint's fiscal problems were addressed through the same neoliberal playbook, with an unaccountable technocrat making decisions, all the while with a bottom-line myopia that blinded him to the human causalities; these decisions would erase certain social contracts in order to pay for contracts with creditors. Yet the political discourse around Flint has become a simplistic battle about political personalities, with the Democrats accusing the Republican governor and the Republicans playing defense. In fact, both parties are culpable because they both peddle the same neoliberal logic. The problem is not a person or a party. It is the logic of the game everyone is forced to play, a game where democracy and accountability are merely "hollowed-out" words (Roy 2012).

## Higher Education

The extraeconomic violence that destroyed Baghdad and the economic violence levied on Detroit can only continue if it is not seen as violence. If they are to be accepted, these events must be seen as normal. Here is perhaps where education is a key ideological and material battlefront. We are in the midst of a process that will transform higher education away from a public site in the service of civil society to yet another place to train and prepare the population for the economic needs of the market and to create the servile political subject willing to consent to the new neoliberal social contract.

Higher education and liberal arts were for the larger part of modern history a privilege afforded to elites. Higher education was a site of social reproduction for elite classes. In her recent book *Undoing the Demos*, Wendy Brown highlights a momentous transition in the post–World War II era, where in the United States for the first time, liberal arts education was made available in public higher education institutions to masses of people:

> The notion that all colleges and universities ought to offer a liberal
> arts degree and that such a degree is one to which all intellectually
> qualified citizens should have access heralded an order in which the
> masses would be educated for freedom. Regardless of the quantitative
> and qualitative limits on its realization, the radicalism of this event
> cannot be overstated: for the first time in human history, higher

educational policy and practice were oriented toward the many, tacitly destining them for intelligent engagement with the world, rather than economic servitude or mere survival. . . . Rather, the ideal of democracy was being realized in a new way insofar as the demos was being prepared through education for a life of freedom, understood as both individual sovereignty (choosing and pursuing one's ends) and participation in collective self-rule. (Brown 2015, 185)

Brown reminds us that the generation brought up in this setting joined the civil rights movement, the antiwar movement, and the free speech movement in the United States. This generation made feminism and ethnic studies academic disciplines and introduced analytical terms now used in public discourse to detect and analyze power—and to push back against it. Of course, there are many reasons for these developments, but surely access to a higher educational system built around providing liberal arts education to nurture a citizenry ready for democratic life—no matter how limited or problem ridden—was a significant factor. But, alas, this too has gone the way of social safety nets. Higher education—indeed, all of education—has come under the sustained attack of neoliberal reforms. Here I will focus explicitly on recent higher-ed policies in California.

In the era of Donald Trump and his education secretary Betsy DeVos, it might seem odd to talk about education policy in California. After all, DeVos's plans for privatizing education are well known (Barkan 2017, Mead, 2016), but California's governor has positioned his state as the anti-Trump model (Lah 2017, Siders and Marinucci 2017). While indeed it is important to see how the Trump administration's explicit nativism, racism, xenophobia, and militarism represent a rupture in how the American presidency operates and portrays itself, it is just as important to be aware of the continuities with U.S. history. For this reason, it is instructive to analyze the state that perhaps is the bastion of progressive politics in order to investigate how the structural forces we saw in Baghdad and Detroit can also operate in a dangerously mundane and uncontroversial manner.

## California's Public Higher Education System

The 2008 economic recession was the perfect crisis, a state of exception of sorts, that allowed these sustained attacks to take root. The neoliberal reforms in education, like the previous two sites discussed above, could not be implemented willingly or democratically. In 2013, Governor Jerry Brown warned against efforts by the three public higher educational systems in the state—the University of California, the California State University, and the community college systems—to reverse the draconian cuts to their budgets that occurred in the years following the 2008 recession (Enacted Budget Summary 2014). The Legislative Analysts Office (LAO), "the California legislature's non-partisan fiscal and policy advisor," applauded his stance (Taylor 2013).

Reversing these cuts was seen as a bad idea because state expenditures should not be expected to increase (Taylor 2013, 10). This is not uncommon. During times of economic crises, which in the 2008 case was caused by the global investor class, the public is forced to swallow austerity. Public anger is mitigated by rhetoric invoking "exceptional times." Neoliberalism, however, is about making those exceptions everyday realities. It is about institutionalizing the otherwise exceptional state, whether in Baghdad, Detroit, or Sacramento. In exceptional times, you might not have enough money to operate a certain public sector, but by privatizing it and enshrining market-oriented policies, you institutionalize the erosion of the public sector.

In the same way, draconian cuts to public education during a recession become the new bar for state expenditures.[8] To try to go back to pre-exceptional times is then seen as financially irresponsible. Neoliberalism banks on the public simply forgetting the past as a dream too idealistic to aspire to. "You have to be realistic and pragmatic," we are told.

## PREVALENCE OF ONLINE COURSES

Consistent insistence on cost cutting, efficiency, productivity, and performance are justified based on an economic framework. The reasoning that "education costs are increasing at unsustainable rates" (Surowiecki 2011) intentionally distracts from the fact that there has been a disinvestment in education (Newfield 2016, 152–160; Schoen 2015). This economic mantra also masks the fundamental reorganization of higher education, much the same way "development" discourse masked the neoliberal reorganization of the Iraqi state. For example, the LAO makes the following bold claim just in passing:

> The traditional higher education delivery model—based on a faculty
> member with an advanced degree teaching a relatively small number
> of students in a physical setting—is high cost relative to other potential
> higher education and industry models. (Taylor 2014, 3)

A university education is defined by an intimate and in-depth analysis of subject matter guided by a highly educated teacher with expertise in the respective field. That is not a radical statement; it is at the core of higher education. So what are these mysterious, "potential" "industry models" that have magical cost-cutting powers?

The only magic here is salesmanship. The low-cost methods alluded to are online classes, MOOCs,[9] and finding ways to pay faculty less to do the same amount of work. Online classes are seen as the technological silver bullet to cut costs, despite the dearth of research or data to support the claim that online teaching by itself can improve student learning (Newfield 2016, 244–245). Online courses are often seen as a replacement for, or in the case of MOOCs a way to revolutionize, traditional in-person teaching (Koller 2012). What is ignored is that online courses decrease the quality of education. While online classes surely save money by cutting facilities costs, and the upkeep cost of servers and technology is lower than lighting buildings and maintaining campuses, the instructor still has to provide instruction, facilitate discussion, and grade. In other words, the difference is the medium, not the workload.

There are only two ways that online classes can be seen as the cure for cutting the costs of a "high-cost delivery model." The first is to develop a policy whereby the university can own the online subject matter and thus repeatedly provide the course developed by a "faculty member with a high degree" every semester to a new group of students without paying for that faculty member. In other words, actual instruction has to be removed. The LAO makes a direct case for this by criticizing sharing among different campuses. "Traditionally, faculty that develop curriculum for face-to-face courses do not share it with faculty at other campuses (either within their segment or across the segments). Generally, we find this practice has carried over to online courses at the segments—despite the relative ease with which such coursework can be made available to colleagues" (Taylor 2013, 27). For example, they suggest that competitive grants should be given out for faculty to develop courses, which are then shared. The jump from sharing to reuse is not far. This is a process where an institution owns knowledge but where the instruction of that knowledge is deskilled and devalued. It is also a way of making adjunct work a more prevalent and permanent feature of the academy (Newfield 2016, 293).

The second way online classes cut costs is through enrolling a much higher number of students (because physical capacity is no longer an issue). This increases class size, which only exacerbates the problem of decreased teacher-student interaction inherent to the medium of online learning. I am not arguing that online learning is not useful but rather that it cannot be seen as a replacement for traditional pedagogical practices.

Newfield (2016, 245) argues that there is value in blended courses utilizing technology. But he cautions that the value does not come from the technology but rather "it was to upgrade studying—to repeat, learner control, more time, more learning resources, and more active learning, including feedback. The need to upgrade studying and feedback was in danger of getting lost in the focus on the technology." Ultimately, online learning must be seen as an additional learning tool, not a replacement.

The other proposal to mitigate costs is to provide more courses through extension programs. However, these programs are increasingly run by relatively autonomous parts of universities with a parallel structure that operates much like for-profit institutions and are often more expensive than regular courses. This trend increases the role of the privatized portion of public universities and is part of a wider trend in public universities that are in the midst of cutbacks in their funding. Universities leverage the history and prestige of their names to compete with for-profit institutions such as the University of Phoenix. Empowering private parts of public universities is a form of privatization. This is part of the slow transformation of the university away from a democratic mission to a market-oriented mission of selling a commodity to a consumer.

## Wall Street and the UC System

As public funds dwindle, colleges are moving toward private financing and as a result are further integrating themselves into the financial market. The University of California's use of tuition-backed bonds to raise private capital is a clear case of this practice. The UC has pledged student tuition to its bondholders to get lower interest rates, raise more funds, and guarantee good bond ratings. The UC pledged the money it receives from student tuitions to a bond trustee (Bank of New York Mellon Trust), where if for whatever reason it cannot pay its debt service, its creditors can directly access those funds (Meister 2009).

Funds collected from student tuitions have fewer strings attached than funds allocated by the state. By using these funds to raise private financing, the UC has made itself susceptible to the demands of the financial market. Cash-strapped state institutions look to the financial market and its creative financial instruments to raise funds. We have already seen this story play out in Detroit. The financial market is thus able to penetrate a new source of funding and a new market. Even the LAO has begun sounding alarms at the increasing reliance of the UC on these bonds and its plan to extend its repayment plan to forty years (Taylor 2014, 21).

At an analytical level, the UC has handed over power to the creditor class, who now, given the bond trustee (Bank of New York Mellon Trust) and its bond-rating companies (Standard & Poor's and Moody's), have a structural position of power within the university.

## PERFORMANCE-BASED FUNDING

Institutions of public higher education are utilizing neoliberal methods of allocating funds. The state of California is moving toward performance-based funding methods. The traditional enrollment funding bases funding levels on the number of students enrolled at any given institution; in other words, funding is based on the needs of the institution. Alternatively, performance-based funding ties funding to student outcomes such as graduation rates or year-to-degree metrics (Murphy et al. 2014). Why should there be a move away from providing higher education based on need to one where it is based on "performance?" Research has shown that performance-based funding has not shown a change in performance itself (Tandberg and Hillman 2013). This is a market-based approach to discipline public institutions. It is a way to force institutions to compete with one another for funding.

Performance-based funding is based on the logic of efficiency, which is a relationship between costs of overhead, whereby the lower the overhead cost or cost of labor, the higher the profit. Education has to emulate business, and students themselves are encouraged to view themselves as a business. So a student is constantly told which educational route is more efficient for her to get a degree. The idea of which class to take based on the readings and type of information offered, as well as the models of engagement practiced, are an afterthought to how efficient it is to take that particular course, given the overall educational plan of that student and her need to graduate within a given period of time.

Sure, one can argue that such funding practices can increase accountability. This is the same argument around school testing, or the new and highly touted Student Success Initiative in California's community colleges, where poor students' financial aid eligibility is tied to meeting certain criteria successfully (Advancing Student Success in the California Community Colleges 2012). The problem, of course, is when accountability is a zero-sum game. If your performance is not up to par, then you must be punished, regardless of the circumstances. Through this incentive structure, institutions and individuals are made accountable to efficiency itself rather than to the substantive goal of providing services or learning key content. This is the prioritization of the technical over the substantive.

Leveraging tuition funds to private capital is egregious, but the type of education being delivered is also being transformed. As colleges are pressured to graduate students faster and faster, students are forced to make up their minds on majors quickly and develop efficient educational plans to get them out in a "timely" manner (Horton 2016).[10] Under this nauseating obsession with efficiency, students are preached to about the connection of their degrees to the job market (Otani 2015, Rawes, 2015). Majors are advertised not based on the type of questions they aim to answer or the methodological approaches they use in that quest but on what type of jobs they can lead to. As the window to choose a major shortens, students are left making decisions not based on what they want to learn but on what type of job they seek. This is despite the fact that a bachelor's degree no longer guarantees entry into the jobs that each major advertises (Pappano 2011, Rampell 2014). Former Secretary of Education Arne Duncan recently remarked, "We need to build a system in which student learning, graduation and going on to get good jobs count most. That's what it means to focus on outcomes" (Duncan 2015). Ultimately, higher education is only a tool to get a job; it is not an end but a means to enter the job market. Neoliberalism instrumentalizes education.

I have offered a cursory case for how the neoliberal processes play out in Baghdad, Detroit, and in educational policy in the California higher educational system. Neoliberal restructuring was pushed through under the guise of crisis and then made permanent in subsequent budgeting policy. This was budgetary blackmail. The neoliberal restructuring included the very way that the university functioned on an everyday level—all sold under the mantra of cost cutting. First we were told budgets had to be reduced, then we were told that education was getting too expensive and needed to be done cheaper. Creditors and the global investor class were brought into the fold and given power over the universities as they, too, became sources of funding. This is the slow process of once again enclosing another public space for profit-seeking investors to rummage through.

## Conclusion

The federal government did not come to Detroit's aid. The only aid it provided was to support a plan spearheaded by the billionaire businessman Dan Gilbert to demolish dilapidated buildings and convert them to high-end commercial and residential spaces. The poor of Detroit who were left to fend for themselves will now be moved to make way for younger and richer newcomers (Halperin 2015). Every war creates refugees. These residents will be America's internally displaced. Their plight is not considered by new developers or the creditors that squeezed the city. These same creditors are now eager for the security situation to improve in Baghdad, so they can pounce on the newly minted free market of Iraq. They have set up offices in Erbil, Amman, and Dubai, circling like vultures and waiting for the right opportunity to jump in. Those that live in these cities, in the battlefronts of this global war, wage a daily struggle to exist with their dignity intact. All the while, we "over here" have become too comfortable with the misery "over there."

The social theorist Herbert Marcuse critiqued what he referred to as "technological rationality." This rationality was about efficiently pursuing a given task. The path is already laid out: go to x college, get y degree, to get z job. A system of costs, debts, and mortgages are laid out on the path to discipline any who try to divert. The path is seen as rational and above critique. It is "neutral" and not ideological. It is scientific, reasoned, and driven by statistics (Marcuse 1964, 145–147). Standardized testing, performance-based funding, balanced-budget austerity, market-based development, best practices, and the social benefits of private competitive enterprise are all predicated on this "neutral" "common-sense" reasoning.

"The point is that today the apparatus to which the individual is to adjust and adopt himself is so rational that individual protest and liberation appear not only as hopeless but as utterly irrational" (Marcuse 1941, 67). The educational system teaches this technological rationality even as it structures itself through it. Technological rationality is in contradistinction to substantive rationality, what Max Weber referred to "value rationality" (Brown 2015, 119).

Neoliberalism as a way of life, with its entrepreneurial spirit as its divine calling, is the latest stage and perhaps the pinnacle of this technological reasoning. Seen as objective reality, as postideological, and as pure economic science based on the human essence, the actions of neoliberalism are not just tolerated but accepted, justified, and, even worse, simply ignored as a "matter of fact." Baghdad needs our help to develop. Even if you are poor in Detroit, you still have to pay for drinking water. Education is getting too expensive, and we cannot just spend more and more. It is common sense.

Therefore we are brought up and are bringing up a generation that will pay no attention to the casualties of today's global war, be it here or "over there." The only path to peace is to break with neoliberalism in all of its political, economic, and social iterations. It is to proclaim independence from the market. We need to call out the biggest myth of neoliberal capitalism—that there is nothing outside of it. We need to reignite our imagination, reawaken our freedom instincts, and begin to reason substantively about how we ought to live (Gordon 2004, 124). This is a task for all of us educators in our classrooms. We need to reclaim our classrooms and make them what they need to be—a space for imaginative and critical thought.

NOTES

1. For a detailed elaboration of the different strategies of neoliberal global capitalism, including financial speculation, militarization in both policing and foreign intervention, and policing of migrants and refugees, see Robinson (2014, chaps 4–5).

2. I will use "TCC," "global investor class," and "the creditor class" interchangeably. TCC is a broader category in which the latter two are smaller class fractions. The investor class and the creditor class, however, are all part of the TCC.

3. For a detailed look at these changes within a corporation as exemplified by the NIKE corporation, see Gereffi and Korzeniewicz (1994).

4. The prevailing mainstream position against "stimulus spending," or government spending, argues that economic growth is not connected to consumption but rather production. In other words, the only way to secure economic growth is to create a business-friendly environment where investors support the economy and create jobs. In fact, government subsidies or welfare programs that seek to help people by enabling them to have more purchasing power have a negative effect, by undermining economic trends' natural movements (Higgs 1997, Popola 2013).

5. I borrow the metaphor of the "entrepreneur" from Wendy Brown's (2015) discussion of Michel Foucault's "homo œconomicus," where she argues that the neoliberal subject functions not only as an economic actor but also that the neoliberal ethos becomes salient in all social interactions, including at the personal and family levels.

6. Naomi Klein (2007) describes how the war effort itself was done in neoliberal fashion: Secretary of Defense Donald Rumsfeld outsourced and subcontracted many responsibilities that had been carried out by the military up to that point. The act of war making was a market to profit from.

7. For drafts of the Iraqi constitution, see N. J. Brown (2005).

8. The "sequester cuts" that were made in the federal government are another example of using cutbacks during recession to implement permanent changes to the public sector. It is perpetual austerity. You can read

more about these cuts at https://obamawhitehouse.archives.gov/issues/ sequester.

9. Massive Open Online Courses, or MOOCs, took off in 2012, to great fanfare. Prognosticators told us that they would fundamentally alter traditional college education, just as Uber had revolutionized the taxi industry. Like most online education, the hype was better than the real thing. See Pappano (2012) and Watters (2015).

10. See the California State University system's Graduation Initiative 2025 for an example of such programs: https://www2.calstate.edu/csu -system/why-the-csu-matters/graduation-initiative-2025/Pages/default.aspx.

### REFERENCES

Abbey-Lambertz, K. 2014. Activists beg United Nations for help after Detroit shuts off water for thousands. *Huffington Post*, June 24. http:// www.huffingtonpost.com/2014/06/24/detroit-water-shut-offs-human -rights_n_5526678.html.

Adler, J. H. 2000. *Ecology, liberty, and property: A free market environmental reader.* Washington, D.C.: Competitive Enterprise Institute.

Advancing Student Success in the California Community Colleges. 2012. http://californiacommunitycolleges.cccco.edu/Portals/0/Executive/ StudentSuccessTaskForce/SSTF_Final_Report_1-17-12_Print.pdf.

Anderson, T. L., and D. Leal. 2015. *Free market environmentalism for the next generation.* New York: Palgrave Macmillan.

Anderson, T. L., and G. D. Libecap. 2014. *Environmental markets: A property rights approach.* New York: Cambridge University Press.

Barkan, J. 2017. Milton Friedman, Betsy DeVos, and the privatization of public education. *Dissent*, January 17. https://www.dissentmagazine.org/ online_articles/betsy-devos-milton-friedman-public-education -privatization.

Barrionuevo, A. 2016. Detroit's billionaires hope to change downtown with development spree. *Curbed Detroit*, March 30. http://detroit.curbed.com/ 2016/3/30/11327192/detroit-downtown-development-dan-gilbert.

Bomey, N., and J. Gallagher. 2013. How Detroit went broke: The answers may surprise you—and don't blame Coleman Young. *Detroit Free Press*, September 15. http://archive.freep.com/interactive/article/20130915/NEWS01/ 130801004/Detroit-Bankruptcy-history-1950-debt-pension-revenue.

Boutros-Ghali, B., and the United Nations. 1996. *The United Nations and the Iraq-Kuwait conflict, 1990–1996.* New York: UN Department of Public Information.

Boyle, K. 2001. The ruins of Detroit: Exploring the urban crisis in the motor city. *Michigan Historical Review* 27 (1): 109–127.

Brown, N. J. 2005. Constitution of Iraq: Draft bill of rights. *Carnegie Endowment for International Peace.* http://carnegieendowment.org/files/BillofRights.pdf.

Brown, W. 2011. The end of educated democracy. *Representations* 116 (1): 19–41.

———. 2015. *Undoing the demos: Neoliberalism's stealth revolution.* New York: Zone.

Calmes, J. 2013. $300 million in Detroit aid, but no bailout. *New York Times,* September 26. http://www.nytimes.com/2013/09/27/us/300-million-in-detroit-aid-but-no-bailout.html.

Chiaramonte, P. 2013. Detroit bankruptcy proposal would leave pensioners with 16 cents on the dollar. *Fox News,* October 30. http://www.foxnews.com/us/2013/10/30/detroit-bankruptcy-proposal-would-leave-pensioners-with-16-cents-on-dollar/.

Daulatzai, S. 2012. *Black star, crescent moon: The Muslim International and Black freedom beyond America.* Minneapolis: University of Minnesota Press.

Dicken, P. 2007. *Global shift: Mapping the changing contours of the world economy.* 5th ed. New York: Guilford.

Dixon, J. 2016. How Flint's water crisis unfolded. *Detroit Free Press.* http://www.freep.com/pages/interactives/flint-water-crisis-timeline/.

Duncan, A. 2015. Toward a new focus on outcomes in higher education: Remarks by Secretary of Education. Washington, D.C.: U.S. Department of Education. https://www.ed.gov/news/speeches/toward-new-focus-outcomes-higher-education.

DWSD. 2014a. *Agreement to create water authority guarantees funding to rebuild regional system and to assist customers in need.* Detroit Water and Sewerage Department.

———. 2014b. *Mayor and DWSD to release full plan on water shutoffs Thursday.* Detroit Water and Sewerage Department.

Enacted Budget Summary. 2014. http://www.ebudget.ca.gov/2013-14/pdf/Enacted/BudgetSummary/HigherEducation.pdf.

Finley, A. 2013. Kevyn Orr: How Detroit can rise again. *Wall Street Journal,* August 2.

Gelvin, J. L. 2012. American global economic policy and the civic order in the Middle East. In *Is there a Middle East? The evolution of a geopolitical concept,* ed. M. Bonine, A. Amanat, and M. Gasper, 191–207. Stanford, Calif.: Stanford University Press.

Gereffi, G., and M. Korzeniewicz. 1994. *Commodity chains and global capitalism.* Westport, Conn.: Greenwood.

Gill, S. 1998. New constitutionalism, democratisation, and global political economy. *Global Change, Peace, and Security* 10 (1): 23–38.

Giroux, H. A. 2014. *Neoliberalism's war on higher education.* Chicago: Haymarket.

Gordon, A. 2004. Some thoughts on the utopian. In *Keeping good time: Reflections on knowledge, power, and people,* 113–132). Boulder, Colo.: Paradigm.

Guillen, J. 2013a. Pact would reunite Detroit EFM Kevyn Orr with former boss at Jones Day. *Detroit Free Press,* April 16. http://archive.freep.com/article/20130416/NEWS01/304160075/kevyn-orr-jones-day-stephen-brogan-contract-detroit-city-council.

———. 2013b. City of Detroit to pay $65M less to banks in new bankruptcy settlement. *Detroit Free Press,* December 24. http://www.freep.com/apps/pbcs.dll/article?AID=2013312240064.

Halperin, A. 2015. How Motor City came back from the brink . . . and left most Detroiters behind. *Mother Jones,* July 6. http://www.motherjones.com/politics/2015/06/motor-city-after-bankruptcy-and-detroiters-left-behind.

Harvey, D. 2005. *A brief history of neoliberalism.* New York: Oxford University Press.

Higgs, R. 1997. Regime uncertainty: Why the Great Depression lasted so long and why prosperity resumed after the war. *Independent Review* 1 (4): 561–590. http://www.independent.org/pdf/tir/tir_01_4_higgs.pdf.

Highsmith, A. R. 2015. *Demolition means progress: Flint, Michigan, and the fate of the American metropolis.* Chicago: University of Chicago Press.

Horton, M. J. 2016. Why students should take at least 15 units every semester. *CSU News,* December 9. https://www2.calstate.edu/csu-system/news/Pages/Why-Students-Should-Take-15-or-More-Units-Every-Semester-.aspx.

Hursh, D. W. 2016. *The end of public schools: The corporate reform agenda to privatize education.* New York: Routledge.

Iman, M. 2005. Draft constitution gained, but an important opportunity was lost. *United States Institute of Peace,* October 11. http://www.usip.org/newsmedia/releases/2005/1011_draft.html.

Klein, N. 2007. *The shock doctrine: The rise of disaster capitalism.* New York: Picador.

Koller, D. 2012. *What we're learning from online education* [Video]. https://www.ted.com/talks/daphne_koller_what_we_re_learning_from_online_education/transcript?language=en.

Krugman, P. 2008. New deal economics. *New York Times,* November 8. https://krugman.blogs.nytimes.com/2008/11/08/new-deal-economics/.

Lah, K. 2017. Governor to Trump: "California is not turning back. Not now, not ever." *CNN,* January 24. http://www.cnn.com/2017/01/24/politics/jerry-brown-california-donald-trump/.

Linebaugh, K. 2009. Detroit's pain begins to spread into wealthy suburbs and schools. *Wall Street Journal*, March 17.

Magdoff, H. 1982. Imperialism: A historical survey. In *Introduction to the sociology of "developing societies,"* ed. H. Alavi and T. Shanin, 11–29. New York: Monthly Review.

Marcuse, H. 1941. Some social implications of modern technology. *Studies in Philosophy and Social Science* 9 (3): 414–439.

———. 1964. *One-dimensional man: Studies in the ideology of advanced industrial society.* Boston: Beacon.

Mead, R. 2016. Betsy Devos and the plan to break public schools. *New Yorker*, December 14. http://www.newyorker.com/news/daily-comment/betsy-devos-and-the-plan-to-break-public-schools.

Meister, B. 2009. They pledged your tuition. *Council of UC Faculty Associations.* http://cucfa.org/news/2009_oct11.php.

Midnight Notes Collective. 1992. *Midnight oil: Work, energy, war, 1973–1992.* Jamaica Plain, Mass.: Autonomedia.

Morrow, J. 2005. *Iraq's constitutional process II: An opportunity lost* (report no. 155). Washington, D.C.: United States Institute of Peace. http://www.usip.org/publications/iraqs-constitutional-process-ii-opportunity-lost.

Murphy, P., K. Cook, H. Johnson, and M. Weston. 2014. *Higher education in California: Performance budgeting.* http://www.ppic.org/main/publication_quick.asp?i=1120.

Newfield, C. 2016. *The great mistake: How we wrecked public universities and how we can fix them.* Baltimore, Md.: Johns Hopkins University Press.

Otani, A. 2015. The college majors that make the most money. *Bloomberg News*, May 7. https://www.bloomberg.com/news/articles/2015-05-07/here-are-the-college-majors-that-make-the-most-money.

Pappano, L. 2011. The master's as the new bachelor's. *New York Times*, July 22. http://www.nytimes.com/2011/07/24/education/edlife/edl-24masters-t.html.

———. 2012. The year of the MOOC. *New York Times*, November 2. http://www.nytimes.com/2012/11/04/education/edlife/massive-open-online-courses-are-multiplying-at-a-rapid-pace.html.

Popola, J. 2013. Think consumption is the "engine" of our economy? Think again. *Forbes*, January 30.

Prashad, V. 2005. Second-hand dreams. *Social Analysis* 49 (2): 191–198.

———. 2007. *The darker nations: A people's history of the Third World.* New York: New Press.

Rampell, C. 2014. The college degree has become the new high school degree. *Washington Post*, September 9.

Rawes, E. 2015. The 5 highest paying degrees of 2015. *USA Today*, January 31. http://www.usatoday.com/story/money/personalfinance/2015/01/31/cheat -sheet-highest-paying-degrees/22478439/.

Robinson, W. I. 2004. *A theory of global capitalism: Production, class, and state in a transnational world*. Baltimore, Md.: Johns Hopkins University Press.

———. 2006. Beyond the theory of imperialism: Global capitalism and the transnational state. *Societies without Borders* 2 (1): 5–26.

———. 2014. *Global capitalism and the crisis of humanity*. New York: Cambridge University Press.

Roy, A. 2012. We call this progress. *Guernica*, December 17. https://www .guernicamag.com/we-call-this-progress/.

Ruggie, J. G. 1982. International regimes, transactions, and change: Embed-ded liberalism in the postwar economic order. *International organization* 36 (2): 379–415.

Sassen, S. 2001. *The global city: New York, London, Tokyo*. 2nd ed. Princeton, N.J.: Princeton University Press.

Schoen, J. W. 2015. Why does a college degree cost so much? *CNBC*, June 16. http://www.cnbc.com/2015/06/16/why-college-costs-are-so-high -and-rising.html.

Shapiro, T. M. 2004. *The hidden cost of being African American: How wealth perpetuates inequality*. New York: Oxford University Press.

Sheehan, P. 2015. Revitalization by gentrification. *Jacobin*, May 11. https:// www.jacobinmag.com/2015/05/detroit-foreclosure-redlining-evictions/.

Siders, D., and C. Marinucci. 2017. Jerry Brown delivers anti-Trump manifesto. *Politico*, January 24. http://www.politico.com/states/california/ story/2017/01/jerry-brown-warring-with-donald-trump-back-on-national -stage-108988.

Sklair, L. 2001. *The transnational capitalist class*. Malden, Mass.: Blackwell.

Sugrue, T. J. 2005. *The origins of the urban crisis: Race and inequality in postwar Detroit*. Princeton, N.J.: Princeton University Press.

Surowiecki, J. 2011. Debt by degrees. *New Yorker*, November 21. http://www .newyorker.com/magazine/2011/11/21/debt-by-degrees.

Tandberg, D. A., and N. W. Hillman. 2013. *State performance funding for higher education: Silver bullet or red herring?* http://wiscape.wisc.edu/docs/ WebDispenser/wiscapedocuments/pb018.pdf.

Tanner, K. 2016. All Flint's children must be treated as exposed to lead. *Detroit Free Press*, January 16. http://www.freep.com/story/opinion/ contributors/raw-data/2016/01/16/map-8657-flints-youngest-children -exposed-lead/78818888/.

Taylor, M. 2013. *The 2013–2014 budget: Analysis of the higher education budget.*
    http://lao.ca.gov/Publications/Detail/2686.
———. 2014. *A review of state budgetary practices for UC and CSU.* http://lao
    .ca.gov/Publications/Detail/2913.
UN High Commissioner on Human Rights. 2014. Detroit: Disconnecting
    water from people who cannot pay an affront to human rights, say UN
    experts. Press release. June 25. http://www.ohchr.org/EN/NewsEvents/
    Pages/DisplayNews.aspx?NewsID=14777.
Watters, A. 2015. The MOOC revolution that wasn't. *The Kernel*, August 23.
    Retrieved from http://kernelmag.dailydot.com/issue-sections/headline
    -story/14046/mooc-revolution-uber-for-education/.

# Kony 2012 as Citizenship Education: A Grassroots Revolution or a Strategy of Warfare?

*Chandni Desai*

On March 5, 2012, a video entitled *Kony 2012* was released by Invisible Children, a U.S.-based nongovernmental organization (NGO) that operates in Uganda. The video garnered unprecedented attention: It went viral on the Internet via social media, made headlines around the world, and was viewed by over 100 million people globally in under one week. In the emotionally compelling video, Jason Russell (the founder of Invisible Children) tells his son Gavin about the work he does in Uganda. He specifically teaches his son about Joseph Kony, the leader of the Lord's Resistance Army (LRA), a rebel militia that forces children into its army and commits horrible atrocities such as rape, mutilation, and murder. The purpose of the film is to promote the NGO Invisible Children's "Stop Kony" campaign and have Joseph Kony known globally in order to have him arrested and tried at the International Criminal Court in The Hague. In the video, Jason Russell encourages people to become "global citizens" and join the revolution by buying bracelets and T-shirts, donating money to the organization, and otherwise supporting the cause via the click of their mouse. As the *Kony 2012* video spread, educators began discussing ways in which they could use the video and campaign to teach their students about Joseph Kony's war with the Ugandan army.

During this time, I was teaching a course at the Ontario Institute for Studies in Education (OISE) at the University of Toronto; my students were primarily public school teachers. Upon the launch of *Kony 2012*, many of the teachers I was teaching believed that by educating young people about Kony they would be influencing their students to engage in global citizenship education effectively, by encouraging them to participate in taking action against a serious global issue—child soldiers.

## *Citizenship Education and* Kony 2012

In the twenty-first century, educating for global citizenship has become a shared goal for educators, educational institutions, and governments. Globalization and the digital era have compressed time, space, and nations together (Harvey 1990), linking the global community through issues such as climate change, poverty, war, terrorism, and epidemics. To respond to such problems, Lapayese (2003) underscores that education as a field has been called upon to prepare people for various evolving forms of activity as citizens. In particular, she notes:

> Global citizenship education has been suggested as a way in which universities can respond to the demand for opportunities to engage in relevant, meaningful activities that enhance students' global perspectives and help them to contribute to a more peaceful, environmentally secure and just world. (Shultz and Jorgenson n.d., 1)

Many universities across North America have invested resources to develop programs of global-citizenship education (Shultz and Jorgenson n.d.). In Canada, moreover, every province and territory has made some form of citizenship education a part of its core curriculum for elementary and secondary students (Evans and Reynolds n.d.), which emphasizes "active" and responsible "citizenship" in response to youth disengagement from the formal political process (for example, voting) (Bickmore 2014). Drawing from research evidence from various studies of teachers and students in schools, Bickmore (2014, 261) argues that the "Canadian curriculum in practice often reflects older, less democracy-orientated versions of citizenship education, and that this education does not seem to inspire in students, ethical, critical awareness or intent to participate politically."

Furthermore, Sears and Hughes (2006) argue that both discourse and practice in the field of citizenship education exists in a state of tension between education and indoctrination. They underscore that an education approach would deepen the public discussion of the role of citizenship education, broaden conceptions of citizenship and participation, and develop a substantial knowledge base on the topic. In contrast, indoctrination "pushes for uncritical acceptance of ideas and beliefs and ignores or disregards evidence" and can be found in a "commitment to slogans and dogma, a rush to reform and to find the quick fix, and in some places a tradition of didactic teaching that focuses upon an encyclopaedic coverage of details without particular regard to their meaning for pupils" (3). While Sears and Hughes underscore some very good examples of citizenship education in England and Australia that open up possibilities for teaching for a democratic society, the authors remain critical of citizenship education within the context of Canada.

Moreover, Richardson and Abbott (2009) assert that most citizenship education in Canada often reinforces a nationalist perspective through dominant Eurocentric narratives that marginalize other experiences and viewpoints. Bickmore's (2014, 266) research on curriculum policies and texts suggests that "although transnational issues and perspectives are included more [now] than in previous years, some Canadian school curricula may reinforce ignorance and stereotypes about other nations and peoples and about the causes and effects of global problems such as war." Weber (2012) and Bickmore (2014) claim that "a large proportion of the visible global citizenship education activity in Canadian schools seems to be focused on co-curricular activities, often emphasizing awareness and charity fundraising campaigns" (Bickmore 2014), reinforcing Canadian superiority by undermining the structural causes that produce social, political, and economic issues in other parts of the world. As well, many curriculum resources designed for teachers on the subject of citizenship education, such as *Educating for Global Citizenship in a Changing World*, outline that this particular resource would be useful for secondary school teachers in order to address specific learning expectations on citizenship education. The expectations include some of the following:

> Increase knowledge of international-development and cooperation issues (e.g., rights of children, gender inequities, human rights, environmental global issues).
>
> Instill an understanding of global interdependence and Canada's responsibilities as a member of the global village (and other related concepts, e.g., globalization, rights and responsibilities, social justice, diversity, peace and conflict).

Raise awareness of the role Canadian individuals and organizations
play in overseas relief and development assistance.

(EXCERPTED FROM EVANS AND REYNOLDS N.D.)

These learning expectations underscore a close relationship between
citizenship education and the field of international development. The Canadian Development Agency (CIDA)—which is committed to charitable
and international bilateral development work—has a number of initiatives
designed to help educators explore topics of global interest in their classroom and ensure that their students broaden their awareness of international issues. Building on the critiques outlined by various scholars working
on the area of citizenship education that I have outlined, I will analyze the
*Kony 2012* campaign, which many teachers have taught in their classrooms
as a form of "citizenship"/"global" education. I analyze the *Kony 2012* campaign as an example of how uncritical attempts to teach for/about/on
"citizenship" can lead to indoctrination rather than education.

Immediately after the *Kony 2012* campaign video was released, a wide
range of expert analysts leveled criticisms at both the film and its producers (see de Waal 2012, Harding 2012, Schomerus 2012). Most of the *Kony
2012* critiques centered on the misrepresentation of the situation in Uganda
(Kony left Uganda in 2005), the oversimplification of the issue, and the
erasure of Ugandan voices from the video or larger NGO strategy. In addition, another important critique missing from the mainstream media was
the relationship between Invisible Children's *Kony 2012* campaign and the
political economy of development's relationship to education, militarization, and war. Therefore, here I offer an analysis that demonstrates the
relationship between citizenship education, pedagogy, and international
development. Though further empirical research is required to demonstrate the relationship between citizenship education and international
development, by focusing this chapter on Uganda I will analytically offer
insight on how teaching for "citizenship" can facilitate supporting imperialist and neocolonial foreign policy agendas that may be detrimental to entire nations. I interrogate the *Kony 2012* video/campaign, the discourses
of development that operate within Invisible Children's work to gain popular support for its campaign, and how this development project animates
"a pedagogy of war" (Desai 2016) that furthers imperialism, racial capitalism, and neocolonialism. I argue that those who uncritically teach about
Joseph Kony and Uganda also animate a pedagogy of war. I argue that it
is important for educators to be critical when teaching global issues because
of the implications—namely, indoctrination—their teaching can have on

their students and society at large. I conclude with considerations that would enable teaching critically about global and political issues for education rather than indoctrination.

I will draw on antiracist, anti-imperialist feminism as the theoretical lens through which to view how the *Kony 2012* video/campaign animates a pedagogy of war. An antiracist, anti-imperialist, feminist critique is necessary for any interrogation of the continuity of the imperialist project, as it helps us expose the war/peace binaries as two opposites of one unity— the racist-masculine-imperialist peace is the continuation and reappearance of the racist-masculine-imperialist war. It is precisely within this entanglement that Chandra Mohanty (2006) rightly insists on a feminist anti-imperialist praxis rooted in a politics of dissent, which insists on investigating the neoliberal underpinnings of racist-masculine-imperial peace that unravels the contradictions of the dialectics of peace and war.

## Overlapping Racial and Imperial Discourses in Citizenship Education and International Development

Upon the release of the *Kony 2012* video, many teachers believed that this campaign would be a great resource for global-citizenship education. Teachers could raise awareness about the children of Uganda (in particular, child soldiers) by showing their students the video and encouraging them to be engaged with charity work, for example, taking action through raising awareness and money, activities that both Bickmore (2014) and Weber (2012) underscore as the focus of what citizenship-education activity in Canadian schools looks like. While the intentions of various teachers was well meaning, through our conversations it became evident that most of them lacked any critical analysis on the development industry also known as the nonprofit-industrial complex (Smith 2009) and the ways in which this industry and its discourses often do more harm than good. Development is about ideology and the production and transmission of policies and discourses. Therefore to understand fully what is at stake in this transmission, we need to understand how particular notions of development are diffused, disseminated, and popularized. Discourse is not simply about representation; it also encompasses material effects.

International development is premised on specific discourses, particularly those from modernization theory, that govern relations between the North and South/First and Third Worlds, which came out of Orientalist colonial representations about "other" cultures and people that were not white (Said 1979). Modernization theory and its discourses were most salient in the field post–World War II until the 1970s, particularly the discourse of lack, which required the modernization of the deficient other (McEwan 2009). Discourses of indolence—in which people were deemed to be childlike—were used as a way to enact the White Man's Burden, to awaken colonized peoples from their passive and lazy dispositions (McEwan 2009). Though development discourse shifted to critique modernization theory in the 1970s, in practice I would argue that modernization discourses of lack and indolence are still very prevalent in much of the work that NGOs do. These themes are certainly evident in the work of Invisible Children and their *Kony 2012* video and campaign.

For example, in the *Kony 2012* video, the discourse of othering is shown through Jason Russell's discussion with his son Gavin, as Jason explains his encounters with the former LRA child solider Jacob Acaye and other child soldiers, whom Jason calls "his friends," as opposed to Joseph Kony, whom he terms "the monster." The story and images of the "Black other" are depicted as either "violent" and "scary"—Kony—or "lacking" and "childlike" and in need of "saving"—Jacob. Othering is also evident in the way Ugandan child soldiers are described as "invisible," which expresses the Western, white male gaze of not seeing the other because of their lack and indolence. For many Africans and others around the world, the plight of these children has never been invisible and has always been known. Development discourses of lack and indolence are not innocent; rather, they influence the way in which knowledge about (other) nations and peoples are transmitted. These discourses have seeped into citizenship education, specifically in relation to how educators and students from the West perceive people in the "developing world" as "underdeveloped" and needing "saving" (Richardson and Abbott 2009).

Citizenship-education discourses are also framed similar to dominant development discourses. Richardson and Abbott (2009) argue that in Canada, the nationalistic orientation of global-citizenship education is framed within an imperial imaginary rooted in Canada's historical membership in the British Empire and subsequently in the Commonwealth (Willinsky 1998). Within this imperial imaginary, Canadian social studies curricula reflected postwar ideologies:

> The third world or developing world was used as a kind of marker against which both Canada and the West measure its own progress and established its own sense of identity, while the development of nations in the non-West was measured on the basis of the degree to

which they Westernized their economic and political institutions. (Richardson and Abbott 2009, 381–382)

As Bickmore (2014) suggests, ignorant stereotypes are the basis for the way students superficially understand the causes and effects of global problems such as war. Richardson and Abbott (2009) state that "though global citizenship education has become less overtly Eurocentric and racist over time, it remains part of an imperial project aimed primarily at a process through which students learn to divide the world." In particular, in the post-9/11 climate students have been taught to divide the world via a "clash of civilizations" discourse. (Samuel P. Huntington proposed in 1996 the "Clash of Civilizations," the theory that people's cultural and religious identities will be the primary source of conflict in the post–Cold War world.) In an exploratory study, Stephane Levesque (2003) assessed students' capacity to understand terrorism post-9/11 in one Ontario high school. The following responses from students in Levesque's (2003) study underscore the process of othering that divides the Western world from the non-Western world.

> Terrorists run on hate because how else could a person of this world do such terrible acts of murder [referring to 9/11]. The terrorists were angry or jealous of the Western World's economy and life style.
>
> People in the Middle East are expressing anti-Western feelings, I think, because our countries are more advanced, high-tech, and developed than those in the Middle East.

Such responses demonstrate the way in which some students perceive the Western world, in particular North America, as the "benchmark" or standard by which other cultures and peoples are judged, denigrated, and believed to have different values, a stance founded on an imminent clash of civilizations.

Invisible Children deployed the "clash of civilization" discourse in their short film, which articulates an intervention to "capture the bad monster Kony" in order to bring peace to Uganda. The clash of civilizations was evoked through the figure of the terrorist, who is a constant threat that needs to be removed forcefully from society and the world. The *Kony 2012* campaign centered their entire video on the "figure of the terrorist"— Kony. Their promotional materials, in particular one poster, shadowed Joseph Kony's face with the image of Osama bin Laden and Adolf Hitler.

In comparing Kony to bin Laden and Hitler, the campaign not only dehistorized where Joseph Kony came from but dangerously collapsed the historical context of the Holocaust and 9/11 as synonymous to the political situation in Uganda. In doing so, the historical and contemporary discourses of terror are manipulated to suggest that northern Ugandans are in a similar state of crisis and terror as the Jews during the Holocaust—as well as the way Americans were post-9/11—to invoke sympathy and urgent military intervention. These tactics of masculine-imperialist warfare fought in the name of bringing peace are not new; they have been used before. For example, this includes "let's get rid of Saddam Hussein and his weapons of mass destruction in Iraq," capturing the Taliban and Osama bin Laden in Afghanistan, saving Afghan women from the Taliban, and getting rid of Hamas in Gaza. In these instances, the figure of the terrorist has been used to wage imperialist wars that have devastated these regions and their peoples.

Since the September 11, 2011, attacks on the World Trade Center and Pentagon, there has been a shift in development discourse toward terror and security as primary to development agendas. The discourse of terror and security are framed by a politically sanctioned vocabulary, such as "axis of evil," "evil doers," and "freedom-loving peoples" (Jackson 2005), which then assists in establishing criteria to judge particular actions and policy. Though the agenda of security in development is not new (and dates back to the Cold War), the current shift in development is a development-security nexus "where security is conceptualised as both objective of, and an instrument for, development" (McEwan 2009). As an instrument of development, security now sits at the top of developmental agendas, while as an objective of development, the security focus is upon fragile states, humanitarian action, humanitarian intervention, and peace building. Many NGOs are shifting to make security a priority in their work in order to secure large tranches of funding, particularly from government aid agencies such as USAID and CIDA.

Therefore, by casting Kony as an evil monster and terrorist from which Ugandans need saving, Uganda is portrayed and simultaneously seen as needing urgent intervention through securitization and protection. The urgency of military intervention is portrayed by evoking tragic historical moments such as the Rwandan genocide and the Holocaust. In the *Kony 2012* video, images of the concentration camps, massacred Tutsi bodies spilled through the streets of Rwanda, and skulls depict the tragedy of the Rwandan genocide and the Holocaust. After showing these painful images, in the video Jason Russell says, "When we look back at history, to these genocides, even if we cared, we didn't know what to do." He continues, "The people of the world see each other now and can protect each other. . . .

We are living in a new world in which 750 million people share ideas, not thinking in borders; it's a global community" (*Kony 2012*) thanks to social networking sites such as Facebook and Twitter.

Jason Russell invokes the notion of global citizenship and believes that the connectivity that has resulted because of the Internet and social media can help spread awareness and create responsible global citizens that care, all to help end a twenty-eight-year war by "joining the *Kony 2012* revolution." The video articulates that ignorance is the problem, and therefore the answer is education—education about the issue and education on the solution. As such, Invisible Children suggests that raising awareness through the film and "making *Kony* popular" will potentially prevent a future genocide by garnering the support of the American people for the decision to deploy U.S. troops in the region. Russell explains, "Although in 2011, Barack Obama deployed one hundred troops ('advisors'), the mission will be cancelled without popular support" (*Kony 2012*). The messaging is clear—the "good global citizen" in the West can stop this twenty-eight-year-long war.

Those teachers that taught *Kony 2012* uncritically and believed that their students would make a difference by engaging in this campaign were easily indoctrinated by the video, as they believed that teaching the issue to people in the West could bring about peace in Uganda. What privileges and imperial imaginaries do these teachers have, to believe that they could stop a war from happening simply through raising awareness? Which citizens can engage in global affairs and enact their power of citizenship? If we take a closer look at the *Kony 2012* video and Invisible Children's strategy, what becomes clear is that only those deemed human can partake in this global citizenship. Since racialized and Indigenous communities are deemed backward and unhuman, as per the discourses of modernization (McEwan 2009), Ugandan subjectivity, agency, resistance, organizing, and strategies toward peace, conflict resolution, and reconciliation did not seem to matter and are erased and denied. Thereby global (Western) citizens must seemingly solve Ugandan issues as opposed to the Ugandans themselves. Ugandans' agency and their commitment and struggle for peace—which they have been engaged in for decades—was erased, and their efforts in the Juba peace talks that began in 2006, which was primarily responsible for the relative calm being experienced in northern Uganda today, was also effaced by the Kony video.

Thus when teachers uncritically use cultural artifacts such as the *Kony 2012* video and campaign to teach practices of global citizenship, a reification of the (Western) nation takes place. As students develop global

civic competencies directed toward learning, they are consequently indoctrinated to believe that their nation is unique and morally, economically,
and politically superior, justifying Western intervention and imperialism
in the developing world (Richardson and Abbott 2009, Willinsky 1998).
As well, young people are indoctrinated to believe that international development projects always do "good" and help save others less fortunate
and in need.

## Pedagogy of War

Teachers that educate on global issues must be mindful of the ways in which
their curriculum and pedagogy could have detrimental effects on society
(that is, indoctrination) when done uncritically. Those teachers that jumped
on the bandwagon of teaching *Kony 2012* because it became popular and
circulated all over social media may have, or could become, implicated in
furthering racist-imperialist projects of war. The *Kony 2012* campaign animates a pedagogy of war by calling for and justifying military (U.S.) intervention into Uganda. This is because a "Western" solution was imagined
and proposed to solve a twenty-eight-year conflict. Jason Russell says, "For
the first time in history, the United States took that kind of action [to deploy one hundred advisors] because the people demanded it, not for the
U.S.'s self-defense or self-interests, but because it was right" (*Kony 2012*).
Here a moral claim is put forth on the U.S decision to deploy troops to
Uganda because of their "righteousness" and "global responsibility" toward
others, in particular marginalized peoples. However, I want to interrogate
the contradictions of peace and the discourse of global citizenship here by
suggesting that the *Kony 2012* campaign and video are a means by which
the development-security nexus is furthering imperialism through the
support of the militarization of Africa.

By proposing a military solution, Invisible Children and their *Kony 2012*
campaign are further legitimizing and popularizing U.S. support for
African Command (AFRICOM). According to its official website,
AFRICOM is a development agency whose goals are to promote stability
through humanitarian aid on the African continent and to increase the capacity of African militaries by "helping Africans help themselves. What
this means is: the ability to set up military bases, with U.S. soldiers, all over
the African continent" (Resist Africom 2008). The *Kony 2012* campaign is
linked to the U.S. government's foreign policy agenda of militarizing Africa through the Africa Command. There are several reasons why this
video/campaign/NGO leads me to believe that, in the name of "peace" and

"development," humanitarian imperialism is the essence of what is actually taking place.

In a July 2011 meeting, the AFRICOM commander Carter Ham called Uganda a "major partner" in achieving U.S. objectives in the region, particularly after Uganda discovered oil prospects. Escobar (2011) explains that Heritage Oil discovered that Uganda may hold "several billion barrels of oil, the largest-ever onshore oil discovery in sub-Saharan Africa." Escobar suggests that this implies overt U.S. involvement: "the construction of a $1.5 billion, 1,200 kilometer long pipeline to Kampala and the coast of Kenya. Then there's another pipeline from 'liberated' South Sudan. Since this discovery the U.S. became very interested in the Lord's Resistance Army." Washington wants to make sure access to these raw materials and oil will be exclusively available for the United States and European allies. Also, Kony and the LRA operate across the borders in the territories of several countries (as the war has spilled over to neighboring nations, including South Sudan, Congo, Burundi, and the Central African Republic), which are also of particular interest to the United States because they are resource rich in copper, gold, coltan, diamonds, timber, uranium, and oil. As such, Kony and the LRA became strategic targets for U.S. imperialist greed for minerals and raw materials. Moreover, since China has infiltrated the African continent through development aid, trade, and commerce partnerships, the ultimate objective of AFRICOM would allow the United States to be able to counter resource-hungry China by having boots on the ground near the oil-rich northern part of Uganda, South Sudan, the Congo, and the Central African Republic.

Though the military option to defeat Kony has been explored numerous times in the past, notably Operation North (1991), Operation Iron Fist (2002), and Operation Lightning Thunder (2008–2009), each failed and led to massive reprisals against civilians (Internal Displacement Monitoring Center Report Uganda 2010). Therefore, to legitimize entrance into Uganda, the NGO Invisible Children was being used by the U.S. government to disguise their war agenda, in order to gain popular support for an invasion by invoking discourses of terrorism and security. Who would object if the United States sends one hundred U.S. "advisers" if they are helping and saving Ugandans, especially young children, from terror? Thus military intervention into the region is not about "righteousness" and "U.S. goodness," as Jason Russell suggests; it is about U.S. imperialist and capitalist interests in the region.

I want to make clear that I do not support the activities of the LRA and Kony's violence. However, it is important to clarify that the LRA is not a military power. "The LRA are a few hundred at most, poorly equipped, poorly armed, and poorly trained children that were kidnapped and turned into tormentors" (Mamdani 2012). In short, addressing the problem called the LRA does not call for a regionwide military operation. Thus, educators must critically ask why Invisible Children is advocating a military solution. Invisible Children calls for a military operation because by following the development-security nexus, it can secure large amounts of funding. This is highly problematic because the support of this discourse not only encourages and reinforces the acceptability of the United States' commitment to violent security practices but also further legitimates and naturalizes the racist knowledge upon which it is based. This suggests that Invisible Children is not a revolutionary, grassroots movement as it claims to be; rather, it is part of the nonprofit-industrial complex that is closely linked to the state and animates a pedagogy of war by "stealing the pain of others" (Razack 2007) to garner support for its political objectives.

If campaigns such as *Kony 2012* are taken at face value, teachers become implicated in animating a pedagogy of war and teaching without critically thinking, especially if the educator is not familiar with that geographic location, the history of that country, and the complexities regarding the political issues there. "A tradition of didactic teaching that focuses upon an encyclopedic coverage of details" is indoctrination (Sears and Hughes 2006, 3). Therefore, the *Kony 2012* video and campaign is not a progressive activist struggle but a product that is being sold by invoking fear and global citizenship as a means to teach war and mobilize supporters for war.

## Factors to Consider When Teaching Political/Global Issues Critically

It is important for teachers to consider many things when teaching complex historical and contemporary political issues, whether regarding Joseph Kony, the Israeli occupation of Palestine, the U.S. imperialist destruction of Iraq, the Syrian war and refugee crisis, or immigration policies such as President Donald Trump's "Muslim ban" in the name of "eradicating radical Islam." Specifically, in the contemporary political climate, where a white supremacist (fascist) government has taken public office in the United States, teachers have a critical role to ensure that they do not partake in promoting a pedagogy of war either at home or abroad. While a white supremacist, right-wing government has changed the conditions of life for U.S. citizens, current U.S. foreign policy in Africa and the Middle East, which perpetrates war to advance U.S. capitalist interests, is simply a continuation of previous administrations' policies. Time and again we have learned that wars abroad reverberate negative stereotypes about the "Other" from over there into Western discourses. In turn, this has consequences for racialized people, specifically Muslims and people whose origins, family ties, or political affiliations are to countries that the United States is waging war upon. As such, the war over there will also play out in the streets, courtrooms, borders, and classrooms in North America. Hate crimes increased post-9/11 and are seen to be increasing in the post-Trump moment. As such, the following factors should be considered when teaching political and global issues, as they will help teachers move away from indoctrination and focus on education.

1. **Historicize the Issue**

   When teaching about global/political issues, in particular issues regarding nations the educator is not familiar with or does not know much about, it is important to understand the history of that nation/issue. Historical context provides a more complicated analysis to understanding contemporary issues and enables looking at the causes of conflicts/issues rather than simply what is told in a video like *Kony 2012* or by the corporate media.

2. **Provide Various Perspectives on the Issue through a Contrapuntal Reading of Texts**

   Educators must research the issue they will be teaching from various perspectives. Often a global issue/conflict may garner various viewpoints; it is important to seek out the various perspectives that people have and what they say or think about that topic. Educators should engage in a contrapuntal reading of the myriad texts— articles, videos, artwork, news interviews—that they gather on the topic. As a practice, a contrapuntal reading "goes directly against the grain of readings and writing to erect barriers between texts or to create monuments out of texts" (Said 2002, 137). Contrapuntal reading enables the unraveling of what is under the surface by paying attention to the hierarchies and power-knowledge nexuses embedded in them, through an interrogation of history and the assumptions that uphold traditional curricula and pedagogies (Desai and Gaztambide-Fernández 2013).

3. **Recognize the Voices of Those Most Affected by the Issue/Conflict**

   It is important for educators to show and share with students what people's lived experiences are. What do those most affected by the

issue/conflict feel and think? For example, in the *Kony 2012* video,
the Ugandan peoples' voices were completely left out, silencing
what the people facing the issue feel about the topic. Using personal
testimonies about the experiences of various people that lived
through the violence could enhance and provide nuance to what
might be happening in a particular place; this will also show how
different people are affected by the issue. It is important to consider
the social categories of race, class, gender, sexuality, nationality,
and ethnicity, among others, when choosing and discussing how
people experience an issue. These social categories will affect how
a group or individual experiences the issue/conflict. For example,
the Acholi people, who were directly affected by the LRA, will have
a very different experience of the conflict than an upper-class
business person/family in Uganda that might not be very closely
linked to the violence. Thus, when sharing resources on the topic,
teachers should locate the writers' or speakers' positions if that
information is available.

4. **Ask Critical Questions about the Texts and Media That You Incorporate into the Curriculum**
   As teachers incorporate various materials into their curriculum,
   ask critical questions about the material/artifact itself. Who has
   produced the material/artifact? Whose voices are heard? Whose
   voices are not heard? What is the key message in the material/
   artifact? What are the main topics that the material/artifact
   outlines? What might be left out of this material/artifact?

5. **Encourage Your Students to Think Critically**
   Upon gathering all the information and materials educators need
   to develop lesson/unit plans that are critical, diverse, informed, and
   historicized, ensure that the material is engaging for students. Use
   materials that will engage students, such as videos, newspaper
   articles, documentaries, news podcasts, and music/art pieces.
   Encourage your students to come up with their own perspectives
   on what they think about a particular issue/conflict by providing
   them with resources that have been carefully selected by the
   educator. Ask your students critical questions about the texts/
   media/cultural artifact and engage them in activities in which they
   develop their critical thinking skills and are able to discuss and
   share what they think and believe about a particular topic or
   issue.

6. **Create Learning Spaces That Are Safe**

   There are no learning spaces that are 100 percent safe. However, when teaching about political/social issues it is important to create a space that will allow different voices and perspectives to be heard and in which students and the educator feel they will not be attacked. Before the lesson/unit, the educator should develop strategies on how to address conflict(s) if they emerge and brainstorm ways to facilitate a conversation that has differing, conflictual perspectives. Most importantly, know where your students come from, as they could be triggered by the topic/issue you are teaching, especially if your students come from war zones/zones of conflict or are survivors of trauma. Be prepared to deal with students who might be triggered by the topic/issue you are teaching about and plan on how best to support them.

7. **Ask Questions**

   Always ask questions about a topic/issue one is not sure about. One can ask experts in that field of study, organizations working on that topic/issue, or anyone else that might be well versed on the issue/topic. Encourage your students to ask questions, as well.

8. **Critically Examine One's Own Subject Position**

   When educators teach political/global issues, it is important to consider one's own subject position in relation to the various social categories of race, class, gender, sexuality, religion, nationality, ethnicity, and language, among others. In what ways are you privileged and/or marginalized in relation to the social categories? In what ways do you think your social position limits or helps you understand the issue/nation/topic you are teaching? What biases or blind spots might you have about a particular issue/topic/nation because of your subject position? Considering one's subject position is important because it will make one mindful of the ways in which one may be implicated in perpetuating a problem (for example, animating a pedagogy of war or reproducing racist notions about other places/people) or how one may be contributing to the alleviation of an issue/conflict.

9. **Consider Your Theoretical/Political Frameworks and Lens for Teaching**

   Ask yourself what your theoretical/political orientation is at the outset of teaching. Is it anticolonial, anti-imperialist, antiracist,

antiheteropatriarchy, anticapitalist? If yes, consider how you
will address steps 1 through 8 in a manner that seeks a different
world.

Educators can teach for a more just, equitable, and democratic world
and inspire young people to get involved locally, nationally, and globally.
Being critical, mindful, and responsible are the primary factors that educators need to consider when teaching about global citizenship, justice,
peace, and social change.

## REFERENCES

Ast, D., and K. Bickmore. 2014. Critical global citizenship education:
    Cultivating teacher efficacy through professional collaboration. In *Inquiry
    into practice: Teaching global matters in local classrooms*, ed. D. Montemurro
    et al., 41–49. Ontario: OISE.
Desai, C. 2016. "We teach life": Exile, hip hop, and the radical tradition of
    Palestinian cultural resistance. Ph.D. dissertation. University of
    Toronto.
Desai, C., and R. Gaztambide-Fernández. 2013. Edward Saïd: An exilic
    pedagogue. In *Thirty-three critical pedagogues we need to know*, ed. J. Kirylo.
    New York: Peter Lang.
Escobar, P. 2011. Obama, the king of Africa. *Asia Times*, October 18.
    http://www.atimes.com/atimes/Global_Economy/MJ18Djo6.html.
Evans, M., and C. Reynolds. N.d. Introduction: Educating for global
    citizenship in a changing world. http://www.oise.utoronto.ca/cidec/
    UserFiles/File/Research/Global_Citizenship_Education/intro.pdf.
Harvey, D. 1990. *The condition of postmodernity: An enquiry into the origins of
    cultural change*. Cambridge, Mass.: Blackwell.
Huntington, S. 1996. *The clash of civilizations and the remaking of world order*.
    New York: Simon & Schuster.
Internal Displacement Monitoring Center Uganda Report. 2010. Difficulties
    continue for returnees and remaining IDPs as develop phase begins.
    http://www.internal-displacement.org/assets/library/Africa/Uganda/pdf/
    Uganda-December-2010.pdf.
Jackson, R. 2005. *Writing the war on terrorism: Language, politics and counter-
    terrorism*. Manchester: Manchester University Press.
*Kony 2012*. 2012. https://www.youtube.com/watch?v=Y4MnpzG5Sqc.
Lapayese, Y. 2003. Toward a critical global citizenship education. *Comparative
    Education Review* 47 (4): 493–501.
Levesque, S. 2003. Bin Laden is responsible; it was shown on tape: Canadian
    high school students' historical understanding of terrorism. *Theory and
    Research in Social Education* 31 (2): 174–202.

Mamdani, M. 2012. The downside of the *Kony 2012* video. *Pambazuka News.* http://www.pambazuka.org/en/category/features/80714/print.

McEwan, C. 2009. *Postcolonialism and development.* New York: Routledge.

Mohanty, C. 2006. U.S. empire and the project of women's studies: Stories of citizenship, complicity, and dissent. *Gender, Place, and Culture* 13 (1): 7–20.

Razack, S. 2007. Stealing the pain of others: Reflections on Canadian humanitarian responses. *Review of Education, Pedagogy, and Cultural Studies* 29 (4): 375–394.

Resist Africom. 2008. https://www.youtube.com/watch?v=JRCZk8mM1EU.

Richardson, G., and L. Abbott. 2009. Between the national and the global: Exploring tensions in Canadian citizenship education. *Studies in Ethnicity and Nationalism* 9 (3): 377–394.

Said, E. 1979. *Orientalism.* New York: Vintage.

———. 2002. *Reflections on exile and other essays.* Convergences: Inventories of the Present. Cambridge, Mass: Harvard University Press.

Shultz, L., and S. Jorgenson. N.d. Global citizenship education in post-secondary institutions: A review of the literature. http://www.gccd .ualberta.ca/en/~/media/gccd/Documents/GCE_lit_review.pdf.

Sears, A., and A. Hughes. 2006. Citizenship: Education and indoctrination. *Citizenship Teaching and Learning* 2 (1): 3–17.

Smith, A. 2009. The NGOization of the Palestine Liberation Movement: Interviews with Hatem Bazian, Noura Erekat, Atef Said, and Zeina Zaatari. In *The revolution will not be funded: Beyond the nonprofit industrial complex,* 165–184. Boston, Mass.: South End.

Weber, N. 2012. *NGO-produced global education programming in Canada and the United Kingdom: Reconciling global education ideals with national and international interests.* Toronto: University of Toronto.

Willinsky, J. 1998. *Learning to divide the world: Education at empire's end.* Minneapolis: University of Minnesota Press.

# Reflections on the Perpetual War: School Closings, Public Housing, Law Enforcement, and the Future of Black Life

*David Stovall*

## *The War Cannot Be Reduced to a Rhetorical Exercise*

I am thankful to the editors for the invitation to participate in this project for several reasons. First is the fact that current popular war rhetoric in the United States omits the domestic theater of war. Beyond hyperbolic rhetoric in the mode of the "war" on drugs or a "war" on poverty, the editors of this volume understand war as both a literal and contested term, speaking to the realities of many K–12 schools serving students of color in urban centers. Second, the editors explicitly understand the concept of postraciality as a false construct in the colonial mode of pacification and paternalism. Rounding out my feelings of gratitude toward the editors is that in part thanks to them I am not paranoid in my use of the term *war* to describe the conditions faced by hosts of students and families of color in K–12 city schools. From my understanding, the current war on students and families of color in U.S. K–12 schools is active, perpetual, and largely facilitated by apparatuses of the state. With this in mind, the proposed chapter organizes critical race theory (CRT), postcolonial theory, and theories of anti-Blackness to interrogate state-sanctioned violence, urban space, and the politics of exclusion. Countering the narrative of "hyperviolent youth," my project draws attention to policy formation and implementation as ideological rationales for containment and marginalization. Coupled with the destruction of public housing and federal corruption statutes, education is grouped with the aforementioned under the logic of state-sanctioned instability. Later referred to as "engineered conflict," here I provide a framework to examine conditions of urban space for African American and Latinx residents.

As a scholar and concerned community member who has utilized CRT over the last twenty years, I use the concept of counterstory to frame the current conditions in Chicago and their global connection to the larger neoliberal project of exclusion and marginalization of low-income People of Color. Countering the narrative of hyperviolent, despondent urban youth, the conditions in cities often create a complex set of circumstances that require more nuanced analysis. In recognition of these complexities, it is important to note that this document is reflective of a larger project, one in its infancy. For these reasons, the majority of this document remains theoretical and conceptual. As race studies scholars in education remain explicit in their analysis of the racialization of bodies in classrooms and school policy, they continue to explicate the intersectional relationship of race to urban geography, political economy, and gender (Bonilla Silva 2015, Buras 2015, Matias and Allen 2013, Wun 2014).

In solidarity with this line of inquiry, this chapter is organized into sections that speak to both the personal and external realities of the war theater and its relationship to education. Although it is impossible to provide a comprehensive account of the complexities of Black life in Chicago here, my condensed account comprises three sections. The first positions my own living condition in relation to containment, marginalization, and militarization. The second is dedicated to the concept of engineered conflict as the rationale for housing, education, and law enforcement policies. The final section is dedicated to futurity by embracing a radical imaginary to combat hopelessness in deeply trying times.

### *Where I'm From and Where I Live: Positioning the Colonial Project of Containment in Chicago*

I was born and raised and currently reside in one of the most segregated cities in the United States. Out of seventy-seven Chicago neighborhoods, twenty have populations that are over 90 percent African American (Swerd-low 2014). The schools in these areas reflect the same demographics. I often joke with visitors to the city that Chicago purports to be a community of neighborhoods, when it is actually a city of universes. It is not uncommon for residents of some neighborhoods rarely to leave those neighborhoods. Depending on where you are in the city, crossing one street can take you into an entirely different space, one with completely different demograph-ics from the area you just left. Beyond the pathology rhetoric that fuels common tropes of a "culture of poverty," Chicago is a city deeply affected by displacement, disinvestment, and neoliberal urbanism (Lipman 2011). Since 2000, the city has lost 200,000 residents, of which 178,000 were Black. In the same timeframe, over 80 percent of the city's public housing (which is 90 percent African American) has been razed.

Originally promising right of return and new housing accommodations to its residents, the Chicago Housing Authority (CHA) has only been able to replace 20 percent of its demolished housing stock (Hunt 2009). In a municipality that positions itself as a "global city," local and international investment capital permeates the mayor's office and the central business district, deeply influencing housing, education, and law enforcement policy. Neoliberal rhetoric runs rampant via monikers of "choice," "options," and "renewed opportunities." Once shunned neighborhoods rapidly become optimal sites for residences and retail as property taxes skyrocket, result-ing in raised rents and inflated real estate speculation. This dynamic leaves many long-term residents with few options beyond leaving the com-munity entirely. As people are displaced and their former neighborhoods become gentrified, African American residents who are able to remain in the city often relocate to already segregated portions of the city, creating instances of hypersegregation.

In some communities, the phases of gentrification are incomplete. I cur-rently live in one of those communities in transition. Known as Wood-lawn, the community is adjacent to the neighborhood of Hyde Park, home to the University of Chicago (U of C). Once a community of recently ar-rived European immigrants, the coupling of systemic racism by way of un-fair housing practices with the second iteration of the Great Migration prompted massive white flight, leaving Woodlawn devoid of city services and infrastructure. Documented extensively in Moore and Williams's (2012) ethnography of the genesis of a large Chicago street organization (gang), the lack of education and employment infrastructure deeply influ-enced the growth and development of one of the largest African American street organizations in the city, the Black P-Stone Rangers. Following the rise and fall of the Black P-Stones, numerous shifts took place in Woodlawn (deindustrialization, federal recessions, depletion of the social safety net, the disappearance of long-term living wage employment, etc.), resulting in depopulation and further disinvestment.

Directly in concert with Harvey's (2007) concept of "accumulation by dispossession," the story of Woodlawn grows deeper in complexity. As the area began to depopulate in the late 1980s and early 1990s, housing stock was either demolished or abandoned. Soon after, because the eastern sector of the community is proximal to the lakefront, developers targeted vacant land for new housing developments. During this time, a small plot of land was brokered by a local church and community organization. A small pocket of affordable housing was built, but it has been poorly maintained over the years. In addition to its proximity to the lakefront, the eastern portion of Woodlawn has direct access to public rail transit (providing swift travel to and from the downtown central business district). Despite the housing bubble and financial crisis of 2008, abandoned buildings are still being repurposed, transforming into luxury condominiums and/or expensive single-family homes. Additionally, over the past five years a public housing development (Grove Parc Place) that used to sit at the entrance of the local train station has been razed. The development has been replaced by a set of mixed-income properties, which require low-income residents to "qualify" for acceptance. In the new development, only low-income renters are required to work at least thirty hours per week, cannot have a recent felony conviction, and cannot have a recent history of drug addiction. Where some may view this as providing "needed improvements" to the area, the narratives of race and class are intimate partners in the sordid story of the dispossession of long-term, working-class and low-income African American residents of Woodlawn.

Simultaneously, the U of C has emerged as one of the primary beneficiaries of this accumulation by dispossession. As much of this new "development" is marketed to faculty, staff, and students, the U of C shuttle bus currently makes stops throughout the southeastern corridor of Woodlawn. Continuing U of C's vision to expand its corridor beyond the neighborhood's southern boundary, at Sixty-First Street, a squash center has been built on land where a section of Grove Parc Place once stood. As U of C is one of the primary landholders on the main corridor in East Woodlawn (Sixty-Third Street), much of the land is held in trust until a suitor of its choosing makes a bid on the vacant lot. Despite the transition, these not-so-subtle developments fuel displacement throughout the neighbor-hood. Although the process has slowed since the financial crisis of 2008, it is returning to the levels witnessed before the crash.

To ensure continued interest in the community, a significant police presence is felt throughout Woodlawn's eastern corridor. Depending on the time of day, there can be one to three parked police cruisers on my block. Beginning in 2014, the Chicago Police Department began a prac-tice of using the neighborhood as the training ground for first-year offi-cers. This has been a trend across the city in select African American neighborhoods, as city officials feel pressure to address "high-crime" areas. At the current moment in East Woodlawn, police sergeants hold meetings with street teams of officers in the middle of the block as a demonstration of police presence for new residents. Police bike patrols ride through the neighborhood no fewer than six officers at a time. In the summer of 2014, first-year patrol officers could be found walking in groups of three along Woodlawn alleys. In the summer of 2015, beat patrol officers walked the streets of Woodlawn, again in groups of three, to demonstrate to com-munity members that the eastern corridor will be protected. Instead of producing a sense of safety, a reframing of the situation would consider this show of power as a sign of containment, serving notice to certain residents that they are now being watched and no longer wanted in the community.

Simultaneously, it is important not to downplay the effect (and affects) of violence in the city and, in this case, throughout Woodlawn. From July 1–8, 2015, there were over three hundred shootings throughout the city and over sixty homicides. The week of September 29, 2015, began with fifteen people shot in fourteen hours (Grenoble 2015). It is important to understand both the tragedy and trauma of shootings and death by gun violence. At the same time, however, I want to pose the challenge to read-ers that this type of violence can also be facilitated by the state. The state's narrative of hyperviolent youth in hyperviolent communities allows war to be declared on them.

### *To Engineer Conflict: The War Is Real, Not Imagined*

Over the last few years, I have made it a practice in my classrooms, work-shops, and guest lectures to ask a basic question: *What is the best way to start a fight that you don't take part in?* The answers range from "instigating" to "starting a rumor" to "lying." After people offer their suggestions, I give them the image of two rival schools. If people are seated in rows, I start the exercise by having them imagine the room being divided in two.

I continue to have the group imagine that both sides are rival high schools. Concluding the exercise, I ask the group what would happen if one side of the room's high school was closed and everyone in it was sent to the rival high school (in this case, the people on the other side of the room). The very first answer they give me is invariably "fights." My following question to the group is, "What if you did that forty-nine times in one summer?" I like to begin with this example because it allows people who are unfamiliar with the situation in Chicago to imagine the conditions that certain groups of young people and their families endure. If it is common-sense knowledge that conflict is most likely to ensue if students unfamiliar with one another are placed in the same space, then why would a city implement such a policy with working-class/low-income sectors of the population that are almost entirely African American and Latinx?

In the summer of 2013, Chicago Public Schools (CPS) closed forty-nine schools. Of these forty-nine, over 90 percent were schools that served predominantly African American students from low-income families. Of the 56,000 students directly affected by the closure, 4,600 of the students were students with special needs, all of whom are required to have Individualized Education Plans (IEPs) (Waitoller et al. 2014).

In years past, I have discussed a "politics of disposability" with regard to People of Color in urban spaces. The assumption of criminality is often placed on Black and Latinx youth before any belief in their capacities as human beings to change and improve their conditions. Recent reporting of the death of unarmed Black residents in large U.S. cities have brought this to the fore, but we also need to consider the analysis brought forth by CRT—*the presumption of Black criminality is endemic to the policy architecture of the United States since its inception.* From voting suppression to overt policy-based discrimination in the housing market, Chicago has served as a prima facie example of the continued marginalization, containment, and isolation of certain Black bodies (Coates 2014).

Coates's analysis also allows us to complicate the issue of "gang violence." Where the majority of shootings in Chicago are attributed to gang disputes, a number of factors complicate this assumption. Originating in the mid-1990s, the Chicago Police Department teamed with the Federal Bureau of Investigation to enforce the Racketeering Influenced and Corrupt Organizations Act (RICO) on suspected gang chiefs in the city. Once used as legislation to create large dragnet operations in the 1950s and 1960s to halt Mafia activities, both law enforcement agencies assumed they would have similar success with gangs throughout Chicago. To their dismay, the exact opposite occurred. What the police and FBI did not take into account was the fact that hypersegregation often *precludes* gang disputes. Because some communities have tensions that may combine affiliations with neighborhood residency, animosities have the potential to be awakened tenfold when members of communities are forced to engage with others they may not know. As always, this should be complicated and understood within the colonial frame of dispossessing people of knowledge of themselves and their conditions, but it has to be taken into account when understanding state-sanctioned violence via planned instability. When purported gang chiefs were arrested as part of RICO enforcement, the result was a bifurcation of traditional gang allegiances. What once stood as coalitions across geographic areas became dispersed to individual geographic blocks in neighborhoods. Despite the negative connotations of gang life, it is important to know that the presence of older members in some cases gave order to the particular set (gang). Once this disappeared, weapons remained on the blocks, but now with little regulation from respected members of the set. Coupled with a fledgling drug trade in some communities, tensions were heightened.

In relation to the larger project of colonialism, the realities of housing, education, and law enforcement, paired with gun violence, create an instance where these communities have the greatest potential to become collective open-air cages for people to exterminate one another in. The areas farthest away from rail transit and the central business district operate as the "cages." Neighborhoods closest to rail and downtown that have not been completely gentrified serve as the spaces to be "cleansed" of unwanted elements, facilitating the transition from cage to desirable community. In the case of Woodlawn, it has become the latter. The convergence of geographic amenities (lakefront area, museum campuses, and more) with access to infrastructure (rail transit, high-end housing stock, and so forth) has created an instance where facilitators of investment capital patiently wait for the cycle of cleansing to complete itself.

Contrary to popular-media accounts of gun violence and school closings due to budgetary constraints, I understand these dynamics as engineered conflict. The city of Chicago has paired a set of neoliberal policies (school closings and the lack of affordable housing) with RICO enforcement, resulting in the destabilization of many low-income African American and Latinx communities. Using loss of population density and budget constraints as the rationale to enforce policy, populations are declared disposable and are systemically "cleansed" from the city boundaries. Because Chicago is used as a national template for school and housing reform, the inclusion of law enforcement in this intersection provides the opportunity to inform existing struggles against displacement, corporate educational reform, and marginalization. Operating as a form of state-sanctioned violence, the aforementioned policy architecture exacerbates deeply rooted conflicts in a hypersegregated city, resulting in tragic results for schools and families.

Even as the final number of shuttered schools was reduced to forty-nine (originally from 124 to fifty-four and then to forty-nine), many of these communities have experienced mass depletion of resources and infrastructure, while funds have been reallocated to revitalization projects aimed in making Chicago a "global city." As schools are closed, express bus lanes, multimillion-dollar art projects, and tourism campaigns are allocated to the central business district. Simultaneously, garbage services and road maintenance have been reduced in the areas where the schools are being closed. The maintenance of parking meters has been privatized, but the city is still able to secure a revenue stream through the collection of fees for parking tickets, making the city even less affordable and accessible for low-income families. From this type of disinvestment, the city has deemed its outskirts to be a nondesirable periphery solely designated for those who will be relegated to it, with minimal access to the core.

Deepening the concept of the disposability of low-income families, CPS hired Tom Tyrrell, a former Marine colonel whose claim to fame is his success with hostage negotiation during the Kosovo conflict in the mid-1990s. For me this raises a particular question: If the city is equating its low-income communities with war-torn countries, what does it say about the residents of these areas? Are they refugees? Prisoners of war? Enemy combatants? If so, what policies do you put in place for this group of young people? Unfortunately, the city has proven itself to have a unilateral answer to these questions: *In this particular war, they are disposable . . . if they do not comply, extermination awaits.*

On the ground, community residents who are living the realities of engineered conflict can argue for an intensified police presence, often resulting in further social, political, and economic isolation. Ideologically and materially, the city has deemed the most viable place for young people caught in this conflict to be the Department of Corrections. As eyes are currently on Chicago with respect to gun violence, few critiques have posited the current wave of violence as indicative of chronic disinvestment, structural racism, poverty, and food insecurity. At this moment, crime-fighting strategies are focused on "getting bad guys off the street" without a systemic understanding of the aforementioned concerns as central to violence.

From both an ideological and structural perspective, the closure of forty-nine schools has the greatest potential to increase violence in these communities. Not because of hyperviolent or inherently deficient youth but because one of the consequences of hypersegregation via local residential policies is that communities don't know one another. As a historical consequence, tensions are "engineered" when communities resort to protectionism. In an environment where individuals are stressed from a lack of infrastructure (housing and education) along with a lack of access to basic services, this becomes a perfect storm for conflict.

### *Toward Futurity: Black Life in the Radical Imaginary*

School closings should be understood not only as a tired excuse by CPS to address budget shortfalls but as part and parcel of a larger project that involves the mass disinvestment, displacement, and state-sanctioned disposability of low-income African American and Latinx communities. Key to these concerns is the view that to make schools "cost effective," competitive, and efficient, there have to be "winners" and "losers." According to CPS, the losers continue to be from groups that have been historically marginalized and isolated.

In light of the realities of the presidential administration of Donald Trump and the convergence of housing, education, and law enforcement in Chicago, my commitment to a radical imaginary draws my focus to the population of African American and Latinx residents that are able to remain in the city. While the vast majority of said residents remain in areas that have little proximity to the rail systems and the central business district and have a history of community disinvestment by the city, some African American and Latinx residents were able to keep their homes or apartments in areas targeted for development. To their credit, these families are not taking the aforementioned policy architecture lying down but are instead collectivizing their efforts to secure quality education, affordable housing, and human dignity. Despite the challenges of their struggle, their efforts have gained support across the country and internationally.

As a project of the radical imaginary, I seek to work with others to confront the world as it is. The future of the lives of African American and Latinx youth in Chicago is not hopeless. After years of work as an engaged scholar, I often express my worry to my students that my initial inquiries can instill a sense of hopelessness in them. To the contrary, despite the many trials that youth must endure in the city, young people and community residents are organizing to change their conditions. For thirty-four days, a group of twelve community members engaged in a hunger strike demanding quality education for their community. Known as the Dyett Twelve, their demands on the city gained national attention in challenging the city to provide quality education for its residents (www.teachers forjustice.org).

Operating from a Black feminist analysis, the Black Youth Project 100 has taken a stance against youth criminalization, unfair wages, and substandard education (www.byp100.org). Critical to their work is the ability to envision "a world where all Black people have social, political, and educational freedom." Understanding the intensity of the current situation, groups like the Dyett Twelve and BYP 100 are taking the steps necessary to support young people in the process of creating new realities during extremely serious times.

Although the recent election of Donald Trump as president of the United States is an absurdity, the situation has become even more challenging and serious as a result. His appointment of Betsy DeVos as secretary of education epitomizes the aforementioned hyper form of white, Protestant, patriarchal, able-bodied, heteronormative neoliberalism. From vouchers to the myth of school choice, DeVos's rhetoric feeds into a sentiment that positions quality education as a commodity only reserved for the "deserving"; her blunders in the first month and a half of the presidency only presage the days ahead. By all means, the need for antiracist educational justice remains, but the work has definitely become more challenging. Nevertheless, in times of extreme and overt repression, the window for resistance opens a bit wider. The stark and dire nature of Trump's advisors' and cabinet members' support for immigration suppression (including Steve Bannon, among others), climate change denial (Scott Pruitt), voter suppression of People of Color (Jefferson Sessions), false claims of wiretapping (Sean Spicer), and false claims of voter fraud (Kellyanne Conway) can provide a window for people to understand the long-term effects of the perpetual war waged against People of Color in the United States. At the same time, this window to understand struggle will not be open for long. As many have begun to ride the wave of protest of the Trump election, a more sustained resistance is necessary in the development of strategies, tactics, and formations that allow us to engage this fight for the long haul. If we do not, it will not just result in more of the same. This time it will be worse.

## REFERENCES

Arrastia, L. 2007. Capital's daisy chain: Exposing Chicago's corporate coalition. *Journal of Critical Education Policy Studies* 5 (1).

Ball, S. J. 2007. *Education plc: Understanding private sector participation in public sector education.* New York: Routledge.

Bell, D. 1980. *Brown v. Board of Education* and the interest convergence dilemma. *Harvard Law Review* 93:518–533.

Bennett, L., J. Smith, and P. Wright, eds. 2006. *Where are poor people to live? Transforming public housing communities.* London: M. E. Sharpe.

Bonilla-Silva, E. 2015. More than prejudice: Restatement, reflections, and new directions in critical race theory. *Sociology of Race and Ethnicity* 1 (1): 75–89.

Boyd, M. R. 2008. *Jim Crow nostalgia: Reconstructing race in Bronzeville.* Minneapolis: University of Minnesota Press.

Brown, L., and E. Gutstein. 2009. The charter difference: A comparison of Chicago charter and neighborhood high schools. *Collaborative for Equity and Justice in Education,* February 17.

Buras, K. L. 2015. *Charter schools, race, and urban space: Where the market meets grassroots resistance.* New York: Routledge.

Buras, K. L., J. Randels, and K. Y. Salaam. 2009. *Pedagogy, policy, and the privatized city: Stories of dispossession and defiance from New Orleans.* New York: Teachers College Press.

Burch, P. 2009. *Hidden markets: The new education privatization.* New York: Routledge.

Civic Committee of the Commercial Club of Chicago. 2003. Left behind: Student achievement in Chicago's public schools. Commercial Club of Chicago.

Coates, T. 2014. The case for reparations. *The Atlantic,* June.

Crenshaw, K., N. Gotanda, G. Peller, and K. Thomas. 1995. *Critical race theory: The key writings that formed the movement.* New York: The New Press.

Delgado, R. 2003. Cross and blind alleys: A critical examination of recent writing about race. *Texas Law Review* 82 (1): 121–152.

Delgado, R., and J. Stefancic. 2001. *Critical race theory: An introduction.* New York: New York University.

Duncan-Andrade, J. M. R. 2009. Note to educators: Hope required when growing roses in concrete. *Harvard Educational Review* 79 (2): 1–13.

Fine, M., and M. Fabricant. 2012. *Charter schools and the corporate makeover of public education: What's at stake?* New York: Teachers College Press.

Glanton, D., W. Mullen, and A. Olivio. 2011. Neighborhood population drain: Census shows central Chicago grew while outlying areas lost. *Chicago Tribune,* February 18.

Grenoble, R. 2015. Chicago starts the week with 14 shot in 15 hours. *Huffington Post,* September 30. http://www.huffingtonpost.com/entry/chicago-shootings-gun-violence_560afobfe4bodd8503099034.

Freire, P. 2003. *Education for critical consciousness.* New York: Continuum.

Harvey, D. 2007. *A brief history of neoliberalism.* New York: Oxford University Press.

Hunt, D. B. 2009. *Blueprint for disaster: The unraveling of Chicago public housing.* Chicago: University of Chicago Press.

Koval, J. P., L. Bennett, M. I. J. Bennett, et al., eds. 2006. *The new Chicago: A social and cultural analysis.* Philadelphia: Temple University Press.

Lipman, P. 2003. Chicago school policy: Regulating Black and Latino youth in the global city. *Race, Ethnicity, and Education* 6 (4): 331–355.

———. 2004. *High stakes education: Inequality, globalization, and urban school reform.* New York: Routledge.

———. 2011. *The new political economy of urban education: Neoliberalism, race, and the right to the city.* New York: Routledge.

Lipman, P., J. Smith, E. Gutstein, and L. Dallacqua. 2012. Examining CPS' plan to close, turnaround, or phase out 17 schools. *Collaborative for Equity and Justice in Education*, February 21.

Lynn, M. 1999. Toward a critical race pedagogy: A research note. *Urban Education* 33 (5): 606–627.

Matias, C., and R. L. Allen. 2013. Loving Whiteness to death: Sadomasochism, emotionality, and possibly of humanizing love. *Berkeley Review of Education* 4 (2): 285–309.

Mills, C. 2003. *From class to race: Essays in White Marxism and Black radicalism.* New York: Rowman & Littlefield.

Moore, N., and L. Williams. 2012. *The almighty Black P-Stone nation: The rise, fall, and resurgence of an American gang.* Chicago: Chicago Review.

Olivio, A. 2004. New CHA housing is tied to jobs: Adults must work 30 hours a week. *Chicago Tribune*, September 22.

Olszewski, L. 2004. 10 city schools targeted to close: Low enrollment, building condition used as criteria. *Chicago Tribune*, June 4.

Olszewski, L., and C. Sadovi. 2003. Rebirth of schools set for South side CHA and a list of institutions have big plans. *Chicago Tribune*, December 19.

Pedroni, T. 2007. *Market movements: African-American involvement in school voucher reform.* New York: Routledge.

Popkin, S., B. Katz, M. Cunningham, et al. 2004. *A decade of HOPE VI: Research findings and policy challenges.* Washington, D.C.: The Urban Institute and the Brookings Institution.

Rossi, R. 2012. Minister in rent-a-protester flap offers to open his books. *Chicago Sun-Times*, January 27.

Schlikerman, B. 2015a. CPS enrollment down 2 percent: 367,499 students in school system; charter schools show slight increase. *Chicago Sun-Times*, September 26.

————. 2015b. CPS sets hearings for proposed new charter schools. *Chicago Sun-Times*, September 26.

Schmich, M. 2004. Dream faces bumpy road: Future as mixed-income community may pass some neighbors by. *Chicago Tribune*, July 18.

Smith, J., and D. Stovall. 2008. Coming home to new homes and new schools: Critical race theory and the new politics of containment. *Journal of Education Policy* 23 (2): 135–152.

Swerdlow, S. 2014. How segregated is Chicago and does it matter? *Chicago Sun-Times*, May 27.

Taylor, S., F. Rizvi, B. Lingard, and M. Henry. 1997. *Educational policy and the politics of change*. New York: Routledge.

Wun, C. 2014a. The anti-Black order of No Child Left Behind: Using Lacanian psychoanalysis and critical race theory to examine NCLB. *Educational Philosophy and Theory* 45 (5): 462–474.

————. 2014b. Unaccounted foundations: Black girls, anti-Black racism, and punishment in schools. *Critical Sociology* 1 (1): 1–14.

Waitoller, F., J. Radinsky, A. Trzaska, and D. Maggin. 2014. *A longitudinal comparison of enrollment patterns of students receiving special education services in Chicago charter and neighborhood public schools*. Chicago: Collaborative for Equity and Justice in Education, University of Illinois at Chicago.

Yamamoto, E. 1999. *Interracial justice: Conflict and reconciliation in post–civil rights America*. New York: New York University Press.

Yosso, T. 2005. Whose culture has capital? A critical race theory discussion of community cultural wealth. *Race, Ethnicity, and Education* 8 (1): 69–91.

# Caste Education in Neoliberal Society: Branding ADHD and Value-Added Students through the Tactics of "Population Racism"

*Clayton Pierce*

*Racism, always the game of a reactionary governing class,*
*is being played for much higher stakes today.*

—HARRY HAYWOOD, *Negro Liberation*, 1948

Neoliberalism has been broadly defined as a set of radical free-market economic and social policies designed to abolish Keynesian Depression-era responses by the state to drastic poverty and wealth disparities in the United States (Foucault 2010; Harvey 2005a, 2005b; Klein 2008; Ong 2007). The privatization of public sectors such as education and health care, disciplining labor through union busting, and deregulation of financial capital (for example, the infamous credit default swaps that helped precipitate the 2008 financial crisis) all represent the successes of the neoliberal economic and social reform that began in earnest in the late 1970s in the United States, United Kingdom, Latin America, and across the globe (Harvey 2005a). As an economic and social doctrine, however, neoliberalism should not be understood as a "new" phase or rupture with capitalism; rather, it is simply the most recent set of economic and political strategies utilized by the white ruling elite to control and regulate what the Occupy movement has called the "99 percent of the population" in ways that maintain historical differences and inequities (forms of white privilege, for example) while also reconcentrating astronomical amounts of wealth to a sliver of the world's population (Piketty 2014).[1]

Up to this point, traditional Marxist approaches in education focusing on class formation have not adequately shown how capitalism and racism in the United States are coevolutionary partners and thus must be understood in dialectical relation (Brown and De Lissovoy 2011; Leonardo 2004, 2012).[2] Neo-Marxist educational theorists, in other words, privilege class when analyzing problems of schooling—such as the "dropout" student— and consequently lose sight of other important power relations that play a pivotal role in the processes of capital accumulation and white supremacy (Allman 2001, Bowles and Gintis 1977, Cole 2007, Freire 2000, McLaren 2005, Willis 1981). Differing from neo-Marxist approaches to analyzing schooling in our neoliberal moment, I argue that neoliberal governing strategies utilized by state/corporate networks of power have evolved out of the needs of the United States as a racial capitalist state.

As such, I suggest that a better-equipped historical-materialist approach would attend to the ways race, class, gender, and sexuality are mobilized by state and corporate actors through sets of biopolitical strategies that focus on controlling and regulating populations within the nation in line with the laws of capitalist accumulation and the maintenance of white supremacy.[3] This chapter aims to articulate a racial capitalist analysis of schooling that highlights biopolitical governing strategies by turning to Du Bois's work on caste education. Looking to Du Bois's analytic of caste education, I argue, provides a point of departure for better understanding the dialectic relationship existing between racism and capitalism in the United States, in particular how it has been embedded in the nation's school system. In today's neoliberal reform context, however, I am also arguing that we need to understand how caste education operates through the intersecting radical free-market reform strategies and the needs of the racial capitalist state. In the examples of the ADHD and value-added metric debates, I argue that core features of racial capitalist schooling are present: The regulation of populations of students into manageable forms of biocapital maintains and reproduces the cogenerative projects of accumulation and white supremacy. First, however, it will be helpful to clarify how Du Bois's caste analytic of schooling is rooted in his larger understanding of racial capitalist society.

## The Role of Schooling in Racial Capitalist Society

Racial capitalism is a historical-materialist analysis Du Bois developed in his body of work that highlights how racism is fused to the historical expansion of capitalist accumulation as opposed to being an external, separate problem that emerged after capitalist development began in the United States (Du Bois 1935, Robinson 2000).[4] For Du Bois, one of the most damaging (and effective) ways racial capitalist relations have been preserved in the United States is through the institution of public schools (Pierce 2017). Specifically, he articulates how the construction of public schools after the Civil War put in place a caste education system—a continuation of the former caste system established in plantation society. For Du Bois, during and after Reconstruction schools provided the racial capitalist state a tool of population management for the white ruling oligarchy to enact accumulation strategies upon working-class populations. For Du Bois, caste education is the racial capitalist expression of schooling in the United States.

Du Bois identified two primary goals that the caste education system helped bring to fruition in racial capitalist society. The first goal entails the need to reproduce racial divisions among the working-class populations through institutions such as schools that simultaneously strengthen white supremacy across class lines (white workers and industrialists united in their racial solidarity) while also creating a labor underclass in the nonwhite worker. What Du Bois called "the psychological wages of whiteness" were paid through segregated schooling by teaching white, working-class students that they enjoyed social and political rights and privileges not granted to the inferior subgroup of humans that attended schools for People of Color.[5] In turn, the second related goal of the caste education system for Du Bois has to do with how a segregated and unequal schooling system helps maximize the extractive value of surplus labor from working-class populations. Put differently, wealth accumulation for white state/corporate elites requires that the schooling system preserve a racially divided competitive wage-labor system (Du Bois 1935).

The "psychological wages of whiteness" works for Du Bois on two levels in racial capitalist society. On the one hand, being white generally affords workers with better paying, safer, and overseer positions that were based on whites' perceived racial superiority and protected through segregated workplaces and union policies (Roediger 1991). Yet whites also profit from wages of whiteness in social spaces where white individuals feel empowered and entitled—riding on a Jim Crow bus or train, for example—because their sense of being in the world is positively affirmed through the visible recognition that their economic and social situation is better than the racially inferior "nonwhite." For Du Bois, in other words, whites learn not only in school that they are a superior caste to People of Color. White folks also learn through a racialized social and political experience that the state and its institutions protect and reward white supremacy—it is learned that being white is a more "valuable" form of life, one to be protected at all costs (Lipsitz 2006).

Du Bois (1935) named this process of white subjectification "caste psychology," that is, how whites learn to behave and act in the white world in relation to the dark world. From these core dynamics animating racial capitalism—creating the structural conditions for a racially divided working class and the subjective education of white supremacy within the white working class—Du Bois situates the public schooling system created during Reconstruction within a broader set of strategies of social control that emerged with the unification of the white ruling groups of the North (industrialists and bankers) and South (the former labor-camp aristocracy). Therefore, understanding these central mechanisms of racial capitalism is especially relevant today in light of major recent studies on the growth of economic and racial inequality over the past half-century and the role schools have played in contributing to such trends (Harvey 2011, Marsh 2011, Piketty 2014).

With these two goals of racial capitalism in mind, I argue it is imperative to ask: How do contemporary neoliberal tools of caste education work, and what do they look like? Identifying the ways caste education strategies work today is important because it gives us points onto which to focus strategies of resistance, especially in a historical moment when colorblind racism is facilitated through the free-market language of personal responsibility and individual competition—both underlying discourses to the ADHD and value-added debates. Yet it is equally necessary to understand how caste formation works through free-market discourses and values coded through tactics of population racism and the "technical solutions" that provide the pretext for assembling and branding bodies and populations.

### Population Racism and Its Technologies

Population racism is a concept that the social theorists Patricia Ticineto Clough and Craig Willse (2011) developed out of Foucault's work on biopolitics. Biopolitics, as Foucault theorized it in his writings and research on modern state governance, is a model of politics modern states use to regulate and manage populations within their borders to meet the needs of labor and normative cultural values. For Foucault, what makes the modern state "biopolitical," that is, having a politics focused on the management of life within a state's territory, was a shift in how governing began to focus on problems of population health and productivity. States in the modern period, according to Foucault, began to focus their social and political policies on how to make a more productive workforce, on which citizens were to be considered racially pure and impure (that is, eugenic social policies such as miscegenation laws or one-drop blood laws), on how legal/penal institutions and police forces should treat and discipline criminals within the population, and on what ways citizens were to be educated (Foucault 2009, 2010; also see Dean 2010; Lemke 2011; Stoler 1995).

Within Foucault's biopolitical understanding of modern state governance, race plays a particularly important role. Racial and ethnic divisions among European populations that have developed over centuries served as antagonisms states could use to manipulate their populations for the labor needs of growing industries and to discipline dominant cultural norms surrounding concerns such as reproduction in the Christian heteronormative family. Anti-Semitism, for instance, or hatred of Muslim ethnic groups in "Christian" nations are types of racism states use to regulate their population through immigration policies, the formation of ghettos, and generally to construct an idea of the "pure" citizen against the perceived debased and potentially dangerous segments of the population. Importantly, for Foucault, biological or genetic forms of racism undergird biopolitical governing strategies. In Foucault's biopolitical analysis of the state, in other words, governing practices can only function if states maintain a population of biologically different races within and outside their territorial boundaries. Consider, for instance, how American Indian boarding schools and other "civilizing" projects of the U.S. government sought to "kill the Indian and save the man" (Churchill 2004). The biological racist rationality that was normalized through federal policies such as boarding-school strategies—or, in a more contemporary context, colonial curricula embedded in textbooks that are used to Westernize American Indian nations—provides the pretext in which to kill one form of life and replace it with a form more controllable and useful to the nation-state (Calderón 2014).

It is also important to point out, however, that Foucault's biopolitical analysis focused exclusively on European forms of racism and its paradigmatic form in the Nazi state (Foucault 2003). As Alexander Weheliye (2014) has argued, Foucault's European biopolitical theory of racism leaves out or ignores how racism developed differently in the U.S. colonial/plantation context. In this sense, Du Bois's analysis of racial capitalist schooling in the form of caste education offers a stronger and more appropriate biopolitical theory of race and schooling in the United States because it is rooted in a specific historical materialism unique to the colonial and plantation foundations of this country.

Clough and Willse's concept of population racism builds out from Foucault's concept of biopolitics and connects to Du Bois's biopolitical analysis of schooling in the United States in some important ways. Yet population racism, as Clough and Willse theorize it, is different from Foucault and Du Bois and takes on some unique qualities within neoliberal societies:

> Population racism in neoliberalism functions in a field of many populations, all of which are differently targeted for manipulation through technical solution. Technical solutions take part in and thereby give support to population racism not only as a matter of governance, but as a matter of economy as well. That is to say, population racism functions on behalf of capital accumulation by enacting a fragmentation of the biological field, enabling differences to be cut into the biological, which, as life-itself, had been made abstract. The calculation of biological differences enables a process of value production in the differences of race, or in the differences of life capacities rendered as racial probabilities to be circulated as data. Not only do probability statistics activate a population, the probabilities draw future possibilities of life and death into the present, and in so doing generate and circulate value, or what might be better called the biovalue of risk or life and death chances. (Clough and Willse 2011, 51)

Before I go further, it will be helpful to break down Clough and Willse's definition of population racism into its component parts in order to see better how it connects to neoliberal caste tools of education and how they operate today.

The first part of Clough and Willse's concept of population racism relevant to my analysis of neoliberal caste tools of education is its assumption that neoliberal societies already have racially and ethnically divided populations. Within the context of the United States, this assumption stands on pretty solid ground. Cities and schools, for example, have not seen the current levels of segregation since before the *Brown v. Board of Education* ruling (347 U.S. 483, 1954). Moreover, discourses around immigration in the United States signal another way that distinct racial and ethnic groups are maintained as "outsider" populations. Asian, Latinx, and Muslim communities, for instance, are constructed through media and surveillance technologies as well as through immigration policies that turn these groups into threats such as potential terrorists or strains on our country's health care infrastructure (Ali 2014, Ong 2006). This is all to say that since the United States is one of the most racially and ethnically divided and segmented nations in the Western world, it is fertile soil for governing strategies designed to exploit and expand these differences, differences that are themselves a result of the racial capitalist history of the country. Du Bois's analysis of the reconfiguration of racial capitalism during Reconstruction is one of the best historical examples of how U.S. social and political life is already primed for such governing policies and for the establishment of institutions (here, schools) that build on racial and ethnic differences established over the country's colonial-plantation, Jim Crow, and now neoliberal period.

Up until the middle of the twentieth century, many social policies dealing with the poor, communities of color, immigrants, and indigenous populations in the United States were explicitly rationalized through eugenic science that posited the biological inferiority of nonwhite population groups. Even white European immigrant groups, such as the Poles, Irish, Italians, and Jews, had to "earn" their whiteness and distinguish themselves from established darker, more impure races in the U.S. nation-state (Ignatiev 2008). As another example, the sterilization of poor African American or indigenous women was carried out with the express intent of limiting and regulating the reproductive abilities of the perceived biologically inferior caste (understood to be a threat to the genetic purity of the white, Anglo, Christian blood of the superior caste of the nation) (Davis 1983). In a similar vein, the prison-industrial complex has always been one of the most important governing tools, in that it provides the racial capitalist state a way to remove and incarcerate "problem" portions of the population (Alexander 2012, Davis 2003). These would all be examples of previous forms of what Clough and Willse call "technical solutions" to population management problems, something they suggest continues through new methods of governing in neoliberal societies. Yet since neoliberal societies cannot openly use biologically racist rationalizations for social and political policies because they were largely eradicated through civil rights legal reform and the social movements of that era, according to Clough and Willse, biological racism had to be reconfigured into new regimes of knowledge and power that allowed states to continue to govern the population through racial and class divisions in disguised ways.

We can detect such new governing regimes that turn biological racism into acceptable colorblind forms by how they frame problems within the population as needing technical solutions, which solutions, in turn, call for measurement devices necessary to distinguish among the more valuable and more disposable (that is, more dangerous and less productive strains on the economy, and so on) types of life within the nation. From Clough and Willse's point of view, population racism works today not on the basis of blood quantum laws, a governing practice of the eugenic period of U.S. history, but rather on the construction of discourses and practices around state- and expert-identified problems such as the achievement gap and on other laws and policies deployed as technical solutions used to manage such problems in ways that maintain racial capitalist social relations.

Since neoliberal societies, and more specifically their governing strategies, cannot rely on biological racism as a rationality, they instead build on the foundation these policies and laws lay by focusing on newly defined "technical solutions" within the population, such as human capital development. By using the discourse and practices of technical solutions, neoliberal societies are able to manage identified problems within the population through expert regimes that not only name the problem (for example, failing schools falling behind other advanced industrialized nations in the production of a high-tech competitive workforce) but also get to manage the problem through a limited set of solutions defined by powerful actors such as the Bill and Melinda Gates Foundation or the Walton Family Foundation. In terms of how population racism is created through a technical-solution approach to governing expert-identified population problems, it is important not to lose sight that amid this neoliberal educational restructuring, urban communities of color are at ground zero. Here we can see how groups within the population who were previously the target of biologically racist governing strategies are now similarly being targeted through the sanitizing matrix of probability data and risk-management studies.

In neoliberal societies, population racism translates the problem of school failure through measurement metrics that create data around dropout rates, graduation rates, academic performance by subject, achievement gap, the amount of students qualified for free and reduced lunches, teacher performance, and so on. Here we can see how from a perceived "nonracial" problem a whole economy of data is created through which the justification and rationality for reconstructing schools through privatization schemes takes place. Once these data economies around school reform are established, decisions are made around the value of life in urban communities in ways that sort groups along a continuum running from "valuable" to "disposable." Here, for instance, the dropout student falls on the disposable end, while the small percentage that navigate the system successfully are then faced with a very low statistical probability of making it through predominantly white institutions of higher education, where they will be met with a whole new host of challenges, such as unhealthy racial climates (Buenavista 2010; Solórzano, Ceja, and Yosso 2000).

Clough and Willse's concept of population racism is extremely useful for understanding and interpreting the ways neoliberal education reform operates in the U.S. context. In particular, it helps us see how caste is reconstructed through the data economies established through the technical-solutions governance approach of neoliberal educational actors such as the National Governors' Association or corporate management companies that run charter schools—both of which, like all the other major corporate education philanthropists, are elite whites not unlike the Carnegies, Rockefellers, and other Industrial Era philanthropists (Au and Ferrare 2015, Brown 2015). Once student populations such as those in the Philadelphia, New Orleans, New York, Washington, and Chicago school districts are translated into actionable economies of probability statistics, the stage is set to manipulate communities of color in line with the needs of the racial capitalist state. Namely, antagonistic and competitive relations between working-class communities of color and more affluent white communities are preserved through the dual discourses of school choice and individual responsibility, where it is up to individual families to utilize school data to make their best consumer choices in the educational marketplace. The illusion of school choice, in this example of neoliberal education governance, dictates the reality of limited choice, which is shaped by the population racism of neoliberal education governance regulated through data-economy regimes.

Population racism, as the examples above indicate, work in conjunction with neoliberal education-restructuring policies to preserve caste relations in society. Although there has been an extensive amount of research on school choice and charter systems showing how racial and class inequality is maintained through these policies, little work has looked at how other data economies have been created for deepening the biopolitical management of bodies and populations in racial capitalist society. To understand caste education in the neoliberal era, I am suggesting, we also need to connect strategies such as school choice to new technologies of control that work through neurological intervention as well as population "quality" metrics devised in the genetically engineered crop field and subsequently deployed in the classroom.

*The ADHD Student: A Biopolitical War on Bodies*
*and Populations of Color*

The skyrocketing Attention Deficit Hyperactivity Disorder (ADHD) rate is one of the most alarming examples of the biopolitical war on bodies and People of Color in the neoliberal education-reform context. In a recent study performed by the clinical psychologist Steven Hinshaw and health economist Richard Scheffler (2014), child ADHD diagnoses rates are shown to be dramatically higher in states that have adopted accountability policies (such as Race to the Top) that severely penalize schools for student and teacher "underperformance." Hinshaw and Scheffler analyzed Center for Disease Control (CDC) data and corroborate previous research I have done on the subject, which found that, especially in working-class communities of color, the explosive growth trend of ADHD diagnoses in U.S. schoolchildren is directly connected to radical free-market reform strategies aimed at school districts across the country (Pierce 2013). Hinshaw and Scheffler's recent findings are particularly troubling when considering the powerful network of actors that compose the public outreach and advertising apparatus that teaches teachers, school psychologists, nurses, parents, and school personnel (and the public in general) about sicknesses like ADHD and its pharmaceutical solution through products such as Adderall and Ritalin. Big Pharma, the National Institute of Health, the Department of Education, prominent psychologists, and other actors have spent the past two decades or more creating an entire knowledge industry around the benefits of ADHD drugs for schoolchildren (and their parents). Within the context of the high-stakes testing culture that urban schools have been turned into, the technical problem of ADHD has emerged as an educational problem that can only be solved by constructing a data economy based largely on brain images and clinical studies of children. Research done by some of the most powerful corporate and scientific experts in the nation, in other words, drives the practices schools employ in dealing with ADHD students.[6]

It is not a coincidence, as the former editor-in-chief of the *New England Journal of Medicine* Marcia Angell (2005) notes in her book, that pharmaceutical companies spend more on advertising than on research and development. The linking of the pharmaceutical industry actor network with the aggressive corporate education-reform network driving policy in this country today creates a win-win situation for profiteering entities in the business of selling cures for behavioral disorders *and* educational underperformance. Here the exploding ADHD rates in schoolchildren in the

United States can be read through Clough and Willse's concept of population racism and, in particular, as a problem in the educational population that can only be solved through a technical solution. Circulated into other data economies such as academic performance measures on tests, ADHD diagnoses (which are understood through scientific regimes closely tied to the pharmaceutical industry) in students become another way for schools to manage bodies that threaten the high-stakes testing culture of urban classrooms and the national human capital development crisis that almost every educational reformer invokes when given a chance to speak about the educational challenges this country faces. Additionally, recent CDC (2011) data also shows that African American and Latino male students are quickly catching up to middle-class white male students as the most diagnosed ADHD group in the nation. Terrence Fitzgerald (2010) rightly argues that ADHD drugs and their use on students of color intersect with the long and violent history of white expert elites controlling the bodies and minds of African Americans in compulsory spaces such as schools.

In one of the most stunning findings from the study, "ADHD diagnoses of public school students within 200 percent of the federal poverty level jumped 59 percent after accountability legislation passed, Hinshaw reports, compared with less than 10 percent for middle-and high-income children" (Miller 2014). Hinshaw and Scheffler go on to show that their data point to a logical explanation to the ADHD diagnoses rate explosion among U.S. schoolchildren. When one considers the data alongside the accountability and testing regimes schools have been forced to adopt, where teachers, principals, staff, and personnel jobs are literally on the line, an incentive structure is also created to utilize medicalized conditions in order to maximize the potential for high-achieving students in a school—students are turned into manageable forms of biocapital measured by their ability or inability to accrue human capital skills. The market culture that schools are being forced to adopt, in other words, produces adjustments in how students' bodies are treated as potential risks or assets as test takers. One of the most damaging ways schools have responded under the radical market restructuring strategies that have gripped cities like Chicago, New York, Washington, and Atlanta is to turn to new technological solutions, for example, the biotechnological solution of psychotropic drugs such as Ritalin and Adderall.

Ultimately, what the new study analyzing data on ADHD diagnoses rates shows is this: Interpreted alongside states with the most intense punitive assessment policies, there is a clear correlation between new biotechnological forms of control (that is, Adderall and Ritalin) and state and national educational strategies focused on increasing academic performance in schools (and in the global economic marketplace). As I have argued elsewhere (Pierce 2013), the convergence of new biotechnologies that can control the biochemical makeup of students *and* radical free-market educational reform strategies marks a horrifying turning point in how schools can adjust students' bodies to the performative standards of "racing to the top" at all costs. The connection between high-stakes urban school environments with exploding ADHD diagnoses rates of African American and Latinx children also illuminates an important dimension of how population racism manifests within the caste education model of neoliberal society. Caste, in other words, is being reconstructed not through old biological racist paradigms associated with the eugenic era, such as IQ tests, but rather through new genetic sciences that allow for the managing of the ADHD child and the populations they belong to by considering their bodies not biologically inferior but rather neurologically abnormal.

In this sense, the opening up of the neural pathways and biochemical messaging systems of schoolchildren's bodies to market-driven reform strategies is one of the most troubling phenomena to emerge from the neoliberal educational restructuring project that has been underway for the past thirty years. Once the biological processes of children become enmeshed with the question of academic performance and human capital development in a high-stakes schooling culture, a deeper control of life in schools is achieved. Since government and corporate scientific experts primarily shape how the public understands problems such as ADHD diagnoses in schoolchildren, it is only natural that a whole new data economy built around ADHD students and their symptoms is being integrated into systems of neoliberal educational restructuring, thus helping preserve caste roles in schools. Within such a context, the abnormal ADHD student becomes a test risk and therefore a liability for the teachers, principals, and administrators who are held accountable to the measureable performance of their measured student populations. Similar to the way African American students are overrepresented in special education classes, the ADHD student is another way to control populations within a competitive educational environment by mitigating the risk potential they represent to the test data economy, which already holds so much power over the lives of students and teachers in school (Artiles et al. 2002, Harry and Anderson 1994).

It is important to make clear, however, that I am not suggesting ADHD is a fabricated or nonexistent condition. What I am suggesting, rather, is that around the condition of ADHD within the high-stakes testing cultures of urban schools there is a strong indication that diagnoses rates and neoliberal economic disciplining mechanisms have converged on students' bodies in ways that mirror previous biopolitical tools of control used in schools, tools such as IQ testing and other eugenic metrics. Again, one of the signature characteristics of neoliberal caste education tools, I would like to make clear here, is their ability to resurrect what was achieved in earlier historical phases of caste education through biological racism into the now acceptable language of the genetic (connected to human capital discourses around human nature) or neurological problem. As I argue in the next section, looking at another neoliberal caste education tool, racial capitalist governing strategies that reproduce the caste education system in the United States also draw upon technologies created to measure the agricultural productivity of genetically engineered crops. Here the symmetry between governing rationalities focused on the genetic control of crops in the field and students in the classroom demonstrates how population racism operates through the biopolitical management of educational populations through metrics designed to capture human capital growth in human learners.

### *Crop Tools for the Classroom: The Forgotten History of Value-Added Metrics*

During his tenure as secretary, Arne Duncan and the Department of Education enforced value-added metric (VAM) models for evaluating teacher effectiveness on districts across the nation. Since then, policies such as Race to the Top and groups such as the National Governors' Association (one of the chief actors behind the Common Core) have been compelling states to integrate VAMs into their educational plan. For many critics of the accountability movement, however, this story is an old one. A new "revolutionary" or "innovative" evaluation tool comes on the scene with claims of magically curing endemic educational problems such as the achievement gap or underperforming schools. Schools, it seems, especially since the Nation at Risk turning point in the early 1980s, are a testing ground for newfangled technologies of student and, now, teacher assessment. Escalating through the NCLB era, testing regimes have been the primary technology through which student performance has been measured. Many people have also profited in the evaluation industry that produces testing material, curriculums, computer software, and grading services. The Pearson Corporation, for example, brings in more than $9 billion annually from textbook sales (Singer 2013). Add to this giant testing corporations such as CTB/McGraw Hill, ETS, and Houghton Mifflin Harcourt, and many more billions are being harvested from the testing fields that schools in the United States have turned into. The adoption of the Common Core across the nation, which is also forcing the adoption of VAMs, also promises a massive windfall of profits for the computer adaptive testing industry (Horton 2014).

As the latest incarnation of the education evaluation industry are of course VAM models, VAMs provide corporate education reformers the necessary data in which to measure schools and the educational population within the more competitive "flat world" economy. A shift away from year-end student tests on which policies such as NCLB were built, VAMs instead focus on teacher performance. Specifically, they are designed to correlate multiple student tests throughout the year to individual teachers who either "add" or "subtract" value to the student's overall value-added rating score generated from year-long computer adaptive testing. VAMs have also increased the use of merit-pay policies in the teaching profession because they provide data that claim to isolate an individual teacher's ability to add or subtract value from his or her students' intellectual capacities (a quality human capital theory posits as genetic or hereditary; see Pierce 2013). In short, VAMs create the data economy needed in which to discipline teachers—but also students and schools—through ratings and scores that are generated through sophisticated algorithms calculated in data processing centers, which have also become a booming cottage industry.

After five years of wide-scale experimentation in school districts in Washington, New York, Atlanta, Philadelphia, Chicago, New Orleans, and an increasing number of cities across the nation, it is clear that VAMs fail to achieve what they are purportedly best at: providing accurate, evidence-based data from which educational reform decisions should be made. Diane Ravitch (2014), among others, has been closely following the growing number of studies that have recently come out showing in unequivocal terms how VAMs are not delivering what they claim to be designed for: zeroing in on the prime factor of student learning—teacher ability. Given the amount of insurmountable data showing the faultiness and inaccuracy of VAMs as an educational assessment technology, why are such assessment models only growing in use in states across the country? Why do they remain integral to the largest education reform policy since NCLB (Amrein-Beardsley 2014)?[7] Further, from where did such a model emerge, and can its origins tell us something about why it has seized the imaginative capacity of all mainstream educational reformers, whether Democrat or Republican?

The history of VAMs is a fascinating albeit familiar tale. Education reformers have long looked to corporate America for ideas on how to fix inefficient and failing schools. But what makes the history of VAMs unique is how it fuses corporate management science with a biostatistical approach to measuring student performance in classrooms. To understand the history of value-added metrics, you need to begin with the free-market intellectual laboratory started by the Chicago School of Economics professors Milton Friedman, Theodor Schultz, and Gary Becker, during the post–World War II era (Pierce 2013). It is here that you will find the birth of metrics geared toward identifying and measuring the economic value of human life (see, for example, Robert Fogel and Stanley Engerman's [1974] study of the value of slave labor, using their economic metric called "cliometrics"). But here I want to call attention to the forgotten history of VAMs that, building off of the neoliberal economic thinkers of the Chicago School, began in a biostatistical laboratory in Tennessee in the early 1970s.

William Sanders is considered by many to be the modern-day founder of VAMs. Sanders started his academic career as a researcher at the well-known Oak Ridge National Laboratory, the Department of Energy's biggest research facility, where he worked as a biostatistical researcher. From Oak Ridge, Sanders moved to the University of Tennessee, where he took over the statistical analysis center for agricultural research. Shortly after his move to UT, Sanders began applying his skills in measuring crop yields and efficiency to a mixed-methods statistical analysis of classrooms in the state of Tennessee. As Sanders himself put it, he became involved in educational evaluation "in the late 1970s when Governor Lamar Alexander was advocating a merit pay plan for Tennessee teachers. A big issue at the time was, and still is, how are you going to measure teacher effectiveness?" (Clowes 1999). Drawing upon his research in the field of bioagriculture efficiency/productivity, Sanders created the Tennessee Value-Added Assessment System (TVAAS), which has become one of the primary models from which many current VAMs in education are derived.

So why does it matter that someone trained in quantitative genetics and biostatistics is the parent of the most widely used and controversial educational evaluation tool in the United States? For starters, I think we should take great pause from the fact that the nation's top educational reform tool was created from work concerned with how to get the most value out of genetically engineered (GE) crop fields. In other words, are we comfortable equating the "value" of rows of GE corn or soy with children sitting in desk rows in Chicago? More alarming is the fact that even to be able to ask this question means that we as a society have arrived at a moment in history when a major research and development question for industrial agriculture corporations also makes sense when asked about the educational population in the United States. Such questions, I argue, point to the degree to which privatized and corporate reform strategies based around ideas of "productivity" and "efficiency" have become completely normalized through the educational reform industry's governance of public schools. In other words, the application of crop-measurement tools to classrooms in communities of color in particular seems completely rational in a society interested in solving a major economic developmental issue like our country's so-called human capital crisis. If we want better educational crops of human capital—if we want individuals fertilized with "twenty-first-century skills" in our population—then why not turn to corporate experts who have been successful in developing tools in similar arenas, even if these solutions were developed by some of the largest chemical and genetics companies in the world?

Here is where the characters from the history of Sanders, VAMs, neoliberal education reform, and the GE crop field all come together. Both the arenas of the educational crop field and GE farms share a similar problem within the context of a society organized around radical free-market values and notions of freedom. It is ultimately a problem of economic development in spaces where maximizing the yield of valuable goods in a competitive economic environment drives social (that is, educational) policy. To clarify, it is important to look at what technical problem or challenge the development of GE food production seemingly solved. One of the biggest problems that mass-scale, GE industrial food production has tried to solve is producing the *greatest number* of base food commodities at the lowest cost. However, creating an ocean of GE corn, for instance, does not mean that companies like Monsanto are losing money because they have figured out a way to trick nature and make food faster and cheaper. Companies like Monsanto and Syngenta (the owners of Golden Rice) have figured out how to increase the scale of *consumption* of their product as well; in other words, since corn is in almost everything we eat and drink, the corn industry yields massive profit windfalls at almost every stage of our food lives. So while corn may be cheap, it is also everywhere, and thus profit is captured in a cascade across the U.S. food system. Here the development problem of how to make more food cheaper while *also* capturing more profit has been achieved through standardizing food production and technologies capable of rearranging nature more in line with the corporate need to maximize the most value out of life.

It is the optimizing logics of increased productivity and efficiency, I argue, that constitute the same problem-solving matrix at work in technologies like VAMs applied to schools and educational populations in general. Instead of a crop-yield problem, however, schools are understood in the "flat world" global economic race-to-the-top mania as the fertile ground from which human capital crops can be grown and harvested for corporations to compete in the knowledge economy. Here the crossover between the science of the GE crop field and classroom represented by Sanders's VAM tool is a genealogical example of how neoliberal governing strategies target forms of life for optimization in market-competitive societies. Put differently, if the nation is facing a crisis of development in which it does not have enough competitive knowledge workers to outcompete the rest of the world, why not utilize models that have worked in the corporate sector for solving similar development problems? Unfortunately, this question has already been answered by both Arne Duncan and now Betsy DeVos's even more aggressive privatization approach as well as by a host of corporate actors currently applying free-market solutions to the public education system on a national scale.

As the school privatization movement continues to crop dust districts across the country with technologies such as VAMs, new data economies are being constructed through which to control and manipulate district populations across the country, especially urban working-class communities of color. Population racism, viewed through the neoliberal caste tool of VAMs, takes place through neighborhood schools in Chicago marked as "turnaround" schools, where students and teachers rate as low value or noninvestible forms of educational life. As multiple studies looking at the relation between neoliberal education reform and segregation have pointed out, urban communities across the nation are being fragmented into lower- and higher-value population groupings through caste tools such as VAMs—these are the same groups and community formations that the segregated schooling system in the Jim Crow era produced and managed (Lipman 2002, 2011; Novak 2014; Stovall 2013).

## *Neoliberal Caste Education within the History of Racial Capitalist Schooling*

So what do the examples of how ADHD students are managed in high-stakes schooling contexts and VAMs tell us about how caste education operates today in its neoliberal phase? Furthermore, in what ways do neo-liberal caste education tools such as psychotropic drugs (a biotechnologi-cal tool) and educational metrics designed to measure the economic value of life in schools contribute to the maintenance of racial capitalist goals in society? Recall that for Du Bois, two primary goals of racial capitalist so-ciety were built into the governing practices of U.S. states after Recon-struction to preserve existing and previous caste relations, for example, those that were developed on Southern labor camps to control the lives of both enslaved and free African Americans. After Reconstruction and emancipation, states and the governing elite of the United States (white Northern industrialists and the enslaving aristocratic class of the South) faced the problem of how to keep the working-class population divided and fragmented in ways that maintained racial antagonisms between whites and nonwhites established during the founding of the country's government. They also needed to put these divided and antagonistic groups into com-petition with one another in order to maximize wealth accumulation for the ruling white elite caste. As Du Bois reminds us in his magisterial *Black Reconstruction*, the greatest fear of the elite ruling class during Reconstruc-tion was to have poor whites and freed African Americans (as well as other nonwhite working groups) unite against the exploitative conditions forced upon both groups by the industrial wage-labor system.

Here I think it is helpful to bring back Clough and Willse's concept of population racism to understand how schools play an important role in re-alizing the goals of racial capitalist society. In other words, understanding how caste is reconstructed through schooling in the United States today (in a neoliberal reform context) helps us see how caste education is not a problem of the past. In fact, it is a problem of the present, and part of see-ing this truth is to make the continuity clearer between caste education models of the Reconstruction–Jim Crow era and its current neoliberal phase.

Both of the above examples of neoliberal caste education tools share some important governing commonalities that help us understand how ra-cial capitalist schooling is governed today and also how they are part of a longer history of caste control developed within the racial capitalist soci-ety of the United States. The first governing commonality has to do with the fact that both the management of ADHD students in high-stakes schooling environments and the economic metrics used to place measures of value on students and teachers in classrooms rely on the creation and circulation of data economies. For example, as a measurement device, VAMs are designed to produce data streams on both the learning capacities of students and, in an extremely narrow sense of the term, the pedagogical abilities of teachers. School and district ratings (that is, the published grades/ratings of schools in newspapers and by districts), merit pay, admissions tests, and year-long testing regimens can only make sense and be put into practice if there is a legitimized evidence bank of data that can be used to rationalize free-market reform decisions. Similarly, as pointed out above, in high-stakes schooling contexts ADHD rates are connected to a school performance culture that relies on and fetishizes testing data.

Furthermore, in normalizing ADHD as a genetic "problem" in the body of students, an entire (and powerful) regime of scientific knowledge becomes the dominant governing rationality used by teachers, administrators, school psychologists, parents, and school nurses to diagnose students for treatment. In this case, neurological data such as brain scan images become the basis for creating populations of normal and abnormal students or, perhaps more accurately, high-performing and underperforming ones that converge with the human capital productive paradigm (Pierce 2013). The point here is, as Clough and Willse's definition of population racism helps us understand, data economies create a context where governing decisions are made about the lives of students and teachers in ways that continue to divide and fragment the educational population along racial and economic lines. The dropout, the underperforming student, the student with abnormal behavior patterns, the pushed-out student, and the at-risk student are all conjured into existence from data economies that provide the governing rationality by which such divisions are made and normalized within the educational population of the country (Fine 1995). Most of these educational population groups are also largely composed of the same historical groups that previous versions of caste education have helped shape through the segregated schooling system.

The second governing commonality shared between the two examples of neoliberal caste tools I analyzed above stems from how data economies surrounding the "problems" of ADHD and value-added students manage life in schools. Connected to data economies that are constructed as a way to regulate educational populations in the United States is what Clough and Willse (2011) call a kind of "political branding" associated with population racism in neoliberal societies. According to Clough and Willse (2011), population racism "plays an important part in producing affect, as, for example, it circulates fear along with statistical profiles of populations, providing neoliberalism with a rhetoric of motive in the process of political branding" (52). Failing schools in urban communities are the perfect pretext for such a type of political branding to take hold and regulate the problem of the "achievement gap" and "underperforming" teachers and students. For example, take the infamous public shaming ritual that took place in Los Angeles in 2010 surrounding the publication of value-added ratings of teachers across the Los Angeles Unified School District (LAUSD). Aside from the fact that publishing the names of teachers was a corporate education reform political stunt to "prove" the effectiveness of value-added metrics as a way to sort out "good" from "bad" teachers, its true intent was to normalize in the public sphere acceptance of a governing strategy that segmented the educational population of the city by constructing vast swaths of failing students and teachers in LAUSD through a new value-added data regime (Pierce 2013).

Put differently, the publication of teacher ratings based on VAMs and other economic metrics politically branded both teachers and students within the second-largest school district in the United States by turning each into "statistically organized and manipulated as groupings of characteristics, features, or parts" (Clough and Willse 2011, 52).[8] Understood as human capital development components (or, more accurately, biocapital) within VAM reform governing strategies, teachers and students are turned into statistical objects (or bits) of data that allow for greater corporate manipulation of the country's educational population, especially those populations that are understood to be underperforming, at risk, or simply not worthy of educational investment.

Yet there is also another important feature associated with how VAMs politically brand educational populations. Again, Clough and Willse's (2011) analysis of the ways population racism works in neoliberal societies is instructive. From a governing perspective, political branding is part of a set of broader goals associated with neoliberal economic and social reforms that seek "manipulation of populations through a population racism." This manipulation, therefore, "is a manipulation of life capacities, of vitality, and operates as well to produce sensation, affects, and somatic effects that are not only felt at the individual level, but more importantly at the population level through political branding" (52). However, as Clough and Willse also point out, these "manipulations are not meant to produce behavior of the individuals or groups so much as they are meant to produce affective states, states of attention or activation with indeterminate, though already to-be-sensed, future effects" (53). What Clough and Willse mean is that through political branding, population racism works in neoliberal societies by giving government and corporate elites the rationality through which they can decide and enforce which segments of the population should be activated (invested in) and which should be disposed of, simply ignored and left for social death, imprisoned, or subjected to constant police violence and other legal and policing apparatuses associated with criminalized communities. Let me offer one example of how the life capacities of differentiated segments within the educational population of the United States are governed through political branding strategies such as VAM rating scores.

The expansion of the charter school system, as many have pointed out, is one of the fundamental strategies undergirding neoliberal educational restructuring in the United States (Au 2008; Au and Ferrare 2015; Buras 2010; Fabricant and Fine 2012; Saltman 2006, 2007). One of the key strategies corporate reformers such as the Bill and Melinda Gates Foundation have utilized to expand the charter school system has been the use of VAMs, which provide the data on failing and high-performing schools. These data are needed to abolish the public education system and replace it with a more "efficient" privatized model of governance. But what is also being normalized in the process of establishing data economies around the value of life in schools is the emergence of market strategies available to certain groups within the educational population. Consider, for instance, how narratives of school choice undergird the argument of charter school expansion—the general argument posits that more charter schools are needed in the educational market in order to create better educational options for parents, which, in turn, puts pressure on existing public schools to change their ineffective ways of dealing with the human capital crisis the country faces in the twenty-first-century economy (Pierce 2012; Wells, Slayton, and Scott 2002). Since VAM ratings and other economic measurement tools determine which schools are highly rated and which are not through the construction of data economies, school choice in reality is an instance where the market (that is, corporate/government actors) has created an artificial scarcity of "quality" schools, and therefore competition between consumers of schools (parents) is a natural *and* desired outcome of neoliberal reforms.

But how does the example of school choice highlight how population racism and political branding work through neoliberal education reform to reconstruct caste education conditions in the United States? To begin with, we cannot lose sight of the fact that charter school reform is framed as a technical solution to a problem in the population—widespread educational failure especially in the urban centers of the United States. We also cannot forget that the larger claims of school failure are based on narratives of the crisis of human capital that position schools within a global "flat world" economic competition set of discourses—in this sense, schools in Chicago and Washington are part of a larger national security battle being waged against other advanced industrial nations and their educational systems, which are outpacing the United States in terms of producing highly valuable forms of human capital such as STEM knowledge and skills (Lipman 2011, Pierce 2013). Once failing schools are framed as a technical problem through their inability to produce a sufficient human capital surplus in the country's educational population, the only fitting solution is to apply new measurement technologies to the educational population that provides data economies. Through these measurement technologies, government and corporate actors can restructure the educational system in line with the labor and racial needs underlying racial capitalist society.

Here is the other important dimension hiding in plain sight: Population groups are forced to accept the competitive reform environment as if there were no other alternative. So in this sense, divided groups within the population are sorted into unequal groups through what consumptive options parents can attain in trying to outcompete other consumers for their children and families' educational opportunities. Selective charter schools that are rated very high have protective mechanisms built into them such as admissions tests or push-out financial requirements (lab fees, application fees, tardy fees, and more) that privilege white affluent students who generally have greater economic resources with which to play the rigged game (tutoring, transportation freedom, college-educated parents who demand certain responses from school officials, etc.). Here what Clough and Willse describe as producing affective states of attention or activation of indeterminateness is played out in the market-reform environment of education in the United States through competitive population segments that reproduce racial and economic inequalities through schooling. In other words, distinct populations emerge within free-market reform strategies, and some are met with the attention of the market-based education system (that is, access to the best schools and teachers) while others are activated through a kind of educational indeterminateness—a state of free-market purgatory where individuals are to blame if their individual choices fail what the educational market predicates on demands of competition and individual free choice.

I think we are now in a position to see how population racism within neoliberal education reform in the United States might best be understood as a form of biopolitical warfare against communities of color, a war that has been underway for centuries. Using the lens of population racism to interpret the emergence of data economies and their effects on different groups within the educational population of the United States, I suggest that the signature of caste reconstruction in racial capitalist society is visible. That is, the population segmentation created through free-market education reform strategies such as school choice replicates the needs of racial capitalist society in fundamental ways. Who, for instance, is the greatest beneficiary of the increasingly free-market educational system? Which segments of the population are set up to navigate this system best? During the Reconstruction Era and immediately afterward, poor and working-class white communities were happy to accept the marginally better schools than the segregated, grossly underfunded schools students of color were forced to attend, even though both groups were from the same economic class *but* different race. Industrial barons in the North and the ex-slaveholding class in the South benefited greatly from this educational arrangement. Schools naturally bred racial hatred and class antagonism in the poor, working-class white population—in turn, this animosity created an artificial competitive environment that ensured greater dividends to the white industrial oligarchy; a unified and focused working-class was one of their deepest fears (Du Bois 1935).

Today, in the neoliberal caste education environment, a similar scenario is taking place, where white families flee schools filled with ELL students, underperforming students of color, "bad" teachers, and underfunded facilities, all population groups and types of branding that bring down the measures of success symbolized in data economies such as school ratings. Yet all of these decisions made by the white world are not, for the most part, rationalized through notions of biological racism—they are rationalized through the sanitized data economies that form distinct populations who are judged through their ability to compete on the open market of educational consumption. It is no longer "racist" for white parents to want to be in a racially isolated school; the market mechanisms, along with the data economies these markets rely on, render populations absolved from such ethical considerations because these caste tools rationalize colorblind modes of being when it comes to educational decision making for white parents and families. This is the insidious nature of caste education in the neoliberal era and just the latest phase of racial capitalist warfare being waged on urban communities of color *and* white communities that continue to choose racial alliance over potential points of class solidarity. In conclusion, I want to offer some key focal points of what rejecting neoliberal caste education might look like. In other words, from what I have argued above in my analysis of neoliberal caste education, the following three themes are problem sets from which resistance movements to caste reconfiguration through schooling could be developed.

- *Refuse Participation in the Neoliberal Caste Education Data Economy*: As Wayne Au (2015) and others' work has focused on, organizing parents, students, and communities around the opt-out movement to testing is one practical method for refusing the translation of educational life in schools into data bits that can be manipulated for corporate education restructuring.[9] High-stakes testing data is one of the most powerful caste tools the neoliberal state requires; refusing to allow students' and teachers' bodies and populations to be used as data crops is key to resisting neoliberal caste education.
- *Identify and Map New Caste Technologies Used to Govern Life in Schools*: Students, teachers, and communities should focus critical inquiry around research that assesses what types of programs, protocols, and measurements are in place to assure "quality" and efficiency in schools. In particular, community-led research should focus on what types of "subpopulations" are created in schools by programs/ procedures that brand student bodies through discourses such as neurological disorders (ADHD), behavioral problems, or special education. The point here would not be to claim that some students need different types of support; rather, it is to identify what the composition of such populations looks like in terms of racial and gender demographics and *how* these overrepresentations are produced through neoliberal systems of measurement and evaluation.
- *Neoabolitionary Movement around Public Education*: As recent educational scholarship on the intersection of race/class and schools has suggested (Allen 2004; Gillborn 2005; Leonardo 2002, 2009; Watkins 2005), the persistence of caste education in the United States in its neoliberal forms increases the merit in calls for creating a neoabolitionist movement in education. An abolitionary response, in other words, seems to make the most sense when considering the deeply entrenched nature of the public education system with racial capitalism. Here nodal points for an abolitionary politics around education might begin by building on existing resistance movements against the neoliberal takeover of education in this country. For instance, recent struggles in Seattle saw the State of Washington Supreme Court overturn the legal basis for governing schools through a charter system of governance. A citywide teachers' strike against the increased corporate governance of the Seattle school district also accompanied this ruling. The biggest challenge, however, will be to imagine how to abolish the existing public education system while not exacerbating existing forms of racial,

economic, and gender inequality in society. This is why any neoabolitionary movement of education should be led by those communities who have suffered the most from the caste education system of the United States.

The above are what I see as possible starting points for resistance practices against the permanent war the caste education system wages on the working class and communities of color in this nation. Confronting racial capitalism and how it organizes schooling in this country requires a decisive and complete rejection of neoliberal caste tools and the history of racial and economic injustice they embody. One first important step toward the abolition of the current caste education system is for white populations and individuals to reject the wages of whiteness that are being reconstructed through the neoliberal schooling context. Here a natural point of commonality would be to fight against the measurement of educational life in schools and the value that is attributed to it through data economies. Just as Du Bois diagnosed almost three-quarters of a century ago, the biggest fear of the 1 percent is for whites to understand how their existence is tied to the exploitation of the dark world and thus see the entire dehumanizing system of social and labor conditions of racial capitalist society. Choosing to recognize and not replicate caste privileges might start with a refusal to participate in the production and maintenance of data economies used to regulate educational populations in this country.

Such an act would be in line with one of Du Bois's most respected white historical figures, John Brown. John Brown found it morally reprehensible to live without fighting a war against the institution of enslavement, the caste system it enforced in the United States, and its expansion westward as part of the colonial project of the U.S. nation-state. Today's Brownian movement against the caste education system should start with the clarity and seriousness of John Brown's abolition movement's politics. Anything less is living in complicity with a system of caste control that is both adaptive and highly entrenched in the governing mechanisms of the state. I end with Du Bois's (2001, 230) reflection on the legacy of John Brown and his battle against the caste society of his time as a way of beginning to ask what an abolitionary politics of education might look like in the twenty-first century:

> Has John Brown no message—no legacy, then, to the twentieth century? He has and it is this great word: the cost of liberty is greater than the price of repression. The price of repressing the world's darker races is shown in a moral retrogression and an economic waste

unparalleled since the age of the African slave-trade. What would be
the cost of liberty? What would be the cost of giving the great stocks
of mankind every reasonable help and incentive to self-development—
opening the avenues of opportunity freely, spreading knowledge,
suppressing war and cheating, and treating men and women as equals
the world over whenever and wherever they attain equality?

NOTES

1. It is important to keep Angela Davis's (2011) critique of the
99 percent in mind, however. For her, the 99 percent contains important
distinctions that cannot be swept away in a rush to show solidarity against
the 1 percent. That is, for Davis, one's race, gender, sexuality, and class still
figure into what constitutes the 99 percent—so, in this sense, the 99 percent
is a potentially revolutionary starting point but also one that contains privileges that need to be abolished if true revolutionary change is going to occur.

2. Also see David Gillborn's (2010) critiques of neo-Marxist analyses of
education, where he points out the deficiencies of a solely class-based
analysis of schooling and why critical race theory provides a much-needed
corrective. For a strong analysis of the debate around the critical race
theorist of education David Gillborn and Marxist educational theorist
Mike Cole, see Preston (2010).

3. See Zeus Leonardo's (2013) pathbreaking work in educational theory,
where he argues for the bridging of critical race theory and Marxist analyses
of schooling without losing the strengths of either framework. My argument
here takes a different tack to the problem, stemming from segregated
approaches to the study of race and class that Leonardo has pointed out in
the traditions of critical race theory and Marxist analyses of schooling.
Specifically, my argument situates the analysis of race and class within the
framework of racial capitalism developed by thinkers in the Black radical
tradition, such as W. E. B. Du Bois, which holds that white supremacy and
the processes of capital accumulation are evolutionary partners in the
United States. From the standpoint of a racial capitalist analysis, any critique
of schooling that separates how race and class codetermine each other is
limited precisely because to understand white supremacy we must understand
how it has developed in relation to capitalist structures of power that are
built on producing racial antagonisms within the working class. Finally, my
racial capitalist approach to analyzing schooling is different from previous
scholarship on the problem of race and class dynamics in educational
research because I situate Du Bois's racial capitalist analysis of schooling in
the United States within the biopolitical tradition. In other words, I argue
that the racial capitalist framework gives us an analytic focus on how

subjects and populations are produced and regulated by the racial capitalist state.

4. Also see Cedric Robinson's (2000) excellent work developing Du Bois's and other thinkers from the Black radical tradition.

5. For one of the best examinations of Du Bois's concept of "wages of whiteness," see Roediger (1991).

6. See, for example, my (2013) analysis of how the National Institute of Health and Department of Education have relied on brain scan images of the neural pathways of ADHD-diagnosed children to prescribe education and training material for schools and parents.

7. For example, see the special issue in *Teachers College Record* (116 [1], 2014), where researchers provide compelling evidence that value-added measurement is a faulty assessment tool for educational settings.

8. LAUSD is not the only school district to participate in the public shaming ritual of teachers. The New York City school district, Washington, Chicago, and many other large urban school districts utilize the strategy to create momentum for corporate reform strategies such as the expansion of the charter school system.

9. See the United Opt Out organization's work around corporate education resistance: http://unitedoptout.com/.

### REFERENCES

Alexander, M. 2012. *The new Jim Crow: Mass incarceration in the age of colorblindness*. New York: The New Press.

Ali, A. I. 2014. A threat enfleshed: Muslim college students situate their identities amidst portrayals of Muslim violence and terror. *International Journal of Qualitative Studies in Education* 27 (10): 1243–1261.

Allen, R. L. 2004. Whiteness and critical pedagogy. *Educational Philosophy and Theory* 36 (2): 121–136.

Allman, P. 2001. *Revolutionary social transformation: Democratic hopes, political possibilities, and critical education*. Santa Barbara, Calif.: Praeger.

Amrein-Beardsley, A. 2014. *Rethinking value-added models in education: Critical perspectives on tests and assessment-based accountability*. New York: Routledge.

Angell, M. 2005. *The truth about the drug companies: How they deceive us and what to do about it*. New York: Random House.

Artiles, A. J., B. Harry, D. J. Reschly, and P. C. Chinn. 2002. Overidentification of students of color in special education: A critical overview. *Multicultural Perspectives* 4 (1): 3–10.

Au, W. 2008. *Unequal by design: High-stakes testing and the standardization of inequality*. New York: Routledge.

———. 2015. Just whose rights do these civil rights groups think they are protecting? *Washington Post*, May 9. http://www.washingtonpost.com/blogs/answer-sheet/wp/2015/05/09/just-whose-rights-do-these-civil-rights-groups-think-they-are-protecting/.

Au, W., and J. Ferrare. 2015. *Mapping corporate education reform: Power and policy networks in the neoliberal state.* New York: Routledge.

Baptist, E. E. 2014. *The half has never been told: Slavery and the making of American Capitalism.* New York: Basic Books.

Blacker, D. J. 2013. *The falling rate of learning and the neoliberal endgame.* Washington, D.C.: Zero.

Bowles, S., and H. Gintis. 1977. *Schooling in capitalist America: Educational reform and the contradictions of economic life.* New York: Basic Books.

Brown, A. L. 2015. Philanthrocapitalism: Race, political spectacle, and marketplace of beneficence in a New York City school. In *What's race go to do with it? How current school reform policy maintains racial and economic inequality,* ed. B. Picower and E. Mayorga, 147–166. New York: Peter Lang.

Brown, A. L., and N. De Lissovoy. 2011. Economies of racism: Grounding education policy research in the complex dialectic of race, class, and capital. *Journal of Education Policy* 26 (5): 595–619.

Buenavista, T. L. 2010. Issues affecting U.S. Filipino student access to postsecondary education: A critical race theory perspective. *Journal of Education for Students Placed at Risk* 15 (1–2): 114–126.

Buras, K. L. 2010. *Pedagogy, policy, and the privatized city: Stories of dispossession and defiance from New Orleans.* New York: Teachers College Press.

Calderón, D. 2014. Speaking back to Manifest Destinies: A land education-based approach to critical curriculum inquiry. *Environmental Education Research* 20 (1): 24–36.

Center for Disease Control and Prevention. 2011. Rates of parent-reported ADHD increasing. http://www.cdc.gov/mmwr/preview/mmwrhtml/mm5944a3.htm?s_cid=mm5944a3_w.

Churchill, W. 2004. *Kill the Indian, save the man: The genocidal impact of American Indian residential schools.* San Francisco: City Lights.

Clough, P. T., and C. Willse. 2011. Human security/national security: Gender branding and population racism. In *Beyond biopolitics: Essays on the government of life and death,* ed. P. T. Clough and C. Willse, 46–64. Durham, N.C.: Duke University Press.

Clowes, G. A. 1999. Helping teachers raise student achievement: An interview with William L. Sanders. *Heartland Institute.* http://news.heartland.org/newspaper-article/1999/11/01/helping-teachers-raise-student-achievement-interview-william-l-sanders.

Cole, M. 2007. *Marxism and educational theory: Origins and issues.* New York: Routledge.

Davis, A. Y. 1983. *Women, race, and class.* New York: Vintage.

———. 2003. *Are prisons obsolete?* New York: Seven Stories.

———. 2011. The 99 percent: A community of resistance. *Guardian.* http://www.theguardian.com/commentisfree/cifamerica/2011/nov/15/99 -percent-community-resistance.

Dean, M. 2010. *Governmentality: Power and rule in modern society.* Thousand Oaks, Calif.: Sage.

Du Bois, W. E. B. 1909. Evolution of the race problem. In *Proceedings of the National Negro Conference,* 142–158. New York.

———. 1911. The economics of Negro emancipation in the United States. *Sociological Review* 4 (3): 303–313.

———. 1935/1998. *Black Reconstruction in America, 1860–1880.* New York: The Free Press.

———. 1996. *Souls of Black folk.* New York: Penguin.

———. 2001. *John Brown.* New York: Random House.

Dumas, M. J. 2013. "Waiting for Superman" to save Black people: Racial representation and the official antiracism of neoliberal school reform. *Discourse: Studies in the Cultural Politics of Education* 34 (4): 531–547.

Fabricant, M., and M. Fine. 2012. *Charter schools and the corporate makeover of public education: What's at stake.* New York: Teachers College Press.

Fine, M. 1995. The politics of who's "at risk." In *Children and families "at promise": Deconstructing the discourse of risk,* ed. B. B. Swadener and S. Lubeck, 76–94. Albany: SUNY Press.

Fitzgerald, T. D. 2010. *White prescriptions? The dangerous social potential for Ritalin and other psychotropic drugs to harm black males.* Boulder, Colo.: Paradigm.

Fogel, R. W., and S. L. Engerman. 1974. *Time on the cross: The economics of American Negro slavery.* New York: Norton.

Foucault, M. 2003. *Society must be defended: Lectures at the Collège de France 1975–1976.* Trans. G. Burchell. New York: Palgrave Macmillan.

———. 2009. *Security, territory, population: Lectures at the Collège de France 1977–1978.* Trans. G. Burchell. New York: Palgrave Macmillan.

———. 2010. *The birth of biopolitics: Lectures at the Collège de France 1978–1979.* Trans. G. Burchell. New York: Palgrave Macmillan.

Freire, P. 2000. *Pedagogy of the oppressed.* New York: Continuum.

Gillborn, D. 2005. Education policy as an act of White supremacy: Whiteness, critical race theory, and education reform. *Journal of Education Policy* 20 (4): 485–505.

————. 2009. Who's afraid of critical race theory in education? A reply to Mike Cole's "The color-line and class struggle." *Power & Education* 1 (1): 125–131.

————. 2010. The White working class, racism, and respectability: Victims, degenerates, and interest convergence. *British Journal of Educational Studies* 58 (1): 3–25.

Harry, B., and M. G. Anderson. 1994. The disproportionate placement of African American males in special education programs: A critique of the process. *Journal of Negro Education* 63 (4): 602–619.

Harvey, D. 2005a. *A brief history of neoliberalism*. New York: Oxford University Press.

————. 2005b. *The new imperialism*. New York: Oxford University Press.

————. 2011. *The enigma of capital and the crisis of capitalism*. New York: Oxford University Press.

Haworth, C. M. A., K. Asbury, P. S. Dale, and R. Plomin. 2011. Added value measures in education show genetic as well as environmental influence. *PLoS ONE* 6 (2): e16006.

Haywood, H. 1948. *Negro liberation*. New York: International Publishers.

Hinshaw, S. P., and R. M. Scheffler. 2014. *The ADHD explosion: Myths, medication, and today's push for performance*. New York: Oxford University Press.

Horton, P. 2014. Paul Horton: Why the common core is unlike standards of the past. *Education Week*. http://blogs.edweek.org/teachers/living-in -dialogue/2014/02/paul_horton_why_the_common_cor.html.

Ignatiev, N. 2008. *How the Irish became White*. New York: Routledge.

Institute on Metropolitan Opportunity University of Minnesota Law School. 2014. Charter schools in Chicago: No model for education reform. http://www.law.umn.edu/uploads/77/fd/77fd345c608a24b997752a ba3f3of072/Chicago-Charters-FINAL.pdf.

Klein, N. 2008. *The shock doctrine: The rise of disaster capitalism*. New York: Picador.

Kochhar, R., R. Fry, and P. Taylor. 2011. *Wealth gaps rise to record highs between Whites, Blacks, and Hispanics*. Washington, D.C.: PEW Social and Demographic Trends.

Leonardo, Z. 2002. The souls of White folk: Critical pedagogy, Whiteness studies, and globalization discourse. *Race, Ethnicity, and Education* 5 (1): 29–50.

————. 2004. The unhappy marriage between Marxism and race critique: Political economy and the production of racialized knowledge. *Policy Futures in Education* 2 (3/4): 483–493.

————. 2009. *Race, Whiteness, and education*. New York: Routledge.

———. 2012. The race for class: Reflections on a critical raceless theory of education. *Educational Studies* 48 (5): 427–449.

———. 2013. *Race frameworks: A multidimensional theory of racism and education.* New York: Teachers College Press.

Lemke, T. 2011. *Biopolitics: An advanced introduction.* New York: New York University Press.

Lipman, P. 2002. Making the global city, making inequality: The political economy and cultural politics of Chicago Public School Policy. *American Education Research Journal* 39 (2): 379–419.

———. 2011. *The new political economy of urban education: Neoliberalism, race, and the right to the city.* New York: Routledge.

Lipsitz, G. 2006. *The possessive investment in Whiteness: How White people profit from identity politics.* Philadelphia: Temple University Press.

Marsh, J. 2011. *Class dismissed: Why we cannot teach or learn our way out of inequality.* New York: Monthly Review Press.

McLaren, P. 2005. *Capitalist and conquerors: A critical pedagogy against empire.* Lanham, Md.: Rowman & Littlefield.

Miller, C. 2014. The truth about ADHD: Over-diagnosis linked to cause championed by Michelle Rhee. *Salon.* http://www.salon.com/2014/03/01/the_truth_about_adhd_over_diagnosis_linked_to_cause_championed_by_michelle_rhee/.

Morgan, E. S. 2003. *American slavery, American freedom: The ordeal of colonial Virginia.* New York: Norton.

Novak, T. 2014. Whites getting more spots at top Chicago public high schools. *Chicago Sun-Times.*

Ong, A. 2006. *Neoliberalism as exception: Mutations in citizenship and sovereignty.* Durham, N.C.: Duke University Press.

Orfield, G. E., J. Frankenberg, and J. Kuscera. 2014. *Brown* at 60: Great progress, a long retreat, and an uncertain future. Los Angeles: Civil Rights Project/Proyecto Derechos Civiles. http://civilrightsproject.ucla.edu/research/k-12-education/integration-and-diversity/brown-at-60-great-progress-a-long-retreat-and-an-uncertain-future/Brown-at-60-051814.pdf.

Pierce, C. 2012. The promissory future(s) of education: Rethinking scientific literacy in the era of biocapitalism. *Educational Philosophy and Theory* 44 (7): 721–745.

———. 2013. *Education in the age of biocapitalism: Optimizing educational life for a flat world.* New York: Palgrave.

———. 2017. W. E. B. Du Bois and caste education: Racial capitalist schooling from Reconstruction to Jim Crow. *American Educational Research Journal* 54 (1S): 23S–47S.

Piketty, T. 2014. *Capital in the twenty-first century*. New York: Belknap.

Preston, J. 2010. Concrete and abstract racial domination. *Power & Education* 2 (2): 115–125.

Ravitch, D. 2014. Reign of error: The hoax of the privatization movement and the danger to America's public schools. New York: Vintage.

Robinson, C. J. 2000. *Black Marxism: The making of the Black radical tradition*. Chapel Hill: University of North Carolina Press.

Roediger, D. 1991. *The wages of Whiteness: Race and the making of the American working class*. New York: Verso.

Saltman, K. 2006. *The Edison School: Corporate schooling and the assault on public education*. New York: Routledge.

———. 2007. *Capitalizing on disaster: Taking and breaking the public school*. Boulder, Colo.: Paradigm.

Scott, J. T. 2013. A Rosa Parks moment? School choice and the marketization of civil rights. *Critical Studies in Education* 54 (1): 5–18.

Singer, A. 2013. Pearson rakes in profit. *Huffington Post*. http://www.huffingtonpost.com/alan-singer/pearson-education-profits_b_2902642.html.

Solórzano, D., M. Ceja, and T. Yosso. 2000. Critical race theory, racial microaggressions, and campus racial climate: The experiences of African American college students. *Journal of Negro Education* 69 (1/2): 60–73.

Stoler, A. L. 1995. *Race and the education of desire: Foucault's history of sexuality and the colonial order of things*. Durham, N.C.: Duke University Press.

Stovall, D. 2013. Against the politics of desperation: Educational justice, critical race theory, and Chicago school reform. *Critical Studies in Education* 54 (1): 33–43.

Sunder Rajan, K. 2006. *Biocapital: The constitution of postgenomic life*. Durham, N.C.: Duke University Press.

Watkins, W. H., ed. 2005. *Black protest thought and education*. New York: Peter Lang.

Weheliye, A. G. 2014. *Habeas viscus: Racializing assemblages, biopolitics, and Black feminist theories of the human*. Durham, N.C.: Duke University Press.

Wells, A. S., J. Slayton, and J. Scott. 2002. Defining democracy in the Neoliberal Age: Charter school reform and educational consumption. *American Educational Research Journal* 39 (2): 337–361.

# Toward What Ends? A Critical Analysis of Militarism, Equity, and STEM Education

*Shirin Vossoughi and Sepehr Vakil*

> A workforce with robust science, technology, engineering, and mathematics capabilities is critical to the success of the U.S. military mission. The U.S. Army Corps of Engineers, the Department of Defense, and the nation must ensure that there is a pipeline engaged in STEM and prepared for careers in engineering, the natural sciences, and research and development.
>
> —Lt. Gen. Thomas P. Bostick, Commander,
> U.S. Army Corps of Engineers

Lieutenant General Bostick's words reflect a common discourse on STEM education in the United States: Expanding opportunities to engage in robust forms of STEM learning is essential to global economic competitiveness and to the security of "the nation." Like many advocates of STEM education, Bostick also describes increasing diversity among STEM careerists as a central goal. As he states, "diversity is something that makes the Army stronger" (Lopez 2013).

In this chapter, we draw attention to the relationship between two narratives regarding STEM education—one advanced by key military and corporate actors and the other by advocates for equity and diversity in STEM education. As Bostick's statement reflects, from the perspective of the U.S. military, improving and expanding access to STEM education is fundamental to national security and the maintenance of U.S. global power. For advocates of equity and diversity in STEM education (itself a heterogeneous community with its own debates and tensions), expanding access to high-quality STEM education is fundamental to improving educational and career opportunities for students historically underrepresented in STEM fields (Feder et al. 2009). How do we understand these narratives in relation to each other? Do they overlap? Does one get subsumed by the other? Both groups are invested in improving access to high-quality STEM education. But how do the discourses that position STEM as fundamental to U.S. national interests shape what—and how—students are learning? What, for example, are the pedagogical, curricular, and ethical implications of military-funded STEM intervention programs that target students of color in low-income urban neighborhoods? As advocates for educational equity, we are concerned that when we neglect to ask these kinds of questions, we may fail to understand how the broader political contours and goals of STEM education shape and constrain students' learning experiences and possible futures. We also assert that the dearth of public debate and scholarly dialogue on the intersections of STEM education and U.S. military and corporate interests leads to the unwitting, strategic, or even willing adoption of ideological agendas that contradict broader visions of justice and dignity for youth and communities of color around the world.

This convergence of interests (Bell 1979, 2004) between equity narratives and the discourse of STEM education as tied to U.S. economic and military power is partly a result of the growing national emphasis on STEM education and of shifts in funding that both incentivize STEM-oriented research and encourage particular approaches to equity (for example, "broadening participation") as tied to workforce development and global economic competitiveness. A 2010 report by the National Academy of Sciences on Expanding Underrepresented Minority Participation states:

> Underrepresentation of this magnitude in the S&E [Science and Engineering] workforce stems from the underproduction of minorities in S&E at every level of post-secondary education, with a progressive loss of representation as we proceed up the academic ladder.
> In 2007, underrepresented minorities comprised 38.8 percent of K–12 public enrollment, 33.2 percent of the U.S college age population, 26.2 percent of undergraduate enrollment, and 17.7 percent of those earning science and engineering bachelor's degrees. In graduate school, underrepresented minorities comprise 17.7 percent of overall enrollment but are awarded just 14.6 percent of S&E master's degrees and a minuscule 5.4 percent of S&E doctorates. Historically, there has been a strong connection between increasing educational attainment in the United States and the growth in and global leadership of the economy. (National Academy of Sciences, 2010, 3)

The report goes on to frame broadening participation in STEM education as a means to address (a) an uncertain science and engineering workforce, including the need to move away from reliance on non-U.S. citizens; (b) shifting demographics ("Those groups that are most underrepresented in S&E are also the fastest growing in the general population"); and (c) diversity as an asset for "expanding the S&E talent pool, enhancing innovation and improving the nation's global economic leadership" (2–3). From our perspective, this increasingly ubiquitous narrative exemplifies what Walter Seceda (1989) refers to as an "enlightened self-interest" and fails to consider the heterogeneous interests and desires of underrepresented students and communities (Tuck 2009). In light of this context, our analysis of the military and STEM education serves as a case study from which we argue the need for more precise and politically grounded theorizations of equity in STEM education.

At the heart of this discussion lie competing visions for the future embodied in distinct approaches to STEM education. The world reflected in Lieutenant General Bostick's statement is one of expanding U.S. political and military dominance. In this world, STEM careers may be more representative of a diverse population, but the fundamental grounding of those careers in capitalist and militarist social relations remains unchanged. For example, expanding the pool of qualified domestic labor so that U.S. technological innovation can lead markets does not trouble the exploitation of workers that often accompanies the mass production of technological innovations, nor does it address the ways these technologies may be used to carry out new forms of surveillance and control (Giroux 2014). We seek to imagine a different kind of future, one in which young people learn about natural, physical, and technological phenomena as deeply imbued with social and political values, where the production of new scientific and technical knowledge is coupled with the development of a more just world.

This chapter therefore advances a critical analysis of the relationship between the U.S. military and STEM education (K–12 and higher education), with special emphasis on issues of equity, pedagogy, epistemology, and the broader purposes of STEM learning. First, we offer a historical analysis of the explicit and implicit connections between militarism, U.S. foreign policy, and STEM education. Second, we consider the specific implications of the relationship between the U.S. military and STEM education for educational equity. This section includes a brief overview of the literature on equity in STEM education and introduces a framework for discerning the differences and contradictions across various discourses of "diversity." We then reflect on the pedagogical alternatives that emerge from this framework. Together, these sections contribute to imagining and advancing approaches to STEM education that are rooted in a trans-national vision of social justice and human dignity.

## The U.S. Military and STEM Education

Critical theories of education contextualize public schooling within larger sociopolitical and economic contexts, illuminating how schools can be sites of social reproduction as well as potential sites of social transformation (Bourdieu and Passeron 1990, Bowles and Gintis 1976, Giroux 1983, hooks 1994). Only by studying the ways in which larger macrostructures both influence and are influenced by pedagogy, curriculum, and classroom interaction can we begin to understand, with conceptual and empirical specificity, how schooling experiences are part of larger sociopolitical processes. Consider the "school-to-prison pipeline," a powerful construct used to reveal the troubling linkages between disciplinary practices in urban schools and the prison-industrial complex (Alexander 2012, Davis 2011, Wald and Losen 2003). Disciplinary issues within schools, if not examined within the context of the prison-industrial complex, could be conceptualized as a technical or personnel problem to be solved by interventions that neglect the broader structural and racialized contexts in which the discipline gap is embedded. The school-to-prison pipeline has therefore become a powerful conceptual as well as rhetorical device for researchers, teachers, and activists to situate the disciplinary practices of schools within their proper context, namely, the ways in which the disciplining of Black and Brown students is tied to the profit motives of a multibillion-dollar industry as well as to broader forms of social control (Davis 2011).

Compelled by these and other critical analyses of schooling in the United States, we begin with a question: If contextualizing an analysis of discipline within a sociopolitical framework so powerfully illuminates a central feature of racialization in urban schools, what might we learn from inquiring into the sociopolitical factors that shape efforts to expand and diversify STEM education? In particular, how do social, economic, and political interests shape our discourses surrounding the nature and purposes of STEM education, and what implications does this have for the ways students experience STEM diversity initiatives and reforms? Other contributors in this volume focus on distinct aspects of militarism and its relationship to education. By honing in on the relationship between militarism and STEM education, we consider how local curricular decisions and pedagogical practices may be overdetermined by the agendas of business and military personnel rather than by wider visions of the public good. By making these agendas explicit, we hope to contribute to the development of alternative possibilities for equity-oriented work in STEM education.

The remainder of this section will explore the ways in which our educational system (higher education and K–12) has been influenced by the interests and goals of the U.S. military. We begin with an examination of how wartime concerns, dating back to World War I, shaped the nature of science and engineering research at the university level. Building from this discussion, we then offer two examples that shed light on implications for K–12 STEM education. The first is a broad, historical look at how military and other national interests have influenced mathematics and science education at the K–12 level. The second is a look at several military-funded educational programs, with special emphasis on the relationship between the Maker movement and the U.S. military.

## Knowledge Production and the Military-Industrial-Academic Complex

When the postcolonial scholar Edward Said (2005) urged all academics "to enter into sustained and vigorous exchange with the outside world," he was speaking of the role knowledge production can and should play in democratic societies. Yet the "outside world" for many university-based science and engineering programs has been the world of corporations and military contractors. Below, we describe events leading to universities' increasing entanglements with war-related science and technology research.

The emerging links between the U.S. military and industry were formalized during World War I through the War Industries Board, a government agency responsible for purchasing war supplies. The participation of the scientific community in these fledgling relationships was, at the time, limited to individual scientists who served on agencies such as the National Research Council (NRC) and who provided technical advice on scientific and military issues on an as-needed basis. The university as an institution was not fully engaged in these dealings. In the years leading up to World War II, some war-related scientific research was being conducted at the university level, but most of these contracts were temporary in nature and not viewed as central to academics' primary research agendas. In the early twentieth century, university researchers largely relied on government subsidies to conduct their work, and in difficult times, such as during the Depression, research labs increasingly turned to philanthropies and industry for support. During World War II, however, scientists (and their research agendas) became more closely linked to the interests of the U.S. military. In 1940, in an effort to establish a formal relationship between universities and military contractors, President Roosevelt established the National Defense Research Committee (NDRC) and later the Office of Scientific Research and Development (OSRD), agencies through which hundreds of millions of dollars were spent on weapons research. This research directly led to new technologies, including radar, the proximity fuse, guided missiles, and, of course, the first atomic bombs resulting from the Manhattan Project.

It is therefore notable that President Eisenhower's farewell speech called out the "unwarranted influence" of the military-industrial complex in America and warned of the unprecedented power and influence of the "industrial machinery of defense" but was silent on the role of (or impact on) higher education, what was later referred to as the "militarization of academia" (Giroux 2008). Indeed, the "successes" of World War II technologies significantly altered the intellectual life of universities over the next few decades. Entire laboratories were established that reflected the priorities of weapons research—MIT's Lincoln Laboratory for air defense, University of California–Berkeley's Lawrence Livermore Laboratory for research on nuclear weapons, and Stanford's Applied Electronics Laboratory for electronic communications. Several years after Eisenhower's speech, Senator Fulbright decried the increasing influence of the Pentagon on university research in what he called the "military-industrial-academic complex," warning against the encroaching agenda of the war-driven U.S. government on the "higher purposes" of the university. In "The Cold War and American Science," the historian Stuart W. Leslie describes the tripartite alliance between industry, the military, and the university as the "golden triangle," arguing that the state of perpetual war has left deep imprints on the very nature of scientific and technological knowledge production at these and other universities.

From World War II onward, military and business sectors not only used their combined resources and political power to mobilize university research toward highly specified, mission-oriented wartime ends but also fundamentally altered processes of inquiry and imagination. Here it is important to note that the consequences of the military-industrial-academic complex were both material *and* ideological. Materially, specific hardware and software technologies, such as jet engines or surveillance systems, are direct results of the "tripartite alliance." To illustrate how militarization also resulted in new forms of scientific knowledge and modes of inquiry, we offer the example of materials science research, a relatively obscure STEM field that has been central to U.S. military interests.

One of the oldest forms of science and engineering, materials science underwent a transformation from its "esoteric origins in the quantum revolution of the 1920s to its maturation in the 1960s as the most practical of scientific disciplines" (Leslie 1993, 188). The catalyst of this "maturation" and the resulting character of materials science research merit further examination. Materials science was once "esoteric" in the sense that theoretical advancements in this field, closely related to other disciplines such as solid-state physics and quantum mechanics, were treated as ends in and of themselves. Until World War II, neither academics nor military leaders viewed the field as particularly relevant to wartime goals. During the war, radar technology became crucial for detecting "enemies" from hundreds of miles away, and it relied on small crystal semiconductors to capture and convert reflected radio signals for proper viewing. These crystals often "burned out" under the rapidly changing conditions of wartime activity. Theorizing and experimenting with the chemical and physical properties of crystals quickly became a research priority for scientists at a number of institutions vying for government contracts. As Leslie writes, "the war gave a tremendous boost to materials science," resulting in applications such as silicon crystal rectifiers for radar systems but also in the production of new textbooks and curricula (such as the applications of quantum theory to solids in *Introduction to Chemical Physics* [1939]). The character and purposes of materials science as a discipline was therefore profoundly altered by wartime goals and concerns.

The case of materials science illustrates how the militarization of academia shaped both the processes and products of scientific inquiry. We do not intend to suggest, however, that military-funded research precludes scientific advances that have nonmilitary applications or uses. In other words, we want to avoid using a simple good/evil binary as the lens through which we assess science and technology research. We anticipate and recognize perspectives that point to those technological and scientific advancements that originated in military-funded research but had profound social benefit, such as the Internet (which was originally funded through the Defense Advanced Research Projects Agency [DARPA] program). Similarly, while materials science research was initiated for the development of new kinds of crystal semiconductors for radar technology, it later led to the development of the transistor, which many have called the "fundamental building block" of modern electronic devices. Yet while we can acknowledge the benefits of some technoscientific advancements stemming

from war-funded research, we also assert the importance of explicitly naming the role of STEM research in producing the theoretical and practical
knowledge required for the production of destructive and deadly weapons
of war—and of engaging in what we call a *critical wondering* about the scientific possibilities that were foreclosed as a result of the "unwarranted
influence" of the military on science research. Indeed, both of these points
were central to the resistance organized against the encroachment of the
military by university students and professors, particularly during the Vietnam War (Lyman 2009).

## IMPLICATIONS FOR K–12 SCHOOLING

Keeping in mind the relationships between knowledge production at the
university level and U.S. military interests, we now turn our attention to
K–12 schooling. As educators, how do we make sense of a sociopolitical
context in which scientific, mathematical, and technological knowledge is
routinely connected to the logics of war, competition, and national advancement? What are the implications of military-oriented shifts in STEM fields
for the educational experiences of children and youth? We begin with a
broad view of the historical development of mathematics and science education over the past sixty years, with particular attention to the impetus
behind changes in the direction and content of the curriculum.

In "The Math Wars," Alan Schoenfeld (2004), a prominent mathematics
education scholar, historicizes the social forces that have shaped ongoing
debates between "reformists" and "traditionalists" in math education.
"Mathematics has been seen as the foundation for the nation's military and
economic preeminence, and in times of perceived national crisis mathematics curricula have received significant attention" (256). As he goes on
to detail, the Soviet Union's successful launch of *Sputnik* during the Cold
War triggered a strong reaction from foundations such as the National
Science Foundation (NSF) to develop new math and science curricula. In
mathematics, these curricula became known as the "new math" and reflected a shift in content toward more abstract topics such as set theory,
matrices, and modular arithmetic. The mindset during those times was
that a dramatic shift in mathematics curricula could stimulate an increase
in the number of mathematically sophisticated students who would go on
to create innovations in the nation's military and defense apparatus. The
"new math" curricula eventually failed, spurring the "back to basics" movement. This pendulum swing of mathematics reform has received substantial attention from educational researchers (Becker and Jacobs 2000, Boaler

2008), yet the focus has been primarily on the advantages and disadvantages of particular instructional approaches, with less attention to the ideological contours of the debate. The history of mathematics education reveals that U.S. military interests (along with other sociopolitical and economic interests) have played a significant role in shaping what goes on in math classrooms across the nation (Harouni 2014). We therefore argue for explicit attention to the ideologies entangled in current manifestations of mathematics education and to the possibilities that can emerge when math education is rooted in alternative discourses and purposes.

The Cold War also had implications for science education. A growing number of engineers and scientists had been voicing their concerns about the United States falling behind in the "space race," warning Congress that the war was "being fought with slide rules, not rifles" (Dean 2007). But it was not until 1958 (the year after the successful launch of *Sputnik*) that Congress passed the National Defense Act. Part of a broader effort by the Eisenhower administration to boost the scientific and technological sophistication of the nation, the National Defense Act directly targeted K–12 science education. The legislation sought to spark a renewed interest in science through incentives such as scholarships and career fairs. With the direct involvement of many of the nation's top professional engineers and scientists, the National Defense Act also triggered a series of professional development workshops and summer institutes to assist K–12 science teachers in reorganizing their curricula and teaching. Significant funding was provided to equip classrooms with the necessary tools and equipment. Science classrooms were, in effect, given a makeover. In a 2007 *New York Times* article, the journalist Cornelia Dean quoted a student recalling her experiences:

> Here I was, a Black kid in a segregated school that was under-resourced—*Sputnik* kind of crossed the barrier. All of a sudden everybody was talking about it, and science was above the fold in the newspaper, and my teachers went to institutes and really got us all engaged. It was just a time of incredible intensity and attention to science.

The student's words exemplify how the Cold War directly affected science classrooms, and they also illuminate the complexity of equity discourses in science education. On the one hand, the space race led to changes in science education that provided increased opportunities to engage in genuine scientific inquiry and led to increased access for students from historically marginalized communities (in this case, Black students attending severely under-resourced schools in the segregated South). On the other hand, we ought not to lose sight of other possibilities that might have and could in the future exist given a different set of priorities, possibilities of what science education could be if similarly resourced but shaped by a different set of values and goals. Framing changes in science and math education resulting from war-related concerns as a net positive gain for equity risks equating educational equity with the foreign policy interests of the state. To the extent that these interests are in opposition to a transnational view of social justice, equity discourses rooted in militarism are beset with serious moral and political contradictions. Later in the chapter, we will offer a framework and vocabulary we argue is necessary to sharpen our conceptualizations of equity in STEM and that can help us both recognize and confront these contradictions.

Like the Cold War, the "War on Terror" has served as a rationale for ongoing U.S. interventions and expanded military presence in the Middle East and around the world. Deepening relationships between the U.S. military, the defense industry, and universities, the "War on Terror" has also created a demand for new technologies of war, including those used for targeted assassinations, surveillance, and torture (McCoy 2007, Wall and Monohan 2011). In the educational sphere, this context has engendered new developments and contradictions. In 2006, President Bush convened the National Mathematics Advisory Panel (NMAP), which was tasked with reviewing mathematics education research and determining best instructional strategies. The findings of the panel became subject to serious critique from the mathematics education research community. The criticism was leveled primarily on the grounds that the panel favored quantitative research and created a false binary between student-centered and teacher-centered pedagogical models, effectively dismissing decades of research on the nuances of teaching and learning mathematics (Boaler 2008). While these critiques are important and remind us of the anti-intellectualism of the Bush era, they did not take the additional step of interrogating the sociopolitical purposes of math education according to the advisory panel, which were unequivocally rooted in "national security" interests. The executive summary of the final report makes this plain:

> Much of the commentary on mathematics and science in the United
> States focuses on national economic competitiveness and the economic
> well-being of citizens and enterprises. There is reason enough for
> concern about these matters, but it is yet more fundamental to recognize
> that the safety of the nation and the quality of life—not just the
> prosperity of the nation—are at issue. (NMAP 2008, 1)

Amid this heightened focus on natural security, the U.S. military and leaders in the defense industry also expanded their own educational programs as part of a growing effort to strengthen the STEM career pipeline, and in response to a 2009 Department of Defense *STEM Education and Outreach Strategic Plan*. The Department of Defense's STEM-based youth program StarBase, for example, presents a straightforward mission:

> To raise the interest and improve the knowledge and skills of at-risk youth in science, technology, engineering and mathematics, which will provide for a highly educated and skilled American workforce that can meet the advanced technological requirements of the Department of Defense. (15)

StarBase currently operates in fifty-nine locations around the country. Similarly, corporations including Raytheon, Boeing, and Lockheed Martin have developed their own science fairs, robotics competitions, and STEM outreach programs. According to Lockheed Martin's "Engineers in the Classroom" program, the company "provides numerous opportunities for employees to interact with the next generation of engineers and technologists by serving as local school advisors, extracurricular activity mentors and career role models for students in communities where we live and work." These programs both highlight the specific role of the defense sector in STEM education and reflect the broader expansion of corporate influence in educational policy (Au and Ferrare 2015). This includes the increasingly narrow view of students as "human capital" and schools as training grounds for the needs of corporate employers (Spring 2015).

## The Maker Movement

Over the last ten years, the "Maker movement" has also become a major player in STEM education. On the one hand, this movement represents a progressive shift toward hands-on and project-based forms of education that ground STEM learning in purposeful and artistic activity. Sylvia L. Martinez and Gary Stager (2013), the authors of *Invent to Learn: Making, Tinkering, and Engineering in the Classroom*, write:

> The past few decades have been a dark time in many schools. Emphasis on high-stakes standardized testing, teaching to the test, de-professionalizing teachers and depending on data rather than teacher expertise has created classrooms that are increasingly devoid of play, rich materials, and time to do projects. Fortunately, there's a creative revolution underway that may change everything. (1)

While a renewed emphasis on making and tinkering represents a progressive shift away from narrow, test-based educational policies, this "creative revolution" is rife with its own political and economic contradictions (Vossoughi et. al. 2016). Most central to our discussion, this includes the collusion of Maker Media (one of the movement's most visible and well-funded brands) with the agendas and interests of the U.S. military.

In 2012, DARPA awarded Maker Media (in partnership with San Francisco's OtherLab) a large grant, for the explicit purpose of transforming education and facilitating the growth of "Makerspaces" in schools. According to the Department of Defense, the partnership was part of DARPA's Adaptive Vehicle Make (AVM) program, which seeks to compress developmental timelines for future defense vehicles by "democratizing" the innovation process and developing a crowdsourcing infrastructure for the development of vehicle systems (DARPA 2010). To improve what they describe as an expensive and inefficient system of production, DARPA sought to draw on the strengths of the Maker movement (including open-source, socially networked, and democratic forms of innovation) to "crowdsource the next generation of combat vehicles" (Ohab 2011). For DARPA, the partnership aimed to "ensure that high-school-age youths are exposed to the principles of modern prize-based design and foundry-style digital manufacturing." As *MIT News* reports, "a design competition hosted in Phoenix, Ariz., for a new combat support vehicle generated more functional designs in a drastically shorter time span than the traditional DoD contract methods" (Mansfield 2011). The Center for Investigative Reporting's account of the Maker-DARPA partnership was therefore astutely titled "Pentagon Taps Students to Build Robots, Drones."

Maker Media's decision to partner with DARPA drew sharp criticism from within the Maker movement itself. Some accused Maker Media of becoming a tool for the Pentagon to develop "killer geeks" (Finoki et al. 2012). Others claimed that the movement had crossed an ethical line—funding programs that have children compete to make the best weapons and giving military recruiters greater access to schools. (The intersections of STEM outreach efforts and military recruitment are outlined in the Department of Defense's *STEM Education and Outreach Strategic Plan* [2010–2014], and the cover story of a 2011 Army recruitment newsletter reads, "What's all the talk about STEM?") Fiacre O'Duinn, a Canadian librarian involved in hacker/maker culture asked:

> What happened to the transdisciplinary focus of hacker/maker
> communities that make them so innovative? Where are the arts?

> Where are wearables, knitivism, DIY molecular gastronomy? Why do the challenges involve working on unmanned air vehicles or robots, projects that are of interest to DARPA for their military applications? Shouldn't we encourage STEAM rather than STEM? Could it be that regardless of their educational potential, these topics have no possible military application? With such a narrow focus, one could ask which culture will win the day, maker or military? (Finley 2010)

O'Duinn's questions point to a central contradiction: The most visible organization in a movement premised on challenging narrow, test-centric forms of education (and STEM education in particular) participated in advancing a narrow version of "making" that privileges particular scientific pursuits at the expense of others and limits the artistic and interdisciplinary potential of making as an educational practice. This is analogous to the ways military interests and funding have reshaped STEM research in higher education.

Some critics have also expressed concern about the place of critical thinking in an educational model funded by the military. Bryan Finoki, Nick Sowers, and Javier Arbona (a trio of artists, architects, and educators) describe the Pentagon as a "space of hacker/maker persecution, as emblematized most obviously by the criminalization of Bradley [Chelsea] Manning" (Finoki et al. 2011). In his analysis of the surveillance state, Henry Giroux (2014) similarly describes the state's attitude toward the antiauthoritarian currents among young techies:

> [Edward Snowden's] "disclosures have renewed a longstanding concern: that young Internet aficionados whose skills the agencies need for counterterrorism and cyber defense sometimes bring an anti-authority spirit that does not fit the security bureaucracy." . . . Joel F. Brenner, a former inspector general of the NSA, made it very clear that the real challenge Snowden revealed was to make sure that a generation of young people were not taught to think critically or question authority.

Herein lies another central tension: Defense and other STEM-related industries are interested in the development of a workforce that is creative and flexible. The word "innovation" dominates contemporary discourse on STEM education. Both DARPA and Maker Media identify the development of "innovative" makers and thinkers as a core goal. Yet as Giroux points out, this innovative sensibility must be taught *without* the critical thinking and questioning of authority that might lead to more transformative visions of making.

In defense of the decision to partner with DARPA, Maker Media's CEO Dale Doherty advanced three central justifications. First, he cited the long history of relationships between universities and the military, which has not, according to Doherty, overdetermined scientific pursuits: "MIT has been known to produce more than a few hackers." Second, he pointed to the major financial effort that is needed to bring making into schools: "By creating makerspaces in an educational context, students can have access to tools and equipment that they might not have otherwise; they can collaborate on projects that are driven by their own interests, and by doing so, develop the capacity and confidence to innovate." Third, Doherty highlighted the need to expand access to making opportunities for all students: "This maker community has created amazing new opportunities for lots of people to develop their potential as creators, builders, and innovators. I'm proud of that, but I'm also disturbed by who is not in that community." Doherty concludes that this equity goal is shared by both Maker Media and DARPA: "The goals of Make and DARPA align in this instance because we have a mutual interest in seeing a more diverse pool of young people become scientists, engineers, programmers."

We argue that the rhetorical justification of this alliance provides a window into broader tensions surrounding equity and diversity in STEM education, tensions that we believe demand careful attention. For example, Doherty draws on the language of *diversity* and *access* to rationalize collaboration with DARPA. How does this logic function? One interpretation might be that Doherty and others in the Maker movement have inadequately engaged and therefore inappropriately drawn from equity narratives within education circles. A second interpretation, one we wish to examine further, is that the underspecified and generic language around educational equity and diversity legitimates Doherty's appropriation of diversity rationales to justify his organization's partnerships and goals. Indeed, Doherty's statement reflects discourses of "access" that are stripped of their sociopolitical context and divorced from meaningful discussion of the *goals* and *values* of STEM education.

In this vein, we are concerned with trends in STEM education that advance pedagogical models organized around innovation yet deemphasize critical thinking, social analysis, and the arts. As educators and researchers, we argue for a nuanced stance that embraces inquiry and problem solving but critiques notions of innovation that are divorced from youth agency and activism. In fact, we argue that educational projects that seek to cultivate a sophistication of mind while suppressing young people's inclinations to critique, resist, and imagine are more aligned with social reproduction than transformation. Thus, in order for STEM education to find its place within a broader framework of social justice, our visions of equity require greater conceptual precision and a more direct engagement with the contradictions embedded in educational discourses that explicitly or implicitly advance the goals of U.S. empire. Before expanding on this point, we turn to a brief discussion of how these issues are currently framed within STEM education, with particular attention to scholars that have focused their research, teaching, and activism on equity and access.

## ALTERNATIVE VISIONS FOR EDUCATIONAL EQUITY

Though our focus in this chapter is to draw attention to what is absent from the discourse on equity and diversity in STEM education, we believe it is critical to honor and draw from the work of teachers, activists, and scholars who have made significant contributions toward an equitable vision for STEM education. In what follows, we briefly outline these contributions and build on their insights to tease apart and contrast various ways of conceptualizing diversity in STEM education.

One prominent example is the work of the civil rights leader Robert Moses, who has made the compelling argument that math and science literacy are civil rights issues (Moses and Cobb 2001). Moses's long-standing work with the Algebra Project is built on the premise that access to a quality math and science education is a major component of full participation in American society and the key to upward mobility for economically disenfranchised communities.

Alongside Moses, many other teachers, activists, researchers, parents, students, and policy makers have contributed to the advancement of equity and diversity in STEM education. The math education reform movement, for example, of which the National Council of Teachers of Mathematics (NCTM) is a central part, has worked over the past several decades to develop and implement research-supported curricula, assessments, and standards grounded in a deep understanding of mathematical thinking, teaching, and learning. NCTM's (2000) *Principles and Standards for School Mathematics* outlines six principles for school mathematics, of which "equity" is the first—defined in terms of the responsibility educators have to provide adequate support and hold high expectations for all students. The science education community has made similar strides, with recent reforms such as the Next Generation Science Standards (NGSS) promoting curricula, technology, and best practices grounded in research on scientific thinking and authentic practices, with specific attention to issues of fairness, access, and equity.

At the same time, the reformist agendas and policy platforms represented by NCTM and NGSS may constrain more radical critiques and approaches (Martin 2003, Tate 1994). Other critical perspectives on equity in STEM education should also be noted. This research is broad and crosses several disciplines, including work on ethnomathematics that challenges the Eurocentric bias in school mathematics (d'Ambrosio 1985); work that illuminates how race, identity, and culture are intertwined with learning processes (Medin and Bang 2014, Nasir 2002); research examining how structural forces such as racism impede learning opportunities (Martin 2000, 2003, 2011, 2013); and social justice perspectives that attempt to repurpose mathematics and science as tools for community development and social change (Barton 2003, Gutstein 2006, Vakil 2014). Our own work is deeply informed by these perspectives, which collectively assert that equity in STEM education will not be achieved as long as science itself remains pure and beyond examination (Medin and Bang 2014, 240). However, we have found few resources to help us think about the specific role of U.S. military interests in STEM education and its implications for discourses on equity (though recent work by Philip et al. (2017) on "Ideological Convergence in an Engineering Ethics Classroom" offers an important way forward). We therefore aim to build from but also extend critiques of equity in STEM education by drawing attention to the ways in which U.S. military and corporate interests influence content, pedagogy, and the overall framing of STEM education.

To this end, we draw on the work of the race and mathematics scholar Danny Martin. Although Martin does not focus on the military, he offers a framework for critically analyzing the national discourse on equity. Questioning calls for diversity in STEM education, Martin (2009, 298) states:

> The goal of increased participation in mathematics, science, and engineering among African American, Latino, and Native Americans for the purpose of maintaining U.S competitiveness . . . carries with it a short-sighted, enlightened self-interest rather than deep moral concern about, or commitment to, the well-being of these groups.

Martin's statement must be understood within the context of his larger argument—that race, a sociopolitical and ideological construction that fundamentally shapes the social world—has been undertheorized with respect to mathematics education. Inherent in this argument is a recognition that broader structural forces must be contended with to comprehend fully students' experiences of STEM education, particularly for students historically underrepresented in STEM fields. Building from Martin's argument and working to analyze racial politics from an international perspective, we believe that the foreign policy interests of the United States, especially in the increasingly militaristic post-9/11 era, have been generally unexamined with respect to their relationship with STEM education.

To consider what this lens contributes to our understanding and development of arguments for educational equity, we return to the two narratives outlined earlier and explicate the *substantive distinctions* between diversity as rooted in the "enlightened self-interest" of U.S. competitiveness and diversity as rooted in a "deep moral concern" for youth and communities of color. Broadly, we assert that STEM education rooted in "enlightened self-interest" *begins with* and organizes learning around the needs and political agendas of the state, whereas STEM education rooted in "deep moral concern" for issues of equity begins with and organizes learning around the needs, capacities, values, identities, and possible futures of underrepresented students and communities. Grounded in a historical view of capitalism and racial hierarchy, this distinction refuses the implicit narrative that state interests necessarily align with the interests of working-class communities and communities of color. In Table 5.1, we offer an examination of the multiplicity of meanings attached to "diversity," a seemingly ubiquitous idea within conversations about STEM education. To Martin's critique of economic "competitiveness" we add a critique of U.S. hegemony, or political and military predominance (see Table 5.1). While this table is by no means exhaustive, it can serve as a tool for identifying the specific conceptual and pedagogical differences between approaches to equity that are tied up in U.S. hegemony and educational models grounded in "a deep moral concern and commitment to the well being" (Martin 2009) of working-class students and students of color.

Based on the historical and contemporary connections outlined in this chapter, we believe the interests of militarism fit comfortably with the arguments for diversity depicted on the left side of Table 5.1. Historically, the military has also served as a vehicle for economic and social mobility. Disentangling these arguments from the alternative values represented on the right side of the table highlights the need to imagine ways of broadening and deepening participation in STEM education without simultaneously increasing participation in the kinds of scientific knowledge production that contributes to the oppression of young people and communities of color around the world. In other words: What kinds of pathways

Table 5.1

| Diversity as rooted in U.S. competitiveness and hegemony | Diversity as rooted in deep moral concern for students of color |
|---|---|
| 1. Culturally and linguistically diverse STEM workers as tied to expanding markets | 1. Culturally and linguistically diverse knowledge producers as tied to expanding and democratizing the meanings, values, and purposes of STEM education |
| 2. Token representation as tied to perceptions of multicultural democracy | 2. Substantive representation as tied to the redistribution of power and the struggle for social, racial, and educational justice |
| 3. Expanding the pool of qualified domestic labor so that U.S. technological innovation can dominate markets and secure military hegemony | 3. For some, expanding the pool of qualified domestic labor as tied to economic/social mobility and community development. For others, diversifying STEM education as tied to building a future free of racial hierarchy and economic exploitation. |
| 4. Closing the "achievement gap" as tied to improving international measures of STEM excellence | 4. Reimagining and transforming education such that all students (in the United States and around the world) have access to intellectually respectful learning experiences and the resources to fulfill their individual and collective potential |

does STEM learning open up for youth? Are STEM concepts and practices unexamined tools for broader participation in the American hegemonic project, or might they become tools for community development and social transformation? Is science treated as a neutral enterprise or as one steeped in history and politics? Even those criticizing Maker Media's decision to partner with DARPA wrestled with the notion that expanding access to STEM education is undeniably positive. In response to the partnership, Rebecca Jeschke of the San Francisco–based Electronic Frontier Foundation stated, "Anything that helps high schoolers do cool things with science is a good thing . . . technology is cool" (2012). Thus, for Doherty's argument to hold, science and technology education must be framed as a morally benign enterprise—the more of which is better, regardless of the means and irrespective of the ends.

## *Discussion*

Drawing from the critical perspectives outlined here, we argue instead for historicized approaches to STEM education that invite students to interrogate the genealogy of STEM concepts and their uses and that define STEM fields as shaped by sociopolitical contexts and values (Lemke 2001, Medin and Bang 2014). This could involve, for example, interdisciplinary courses and projects that bring together history, social science, and STEM learning to contextualize scientific knowledge as an inherited set of ideas that responds to particular human needs and values. In other words, we imagine intellectually rich and critical spaces where youth are exposed both to the wonder of science and technology and to their moral and human implications.

For example, what would it mean if students learning about the robotics, aerodynamics, and computer programming involved in drone technology were simultaneously learning about the interests that spurred the development of such technologies and about what drone warfare has meant for people in places like Yemen, Pakistan, and Afghanistan? What if they were invited to imagine the alternative uses such technology could have? Such a pedagogical approach might involve looking closely at the specific processes of invention and design that were influenced by the *goals* of drone technology as well as at the new and desensitized forms of warfare they begot. Through such lessons and conversations, young people would be supported to think in metacognitive ways about *all* technology and scientific knowledge as imbued with social and political values (Phillips, et al., 2017).

This critical perception would ideally inform their own engagement as producers of knowledge such that the practices of invention, problem solving, and design at the heart of NGSS would involve questions like: What problems are we solving, and who defined it? Whom does this solution help, and whom might it hurt? Who will have access to this technology, and at what cost? More broadly, what are the human and environmental implications of the ways particular theoretical concepts have been or may be used? What kinds of values and analyses are embedded within particular technological solutions? These questions can be engaged in a variety of contexts: schools, afterschool programs, community and family spaces, and science museums. Such pedagogical sensibilities would not only support more critical engagement with STEM; they would also support the broadening and deepening of participation by substantively engaging with a heterogeneity of worldviews, values, and epistemologies (Bang et al. 2013, Warren et al. 2001). In this vein, student inquiries about "the point" of learning particular concepts would be treated as legitimate and essential to the shared process of wrestling with the broader question: STEM learning *toward what ends?* Within this framework, progressive shifts toward models of STEM education that are aligned with professional activity (a core tenet of NGSS) would treat real-world STEM practices as culturally and politically constituted and open to critique and reimagination.

We argue that engaging directly with these tensions and power structures can give life to more meaningful forms of learning and deeper visions of equity. From our perspective, this includes cultivating and opening up new possibilities for solidarity across communities of color in the United States and around the world. The goals outlined on the left side of Table 5.1 take a fundamentally competitive and hierarchical attitude toward the vast majority of people around the world. The children of historically colonized and oppressed communities are positioned as potential contributors to STEM fields *in so far as* they identify with a narrow view of American national interests. Further, the educational experiences and possible futures of young people outside the United States (and Europe) are either ignored or implicitly framed as threats to U.S. competitiveness. Equity narratives that fail to examine these tensions may therefore take a nationalist rather than internationalist view of educational justice and avert the need to wrestle with our positions as U.S.-based researchers and educators within global North-South relations. These narratives are also harmful to immigrant, diasporic, and indigenous youth within the United States whose own histories of oppression and resistance have more in common with the historical struggles of communities in the global South than with the CEOs of Boeing or Raytheon. Situating STEM learning in its sociopolitical and ideological context allows us to see these divisions and possible connections, which may otherwise be out of sight and out of mind. This would include, for example, naming the often unspoken tensions and moral dilemmas experienced by people working within these industries, which could serve as an untapped resource for the type of dialogue we are arguing for.

Such conversations are necessary to advancing an internationalist approach to equity that would invite students to recognize and embrace their connections to youth and communities of color around the world and provide meaningful opportunities to consider the kinds of knowledge production and labor they want to be a part of, the type of world they want to help build. From this perspective, rejecting notions of equity that are premised on sameness or assimilation would also mean resisting invitations to belong that are premised on the dehumanization of others. Though we are not interested in demonizing individual students for choosing particular professional paths, particularly with regards to economic mobility and opportunity, we are questioning a system that creates such narrow choices and its relationship to dominant discourses rooted in militarism, economic exploitation, and racial hierarchy. Ultimately, we seek to situate the struggle for educational justice as part of a larger historical and international struggle. This would include redefining "educational success" to include sociopolitical understandings of STEM fields as well as the knowledge and skills involved in cultivating this type of solidarity. To answer our own question—*toward what ends?*—this work would serve the larger goal of developing approaches to equity that do not simultaneously reproduce global structures of power and that substantively connect broadening access to high-quality STEM learning with the transformation of STEM fields in the direction of social justice and human dignity.

### REFERENCES

Alexander, M. 2012. *The new Jim Crow: Mass incarceration in the age of colorblindness.* New York: The New Press.

Au, W., and J. J. Ferrare. 2015. *Mapping corporate education reform: Power and policy networks in the neoliberal state.* New York: Routledge.

Bang, M., B. Warren, A. S. Rosebery, and D. Medin. 2013. Desettling expectations in science education. *Human Development* 55 (5/6): 302–318.

Barton, A. C. 2003. *Teaching science for social justice.* New York: Teachers College Press.

Bell, D. A., Jr. 1979. *Brown v. Board of Education* and the interest-convergence dilemma. *Harvard Law Review* 93:518.

———. 2004. *Silent covenants:* Brown v. Board of Education *and the unfulfilled hopes for racial reform.* New York: Oxford University Press.

Boaler, J. 2008. When politics took the place of inquiry: A response to the National Mathematics Advisory Panel's review of instructional practices. *Educational Researcher* 37 (9): 588–594.

Bourdieu, P., and J. C. Passeron. 1990. *Reproduction in education, society, and culture.* 4th ed. Thousand Oaks, Calif.: Sage.

Bowles, S., and H. Gintis. 1976. *Schooling in capitalist America.* New York: Basic Books.

d'Ambrosio, U. 1985. Ethnomathematics and its place in the history and pedagogy of mathematics. *For the Learning of Mathematics* 5 (1): 44–48.

DARPA. 2010. Manufacturing experimentation and outreach (MENTOR). https://www.fbo.gov/index?s=opportunity&mode=form&id=a36a6082390 98b6a6a095778bc8a3f19&tab=core&_cview=1.

Davis, A. Y. 2011. *Are prisons obsolete?* New York: Seven Stories.

Dean, C. 2007. When science suddenly mattered, in space and in class. *New York Times,* September 25.

Department of Defense. 2009. STEM education and outreach strategic plan.

Dougherty, D. 2012. Makerspaces in education and DARPA. *Makezine,* April 4. http://makezine.com/2012/04/04/makerspaces-in-education-and -darpa/.

Feder, M. A., A. W. Shouse, B. Lewenstein, and P. Bell, eds. 2009. *Learning science in informal environments: People, places, and pursuits.* National Academies Press.

Finley, K. 2012. The military-maker complex: DARPA infiltrates the hackerspace movement. *Technoccult,* February 24. http://technoccult.net/ archives/2012/02/24/the-military-maker-complex-darpa-infiltrates-the -hackerspace-movement/.

Finoki, B., N. Sowers, and J. Bryan Arbona. 2011. Make, DARPA and teens: A match made in hackerspace. http://demilit.tumblr.com/post/ 16356948391/make-darpa-and-teens-a-match-made-in-hackerspace.

Giroux, H. A. 1983. Theories of reproduction and resistance in the new sociology of education: A critical analysis. *Harvard Educational Review* 53 (3): 257–293.

———. 2008. The militarization of U.S. higher education after 9/11. *Theory, Culture, and Society* 25 (5): 56–82.

———. 2014. Totalitarian paranoia in the post-Orwellian surveillance state. *Truthout,* February 10. http://www.truth-out.org/opinion/item/21656 -totalitarian-paranoia-in-the-post-orwellian-surveillance-state.

Gutstein, E. 2006. *Reading and writing the world with mathematics: Toward a pedagogy for social justice.* New York: Routledge.

hooks, b. 1994. *Teaching to transgress.* New York: Routledge.

Lemke, J. L. 2001. Articulating communities: Sociocultural perspectives on science education. *Journal of Research in Science Teaching* 38 (3): 296–316.

Leslie, S. W. 1993. *The Cold War and American science: The military-industrial-academic complex at MIT and Stanford.* New York: Columbia University Press.

Lopez, C. T. 2013. STEM grads critical to U.S. military mission. http:// www.army.mil/article/109326/STEM_grads_critical_to_U_S__military _mission/.

Lyman, R. 2009. *Stanford in turmoil: Campus unrest, 1966–1972.* Palo Alto, Calif.: Stanford University Press.

Mansfield, J. 2011. DARPA administrators: Just make it. *MIT News,* December 14. http://newsoffice.mit.edu/2011/darpa-manufacturing-event-1214.

Martin, D. B. 2003. Hidden assumptions and unaddressed questions in mathematics for all rhetoric. *Mathematics Educator* 13 (2).

———. 2009. Researching race in mathematics education. *Teachers College Record* 111 (2): 295–338.

———. 2011. What does quality mean in the context of white institutional space? In *Mapping equity and quality in mathematics education*, 437–450. New York: Springer.

———. 2013. Race, racial projects, and mathematics education. *Journal for Research in Mathematics Education* 44 (1): 316–333.

Martinez, S. L., and G. Stager. 2013. *Invent to learn: Making, tinkering, and engineering in the classroom*. Torrance, Calif.: Constructing Modern Knowledge.

McCoy, A. 2007. *A question of torture: CIA interrogation, from the Cold War to the War on Terror*. New York: Owl.

Medin, D. L., and M. Bang. 2014. *Who's asking?: Native science, Western science, and science education*. Cambridge, Mass.: MIT Press.

Moses, R. P., and C. E. Cobb. 2001. *Radical equations: Math literacy and civil rights*. Boston: Beacon.

Nasir, N. I. S. 2002. Identity, goals, and learning: Mathematics in cultural practice. *Mathematical Thinking and Learning* 4 (2/3): 213–247.

National Academies. 2010. *Expanding underrepresented minority participation*. Washington, D.C.: National Academies Press.

National Mathematics Advisory Panel. 2008. *Foundations for success: The final report of the National Mathematics Advisory Panel*. Washington, D.C.: U.S. Department of Education.

Ohab, J. 2010. DARPA challenging students to design cyber-electro-mechanical systems. http://science.dodlive.mil/2010/09/28/darpa-challenging-students-to-design-cyber-electro-mechanical-systems/.

Said, E. 2005. The public role of writers and intellectuals. In *Nation, Language, and the Ethics of Translation*, ed. S. Berman and M. Wood, 15. Princeton, N.J.: Princeton University Press.

Schoenfeld, A. H. 2004. The math wars. *Educational policy* 18 (1): 253–286.

STARBASE Annual Report. 2013. http://www.starbasemn.org/wp/wp-content/uploads/2014/04/2013-Starbase-Annual-Report-Final.pdf.

Tate, W. F. 1994. Mathematics standards and urban education: Is this the road to recovery? *Educational Forum* 58 (4): 380–390.

Philip, T. M., A. Gupta, A. Elby, and C. Turpen. 2017. Why ideology matters for learning: A case of ideological convergence in an engineering ethics classroom discussion on drone warfare. *Journal of the Learning Sciences*.

Vakil, S. 2014. A critical pedagogy approach for engaging urban youth in mobile app development in an after-school program. *Equity and Excellence in Education* 47 (1): 31–45.

Vossoughi, S., P. K. Hooper, and M. Escudé. 2016. Making through the lens of culture and power: Toward transformative visions for educational equity. *Harvard Educational Review* 86 (2): 206–232.

Wald, J., and D. J. Losen. 2003. Defining and redirecting a school-to-prison pipeline. *New Directions for Youth Development* 99:9–15.

Wall, T., and T. Monahan. 2011. Surveillance and violence from afar: The politics of drones and liminal security-scapes. *Theoretical Criminology* 15 (3): 239–254.

Warren, B., C. Ballenger, M. Ogonowski, et al. 2001. Rethinking diversity in learning science: The logic of everyday sense-making. *Journal of Research in Science Teaching* 38:529–552.

# A Day at the Fair: Marketing Militarism to Students of Color in Elementary Schools

*Suzie M. Abajian*

The decade following 9/11 was marked by a "rapidly increasing militarization of public space and culture" within the United States (Giroux 2004, 211). Militarization permeated various institutions, including public schools (Saltman and Gabbard 2011, Turse 2008). Legislation such as the No Child Left Behind (NCLB) Act of 2001 (Pub. L. No. 107–110, 115 Stat. 1425; signed into law in 2002) and the National Defense Authorization Act of 2004 (XVII U.S.C. §§1701–1705), coupled with the strengthening of existing programs such as JROTC and the Junior Police,[1] the proliferation of military charter schools, and the military's heavily funded public relations campaign, all have contributed to the increased militarization of urban high schools and the recruitment of low-income students of color into the military (Abajian 2013, Ayers 2006, Furumoto 2005, Galaviz et al. 2011, Mariscal 2005, Saltman and Gabbard 2011). In 2010, during the first half of the Obama administration, this trend continued as military spending increased to an unprecedented $691 billion. However, 2010 to 2016 saw a gradual drop in military spending. By 2016, the budget had declined to $580 billion, which was still higher than the average spending during the George W. Bush administration (U.S. Department of Defense 2017).

Recently, the Trump administration stated that it intends to increase military spending by $54 billion (Shear and Steinhauer 2017). Together with the new administration's hypernationalist agenda, this will undoubtedly contribute to the continuing militarization of U.S. society and, by extension, U.S. public schools.

Although the increased militarization of schools at the secondary level has garnered some attention from critical educators, what has gone under the radar is the marketing campaign of the military and the police within urban elementary and middle schools. Lipman's (2004) case study of four elementary schools in Chicago, where the focus of the analysis is NCLB's high-stakes accountability measures, is one of only a small number of academic studies examining the growing militarization of elementary schools. However, her analysis focuses on the implicit disciplining function of high-stakes accountability measures and does not address programs and practices explicitly connected to the promotion of the military and the police within elementary schools. In this chapter, I give an illustration and an analysis of these explicit militarized practices within the context of one urban elementary school in Southern California. Specifically, my discussion focuses on a career day fair held at the elementary school and on the ways in which this event serves to normalize militarism and build positive dispositions among young students toward the military and the police through early exposure and conditioning.

*Background*

The militarization of public education in the United States took a new turn in 2001, particularly within schools serving predominantly low-income communities of color (Ayers 2006, Mariscal 2005). The NCLB Act of 2001 reauthorized the Elementary and Secondary Education Act of 1965, promising to close the "achievement gap" between white students and students of color. Although, while it was in effect, NCLB's high-stakes accountability components stirred up much controversy, not much attention was paid to the provision in the bill that enabled military recruiters to have unprecedented access to high school campuses and private student information (Furumoto 2005, Holm 2007, Schroeder 2004). Under NCLB §9528, schools were obligated to give student names, phone numbers, and addresses to the military in order to receive federal funding—unless parents individually opted their children out—and noncompliant schools faced harsh consequences.[2]

The National Defense Act, officials from the Department of Defense, the local educational agencies' Congressional representatives, their Senators, their governor, and certain Congressional committees [were] notified to intervene in cases of non-compliance. The pressure that would be placed on a non-compliant local educational agency and the consequences of non-compliance would [have been] enormous. Not only would a local educational agency suffer from a lack of federal funding, its elected officials would likely anticipate political repercussions over a loss of federal funding and pressure the agency to comply. (Holm 2007, 584)

As a result, secondary schools receiving Title I[3] funds were under heavy pressure to comply with the military recruitment provision of NCLB. At the same time, these schools also were responsible for informing parents, once a year, about the "opt-out" provision and its deadline. However, many schools would often fail to properly notify parents and inform them of their rights (Furumoto 2005, Holm 2007).

Although §9528 of the NCLB Act of 2001 obligated secondary schools and educational institutions receiving Title I funds to give increased access to military recruiters targeting low-income students, the actual implementation of the law varied significantly from school to school and depended largely on the dispositions of the administration and teachers, who would act as either "gate keepers" or "gate openers" for recruiters (Abajian 2013). Furthermore, the NCLB provision did not apply to elementary or middle schools. Hence, any access given to military representatives at the elementary and middle school levels was not mandated by law but would have been exclusively the prerogative of the educators and administrators at the school sites.

A number of scholars have argued that in addition to NCLB §9528, which was geared toward military recruitment in secondary schools, the high-stakes accountability component of NCLB also contributed to the increased militarization of K–12 schools serving predominantly low-income students of color. For instance, Furumoto (2005) argues that NCLB exacerbated the inequalities present at underfunded and marginalized schools, serving predominantly Black and Latinx students. She also argues that the punitive accountability measures that "punish" these so-called low-performing K–12 schools have conditioned school communities to follow NCLB policies obediently and be disciplined by them. Furumoto (2005) further argues that the control, bureaucratization, and accountability focus of NCLB is an inherently militaristic approach to running an organization and part of the hidden agenda of NCLB.

Lipman (2004) similarly argues that NCLB's high-stakes accountability measures and the Charter School Movement (CSM) have been situated
within "the larger neoliberal project to privatize public institutions and
commodify public and private life while increasing state regulation of individuals and institutions through new forms of accountability, testing,
standards [and] surveillance" (3). She grounds her analysis in the experiences of teachers and students in four public elementary schools in Chicago. One of the conclusions she reaches is that these educational policies
have reified a "system of surveillance and coercion [that] breeds fear and
suppression of dissent and teaches people to silence themselves . . . [which
is] crippling to democracy and critical thought and action" (9). In other
words, these neoliberal policies have served as disciplining tools to keep
teachers and students alike within the confines of a narrowly defined curriculum focused on testing and marked by compliance, uniformity, and a
lack of creativity and critical thought. And by extension, these policies have
reified the school-to–exploited labor pipeline.

Even before NCLB and 9/11, scholars such as Berlowtiz (2000) were as-
serting that neoliberal educational reforms and their privatization agendas were widening economic disparities and contributing to the militarization
of urban schools by "endeavoring to transform [these] schools into military academies [and] target[ing] these 'urban underclass' school children
for recruitment" (394). During Obama's first term in office, these neoliberal educational reforms continued to be shaped by initiatives such as
Race to the Top (2009), the attack on teacher unions and teacher tenure,
and the growth of the Charter School Movement, which continued well
into the second term of the Obama administration (Rotberg 2014, Stern
2013). Among the growing number of charter schools were also a growing number of military academies geared toward instilling a certain brand
of militaristic discipline in students from low-income communities of
color. For example, Chicago was flooded by a surge of military charter
schools (Galaviz et al. 2011). In 2013, the Los Angeles Unified School District approved the first military charter school in its district, serving grades
6–12, which includes middle school students (State Numbered Charter
Schools in California 2015).

In December 2015, President Obama signed his Every Student Succeeds
Act (ESSA; Pub. L. No. 114–95 §114 Stat. 1177 [2015–2016]) into law, which
had bipartisan support and was a sweeping overhaul of NCLB. ESSA was
the latest iteration of the 1965 Elementary and Secondary Education Act.
It eliminated the high-stakes component of school accountability and
NCLB's one-size-fits-all approach to school improvement (Davis 2015,

U.S. Department of Education 2017). ESSA eased some of the militaristic, high-stakes approaches to school accountability. However, ESSA, similar to NCLB, contained a provision in §9529 that continued to give military recruiters access to public schools and private student data.

In addition to ESSA, NCLB, and the CSM, institutionalized programs such as the Junior Reserve Officer's Training Corps (JROTC) have contributed to the militarization of schools. Although JROTC is a century-old program, it grew significantly in the early 1990s because of increased federal funding. According to the *Washington Post* (as referenced in Berlowitz 2000), by the mid-1990s the JROTC budget had more than doubled, and the number of JROTC chapters had increased to 2,267 schools (a 32 percent jump from the beginning of the decade), with over 310,000 students (Bartlett and Lutz 1998). During this time period, the JROTC was experiencing "the most rapid expansion in its history" (Ayers 2006, 595). This trend has continued post-9/11.

An article by Jones (2013) in the *Nation* magazine stated that the Department of Defense had spent $365 million in 2013 to provide uniforms, Pentagon-approved textbooks, and equipment to JROTC programs; this sum does not include the portion of the instructor salaries that the Department of Defense pays. The National Network Opposing the Militarization of Youth (2012) website claimed there were over half a million cadets in 3,429 JROTC units across the country, in addition to an unknown number of students in the Middle School Cadet Corps (MSCC) programs (Abajian 2013; referenced in Abajian and Guzman 2013).

Although the JROTC program is a high school program, it has expanded its reach to middle schools through a growing number of MSCC programs. According to the Chicago Public Schools website (2014), there were twenty MSCC programs within the city. Additionally, thirty-three MSCC chapters across the country were listed on the National Middle School Cadet Corps website in 2014.

There have also been some reports of Elementary School Cadet Corps (ESCC) programs across the country. For instance, Wedekind (2005) documented that in Chicago public schools there were voluntary, afterschool ESCC programs that would meet two or three times a week. The ESCC has been described as a charitable program though which students learn first aid, civics, "citizenship," and character development. Students also take part in field trips to local military bases to learn about military history. The discourses surrounding the justification of the MSCC as well as the ESCC programs, similar to JROTC programs (Abajian 2013, Galaviz et al. 2011), have raced and classed notions of discipline and obedience training considered necessary in urban schools geared toward students of color, who are portrayed as "unruly," "undisciplined," and "lacking motivation" (Abajian 2013).

In addition to MSCC and ESCC programs, many JROTC chapters have partnerships with elementary schools and middle schools through which the JROTC cadets volunteer their time to mentor and tutor younger students. The mentoring component of the program is touted as building leadership skills in JROTC cadets and helping elementary school students with much-needed mentorship and tutoring (Abajian 2013). Even though there might be merits to this argument, one cannot deny that this mentorship program also serves as a promotional tool for the JROTC and, by extension, the military.

In an interview from an earlier study, a JROTC instructor in a Southern California high school stated that his students gained "responsibility" and "self-discipline" through the leadership and teaching roles that they assumed in elementary schools within the JROTC context. He stated that students were required to volunteer for activities such as mentoring and tutoring younger students in elementary and middle schools while wearing their full JROTC uniforms (Abajian 2013).[4] The continual presence of JROTC students in elementary schools as mentors and tutors has extended the reach of the program in building positive dispositions toward militarized practices and programs, starting from the elementary school level.

JROTC has often publicly denied its recruitment agenda. Its supporters "claim that the goal is leadership and citizenship development, dropout prevention, or simply the fun of dressing up and parading around" (Ayers 2006, 595–596). However, in addition to its own literature and its evident militarized practices, the data regarding the percentage of students from the program who join the military suggest otherwise. For instance, approximately 40 to 45 percent of JROTC graduates eventually join the military (Ayers 2006, Berlowitz and Long 2003, Galaviz et al. 2011, Lutz and Bartlett 1995), as compared to 0.5 percent of the U.S. population (Miles 2011). Furthermore, JROTC is included in the recruitment budget of the Pentagon (McDuffee 2008; referenced in Galaviz et al. 2011). Thus, beyond the rhetoric of leadership development, academic success, discipline, and citizenship, JROTC functions as part of the larger public relations campaign of the military to normalize militarized practices and create positive dispositions among students toward the military (Abajian 2013).

Although the military budget decreased during President Obama's second term, this did not result in a reduced number of JROTC chapters.

Today, there are 3,453 JROTC chapters around the country (U.S. Air Force 2017, U.S. Army 2017, U.S. Coast Guard 2017, U.S. Marines 2017, U.S. Navy 2017), and it is likely that this number as well as the number of military charter schools will increase during the Trump administration, given Trump's promise of increased military funding and under the leadership of Secretary of Education Betsy DeVos, a big proponent of charter schools and school voucher programs.

JROTC programs target low-income Black and Latinx students (Ayers 2006, Berlowitz 2000, Galaviz et al. 2011, Lutz and Bartlett 1995), so it is no surprise that these populations have become overrepresented in the program. In 1993, most of the JROTC units were "located in the South (65 percent) and/or in schools with a high proportion of minority students: for example, schools with Army [JROTC] units [had] 48 percent, and those with Navy units 39 percent, African-American and Latino/a students, much higher than the 1991 national average of 27 percent African American and Latino/a students (National Center for Education Statistics, 1993). . . . [Also] Nationwide, 54 percent of JROTC cadets [had] 'minority' status" (Lutz and Bartlett 1995, 125–126). This trend has continued throughout the 1990s and into the present day.

Hence, JROTC partnerships with elementary and middle schools are paving the military path for young students of color through building long-standing relationships with older JROTC students who are military bound. This, in conjunction with the aforementioned MSCC and ESCC programs, forms a web of institutionalized programs that promote and normalize militarized practices and, by extension, the military within elementary and middle schools. However, the promotion and normalization of militarized practices within urban elementary and middle schools go beyond the confines of these formalized programs and often permeate instructional and schooling practices in more implicit and insidious ways. In this chapter, I will give an illustration of these practices through the following narrative of an elementary school career day fair that I attended. My analysis is based on qualitative fieldnotes and reflective memos regarding my experience as a visitor at this career day.

## Methodology

I was invited to attend a career day event at Marshall Elementary (a pseudonym), a public school in Southern California in 2011. Although the event was not open to the public, certain community members and educators, including myself, were invited to attend as guests by the teachers at the school site. Marshall Elementary is located in one of the most economically depressed communities in Southern California. The median household income within this community was approximately $30,000, which is lower than the city and county in which it is located; this is also lower than the median income for the state of California (U.S. Census 2010). Marshall Elementary was a Title I school, with 63 percent of its students qualifying for free or reduced lunch. The student population was predominantly Latinx (97 percent), with a small number of Black students (3 percent).

During the economic crisis of the past decade, the school district in which Marshall Elementary was located experienced a massive layoff of teachers (approximately 25 percent of the entire teaching force was laid off), which destabilized the educational progress of its students (Dillon 2010). Extracurricular activities, arts, and music were the first programs on the chopping block (Abdollah 2012). This disinvestment from public schools was accompanied by the high-stakes accountability measures discussed earlier in this chapter, which worked to severely restrict the curriculum within urban public schools and curb enrichment opportunities offered to students (Berliner 2011, Crocco 2007). This is why I was pleasantly surprised to hear about a school that was offering more than the "basics" to its students. I was intrigued by the notion of an elementary school career day—career days are usually held at high schools—and contemplated the possibilities of such an event in igniting the imaginations of young students in developing different postsecondary interests at an early age.

Immediately following my attendance at the career day, I audiorecorded my recollections and reflections, which were then transcribed into ethnographic fieldnotes. I also wrote three reflective memos regarding my school visit. I employed a grounded theory approach and used inductive coding of my fieldnotes and reflective memos to identify and analyze the themes emerging from my data (Corbin and Strauss 1990).

My methodology was also situated within the autoethnographic (Ellis, Adams, and Bochner 2010) and critical research (Duncan-Andrade and Morrell 2008) frameworks. Ellis et al. (2010, 1) conceptualize autoethnography as a methodology that "seeks to describe and systematically analyze personal experience in order to understand cultural experience. This approach challenges canonical ways of doing research and representing others and treats research as a political, socially-just and socially-conscious act." The critical research framework is described by Duncan-Andrade and Morrell (2008) as research done in collaboration and on behalf of marginalized communities, with the goal of producing knowledge that will in turn inform social action and social change.

Drawing from these frameworks, I used a systematic documentation of my personal experience at Marshall Elementary School's career day as well as my prior research experience on the militarization of schools to analyze and understand the schooling practices that promoted and privileged certain postsecondary paths over others for students at Marshall Elementary. My analysis and writing is from a critical perspective: I attempt to analyze and raise awareness of practices that are connected to issues of equity and access for students of color and/or low-income students in the hope of informing educational practice and policy.

## Findings

### THE SCHOOL'S ROLE IN NURTURING POSITIVE AND UNCRITICAL ASSOCIATIONS WITH THE MILITARY AND POLICE

My findings are organized into four sections. One of the themes that emerged from my data was the school's role in nurturing positive and uncritical associations with the military and police.

Upon arriving at the school site, I was greeted by a staff member, who asked me to sign in at the entrance of the school and directed me to proceed down a long hallway leading to the school cafeteria/auditorium. As I walked down the hallway toward my destination, I noticed that the walls were decorated with student artwork. When I reached the cafeteria/auditorium, I observed more of these student art projects, which had been made into placemats and placed in front of every seat at every cafeteria table—approximately 120 of them. The laminated crayon drawings on construction paper portrayed what students wanted to become when they "grew up." Written at the bottom of each art project was the profession the drawings represented.

I was struck by the variety of careers that were represented in the students' drawings. They demonstrated the extent of exposure that Marshall Elementary students had to different career paths. For example, one of these art pieces depicted a paleontologist looking at a dinosaur skeleton; another similarly depicted a chemist in a laboratory. There were many drawings of teachers in classrooms and of doctors with stethoscopes. However, I was also surprised to see a large number of drawings of soldiers, SWAT teams, and police officers, who were often pointing rifles, guns, or tanks at civilians—it was curious that this was the way students envisioned military service and careers in law enforcement. The most striking drawing was that of a soldier pointing a rifle at the back of an unarmed man's head;

the man was kneeling, with his fingers interlaced behind his head. Approximately one-fourth of the placemats depicted military and police activities.

The placemats were the products of a class project. They served as assessment tools through which students depicted what they knew and had learned about various professions and their respective functions in society. As such, the frequency and manner in which the military and the police were portrayed in these student art projects was indicative, to a certain extent, of what was being taught, celebrated, and reified in classrooms and within the school.

Another demonstration of the school's role in nurturing positive associations with the military and police was in the structuring of the career day program. As I walked through the cafeteria/auditorium doors overlooking the quad, where the career day assembly was taking place, I observed approximately 450 students sitting on the floor with their legs crossed, listening intently to the different guest speakers, who introduced themselves and gave a brief description of their respective professions. Students listened patiently and attentively, clapping as each speaker left the stage.

Following a few such speakers, three men and a woman officer from the Air Force took the stage, fully dressed in their military pilot jumpsuits. As the Air Force pilots began their presentation, the atmosphere of the assembly changed from a subdued lull into electric anticipation. Students began moving restlessly in their seats and leaning forward and over the shoulders of the students in front of them so as not to miss what was being presented on the stage.

The Air Force officers seemed to be experienced public speakers who knew how to engage their young audience. The first speaker abandoned the microphone and instead projected his voice, directly addressing the sea of students: "Hello kids! We're really glad to be here today! [Students cheer]. We're gonna give out an award for the essay contest [more cheers]." Together with the school administration, the Air Force had organized an essay contest for students. The two winners of the essay contest, a male student and a female student, were called to the stage and honored by the Air Force officers in front of the entire student body—they were given Air Force backpacks for their prize.

The act of honoring the essay contest winners set the Air Force pilots apart from all other guest speakers. It gave them an honored and privileged position among the representatives of the different professions at the fair. It also communicated to students that the military was a particularly respected profession and had the full blessing and support of the adults at the school site. Furthermore, the essay contest demonstrated that the Air Force had been actively coordinating with the school administration and teachers for some time previously. The contact that the Air Force officers had with students was not relegated to the career day but rather took the shape of an ongoing and purposeful engagement with the school and the student body, with the full approval of the administration. This was an example of how the school provided increased access and exposure to the military in comparison to other fields, including higher education, and by doing so nurtured positive dispositions among students toward the military.

Following the bestowment of these awards, another one of the Air Force officers announced that they had brought back their "fighter jets," due to popular demand. As soon as the words "fighter jets" were uttered, students were thrown into a frenzy of cheers; many of them got up from their seats in excitement. The officer continued his speech by saying that last year they had only brought one of the fighter jets, but because it was so popular, this year they decided to bring three—communicating again their long-standing relationship with this particular school. The presentation about the mock fighter jets obfuscated the seriousness of the military and served to reinforce the notion that war is entertainment—a narrative often privileged in militarized video games and television (Leonard 2007).

The final Air Force speaker proceeded to talk about the merits of being an Air Force pilot, without mentioning any of the challenges of the profession or any of the realities of war. On the one hand, a discussion of the realities of war, in the context of an elementary school career day, would have been construed as inappropriate because of its serious and adult content. On the other hand, it was highly problematic to give a caricatured and simplistic portrayal of military service in a school setting—even though the military is constantly being portrayed in this light through children's toys, clothing, and television shows (Giroux 2004). The presentation given by the Air Force officers was in essence a lesson that promoted a positive and uncritical view of the military, which was in turn celebrated by the school leadership.

After the Air Force presentation, the principal invited students to disperse and visit the different booths set up around the quad. While students were browsing the booths, I took a moment to survey the list of invited guests. Although among the thirty-five guests and twelve booths were representatives from different career sectors, the largest group of the guests—more than 40 percent—were from multiple military and police agencies. The school administration and faculty were responsible for inviting the guests and organizing the career day. Their choice of guests, the differential treatment that certain guests received, and the content of the presentations were all organized and sanctioned by the school leadership. Within this context, the school nurtured a positive association with militarized practices, military service, and law enforcement for its students.

## The Normalization of Militarism and Policing via Raced and Gendered Practices

The career day not only served to nurture a positive association with the military and the police but also normalized militarism and policing via raced and gendered practices.

Three men and one woman officer gave the aforementioned Air Force presentation. The male officers appeared to occupy a dominant position; they literally and figuratively took center stage. They were positioned in front of their woman colleague and presented the major speaking points. The female officer, by contrast, took a passive role. She did not speak or make any major contributions and stood at the side of the stage. As such, the leadership roles displayed to students during this presentation delineated along normalized gender roles, reifying patriarchy—which some scholars argue is typical of the gendered practices within militarized programs, organizations, and spaces (Kronsell 2005).

The last Air Force presenter, a man, spoke in Spanish about how he had decided to join the reserves. His use of the Spanish language created an intimacy between himself and his predominantly immigrant Latinx student audience. He communicated to them that he was from their community and hence understood their experiences. This act positioned him as a role model for his student audience: He was someone from their community who had achieved a respectable position in society and a certain level of upward mobility. When he also mentioned that during the day he was a police officer in a wealthy suburb, he demonstrated the fluidity and connection between the two career sectors. The Air Force presenter was engaging in normalizing discourses about military service for Latinxs and stated that this was in fact one of the best career choices for the Latinx community. This discourse has been associated with the larger military recruitment campaigns targeting nonwhite communities, such as the "Yo Soy el Army" Spanish-language campaign launched in 2001 (Garza 2015). On the one hand, the military and the police were upheld as desirable career choices for Latinxs; on the other hand, the Latinx community was portrayed as the object of policing and militarized practices.

In addition to the booths ringing the quad, there was a police car parked right in the quad's center for students to explore. A few police officers helped a long line of students as they took turns exploring the vehicle: sitting in the back passenger seats, turning on the sirens, using the walkie-talkies, and trying on the officers' caps and handcuffs. It was problematic to see students sitting in the back seat of a police car and trying on handcuffs, particularly within the context of the hypercriminalization of Black and Latinx youth (Rios 2006), police brutality (Lawrence 2000), racial profiling, and overincarceration. Indeed, within these very communities, Blacks are more than six times as likely and Latinxs twice as likely to be incarcerated as are whites (Hartney 2006). Although designed to promote law enforcement as a career path, this activity also contributed to the normalization of scenes of incarceration for students within a primarily Latinx and Black community.

## THE SPECTACLE OF MILITARY AND POLICE

Alongside of the normalization of the military and the police via raced and gendered practices, another theme I noted was the normalization and celebration of war through militarized spectacles that furthered the public relations campaign of the military and the police to win the hearts and minds of young students.

After the presentations, as I walked around the quad, it was easy to see that the tables and booths that attracted the most student visitors were overwhelmingly those occupied by military and police representatives. Many of them came dressed in their respective uniforms and equipped with many freebees such as stickers and pencils, which they passed out abundantly. They also brought interesting gadgets that they made available for students to play with. For example, one of the Air Force pilots had a helmet that students could wear; she explained how they were equipped with speakers and enabled the pilot to communicate via the attached headset. The helmet was essentially a prop that was used by students to play-act and imagine themselves as Air Force pilots. At another booth, a police officer told students about animals that are utilized in police work as he encouraged them to pet his police dog. These props served not only to promote and normalize the military and the police as enjoyable and exciting professions but also enable students to role-play and visualize themselves within these professions.

Other booths did not attract as many students. For example, a booth next to a Metropolitan Transportation Authority bus in one corner of the quad attracted none of the students present at the career day. The MTA bus was not a particularly exciting or novel item for students to explore: Some of them rode MTA buses to school on a daily basis. An ambulance attracted some student attention, but it did not provide the entertainment value of the military and the police presenters.

In the far left corner of the quad, on the basketball court, three long lines of students waited to ride in the three mock fighter jets that one of the Air Force officers had mentioned in his speech during the assembly. The three Air Force servicemen, with the supervision of a teacher, were helping students board the mock fighter jets, one at a time, and taking them on a ride around the quad. It resembled a scene from an amusement park. I myself felt the draw to ride in one of these to find out how they functioned and feel what the students were experiencing during their ride. These fighter jets were built with motors similar to those used in golf carts and were designed specially for young children.

Halfway through the event, a police helicopter began circling above the quad several times. It flew away, then returned close to the center of the quad, loudly hovering right above the police car. All the students who were visiting different booths dropped what they were doing and ran to the middle of the quad, waving and cheering at the helicopter.

Through this militarized carnival, the military and the police successfully made their respective professions the most attractive and exciting of the career day. Although this spectacle might not have necessarily inspired students to become soldiers and law enforcement officers, it nevertheless was a concerted attempt on the part of the military to win the hearts and minds of these young students at Marshall Elementary. It would have been interesting to interview students to understand their perceptions and perspectives relating to this event; however, I had not received permission to interview them.

## DEDICATION OF RESOURCES

A fourth crucial theme to highlight was the dedication of human resources to the promotion of the military and the police at Marshall Elementary. Throughout the career day, it was striking to see the amount of resources dedicated to the promotion of the military and the police in a severely underfunded school, within an economically depressed neighborhood, in the midst of a nationwide recession.

Unlike the volunteers from the other career sectors, the police and military representatives were on the clock. They were paid employees whose jobs were to attend events such as these and promote their respective professions. This also helps explain the overrepresentation and privileging of military and police recruiters within Marshall Elementary: They were free to attend career days, unlike other guests.

In addition to the dedication of human resources, considerable monetary resources were dedicated to the promotion of the police and the military. For example, both the police car that was parked in the middle of the quad and the police helicopter that buzzed the fair required a significant amount of funding. The freebees that were distributed and the construction and maintenance of the mock fighter jets also represented the dedication of monetary resources to the ends of promoting the military at Marshall Elementary.

Additionally, I found it interesting that the Air Force was the branch of the military present at the career day. Being the most competitive branch of the military, and requiring the most education and the highest scores on the Armed Forces Qualification Test (AFQT), the Air Force is the least likely branch for young men and women from underprivileged backgrounds to join (Abajian 2013). However, the goal of having the Air Force presence at Marshall Elementary was less about specifically promoting the Air Force branch of the military as a viable career path and more about promoting the military in general.

During the fair, I spoke with one of the guests, a docent at the local zoo. She told me that before the schoolwide assembly, guest speakers had been asked to provide forty-minute presentations in different classrooms. This undoubtedly included the guests from the military and the police sectors, and it involved the allocation of a significant portion of the school day's instructional time. Although military and police officers were not officially recruiting in this elementary school, they were nevertheless given a lot of instructional time and opportunities to inspire students to pursue professions in their fields. This also contributed to building positive and uncritical dispositions toward the military and law enforcement among students at Marshall Elementary.

## Discussion

Although the militarization of elementary and middle schools serving low-income communities of color is shaped by institutionalized programs such as the JROTC partnerships with elementary schools, MSCC, ESCC, and the Junior Police, as well as by policies such as the NCLB Act of 2001 and ESSA of 2015, it is also shaped through different schooling practices that are not inherently militaristic. In the case of Marshall Elementary, the career day was a schooling practice that facilitated the promotion of the military and the police. The adults who organized the career day served as "gate openers" for military and law enforcement representatives by inviting them to the school, facilitating their one-on-one access to students via the career day, and giving them an honored position among the other guests.

Elementary schools are highly securitized places. For example, university researchers have difficulty gaining access to students and must obtain parental consent before interviewing, observing, and interacting with them. Given this context, it was surprising to see the extent of access that was given to military and police officers to speak and interact with students at Marshall Elementary without any parental notification and consent. At the same time, it was understandable that the school administration utilized the military and police personnel who were readily available to participate in the career day.

In my own experiences organizing career fairs, during my internship with the Coalition against Militarism in Our Schools (CAMS), I found it incredibly difficult to find guest speakers from different organizations and business sectors who could commit a few hours of their day to a high school career fair. It was hard to convince people to volunteer to take time out of their busy workdays, drive to a school site, and give a presentation to students. Guest visits usually had to be arranged weeks in advance. As military and police recruiters have full-time, paid assignments to do this very thing, it makes them the default people that administrators, counselors, and teachers rely on to fill speaker slots or guest lists at school events. As a result, the police and the military are often overrepresented as guest speakers in classrooms and at school events within urban communities because it is much easier to invite them than it is to collect a broad range of guests from different career sectors.

Also, the extent of access given to military and police representatives depends largely on the dispositions of the "gate openers" toward militarized careers—and on the real and imagined pressures that they face because of the overwhelming promilitary culture within the United States (Abajian 2013). Pentagon-sponsored programs such as the Educator Workshop Program (EWP) and Troops to Teachers (TTT),[5] initiated as a Department of Defense and Department of Education collaboration in 1994, continue to nurture positive dispositions regarding the military among teachers in schools serving predominantly low-income, communities of color—making them more likely to become de facto ambassadors for the military.

As urban school administrators and teachers are overwhelmed by the lack of resources and increasingly difficult working conditions, tapping into the readily available resources, conforming to cultural norms, and uncritically celebrating militarized spectacles becomes the path of least resistance. Although the number of educators and community organizations that have launched counter-recruitment[6] campaigns in urban schools is growing (Abajian and Guzman 2013), the largest responsibility falls on the shoulders of school leadership teams and educators in curtailing the unchecked promotion of militarized practices and the excessive access given to military and law enforcement visitors.

What would the career day have looked like had educators and school administrators made a concerted effort to organize different types of learning experiences and privilege different educational and career paths for students at Marshall Elementary? For example, instead of the spectacle of the mock fighter jets and the police helicopter, the administration and the faculty could have organized a career fair that highlighted scientific experiments, computer programming, or a collective art project offering solutions to a local social and/or environmental problem. The organizers of the fair could have been more selective in inviting a diverse group of professionals who defied racial and gender stereotypes to give students alternatives to dominant representations. The activities of the career day could have been more focused on questioning and critical analysis and less on entertainment and the consumption of the military and police public relations campaign. The school leadership could have nurtured different community and school partnerships and drawn from different community resources to design a career fair that gave students a well-rounded perspective on postsecondary paths.

In an age of diminishing public resources and opportunities, we as critical educators have the responsibility to guard and nurture the experiences of our most vulnerable students inside and outside classrooms. We need to employ a mindful and selective approach in designing educational and learning experiences for our students—experiences that spark their imagination, cultivate their creativity, and open up possibilities beyond what is often ascribed to underserved communities via structural, racial, and economic injustices.

NOTES

1. Abajian (2013) argues that the similarities of practices between the Junior Police and the JROTC shapes a conflation of the two programs and the respective career sectors that they represent among students. This, together with the promotion of the military as a stepping stone to law enforcement, has enabled both the JROTC and the Junior Police to act as proxies for each other.

2. Holm (2007, 585) argues that this policy "strikes at the heart of the constitutional right to privacy" and the legal rights of parents, upheld in a court decision in 2000, to "make decisions regarding the care, custody and control of their children, including who, outside of the nuclear family, may have access to [them]."

3. A designation given to schools serving socioeconomically disadvantaged students that entitles these schools to certain federal supplemental funds through the Elementary and Secondary Education Act.

4. Abajian (2013) argues that JROTC uniforms serve as an advertising tool for the JROTC program. Also, because the JROTC uniforms resemble military uniforms, they, by extension, serve as an advertising tool for the military.

5. The Educator Workshop (EWP) program offers workshops that teachers, counselors, coaches, principals, and other school personnel are invited to in order for them to learn about the Marine Corps, obtain a positive disposition toward the military, and ultimately become unofficial recruiters in the schools as they advise students about their career choices and the benefits of joining the Marine Corps. The Troops to Teachers (TTT) program seeks to help veterans in transitioning from their military work into civilian work by placing them in teaching positions across the country in poor and underserved schools.

6. Abajian and Guzman (2013, 193) describe counter-recruitment as a "pedagogical project that consisted of informing or teaching students and communities about the realities of military service often concealed by recruiters, the aggressive advertising campaign of the military and the corporations involved in the war industry. The primary objective of counter-recruitment campaigns in which we participated was 'recruiting' students away from military careers."

REFERENCES

Abajian, S. M. 2013. Drill and ceremony: A case study of militarism, military recruitment, and the pedagogy of enforcement in an urban school in Southern California. Ph.D. diss. University of California, Los Angeles.

Abajian, S. M., and M. Guzman. 2013. Moving beyond slogans: Possibilities for a more connected and humanizing "counter-recruitment" pedagogy in highly militarized urban schools. *Journal of Curriculum Theorizing* 29 (2): 191–205.

Abdollah, T. 2012. LAUSD arts funding cut 76% in five years. *89.3 KPCC*, October 10. http://www.scpr.org/blogs/education/2012/10/10/10421/lausd -arts-funding-cut-76-five-years/.

Air University. 2017. Air Force Junior ROTC unit locator. http://www .airuniversity.af.mil/Holm-Center/AFJROTC/Display/Article/950637/.

Ayers, W. 2006. Hearts and minds: Military recruitment and the high school battlefield. *Phi Delta Kappan* 87 (8): 594–599.

Bartlett, L., and C. Lutz. 1998. Disciplining social difference: Some cultural politics of military training in public high schools. *Urban Review* 30 (2): 119–136.

Berliner, D. 2011. Rational responses to high-stakes testing: The case of curriculum narrowing and the harm that follows. *Cambridge Journal of Education* 41 (3): 287–302.

Berlowitz, M. J. 2000. Racism and conscription in the JROTC. *Peace Review* 12 (3): 393–398.

Berlowitz, M. J., and N. A. Long. 2003. The proliferation of JROTC: Educational reform or militarization. In *Education as enforcement*, ed. K. J. Saltman and D. A. Gabbard, 163–174. New York: RoutledgeFalmer.

Chicago Public Schools. 2014. http://www.cps.edu/Programs/Academic _and_enrichment/JROTCandMilitary/Pages/JROTCacademies.aspx.

Corbin, J., and A. Strauss. 1990. Grounded theory research: Procedures, canons, and evaluative criteria. *Qualitative Sociology* 13:3–21.

Crocco, M. S. 2007. The narrowing of curriculum and pedagogy in the age of accountability: Urban educators speak out. *Urban Education* 42 (6): 512–535.

Davis, J. H. 2015. President Obama signs into law a rewrite of No Child Left Behind. *New York Times*, December 10.

Dillon, R. M. 2010. LA schools reach deal with ACLU on teacher layoffs. *Los Angeles Daily News*, May 10. http://www.dailynews.com/general-news/ 20101005/la-schools-reach-deal-with-aclu-on-teacher-layoffs.

Duncan-Andrade, J. M., and E. Morrell. 2008. *The art of critical pedagogy: Possibilities for moving from theory to practice in urban schools.* New York: Peter Lang.

Ellis, C., T. Adams, and A. Bochner. 2010. Autoethnography: An overview. *Forum: Qualitative Social Research Sozialforschung* 12 (1).

Furumoto, R. 2005. No poor child left unrecruited: How NCLB codifies and perpetuates urban school militarism. *Equity and Excellence in Education* 38 (3): 200–210.

Galaviz, B., J. Palafox, E. R. Meiners, and T. Quinn. 2011. The militarization and the privatization of public schools. *Berkeley Review of Education* 2 (1): 27–45.

Garza, I. 2015. Advertising patriotism: The "Yo Soy el Army" campaign and the politics of visibility for Latina/o youth. *Latino Studies* 13 (2): 245–268.

Giroux, H. A. 2004. War on terror: The militarizing of public space and culture in the United States. *Third Text* 18 (4): 211–221.

Hartney, C. 2006. *U.S. rates of incarceration: A global perspective.* Washington, D.C.: National Council on Crime and Delinquency. https://www.ncdglobal.org/sites/default/files/publication_pdf/factsheet-us-incarceration.pdf.

Holm, K. D. 2007. No child left behind and military recruitment in high schools: When privacy rights trump a legitimate government interest. *Journal of Law and Education* 36 (4): 581–588.

Jones, A. 2013. America's child soldiers: The Pentagon's JROTC program canvasses public high schools for future soldiers. *The Nation*, December 16. http://www.thenation.com/article/177603/americas-child-soldiers.

Kronsell, A. 2005. Gendered practices in institutions of hegemonic masculinity: Reflections from feminist standpoint theory. *International Feminist Journal of Politics* 7 (2): 280–298.

Lawrence, R. G. 2000. *The politics of force: Media and the construction of police brutality.* Berkeley: University of California Press.

Leonard, D. 2007. Unsettling the military entertainment complex: Video games and a pedagogy of peace. *SIMILE: Studies in Media and Information Literacy Education* 4 (4): 1–8.

Lipman, P. 2004. Education accountability and the repression of democracy post-9/11. *Journal for Critical Education Policy Studies* 2 (1).

Lutz, C., and L. Bartlett. 1995. *Making soldiers in the public schools: An analysis of the Army JROTC curriculum.* National Youth and Militarism Program, American Friends Service Committee.

Mariscal, J. 2005. Homeland security, militarism, and the future of Latinos and Latinas in the United States. *Radical History Review* 93:39–50.

National Middle School Cadet Corps. 2014. http://www.nationalmiddleschoolcadetcorps.com.

National Network Opposing the Militarization of Youth. 2012. *JROTC.* http://www.nnomy.org.

Rios, V. M. 2006. The hyper-criminalization of Black and Latino male youth in the era of mass incarceration. *Souls: A Critical Journal of Black Politics, Culture, and Society* 8 (2): 40–54.

Rotberg, I. C. 2014. Charter schools and the risk of increased segregation. *Phi Delta Kappan* 95 (5): 26–30.

Saltman, K. J., and D. A. Gabbard, eds. 2011. *Education as enforcement: The militarization and corporatization of schools.* 2nd ed. New York: RoutledgeFalmer.

Schroeder, K. 2004. NCLB's trix not for kids. *Education Digest: Essential Readings Condensed for Quick Review* 70 (2): 73–74.

Shear, M. D., and J. Steinhauer. 2017. Trump to seek $54 billion increase in military spending. *New York Times,* February 27. https://www.nytimes .com/2017/02/27/us/politics/trump-budget-military.html.

State Numbered Charter Schools in California (CA Department of Education). N.d. http://www.cde.ca.gov/ds/si/cs/ap/rptresult.asp?name=North Valley Military Institute College Preparatory Academy&Submit=Search.

Stern, M. 2013. Bad teacher: What race to the top learned from the "race to the bottom." *Journal for Critical Education Policy Studies* 11 (3): 194–229.

Turse, N. 2008. *The complex: How the military invades our everyday lives.* New York: Metropolitan Books.

U.S. Army. 2017. *JROTC School Report.* https://sites.google.com/a/ usarmyjrotc.com/u-s-army-jrotc-document-files/home/JROTC percent20School_Report.xls?attredirects=0&d=1.

U.S. Census. 2010. U.S. Census Bureau. http://www.census.gov/2010census/ popmap/.

U.S. Coast Guard. 2017. FAQ. https://www.gocoastguard.com/faq.

U.S. Department of Defense. 2017. *FY 2016 budget proposal.* https://www .defense.gov/News/Special-Reports/FY16-Budget.

U.S. Department of Education. 2017. Every Student Succeeds Act. https:// www.ed.gov/essa?src=rn.

U.S. Marines. 2017. Marine Corps Junior ROTC Training and Education Command. http://www.mcjrotc.marines.mil/Schools/List/.

U.S. Navy. 2017. Navy Junior Reserve Officers Training Corps. http://www .njrotc.navy.mil/host_schools.html.

Wedekind, J. 2005. The children's crusade: Military programs move into middle schools to fish for future soldiers. *In These Times,* June 3. http:// inthesetimes.com/article/2136/the_children_crusade.

# The Paradoxical Implications of Developing Youth in a Chicago Public Military Academy

*Heather L. Horsley*

In Chicago, as in large urban centers nationwide, public schools are experimenting with various educational models intended to improve such school outcomes as graduation rates, performance on standardized achievement tests, and post–secondary education enrollment. The addition of public military academies (PMAs), or military-themed college preparatory public high schools, to the school reform landscape suggests that this educational model is intended to respond to the immediate need for city school systems to provide low-income students of color with greater educational opportunities (Payne 2008). Chicago Public Schools (CPS) is taking the lead in this military education experiment; in 2013, it hosted over half of the PMAs in the nation. CPS Central District officials insist that "the military-themed schools give students more choices and provide an opportunity to enroll in schools that provide structure, discipline and a focus on leadership. The schools emphasize academics, not recruitment" (Banchero and Sadovi 2007). These educational leaders use the "achievement gap" and "failing schools" concepts to justify PMAs publicly as an educational opportunity. While it seems sensible to provide new models of schooling that will provide low-income youth of color greater opportunities for life success, it is troubling that these "opportunities" are directly linked to the military model of education through a partnership between a large inner-city public school district and the Department of Defense.

Without a doubt, the neoliberal context juxtaposed with a public school system that is perceived as failing to educate its students for economic and political citizenship situates the development of the PMA within a polarized debate. Opponents of this model are concerned that these schools will function as vehicles for military recruitment (Berlowitz and Long 2003, EnLoe 2000, Lipman 2004, Lutz and Bartlett 1995); proponents insist that it embodies an equity agenda, as the military is perceived as an avenue for social mobility (Hajjar 2005, Laurence and Ramsberger 1991, Moskos and Butler 1996). Others contemplate the complex contradictions of the opportunity by considering the tensions surrounding the military's commitment to Black achievement (Moskos and Butler 1997) and the development of egalitarian racial and gender roles (Clark Hine 1982, Perez 2006). Based on research I conducted at a Chicago PMA, my own view is that these military-themed high schools represent a paradox of educational opportunity. Student insights helped me understand how contradictions emerge when PMAs simultaneously disempower and empower low-income youth of color by furthering the project of militarization while also offering youth of color an opportunity to transform this oppressive project into a vehicle for self-determination (Horsley 2013).

In the context of this debate, I use student survey data to complement a qualitative case study design to examine the educational experience provided to low-income youth of color attending a Chicago public military academy. Specifically, this study asks two main questions: (1) How do students make sense of the educational opportunities offered to them at a Chicago PMA? (2) How do they view issues of gender and race as these constructs intersect with their experiences of developing within a Chicago PMA?

## *What Is a Public Military Academy?*
### *The Sociopolitical Context*

The social context in which schools develop is significant for understanding society's goals for schooling in relation to what is expected of teachers and students. Schools are shaped by how society is organized and by society's systems of beliefs, and, conversely, schools, through educational policy and reform, can occasionally have an effect on social values and structures (for example, *Brown v. Board of Education* or Title IX). In order to analyze the relationship between military education programs and student outcomes, a brief overview of PMA characteristics is offered, in an effort to provide a common understanding of this educational model within the national and local contexts in which these schools emerged. As of 2013, the United States is home to seventeen PMAs, geographically located in the Northeast, Southeast, Southwest, and Midwest regions. There are three distinctive characteristics shared by all of these PMAs.

First, PMAs are a manifestation of the larger neoliberal school choice movement. Students interested in attending a PMA must enter into a competitive application pool that includes academic selection criteria as well as an interview process. Second, all PMAs are designed to offer a college preparatory curriculum and college-going support structure. Doing so links the academic goals of these high schools to that of the highly selective and academically rigorous public service academies (for example, the U.S. Military Academy [West Point] and the U.S. Naval Academy [Annapolis]) (*U.S. News* 2013). The idea of developing these schools in the image of the highly ranked service academies at the very least sounds impressive and at the very best raises expectations for academic rigor at the military-themed high school.

Third, PMAs require four years of Junior Reserve Officer Training Corps (JROTC) participation, whereas most secondary schools offer JROTC as an elective option for a maximum of two years. PMA students attend a Leadership Education Training (LET) class every day, and they are required to comply with daily military uniform codes. The Department of Defense provides the funding for the uniforms and pays half the salaries of the JROTC instructors, that is, the retired military officers that implement the JROTC curriculum. PMAs, in general, promote the idea that the military model of discipline, leadership, and public service supports the successful academic, social, and emotional development of its student body. Moreover, students who attend PMAs are not required to enlist in the military. Because of the four-year commitment to JROTC and the limited amount of research done on PMAs specifically, a review of the effectiveness of JROTC is beneficial to grounding this case study in what we already know about military education in public schools.

## Literature Review

JROTC aims to "provide a quality citizenship, character, and leadership development program, while fostering partnerships with communities and educational institutions" (U.S. Army Cadet Command). Supporting program objectives include citizenship promotion, leadership development,

Table 7.1: Comparison of JROTC Student Population and General Student Population Achievement Outcomes Nationally

| Metric | ARMY JROTC Students | General Student Population |
|---|---|---|
| Attendance | 93% | 90% |
| Graduation Rate | 91% | 78.2% |
| GPA | 2.8–2.9 | 2.6–2.7 |
| SAT Score | 823 | 821 |
| ACT Score | 20.5 | 19 |

*Source*: National Association of State Boards of Education 2010, National Center for Education Statistics 2010

critical thinking skills development, communication skills enhancement, strengthening of self-esteem, incentives to live drug free, physical fitness improvement, and the promotion of high school graduation and college/work readiness (Corbett and Coumbe 2001, Marks 2004, U.S. Army Cadet Command). Because accountability regimes emphasize learning outcomes over learning inputs (Andersen 2010), attendance rates, grade point averages, ACT/SAT/WorkKeys scores, and graduation rates are the dominant student achievement measures compiled by high schools in the United States. Therefore, JROTC participation and student achievement in relation to these measures is compiled and demonstrates the positive effect JROTC has on student achievement, although the limited amount of studies reporting this data as well as the validity of the research is of concern (see Table 7.1).

In addition to these standardized metrics, research conducted on JROTC's character and leadership education suggests that students benefit from participation. Researchers who administered the Democratic Maturity Test and Leadership Ability Evaluation found that JROTC students develop greater democratic maturity and leadership ability (Cassel and Standifer 2000, Kolstad and Ritter 2000). Researchers who conducted qualitative case studies of JROTC programs provided evidence that JROTC programs support students' college-going aspirations (Vines 2004) as well as being "generally supportive of civility, build[ing] leadership, and ingrain[ing] discipline" (Hajjar 2005, 51). Whether intentional or not, this line of research supports the persistent yet problematic idea that low-income youth of color are best served by an educational environment grounded in a pedagogy of control. When researchers employ notions of how PMAs "set an example of civility" and "develop discipline," they are invoking deficit language that speaks to a pervasive organizing logic that pins a "badge of deviance on urban youth" (Lipman 1998, 13). When this logic goes unquestioned, such research further obscures how such behaviors are stereotypically racialized and classed in ways that suggest there is something wrong with low-income youth of color rather than with the societal structures that marginalize low-income youth of color.

In contrast to the largely celebratory findings from the aforementioned effectiveness studies, Gina Perez (2006) complicates the landscape by conducting ethnographic research that focuses on the gendered experience of JROTC. She wondered why young women who were college bound with scholarships would even consider enlisting in the military. The young Latinas Perez interviewed explained that their JROTC participation offered them freedom from responsibilities at home such as cooking, cleaning, and childcare. While these young Latinas described several beneficial aspects of their JROTC participation, it was these same experiences that also encouraged them to develop a deep appreciation for how military culture is perceived to liberate women from traditional gender roles (Segal 1995).

It is in this regard that JROTC programs support the process of militarization, or the "step-by-step process by which something becomes controlled by, dependent on, or derives its value from the military as an institution or militaristic criteria" (EnLoe 2000, 291). Moreover, militarization is not just about mobilizing people for armed conflict—it also serves to legitimate the military's needs and actions, including seeing violence as acceptable, normal, and even valuable (EnLoe 2000). In other words, militarization consists of blurring the boundaries between what is acceptable in military life and what is acceptable in civilian life (Adelman 2003, Feldman 2002).

The U.S. Army Code explicitly points to the goal of militarization, as it states that JROTC intends to "create favorable attitudes and impressions toward the Services and toward careers in the Armed Forces" (32 CFR 542.5:3c). Appreciation is generated through the formal curriculum, or what the instructors intend to teach, as well as through the informal curriculum, or the unintended lessons that often send subtle yet powerful messages to students. The JROTC formal curriculum includes military history and leadership training coursework as well as explicit exposure to career options that emphasize the honor, incentives, and sense of empowerment that result from military service (Corbett and Coumbe 2001, Funk 2002). The informal curriculum primarily centers on the relationships the JROTC instructors build with their students. Of most significance, they serve as role models who treat their students with respect and recognition

(Corbett and Coumbe 2001, Hajjar 2005, Perez 2006). Whereas the informal curriculum appears beneficial to students, it does not come without the potential consequence of the structural violence that disproportionately encourages the enlistment in the military of students from low-income and historically disadvantaged groups in the United States (Berlowitz and Long 2003).

The reviewed literature points to how the outcomes of JROTC participation can empower and disempower students simultaneously. Students may achieve more academically and socially, but at what cost? Militarized education programs subtly persuade us to believe that the armed forces are essential to upward social mobility, which taps into deeply held individualistic ideals. For example, the economic pressures our youth face, along with their desires for political inclusion and social advancement, such as earning citizenship in some cases and/or being valued as a human being, complicate how many nonhypermilitarized youth end up serving in the armed forces (Mariscal 2007). For example, low-income youth of color who believe in and actively support nonviolence movements in their communities can find themselves enlisting in an effort to seek greater economic and social opportunity. Consequently, they find themselves engaged in combat enacting violence against another similarly low-income soldier of color from another nation. They become programmed to devalue the other in the name of seeking better life chances for themselves, even though the two soldiers likely have more in common with each other than they will ever be allowed to know. The process of militarization strengthens the symbolic value of the military, which normalizes beliefs of unquestioned loyalty and subservience (EnLoe 2000). As a whole, it is well documented that the corporate-military industrial complex relies on convincing us that a global project of war is necessary for economic and national security (Kirk and Okazawa-Rey 2000, Staples 2000). Given that militarized education programs foster the development of complex social processes, my research aims to illuminate the paradoxical implications of developing youth in a Chicago PMA.

## Methodology

To document the educational opportunities provided to the students attending a Chicago PMA, I employed a qualitative case study method that uses a survey to complement the design. The ability to "learn the intricate complexity of one case" makes case study an appropriate design: The military-themed college preparation program is the object of study or case, but the program must be interpreted in the context of the school, the school system, and wider social contexts that bear upon the multiple meanings of the program (Yin 1994).

## Data Sources

To examine how PMA students made sense of the opportunities provided them, I compiled administrative district data and collected qualitative data, which are organized into three phases of research.

### Phase 1: Administrative Data Review

In order to compile school demographic and achievement data, I drew on documents from Chicago Public Schools including but not limited to individual school publications, individual school electronic media/publications, JROTC manuals and resource guides, school report cards, and school performance data. I also reviewed the "5Essentials School Reports." The University of Chicago Consortium on Chicago School Research (CCSR) requests the participation of all secondary CPS students in the "My School, My Voice" survey annually. The survey provides information on how well the school is organized, with the goal of continuous quality improvement. In regards to the Chicago PMA under study, I was most interested in the "essential support" related to issues of "supportive environments," as this domain informs us about school climate. The aforementioned administrative data established the context and academic performance of the Chicago PMA under study.

### Phase 2: Interviews

In order to elicit meaning-making information, I conducted four cycles of four focus group interviews with five students per group in order to encourage male and female youth of color to explore their experiences. I intentionally planned and employed follow-up probes that guard against "groupthink" or overt consensus building among the students (Fontana and Frey 2005, 705). The protocols included five to six general questions intended to serve as probes to "obtain range, specificity, depth and personal context" (Merton 1987). Whereas the student focus group interviews are crucial to understanding the meaning the students give to their experiences attending a PMA, I also conducted interviews with five JROTC instructors and two guidance counselors in order to gain additional insight into the broader educational opportunities within this particular school context. I transcribed the interviews and employed both focused coding and constant comparison as an open-ended thematic coding process after the first round and before each subsequent round, which allowed me to analyze issues across groups in terms of a particular category; thereby I could identify similarities and differences to other data I had previously categorized (Hammersley and Atkinson 1995).

## Phase 3: Observations

Although interviews help researchers understand the beliefs of participants, what people say and what they do are not the same (Blomberg et al. 1993). Field observations, the final phase of data collection, served as a form of triangulation, thereby strengthening the trustworthiness of my research as a framework to confirm or disqualify evidence between what participants reported in interviews and what I actually witnessed in the field. I observed JROTC exercises, core academic classrooms, college awareness events, and ceremonies.

Balancing an effort to build relationships with students and staff while remaining mindful of issues of trustworthiness guided the overall development of my role as an observer. I developed an in-between status: Depending on the context of the observation, I would sometimes play a more passive role; other times, I would adopt a participant-observer role. In addition to recording my own actions during an observation (Emerson, Fretz, and Shaw 1995), I also took notes after an observation, which offered me the opportunity to address the often-hidden elements in my personal background.

## Researcher Positionality: Writing into the Contradictions of My Personal History

Ultimately, I used my postobservation notes to write into the contradictions surrounding my family history and the military. When one of the JROTC instructors shared his stories with me, memories of my sides aching from laughter came back to me from when my grandfather told tales of his military service. I had to acknowledge and remain aware of how my researcher role was interconnected with these fond memories of my grandfather. A CPS graduate and from a German immigrant family of modest means, my grandfather told me that college was not an option for him, because he was not focused and goofed around too much in high school.

But he saw military service as a viable option for making a living and providing service to the country. While my grandfather did not participate in JROTC in high school, his younger brother did. When I asked my great-uncle why he joined JROTC in high school, he said, "the camaraderie with my classmates and mostly, I wanted to play in a prestigious band program." When I asked why he did not follow grandpa into the military, he said, "I had decent employment upon graduation, I was able to attend community college right away, and I felt I no longer needed military experience. Johnny was the adventuresome one of us." At my great-uncle's hundredth birthday celebration, he shared with vigor the honor he had in performing for John Philip Sousa as a member of the Army JROTC Band.

While my grandfather's experience had influenced my thinking, my parents and their generational experience also occupied my mind. I wrote into how my parents told me stories of their experiences in the Peace Corps, their active resistance to war, and their general pacifist philosophies, which tempered my ideas about the exciting military life my grandfather led. When I wrote into how I remember the political disagreements my grandfather and parents had, I reconciled their differences by coming to see how their views both shared strong commitments to serving the public good. In fact, through the research process I came to learn my grandfather did not become career military, because he was beginning to see a shift in the use of the U.S. armed forces for the purpose of oil profiteering for a few over protecting the public good of the many.

With this worldview, I still grapple with knowing that I have benefited from my grandfather's military experience while also becoming appreciative of the military. I continue to wonder to what degree I have been empowered by my family's military service and to what degree that empowerment is negated by how I have also been militarized. As a researcher, I shared these contradictions in my personal background with students and staff so that we could engage in a range of conversations about the military, including critical ones. In the end, I came to understand how my life history gave me a unique perspective in which to conduct a study that assesses the benefits and limitations of the Chicago PMA model of schooling.

### Theoretical Framework

The central problem my research is situated within is a restructuring political-economic context that shapes the type of investments made to support the development of opportunity for youth. Utilizing youth development theory allowed me to value the students' perspectives of opportunity within broader psychological and sociological perspectives of youth development.

## Youth Development Theory

In contrast to developmental psychologists' characterization of adolescence as a traumatic experience (Hall 1909), a characterization that tends still to dominate current U.S. social policy for youth (Furlong 2013), Kate Tilleczek (2011, 8) categorizes youth development within an ecological framework that highlights the social processes of "being, becoming, and belonging." The process of "being" emphasizes how a young person experiences and negotiates identity formation. "Belonging" speaks to how a young person experiences a secure base for the development of trust, autonomy, and initiative (Werner and Smith 1992, Tilleczek 2011). Last, "becoming" is the social process in which youth envision their future possible selves and take steps to aspire to their future selves. Tilleczek further explains that being, becoming, and belonging are critical to the development of protective factors in youth that produce resiliency. Tilleczek's ecological theory encouraged me to consider how the youth attending a Chicago PMA enacted the social processes of "being, belonging, and becoming," especially in light of the U.S. Cadet Command explicitly stating that JROTC is intended for "youth seeking a sense of belonging" (Corbett and Coumbe 2001, Funk 2002).

Although ecological theories offer a lens to think about how youth develop their sense of self, sociological understandings of youth development help locate youth identity in societal structures (Deutsch 2008). From this perspective, the concept of youth is a social construct that has a dialectical relationship with the sociohistorical and politico-economic context of schooling and society (Wyn and White 1997). Although young people represent a common age cohort, other social divisions such as gender, class, race, or ethnicity shape and differentiate the experiences of young people. Such social divisions among youth are related to how some youth experience privilege and others marginalization.

Sociological research on gender, for example, points to how from an early age girls and boys are treated differently based on perceived characteristics of masculine and feminine expectations, even though nothing biological explains or justifies such divisions (Arnot 2002, Orenstein 1995). How young men and women are treated then shapes the kinds of experiences offered to them, which means they often perform differently at

school, follow different educational and career pathways, and face different career structures and wage prospects (Furlong 2013). Outcomes based
on social difference make me consider how race and gender shape the experiences of the youth attending a Chicago PMA, especially as militaries
manipulate social conceptions of difference (D'Amico 2000, 167). This
body of work further "provides focus for discussions of structure and
agency, illustrating the ways in which young people are constrained by
factors such as social class or gender and highlighting the ways in which
they can help break down barriers through their own actions" (Furlong
2013, 6). In this respect, I applied sociological theories of youth development to understand better the ways in which youth attending the Chicago
PMA negotiate this particular structure of educational opportunity within
a neoliberal context.

## *Findings and Analysis*

### The Power of Military Group Cohesion to Support a College-Going Culture

In investigating how Chicago PMA students make sense of the opportunities provided to them, the majority of the students credited JROTC with
giving them experiences that "intensified my academic career," "set me
apart from other students applying to the same college," and "give you that
extra boost." Although many people assume that PMAs serve as a significant vehicle for military recruitment, evidence provided by the postsecondary department of this Chicago PMA case under study indicates that
less than 1 percent of the students enlist in the military upon graduation.
Because the students feel JROTC strengthens their access to college by
contributing to an impressive resume that will set them apart from other
applicants, it appears that the Chicago PMA students have been able use
this military structure to achieve their desired aspirations of attending college (see Table 7.2). Moreover, several students specifically commented on
the importance of their JROTC instructors' ability to motivate them to
set high expectations for themselves. As Benita, a sophomore, said, "They
encourage us and it motivates us . . . to get good grades—yeah. They are
honest too, which is what we need."

The JROTC instructors further confirmed these students' perspectives
as they explained how they have a responsibility to contribute to the
college-bound culture of the school. Sergeant Freeman reflected: "If you
want to take somebody somewhere, like to college, you've got to really un-

Table 7.2: Chicago PMA College Preparatory Performance in 2010

| Metric | Chicago PMA Outcomes |
|---|---|
| Average Attendance Rate | 90% |
| Average GPA | 2.9 |
| Average ACT | 19 |
| Scoring 20+ on ACT | 33% |
| Meets/Exceeds PSAE | 47% |
| Average Graduation Rate | 94% |
| Average College Enrollment Rate* | 51.3% |
| Four-Year Institution Enrollment* | 85% of 51.3% |
| On Track to Matriculate from College* | 93.5% |
| Military Enlistment upon High School Graduation | .07% |

*Source: National Student Clearinghouse, 2010

derstand where they are starting and where they want to go. So I got to know their reality, and together we go far." Additionally, all of the sergeants commented on how they use instructional time to raise awareness about the importance of college, which observations of JROTC class activity confirmed. They also explained that they work closely with the counselors of the postsecondary department, which was also confirmed. One counselor said: "We work hand in hand with JROTC because it just correlates. They talk about character development, leadership, setting goals, and decision making, which fits with what we help our students understand about their purpose in life."

Although not exclusive to JROTC instructors, the "My School, My Voice" (2011) student survey also confirmed high teacher-student trust: 79 percent of just over four hundred students reported they find teachers trustworthy and responsive to their academic needs. Moreover, 71 percent of the students reported they are well supported in planning for college. Taken together, it appears that the expectations the JROTC instructors set for their students contribute to an overall school climate that supports the students' process of becoming, in that their desire to be the student who achieves academically now is supported so that they can become the person they envision.

While the students and staff were able to express the ways in which they believed the college prep and military model of the school go "hand in hand," I often wondered, "Why did they so strongly believe that this military educational model supports a college-going school culture?" The students helped me understand how they felt their school is supportive of their college aspirations. During our second round of focus groups, we were discussing expectations—expectations for themselves, expectations they have for one another, and expectations their teachers and parents have for them. When the students were sharing their goals with me, I asked in follow-up, "How would you describe the way your school supports you in meeting your goals?" Jamal, a freshman explained, "It's like we're one big family, haven't you heard us say that before? It's like the whole school just wants you to feel like you belong here." Ernesto, a sophomore, interrupted Jamal: "Like . . . yesterday it was my birthday. Walking down the hall everyone knew it was my birthday and I was getting punched. Like everyone knows. It's very nice." Jamal resumed, "It's how students get along with each other here, but not just as friends, but like we look out for each other, ya know help each other be the best we can be."

When I asked a focus group of freshman and sophomore female students to describe how they feel supported by their school, they shared similar examples of how the staff and students look out for one another. Benita, a sophomore, for example, said, "Yeah, because when they judge [teachers and JROTC instructors], they don't just judge us individually, they judge us as a whole, so we have a responsibility of setting the example, for all of us to do good work." Sara, a freshman, then commented on how she sets the example of being supportive of her classmates:

> Like the other day in math class there were students who just didn't understand what was going on. Our teacher kept explaining it, but they just didn't get it. So a couple of us including myself went over to show them how to do the problem. It was important to me that we helped them out, that we didn't give up and leave them behind.

I followed up by asking, "Why is that important to you? Who or what encourages you, if anyone or anything to help each other out?" Benita added:

> What I was saying about setting an example, that comes from J-RO [JROTC] because they motivate us to do better for ourselves and for others, for like, uh, the whole school. Our sergeants really look after us like we're their own kids; all of them say that to us. We know he has our back all the time, and I think that encourages all of us. I mean to know that we got each others' backs.

These students describe a sense of how they receive and offer support within their school that speaks to the significance of family to our development. Youth look to their families to provide a source of stability and support through processes of change (Furlong 2013). Early-aged youth depend on their family for guidance, but over time they also begin to want their family to trust in them as they begin to desire greater autonomy (Collins and Laursen 2004). As trends in family structure indicate that youth living in two-parent households has decreased steadily (Livingston 2013), schools have the potential to serve as a surrogate family to hundreds of young people. Similar to national norms, the majority of the students attending this Chicago PMA live in mother-only families. Researchers confirm that youth who live in two-parent households have greater access to resources—better access to health care, quality education, and economic security—which all serve as protective factors leading to the healthier development of youth (Blackwell 2010, Jenson and Fraser 2010).

The supports that students receive from their school help fill the gaps in the support they are able to receive at home. Benita said that the "[JROTC] sergeants really look after us like we're their own kids," and several other students shared similar sentiments with me. Their stories demonstrate the beneficial aspect of a school that creates a climate that the students describe as "one big family." The views of Jamal, Benita, and Sara support research that suggests military-education programs are modeled after the armed forces' concept of "military group cohesion," or the expectation of achievement being defined by not only the success of individuals but also by that of the whole group (Siebold 2007, 286). The students' expression of their PMA as "one big family" suggests that the school promotes and enacts a collective orientation to success.

## THE PROBLEMATIC USE OF MILITARY GROUP COHESION TO SUPPORT A COLLEGE-GOING CULTURE

Although the strength of this Chicago PMA is in its ability to provide youth with support and resources during critical stages of their development, it does not come without limitations. Closer examination of their use of phrases such as "Be the best we can be," "Setting the example," and "We didn't give up and leave them behind" evoke military philosophy. The language the students chose reflects the Army Core Values that are taught to them in their JROTC classes (see Appendix A). Other cases, such as not wanting to give up and leave their classmates behind, more subtly reflects the messaging of "I will never quit, and I will never leave a fallen comrade" found in the Soldier's Creed (see Appendix B). Consequently, the students' expressions reveal how military philosophy subtly influences the students' perspectives of belonging to a school that uses the military model of education to support college preparation. In other words, this Chicago PMA is not just becoming a surrogate family, as other schools may do, but sending a hidden message of how the students can look *specifically* to the military to play the role of a surrogate family.

Although it was common for the students to express the importance of being one big family, the idea of everyone succeeding together is influenced by the philosophy of "military group cohesion" and led the students to reveal important reservations and insights. For instance, while the students shared how their experience with this particular opportunity structure is largely beneficial in relation to what they hope to achieve in life, a tension emerged as the students realized how the competitive nature of college preparation opportunities tends to privilege their Latino and female peers over Black males specifically. And the students' perceptions were accurately reflected in data the counselors in the postsecondary department provided me. Using internal school data, the counselors confirmed that only 18 percent of the Black male seniors earned a minimal amount of the total $1.6 million dollars of scholarships earned that year. Moreover, they also informed me that the female students earn the majority of the citywide college preparation college program slots offered the summer before their senior year.

When asked which college preparation experiences are most valuable to them, the junior and senior students' experience preparing for the ACT as well as seeking out citywide postsecondary preparation opportunities further highlighted racial and gender disparities in the college preparation opportunity structure. Santiago, a senior Mexican American male, said, "I felt pretty prepared for the ACT. The extra test prep in JROTC and tutoring after school helped a lot." Several other junior and senior male students echoed Santiago, several chiming in, "Helped a lot, a lot." Santiago continued, "It's really how you apply yourself in school and in these programs." Deron, a Black senior male, spoke up in aggravation:

> Its like you see things, like seein' our school as a happy family. They [the teachers] want to show you all the good things, but there's always something going on behind the scenes. It's like with racism, it's still alive. [Other students listening but getting uncomfortable.] But what I'm sayin' is, we got the same uniform on, we gotta follow the same rules, we use the same bathroom, we eat the same lunch, we do the same things, and it feels like they treat us, like different. You know, as far as, certain things that they'll let [Deron pauses, puts his hand out to Santiago]—I'm not tryin' [it felt like he was being respectful of Santiago, almost to say "it's not your fault"]. With certain things they'll let Santiago know but not let us know, you feel me.

The young men nodded their heads solemnly in agreement. Whereas the young men agreed that the school-based ACT preparation offered to them was beneficial, they also acknowledged how race and racism complicate opportunity based on individual effort. Deron, while in the minority of the shared perspectives, did get the others to listen and reflect on his penetrating analysis of how access to opportunity is linked to social divisions.

In contrast, the young women most often spoke of the significance of the citywide college preparation programs in preparing them for college. However, their discussion also pointed to limitations of opportunities born out of competition and limited access, as Deidra, a Black senior female with a deeply concerned tone, described:

> So it's like our school is doing a good job of preparing us, but I guess it's just like they need to move faster, because it is pretty competitive. You're going to fight for scholarships and you've got to fight for a spot in college. The thing that gets me is why do some of us get so much and so many others nothing at all? I look at some of my friends here, they try hard so why can't we all get a chance to participate in these programs?

As these complex tensions emerge, the young men and women question how competition conflicts with their sense of working together to achieve success collectively. The students' views and experiences reveal how the concept of "military group cohesion" can work to empower and disempower students along racialized and gendered assumptions simultaneously. Because the military view of success still ultimately lies within building soldiers/students up to take on personal responsibility, this view of success can also obscure the historical, structural forms of racism by offering soldiers/students a new military cultural identity that conforms the group of soldiers/students to core military values.

Although it is clear that all of the students are militarized or develop favorable attitudes to military culture to different degrees while attending this Chicago PMA, the young men were most often fixated on how their future possible selves may end up intersecting with service in the armed forces. During a discussion about what they hope for in life, Camillo, a freshman, shared, "I just hope I get a higher postsecondary education, higher academics, a better standpoint view of like where am I supposed to be, how do I become the best I can be." Rodrigo, a junior, explained that for him:

> There's always a back-up plan, so like after high school probably go
> to college first and then Air Force or Air Force first then college or
> I could really screw up in school, yeah, really screw up in school and
> just end up with a minimum wage job at McDonalds or something.
> There's just a lot of things that happen that you don't really see
> coming.

Upon further thought, Camillo added:

> I figure that I better start buckling down, getting my grades better.
> Like if I don't get a good enough scholarship to go to some good
> college then instead of going to college I would just enlist, because its
> better than just roaming around Chicago with nothing working out so
> if that were to happen, I will just leave and enlist.

Camillo and Rodrigo express real anxiety about what it will take to get
into college and how to make it through college. Although attending college is their first goal, their uncertainty indicates how attending a college
preparatory PMA also makes the option of enlisting a viable contingency
plan.

   With these tensions revealed, I wondered just how much the combination of military group cohesion and the students' developmental need to
belong intersect to form hidden messages about a kind of militarized belonging. Public military academies normalize military culture by serving
as a secure base for youth to develop trust, autonomy, and initiative. This
relatively positive process of belonging allows the armed forces to use
schools to promote a greater militarization of society. Evidence from
this study suggests that the majority of the students, boys and girls, felt a
sense of pride in "belonging" to this Chicago PMA, as indicated by how
they felt supported by their school and how they treated one another like
one big family. However, the evidence also points to the fact that the young
men received a stronger message of "belonging" to the military, especially
if their first choice to attend college did not materialize.

   A notable aspect of the kind of militarized belonging found in this PMA
is that in a school with an overt military culture, these students were often conscious of the ways in which they could, as Adam, a senior white male
put it, "be brain washed by the school." While the young Black men appeared to be more at risk of enlisting after high school, Leon, a Black freshman male, could articulate that the military is not "my main place to
really belong" because of his—again like other students—relatively advanced understanding of the benefits and limitations of trusting in a
supportive surrogate military school family.

## ANALYTICAL COMMENTARY: MILITARIZED BELONGING

The findings of this study reveal a central paradox in that this Chicago PMA provides youth access to educational opportunities while simultaneously making it nearly impossible to avoid becoming militarized. In particular, the students spoke of being "one big family," which points to the significance of the social process of youth developing a sense of belonging within schools. The Chicago PMA students were empowered by experiencing a secure base for the development of trust, autonomy, and initiative, which in turn produced protective factors that enabled their enactment of resiliency (Jenson and Fraser 2010). In itself, "belonging" is a demonstrable human need; the potential problem is in *what* to belong to.

This question is further complicated when considering the political-economic context in which public trust is eroded along intersecting social divisions such as, but not limited to, race, ethnicity, gender, class, or age. For instance, societies' intense focus on "perverse personal and social characteristics (teen pregnancy, drug use, resistance to school, school failure, dropping out, etc.)" has created an organizing logic where youth of color who are labeled "at-risk," such as the young people attending this Chicago PMA, have become a "signifier for race and class and a badge of deviance pinned on urban youth" (Lipman 1998, 13). "At-risk," as coded language for racialized-gendered and class-based stereotypical behavior, further promotes the individualistic idea that youth are "containers of risk," suggesting that there is something wrong with low-income youth and youth of color (Tilleczek 2011). The "at-risk" perspective limits how we understand policy problems because it suggests that we fix individual youth instead of the multitude of problems arising from inequitable social, political, and economic structures of society at large. Public military academies as institutions then serve as a learning context in which low-income youth and youth of color can develop protective factors against problematic life outcomes while also analyzing obstacles within a militarized educational model that produces racist, classist institutions intended to control the behavior and worldview of low-income youth and youth of color.

In addition, we are living within a political-economic landscape intent on denying us any "connection with each other that transcends the selfishness, competitiveness, and brutal self-interests unleashed by an ever-expanding market economy" (Giroux 2001, 29). When we no longer engage with one another as human beings, our relationships are reduced to that of mere competitors. As such, neoliberal economic policy and cultural politics promote a ruthless individualism that "brings out the worst in us"

(Verhaeghe 2014). Our human personality is being rewired through neo-liberal experiences that convince us that there is no alternative to getting ahead at all costs. Furthermore, within this context we come to accept the violence produced by global militarism as normal and necessary to economic prosperity and national security. Consequently, public military academies play a role in reproducing this new ethic of hyperindividualism by maneuvering students to believe that their success depends upon militaristic criteria of collective success that in turn taps into the youth's deep desire for all their classmates to succeed. The cost of developing youth at a Chicago PMA, in particular through forms of militarized belonging, is in how the students are subtly learning that trust, independence, and its corresponding successes derive their value from the military as an institution.

## Developing Nonmilitarized Spaces of Belonging

Within a political-economic context that turns trust into a commodity, youth of color who find themselves in any school that offers ample opportunities to feel trusted and respected will by default value their school experience, even if they are not overly committed to the philosophy guiding the school. If belonging is a human need and trust is required to create secure bases for youth to thrive, what can we do to make public schools develop trust without relying on a militarized way of belonging?

Two decades of research into relational trust provide strong evidence that school leaders must cultivate a climate of mutual respect, positive regard, fairness, inclusivity, reliability, and integrity if schools are to provide students with a successful learning environment (Forsyth et al. 2011, Tschannen-Moran 2014). In fact, several studies suggest that trust between teachers and students fosters academic achievement and social-emotional learning (Adams and Forsyth 2013, Bryk and Schneider 2002, Moore 2010). Leaders and teachers who successfully build trust with students understand that when students initially test their goodwill with defiance, they are demonstrating that they are in need of a secure base of support that has not been experienced consistently during earlier stages of development (Hattie 2012; Johnson, Perez, and Uline 2013). Instead of drawing on behaviorism as a way to control youth, school leaders and teachers who successfully build trust with students turn to theories of attachment to guide their approach.

Rather than creating more unpleasant relational experiences for students, applying attachment theory, or "a motivational system that leads to the development of a close emotional bond among between humans over time and space," in the context of secondary schools gives us the opportunity to socialize students into relationships where they can consistently experience secure, nurturing relationships with one another and with adults (Bowlby 1958). Over time, these new, secure relationships give students an opportunity for corrective experiences. The lesson learned for the case under study is that military group cohesion is not necessarily required to build trust with students. Rather, the Chicago PMA students in this case remind us that they viewed their school as one big family because the students felt that the majority of their core content, civilian teachers, and all of their JROTC instructors, in particular, had honest, open, and reliable relationships with them. These particular teacher-student relationships "disconfirm prior problematic relationship history," which allowed the students to repair the part of their personality that had previously kept them from trusting their school and teachers (Howes and Ritchie 2002, 89). To continue to develop school leaders and teachers in ways where relational trust is seen as a vital aspect of their daily pedagogy is essential to creating a public school system in which low-income youth and youth of color will no longer need to rely on a public military school to find a place of belonging. Additional research is needed in public high schools that are exemplary models of relational trust building over space and time.

## Conclusion

Although the students often shared penetrating analyses of their own experiences, they also often struggled with how to critique a militarized form of belonging that both empowers and disempowers simultaneously. Moreover, the analysis also points to how the young men were inclined to consider military service as a contingency plan if they did not achieve their college aspirations, which points to how the male and female students at this Chicago PMA received messages of militarized belonging in different ways. The paradoxical implications of developing youth in a Chicago public military academy point to the significance of building relational trust in a world where competition trumps cooperation. Building trust within neighborhood public schools is one way to reignite the possibility of societal hope. As trust expands, friendships can emerge as a form of political resistance to the neoliberal structuring of current social relations (May 2012, Ranciere 1999). Public schools are optimal sites for the trust building needed to develop an alternative to the current neoliberal way of being in this world.

APPENDIX A: LIST OF THE ARMY CORE VALUES

Duty: Fulfill your obligations.

Honor: Live up to all the Army values. Honor provides the "moral compass" for character and personal conduct in the Army.

Integrity: Do what's right—legally and morally.

Loyalty: Bear true faith and allegiance to the U.S. Constitution, the Army, your unit, and other soldiers.

Personal Courage: Face fear, danger, or adversity both physical and moral.

Respect: Treat people as they should be treated.

Selfless Service: Put the welfare of the nation, the Army, and your subordinates before your own. Selfless service leads to organizational teamwork and encompasses discipline, self-control, and faith in the system.

APPENDIX B: THE SOLDIER'S CREED

I am an American Soldier.

I am a Warrior and a member of a team.

I serve the people of the United States and live the Army Values.

I will always place the mission first.

I will never accept defeat.

I will never quit.

I will never leave a fallen comrade.

I am disciplined, physically and mentally tough, trained and proficient in my Warrior tasks and drills.

I always maintain my arms, my equipment, and myself.

I am an expert, and I am professional.

I stand ready to deploy, engage, and destroy the enemies of the United States of America in close combat.

I am a guardian of freedom and the American way of life.

I am an American Solider.

REFERENCES

Adelman, M. 2003. The military, militarism, and the militarization of domestic violence. *Violence against Women* 19 (2): 205–228.

Andersen, G. L. 2010. *Advocacy leadership: Toward a post-reform agenda in education*. New York: Routledge.

Apple, M. W. 2004. Creating difference: Neoliberalism, neoconservatism, and the politics of educational reform. *Educational Policy* 18 (1): 12–44.

Arnot, M. 2002. *Reproducing gender: Critical essays on educational theory and feminist politics*. London: RoutledgeFalmer.

Banchero, S., and C. Sadovi. 2007. Reading, writing, recruiting?
   Debate rages as city's newest facility is dedicated. *Chicago Tribune*,
   October 15.

Berlowitz, M. J., and N. A. Long. 2003. Proliferation of JROTC: Educational reform or militarization. In *Education as enforcement*, ed. K.
   Saltman and D. Gabbard, 181–191. New York: RoutledgeFalmer.

Blackwell, D. L. 2010. Family structure and children's health in the United
   States: Findings from the National Health Interview Survey, 2011–2007.
   *Vital Health Statistics* 10 (246).

Blomberg, J, J. Giacomi, A. Mosher, and P. Swenton-Wall. 1993. Ethno-
   graphic field methods and their relation to design. In *Participatory design:
   Principles and practices*, ed. D. Schuler and A. Namioka. Hillsdale, N.J.:
   Laurence Erlbaum Associates.

Bowlby, J. 1958. The nature of the child's tie to his mother. *International
   Journal of Psychoanalysis* 39:350–371.

Bryk, A. S., and B. Schneider. 2002. *Trust in schools: A core resource for school
   improvement*. New York: Russell Sage Foundation.

Cassel, R. N., and T. Standifer. 2000. Comparing the leadership development between high school JROTC cadets and beginning college school
   administrator students. *Education* 120 (3): 422–437.

Clark Hine, D. 1982. Mabel K. Staupers and the integration of Black nurses.
   In *Black leaders of the twentieth century*, ed. J. H. Franklin and A. Meier,
   241–258. Urbana: University of Illinois Press.

Collins, W. A., and B. Laursen. 2004. Parent-adolescent relationships and
   influences. In *Handbook of adolescent psychology*, ed. R. M. Lerner and
   L. Stenberg, 331–394. Hoboken, N.J.: John Wiley & Sons.

Consortium on Chicago School Research. 2011. *"My School, My Voice"
   student survey*. Chicago: University of Chicago Press.

Corbett, J. W., and A. T. Coumbe. 2001. JROTC Recent trends and
   developments. *Military Review*, January/February.

D'Amico, F. 2000. Globalizing forces [Review of *Maneuvers: The international
   politics of militarizing women's lives*, by Cynthia EnLoe]. *Social Justice: A
   Journal of Crime, Conflict, and World Order* 27 (4): 167–172.

Delamont, S. 2002. *Fieldwork in educational settings Methods, pitfalls, and
   perspectives*. 2nd ed. New York: Routledge.

Denzin, N., and Y. Lincoln. 2008. *Collecting and interpreting qualitative
   materials*. 3rd ed. Thousand Oaks, Calif.: Sage.

Deutsch, N. L. 2008. *Pride in the projects: Teens building identities in urban
   contexts*. New York: New York University Press.

Emerson, R. M., R. I. Fretz, and L. L. Shaw. 1995. *Writing ethnographic
   fieldnotes*. Chicago: University of Chicago Press.

EnLoe, C. 2000a. *Bananas, beaches, and bases: Making feminist sense of international politics.* Berkeley: University of California Press.

———. 2000b. *Maneuvers: The international politics of militarizing women's lives.* Berkeley: University of California Press.

Feldman, A. 2002. X-children and the militarization of everyday life: Comparative comments on the politics of youth, victimage, and violence in transitional societies. *International Journal of Social Welfare* 11:286–299.

Fontana, A., and J. H. Frey. 2005. The interview: From neutral stance to political involvement. In *The SAGE handbook of qualitative research*, 3rd ed., ed. N. K. Denzin and Y. S. Lincoln, 695–727. Thousand Oaks, Calif.: Sage.

Forsyth, P. B., C. M. Adams, and W. K. Hoy. 2011. *Collective trust: Why school can't improve without it.* New York: Teachers College Press.

Funk, R. C. 2002. Developing leaders through high school Junior ROTC: Integrating theory with practice. *Journal of Leadership Studies* 8 (4): 43–53.

Furlong, A. 2013. *Youth studies: An introduction.* New York: Routledge.

Giroux, H. 2001. *Public spaces/private lives: Democracy beyond the politics of cynicism.* Lanham, Md.: Rowman & Littlefield.

———. 2009. *Youth in a suspect society: Democracy or disposability.* New York: Palgrave Macmillan.

Hage, G. 2000. *White nation: Fantasies of white supremacy in a multicultural society.* New York: Routledge.

Hajjar, R. 2005. The public military high school: A powerful educational possibility. *Armed Forces and Society* 32 (1): 44–62.

Hall, G. S. 1904. *Adolescence: Its psychology and its relations to physiology, anthropology, sociology, sex, crime, religion, and education.* New York: Appleton.

Hammersley, M., and P. Atkinson. 1995. *Ethnography: Principles in practice.* New York: Routledge.

Harvey, D. 2005. *A brief history of neoliberalism.* New York: Oxford University Press.

Hattie, J. 2012. *Visible learning for teachers: Maximizing impact on learning.* New York: Routledge.

Howes, C., and S. Ritchie. 2002. *A matter of trust.* New York: Teachers College Press.

Jensen, J. M., and M. W. Fraser. 2011. *Social policy for children and families: A risk and resilience perspective.* 2nd ed. Thousand Oaks, Calif.: Sage.

Johnson, J. F., L. G. Perez, and C. L. Uline. 2013. *Teaching practices from America's best urban schools: A guide for school and classroom leaders.* Larchmont, N.Y.: Eye on Education.

Kirk, G., and M. Okazawa-Rey. 2000. Neoliberalism, militarism, and armed conflict. *Social Justice* 27 (4).

Kleiber, P. B. 2004. Focus groups: More than a method of qualitative inquiry. In *Foundations for research: Methods of inquiry in education and the social sciences*, ed. K. deMarrais and S. Lapan, 87–102. Mahwah, N.J.: Laurence Erlbaum Associates.

Kolstad, R., and D. L. Ritter. 2000. Use of Air Force JROTC high school cadets as role models for developing democratic maturity in pre-education teachers. *Education* 120 (3): 416–421.

Laurence, J., and P. Ramsberger. 1991. *Low-aptitude men in the military: Who profits, who pays?* New York: Praeger.

Lipman, P. 1998. *Race, class, and power in school restructuring.* Albany: SUNY Press.

———. 2004. *High stakes education: Inequality, globalization, and urban school reform.* New York: RoutledgeFalmer.

———. 2011. *The new political economy of urban education: Neoliberalism, race, and the right to the city.* New York: Routledge.

Livingston, G. 2013. *Less than half of U.S. kids today live in a "traditional" family.* Washington, D.C.: Pew Research Center.

Lutz, C., and L. Bartlett. 1995. *Making soldiers in the public schools.* Philadelphia: American Friends Service Committee.

Mariscal, J. 2007. The poverty draft: Do military recruiters disproportionately target communities of color and the poor? *Sojourners Magazine* 36 (6): 32–35.

Marks, L. N. 2004. Perceptions of high school principals and senior army instructors concerning the impact of JROTC on rates of dropout and transition to college. Ph.D. diss. East Tennessee State University, Johnson City.

Maxwell, J. A. 1992. Understanding and validity in qualitative research. *Harvard Educational Review* 62 (3): 279–300.

May, T. 2012. *Friendship in an age of economics: Resisting the forces of neoliberalism.* Lanham, Md.: Lexington Books.

Merton, R. K. 1987. The focused interview and focus groups: Continuities and discontinuities. *Public Opinion Quarterly* 51:550–566.

Moskos, C., and J. S. Butler. 1997. *All that we can be: Black leadership and racial integration the army way.* New York: Basic Books.

National Association of State Boards of Education. 2010. *Common ground: Education and the military meeting the needs of students.* Arlington, Va.: National Association of State Boards of Education.

Orenstein, P. 1995. *Schoolgirls: Young women, self-esteem, and the confidence gap.* Jacksonville, Fla.: Anchor.

Payne, C. 2008. *So much reform, so little change: The persistence of failure in urban schools.* Boston: Harvard Education Press.

Perez, G. 2006. How a scholarship girl becomes a soldier: The militarization of Latina/o youth in Chicago Public Schools. *Identities: Global Studies in Culture and Power* 13:53–72.

Putnam, R. 1995. Bowling alone in America's declining social capital. *Journal of Democracy* 6 (1).

Ranciere, J. 1999. *Disagreement*. Minneapolis: University of Minnesota Press.

Sassen, S. 2006. *Cities in a world economy*. Thousand Oaks, Calif.: Pine Forge.

Segal, M. W. 1995. Women's military roles cross-nationally: Past, present, and future. *Gender and Society* 9 (6): 757–755.

Siebold, G. L. 2006. The essence of military group cohesion. *Armed Forces and Society* 33 (2): 286–295.

Silverman, D. 2004. *Qualitative research: Theory, method, and practice*. 2nd ed. Thousand Oaks, Calif.: Sage.

Staples, S. 2000. The relationship between globalization and militarism. *Social Justice* 27 (4).

Tilleczek, K. 2011. *Approaching youth studies: Being, becoming, and belonging*. New York: Oxford University Press.

Tschannen-Moran, M. 2014. *Trust matters: Leadership for successful schools*. 2nd ed. New York: John Wiley & Sons.

U.S. Army Cadet Command. N.d. The Official Home of Army ROTC. http://www.cadetcommand.army.mil/.

U.S. News. 2013. National university rankings in education. *U.S. News*. http://www.usnews.com/educationcolleges/rankings/national-universities.

Verhaeghe, P. 2014. Has neoliberalism turned us all into psychopaths? Our me-first economic system has changed our ethics and our personalities. *Guardian*. http://www.alternet.org/economy/has-neoliberalism-turned-us-all-psychopaths.

Vines, B. 2005. Student perceptions of achievement at a public military academy: A phenomenological study. Ph.D. diss. Roosevelt University, Chicago.

Werner, E., and R. Smith. 1992. *Overcoming the odds: High-risk children from birth to adulthood*. Ithaca, N.Y.: Cornell University Press.

Wyn, J., and R. White. 1997. *Rethinking youth*. London: Sage.

Yin, R. K. 1994. *Case study research: Design and methods*. 2nd ed. Thousand Oaks, Calif.: Sage.

# Raza Communities Organizing against a Culture of War: Lessons from the Education Not Arms Coalition (ENAC) Campaign

*Miguel Zavala*

Raza[1] struggle today is marked by interlocking historical, political, and economic contradictions that manifest presently in the intensification of violence against Raza communities in the Southwest and in major areas where Raza im/migrants[2] reside. Fueled by a rampant xenophobia, extreme Right groups together with mainstream political forces across the United States have proposed or enacted anti-immigrant and anti-Raza legislation. The present set of federal mandates under the Trump administration was preceded by historic numbers of deportations, numbering about 2.5 million, during the Obama administration (Department of Homeland Security 2016). What makes the current nationalism in the era of Trump distinct from the xenophobia of the last two decades is its explicit articulation of white supremacist ideology and campaign of hate targeting Muslims, immigrants, Mexicans, women, and LGBTQ peoples. While Trump's white supremacy is not specifically focused on Raza im/migrants, part of his political and ideological campaign is fueled by an explicit othering and persecution of Mexican undocumented peoples throughout the United States.

Although Raza youth are increasingly criminalized and subject to threats of deportation and incarceration, they are, on the other hand, invited to participate as "civic agents" within a system of social apartheid that further marginalizes them (de Genova 2007, Gonzales 2014, Lawston and Escobar 2010). For instance, proposed policies such as the federal DREAM Act, although supported by many undocumented Raza students and organizations, perpetuate the discourse of "illegality" and target youth as fodder for the military, evidenced in the often-ignored military enlistment stipulation offered as an avenue for legal residence (ARE 2010, Buenavista 2012).

Historically, U.S. public schools have not served the interests of Raza communities (Acuña 1998, Spring 2012). In major urban districts across the United States, the push-out rate for Raza youth is at a soaring 53 percent (Romero 2012). Even when controlling for social class across different ethnic-racialized groups, Raza students have been consistently pushed out at higher rates (Covarrubias 2011). In the San Diego Unified School District, where the Education Not Arms Coalition (ENAC) campaign took place, the 2000 graduation rate for Raza students was at an alarming 43 percent (de Cos 2005, Greene 2001). While the district boasts decreasing the push-out rate for all students during the last decade, Raza youth continue to be underserved, with only 47 percent of graduates meeting basic university enrollment requirements (Betts, Zau, and Bachofer 2013). Pushed out of school at high rates, they enter the low-wage unemployment ranks; many are steered into the prison system. Some scholars have argued that large urban districts therefore function as systems that facilitate and perpetuate the criminalization of Raza youth (Noguera 2003, Rios and Galicia 2013).

Within the present post-9/11 culture of war (Hinkson 2015), which has only been intensified by Trump's anti-Muslim campaign, manifest in a series of executive orders targeting mostly Muslim countries, we see how Raza communities have been subject to state forms of violence—but yet again are invited to "participate" in military-imperialist operations against peoples in the Middle East, most evident in the Department of Defense's propaganda campaign "Yo Soy el Army" that began in 2010 (see Garza 2015). Reframing the issue of Raza enlistment in the military as "under-enrollment," the U.S. Department of Defense launched a controversial strategy targeting Raza youth. Segal and Segal (2007, 1) reported that "the Army has launched a vast recruiting campaign targeting Latino youth, placing ads in Spanish-language media, including magazines, radio, and television." Calculating the growing population of Raza youth in the United States as a significant "recruitment pool," and given the decreasing enlistment of Blacks, who remain largely overrepresented in the U.S. armed forces, the Department of Defense had prioritized the recruitment of poor and working class Raza youth (see Garza 2015, Penn 2011). Over the past three decades, the federal government has been successful in closing the "enlistment gap" by recruiting Raza youth at rates exceeding the population growth of Raza communities in the United States. These rates have soared from 6.5 percent in 1990, 11 percent in 2000, to 16.5 percent in 2010 (Office of the Under Secretary of Defense, Personnel, and Readiness 2010).

In the process, schools have played a fundamental role in the military recruitment of Raza youth by using such strategies as Junior Reserve Officer Training Corps (JROTC) classes, federal policy such as NCLB via reporting of student information to the Pentagon, the formation of corporate-military charter school academies, and excessive military presence in urban high schools (Anderson 2009, Ayers 2006, Furumoto 2005, Galaviz et al. 2011, Leal 2007). These policies negatively affect vulnerable sectors of the Raza community as well as working-class students of color as a whole. Mariscal (2006, 46) reports: "Visit any high school with a large Latino population, and you will find JROTC units, Army-sponsored computer games, and an overabundance of recruiters, often more numerous than career counselors."

But also in response to these efforts, an emerging counter-recruitment movement is underway (Harding and Kershner 2011). What follows is an analysis of the practices that emerged within the Education Not Arms Coalition (ENAC) campaign, a two-year struggle to oust shooting ranges across a major urban district in California. In particular, I argue that grassroots organizations such as ENAC provide important spaces not only of struggle but also for understanding how grassroots organizing projects transform research and youth in humanizing ways. This study is guided by the following research questions: How do key ENAC organizers interpret the mediation of pedagogy and action research in the campaign? And what lessons can we learn from these grassroots strategies in building pedagogical and research projects that challenge the present culture of war?

### The Education Not Arms Coalition (ENAC) Campaign

In the spring of 2007, the ENAC campaign was sparked when the principal at Mission Bay High authorized the removal of a college support program and advanced placement courses, replacing them with JROTC marksmanship classes and the installation of a shooting range. Three months later, the local organizing at Mission Bay to reinstate the college-going program at the campus grew into a full-fledged campaign

when Association of Raza Educators (ARE)[3] teachers and students at another high school across the city joined forces after a shooting range was
installed on the newly created Lincoln High campus. Organizations
such as Project YANO, which had undertaken prior campaign work and
extensive research on the militarization of education, and San Diego
State MEChA also joined, drawing support from the Raza Rights Coalition and Unión del Barrio.[4]

The ENAC campaign lasted from the spring of 2007 to the winter of
2009. This campaign brought together multiple projects, including action
research studies conducted by youth and popular education in the form
of community forums. Although mostly Raza students at Lincoln and
Mission Bay High led the campaign, several teachers at both high schools
played key roles in the political development and activism of their students. Campaign goals included the elimination of weapons training,
active consent from parents prior to enrolling in JROTC classes, and
informing parents and students that JROTC courses do not count for
college admissions.

On February 10, 2009, the San Diego City School Board meeting was
packed with students from Mission Bay High and Lincoln High, along
with representatives from ENAC member organizations. The students had
been waiting all evening and late into the night, holding signs reading "No
Weapons Training," for their agenda item to come to a vote. After almost
two years of grassroots organizing that included education forums, community meetings, the presentation of research, protests, strategic participation at school board meetings, and calls to the media, in February 2009
the Education Not Arms Coalition (ENAC) forced the San Diego City
School Board to terminate Junior Reserve Officer Training Corps
(JROTC) marksmanship classes. Because the struggle took place in San
Diego, a "military town" located near major military bases and where
school officials in the second largest school district in California have a
long history of supporting the U.S. armed forces in recruiting Raza, Black,
and poor whites, this grassroots victory resonated deeply with the students,
teachers, and community organizers involved in this two-year campaign.

## Drawing from the Narratives of ENAC Participants and Key Organizers

In delineating the process by which alternative spaces are created out of
resistance and struggle, I use a set of interpretive strategies in my investi-

gation of the interrelation between community organizing, action research, and social justice teaching. This strategy is informed by my own research coming to understand the development of historically new practices within grassroots spaces (Zavala 2013a, 2013b). The question of the interrelation is dialectical, in the sense that it investigates the ways in which practices converge and create new forms. For example, the student-led research within grassroots spaces such as ENAC is transformed vis-à-vis the broader context that makes the research possible. This broader context is the political campaign itself, which is in turn shaped by the participants. My focus on practices signals an orientation toward understanding not just *individual* transformations but *collective* praxis. In this study, I draw from in-depth interviews with key ENAC members. Throughout this chapter, I use the actual names of organizations and places involved in the ENAC campaign but pseudonyms for the individuals interviewed.

Using a retrospective, semistructured interviewing strategy that elicits organizers' interpretations and reflections on campaign dynamics, this study draws primarily from in-depth interviews with key ENAC organizers and representatives of ENAC member organizations. I interviewed two Association of Raza Educators (ARE) teachers, three student organizers who formed youth organizations on their respective campuses, the lead teacher working to support students at Mission Bay High School, and the director of a community-based organization that has undertaken anti-military recruitment work in San Diego for the past two decades. I use traditional coding techniques (Saldaña 2012) to delineate themes in the interviews and expand on these themes via an analysis of how participants conceptualize the interrelation between three leading practices, namely, community organizing, action research, and social justice pedagogy. This kind of analysis enables both the researcher and readers to understand critically not just how *individuals* come together and organize against the militarization and criminalization of Raza youth but also what *collective praxis* is, that is, how collectives form and what the kinds of practices seeded within these spaces that may be termed "organic structures" are. The organic structures analyzed here have been identified as "grassroots" to signify their social location, that is, emerging with the people and often in opposition to state institutions.

If critical scholars are to map and challenge the ways in which militarism has become a central operating mechanism in the schooling of students of color and how militarism interlocks with the neoliberal privatization of public education today (the "materialism" identified by Martin Luther

King Jr.), it is fundamental that we engage with a particular kind of relational analysis that allows us to draw from the lived experience of key participants. This relational analysis will allow us to link their lived experience back to the kinds of collective practices of resistance generated by individuals engaged in struggle. The kinds of practices generated within organic structures and struggles are quite insightful in highlighting principles for future praxis and resistance to colonial and imperial domination within the United States. ENAC represents an organic grassroots structure that generates practices that are *simultaneously* antimilitaristic, antiracist, and anticapitalist.

### Key Organizers: Profiles

The following participants were selected for this study precisely because they held key leadership positions in their respective organizations. As representatives of ENAC member organizations, they were "insiders" to the struggle and knew intimately well the intricacies of the campaign. Moreover, because of their leadership roles, they were integral to campaign design and development. In my experience as a grassroots organizer, campaign design and development entails a constant movement and definition of the object (collective goal) of the campaign and its strategies (Zavala 2016). It also involves working to build organizations, including politicizing members and the broader community.

At the time of this study, Mr. Lopez had been an ARE member since 2007 and held key leadership positions in ARE. Mr. Lopez was featured as San Diego School District's Teacher of the Year. A ninth-grade teacher at Social Justice High School's Social Justice Academy, he has been instrumental in assisting youth with the formation of student-based organizations at the campus. Mr. Lopez was a key ARE representative in the campaign and was consistently present at school board meetings and in the backstage campaign organizing, which included working with students in his social justice class and mentoring and supporting the student organizations integral to the ENAC campaign.

Ms. Garcia, then–ARE San Diego chapter chair, had been an active ARE member three years prior to the campaign. She became involved during the early stages of the campaign, when community resistance to the installation of a shooting range at Mission Bay High was underway. At the time, Ms. Garcia was teaching at Memorial Academy and was also organizing with a base of ARE teachers at the school to address the racist practices of parent and community exclusion.

Ashanti was a student at Lincoln High School. A student of Mr. Lopez, she was apprenticed into community activism. Ashanti was a cofounder of the African Revolutionary Student Organization (ARSO) at Lincoln High. Through ARSO, Ashanti was able to mobilize youth at her campus. She, along with other students, organized community forums, conference presentations, and other educational functions of the campaign.

Carlos was a student at Lincoln High School. A former JROTC student, Carlos started organizing against JROTC course recruitment at his campus and eventually cofounded MEChA de Social Justice High. Many of the ARE organizers considered Carlos a key player in the campaign.

Adela was a student at UCLA and a former Mission Bay student. While at Mission Bay, Adela cofounded MEChA, a student-run organization, and was an instrumental organizer on her campus. An articulate youth, she undertook research as part of the campaign and assisted the youth with community forums and mobilizations.

Mr. Zarate, a teacher at Mission Bay High School, was recognized as an educator whose students achieved the highest AP exam scores in the district. He is a teacher and community activist and has worked, albeit alone, with students at Mission Bay. Although not belonging to any organization, Mr. Zarate was an integral member of ENAC and helped with the organizing at Mission Bay. His honest reflections and insights on the campaign were important in helping me develop a more nuanced understanding of campaign dynamics.

Mike is the program director for Project YANO, a 501(c)(3) nonprofit antimilitary recruitment organization located in San Diego. Mike was Project YANO's organization representative in the coalition. He provided extensive research support and assistance with media and writing on behalf of ENAC. Mike worked closely with Mission Bay and Lincoln High and had worked on antimilitary recruitment campaigns at other campuses.

### Action Research in the Campaign: "The Students Were, Like, Putting It into Action"

Qualitative shifts in the meaning and practice of research within spaces like ENAC, ARE, MEChA, ARSO, and other organic, grassroots structures are paralleled by qualitative shifts in other practices, such as education, research, and organizing itself. The politicization of youth within spaces like ARSO and MEChA grows with the conditions that shape those spaces. While these historical conditions are "carried" forward by the participants, these conditions cannot be reduced to the individuals themselves. Here, I develop three salient themes. First, the idea that action research is "political" by virtue of the space/context that makes it possible. Second, the idea that action research functions as "organic popular education," meaning that it is educational and organic to communities involved in organized struggles. Third, the idea that action research is transformative praxis. I end with a discussion of the apprenticeship of students into community organizing as the "knot" between the three practices (pedagogy, research, and organizing).

## ACTION RESEARCH AS POLITICAL

Although various approaches to research were used in the campaign, from deliberate and structured, as was the case at Mission Bay and Project YANO, to unstructured and informal, such as at Lincoln High, all the interviewees agreed that research within the campaign was a resource or tactic within a broader political strategy to educate the community and orient the attention of school officials. During the early planning stages of the campaign, Mike, the director of Project YANO, reported that the coalition reached the consensus that coalition arguments had to be supported with evidence and that all coalition members needed to be fully informed and knowledgeable about the issues.

Within the ENAC campaign, research took on various forms and assumed a dynamic character. For this reason, I characterize the research as being in motion: as being transformed by and transforming other practices. Based on the collective insights by campaign organizers, research assumed traditional strategies, from statistical analyses of student enrollment in JROTC classes across different schools to the collection of testimonials based on students' experiences with military recruiters and JROTC courses. However, most of this research was done by individual organizations and was not undertaken by the coalition as a whole. In other words, the research was organic and deliberate in relation to the respective member organizations taking a lead on the research, but there was no formal space within the coalition that designed and conducted said research. For instance, student representatives from MEChA de Mission Bay High undertook research on AP versus JROTC course enrollments and collected testimonials of students' experiences in these different programs. Adela, a student organizer at Mission Bay, said that this information, after being presented to the school board, was instrumental in achieving one of the campaign's objectives, which was that parents needed to be informed about their rights with respect to student enrollment in JROTC.

Within the context of community activism, knowledge derived from research is used both to organize the attention of people in power, such as the school board, and to educate the general community in nontraditional ways. All interviewees concurred that education was important to the campaign. However, this education did not happen for the sake of educating. The education that grew out of the research and that took place in organizational meetings, conferences, community forums, and school board meetings was driven by a broader political strategy. In these spaces, the diffusion of information and knowledge vis-à-vis the process of education was already politically charged. For Mike, research functioned to organize people's attention around an issue:

> I think you know research is a tool for the campaign. So, it's usually a tool that is necessary. I won't rule out the possibility that research might be only a minor component in some cases, but effective campaigns, they use information. They use information that has to be accurate and thorough, and so research has to be usually done. How deeply you have to go with the research, it just depends on different issues, different approaches. It's the thing that provides the quote unquote weapons, the arsenal that you have to have to persuade people, and if you don't have it, you're easy to dismiss.

Others appreciated the importance in redirecting knowledge and using it as a "tool for the campaign" but also saw another fundamental function of research: building consciousness. Mr. Lopez describes:

> It's like the students had to read, and read, and read and research, and research in order to be able to understand this issue and every single intricacy. They had to understand what militarization in the schools was, not just understand the contradiction between a gun on campus being brought by a student and one being handed to a student by a staff member. They had to understand what militarization is; they needed to understand what was happening in Iraq. It went to levels far beyond the weapons training. So a lot of them became peace activists; a lot of them are still involved in Project YANO. *Creo una consciencia y un entendimiento* [A consciousness and understanding was created] that went far beyond.

ACTION RESEARCH AS ORGANIC POPULAR EDUCATION

Research played a pedagogical role in that it assisted with educating students and the general community on the expansion of JROTC shooting ranges in the district, exposing contradictions that were not immediately visible or known. Mr. Lopez, an ARE member and teacher at Lincoln High, characterized the research as "political education" for the students and school board.

> Yeah, the students, I mean, like it was a total political education. In order for them to understand the arguments the opposition would bring, they had to know the ins and outs about that issue. They had to totally understand in order for them to be able to counter somebody's— to understand, to predict the argument of the opposition and then be able to counter that argument, I mean just imagine the amount of research that takes place. I mean that's the highest level, highest level of education like the night, that night right before the decision was about to go down, one of the [school] board members says, this is the best political—cuz the students would come up, each side, poom, poom, poom, poom, proposing their arguments. And the place was packed, *ya heran las diez de la noche* [it was ten o'clock at night] and one of the board members said, this is the best political science class I have ever attended. The students were, like, putting it into action.

Indeed, action research was used to educate the community wherever possible. Throughout the campaign, students conducted workshops at their respective high schools, on their college campuses, and at strategically selected conferences. For Mr. Lopez, however, students didn't just learn about organizing, the details of how school boards function, or the institutional history of JROTC. For him, a particular kind of experiential education grows out of these community organizing contexts: "It was a total political education . . . the students had to read, and read, and read and research and research in order to be able to understand the issue." Political education, as the term is used by Mr. Lopez and other ARE members, entails more than a critical social consciousness. Political education involves "political clarity," which "refers to the ongoing process by which individuals achieve ever-deepening consciousness of the sociopolitical and economic realities that shape their lives and their capacity to transform such material and symbolic conditions" (Bartolomé 2004, 98). Yet this consciousness grows out of the students' (and teachers') community organizing. In this sense, political education is both popular and organic, meaning that it develops out of grassroots structures—and it functions to apprentice participants into community activism.

The three student organizers all concurred that teaching and learning were integral to the campaign. Whether it was students mentoring other students or educating the general community or key stakeholders, education was ongoing throughout the campaign. In particular, when asked if they had learned about community organizing itself, all the students answered in the affirmative. Adela iterated that she learned after the first year of the campaign about the way school board decision making works and that how to organize to change their vote was a living lesson. Carlos commented that he learned how to organize by watching more experienced organizers. And finally, Ashanti said that the ENAC campaign has given her experience and the practical knowledge that comes with being immersed in organized struggle. One of the student organizers provides more insight on the pedagogical role that research took. Carlos noted that research assumed a form of self-education around not just JROTC but political organizing itself:

> If you don't have research, we can't really prove our points. You know we had to, I mean we spent time like looking at articles that talked about eliminations of gun shooting ranges. Chicago eliminated shooting ranges, and that really gave us an idea of how to do it. So we researched it so we could understand what was going on, how do we do it as students, how do we find out? I mean—I think two main components of our struggle, the research and the campaign, they're like tied together, they're very important, we really need them to like explain or talk about our opinions.

Students studied the history of JROTC and needed to understand the intricacies of the program and how best to support their arguments. They also felt the need to investigate and learn from other organizing efforts. In the case of Chicago, students read extensively about the organizing tactics, the political framing, and the mistakes made. In these examples, research was student led and is transformed into a form of political education. By this I mean that students engage in reading about pertinent issues with an eye toward educating themselves and at the same time developing organizing strategies that support their local efforts. It is political education in the sense that the education leads to a critical social consciousness and is manifest in their apprenticeship into becoming community organizers.

Ms. Garcia, an ARE member, described the campaign as a "two-year long lesson":

> If you saw one of the clips on the news on Fox, I think it's Juan's daughter who says two years of hard work and we won the battle. Definitely for the students it was a two-year long lesson where they're organizing, they would attend board meetings, they would sit there for five hours sometimes or six hours and they wouldn't even speak on the item. So it was the struggle, the organizing, and the persistence. Mr. Lopez told them from the beginning especially as students, be prepared to fail. Be prepared to fail, don't expect to attend the first board meeting and have them approve it right away. This is a long process. I think that in itself established the curriculum. There's no specific curriculum or book or a lesson plan that has ever been written or that was written. Just the experience, just like with organizing for me, I think that's been the experience.

Here Ms. Garcia points to an important lesson in organizing: campaign work is often enduring, and campaigns are won by being organized and persistent. The Campaign, according to Ms. Garcia's interpretation, functions as a space that generates popular forms of education. With no formal, deliberate teaching going on, the experiences themselves serve as the lived curriculum for the participants. It is in this light that we can understand counter-recruitment and antimilitary organizing as an organic process. Students' take-up of research challenges instrumentalist discourses that dehumanize students by positioning them as "instruments" for social change. In counter-recruitment organizing there is an identified tendency to enact the "strategies and tactics" of the military and reduce education to propaganda (Abajian and Guzman 2013).

## Action Research in Transition versus Action Research in Motion

One of the functions of research is to generate new knowledge and information. This can be said of research within the academy as well as of the research that grows out of community organizing spaces. However, a qualitative shift emerges that changes the nature of the practice of research itself: This shift grows out of the context, here, the grassroots spaces of their organizations and ENAC, in which the research takes form. Yes, students were engaged in the practice of research, yet their participation was guided by the political goals of the campaign itself. A qualitative difference between research in the academy and research in spaces like ENAC grows out of the *object* of their respective activities. ENAC was a political project through and through. More specifically, ENAC was itself an organic structure and medium for organizations to build collectively and struggle for their demands. By *object* I take to mean, borrowing from cultural-historical activity theory (Engeström 1999), the collective goal of any object-oriented collective activity. The object is more than the sum of the goals that individuals or, in this instance, the political goals of ENAC member organizations, bring into the activity.

Within ENAC, a distinct object is forged. Students, for instance, are apprenticed into the practice of becoming critical researchers *and* community activists. When doing research, this is done both to engage with research that self-educates but also to diffuse knowledge and information so as to strengthen themselves as organizers. In a discussion with Mr. Lopez, we touch on this when he identifies a particular type of "internal education."

> Mr. Lopez: Well there was talking points that were developed within the Ed Not Arms coalition that were handed out to everybody, for example, there was an internal education, like the leadership got educated in order for them to [take] back to their collectives, and share the information that was researched. And so that was taking place in Ed Not Arms. And then the ARSO students would go to ARSO and educate the rest of ARSO, you know what I'm saying. ARE members would go back to ARE and educate the rest of ARE, and so on and so forth. It was different levels of education taking place.
> Miguel: And the research that is flowing through those.
> Mr. Lopez: Yeah.

This type of "internal" education has, historically, taken form within *comunidades de base* (base communities). This type of education is animated by the need to strengthen *cuadros* (cadre) and *bases* (bases). In my observation of subsequent ARSO student meetings, I was struck by the ways students developed a critical understanding of the conditions affecting Black and Raza youth and how these conditions are interconnected with U.S. imperialism in the Middle East. In this meeting, Mr. Lopez and another teacher were present as mentors, providing students with the tools for understanding disparate events across the world as processes of imperialism and colonialism today.

## Apprenticeship into Community Organizing

The youth organizers I interviewed were all apprenticed into the practice of community activism. Although they report that their activism was triggered by an experience that woke a need to commit to organized struggle, they identified Mr. Lopez's and Mr. Zarate's classes as fundamental to their continued engagement. Moreover, while these teachers did not develop a curriculum that tied directly to the ENAC campaign, they both articulated a connection between their pedagogy and the community activism of their students. This articulation is worth discussing.

A function of Mr. Zarate's class is building a *"conciencia social"* (social consciousness), which becomes a vehicle for youth mobilization. All three teacher-organizers interviewed emphasized something similar: Their role was to teach and mentor students through their own participation in organized struggle, seeing the activism as a vehicle by which to apprentice students into community organizing. Ashanti, Carlos, and Adela all went on to found student organizations at their campuses. In the case of Carlos, his personal story as the founder of MEChA de Lincoln High is interconnected with his departure from JROTC. With the guidance of Mr. Lopez, he was able to take on a school-based campaign against JROTC's uniform requirements. Throughout this struggle, he saw the need to work collectively instead of alone, and it was thus that MEChA was founded at his school.

In sum, classroom pedagogy is connected to community activism and, in particular, the ENAC campaign through the apprenticeship of students to community organizers. Classroom pedagogy functions indirectly, with the "implicit" goal, as Mr. Lopez stated, for developing youth organizers. In particular, Mr. Lopez's yearlong efforts were geared toward bringing students closer to community organizing work. Moreover, through their direct engagement in community organizing, Mr. Lopez and Mr. Zarate serve as role models for their students and, with their skills, have assisted them in organizing and building youth organizations at their respective campuses.

## Lessons Learned

The investigation of the intersection of leading practices within ENAC revealed the generation of organic practices. The praxis of community organizing and political struggle transformed traditional forms of research undertaken by students into action research, leading to what I term *organic base research* (Zavala 2013a); in turn, the action research mediates "popular" forms of education both for ENAC members and the general community, giving birth to *organic popular education*. Moreover, although social justice teaching was not directly linked to the ENAC campaign and took shape within institutional settings, that is, Lincoln High and Mission Bay High, which were the two high schools involved directly in the campaign, the apprenticeship of students as community organizers, I argue, is the "knot" that links social justice teaching to the campaign. Finally, community organizing and political work in the campaign function as pedagogical and educational spaces, offering students and teachers learning opportunities about militarism and campaign development, the knowledge of which contributes not just to participants' politicization but to a general shift in their development as community organizers.

This study, by tracing the development of grassroots spaces and the formation of grassroots action research, makes significant contributions to the fields of youth participatory action research (YPAR) (Morrell 2008, Tuck et al. 2008) and decolonizing research (Fals-Borda 1985, Smith 1999), which have struggled with the question of the constitution of community-based research and projects, both how they are mediated and how they mediate other practices and processes in rehumanizing ways. Moreover, the study of the dialogical opening of grassroots spaces and processes, whether popular forms of education or youth-led action research, takes historical form within the present context of militarism and schooling that is pushing Raza youth out of school and into the military. Thus, this interpretive study offers insights into the production of spaces of organized resistance that materialize within/against the present criminalization and militarization of the Raza youth body yet are transformed (and transform its participants) through a reinvented Latin American strategy of grassroots organizing resistance within the United States.

One major lesson learned is that the rehumanizing spaces that make the research and mobilizing possible matter as much as the strategies themselves. In our attempt to challenge the militarization and criminalization of Raza and other students of color, especially during a resurgent white supremacy manifest in the election of Donald Trump, scholar-activists are leveraging new forms of solidarity, organizing *with* rather than *for* the grassroots. It is this call for participatory democracy that may transform our fundamental view of what counts as research. More significant is the potential to shift what matters radically, for scholar-activists to engage in struggles for community, because "we urgently need to bring to our communities the limitless capacity to love, serve, and create for each other" (Boggs 2012, 47).

1. Historically, the term "Chicano/a" was reclaimed during the late 1960s and early 1970s as a marker for cultural identity and political ideology of the *Mexicano* in the United States. The term Raza was reintroduced in the early Chicano/a struggles as the general signifier for "the people." More recently, the term "Chicano/a" has been replaced by "Latino/a" in an effort to include the groups and experiences of people from other parts of Latin America, e.g., *Salvadoreño*, *Guatemalteco*, etc. I use the term Raza strategically, as a broader sociocultural identity, which includes the standpoint of the indigenous, mestizo, and working-class peoples from Latin America. From this vantage point, the southwestern part of the United States can be conceptualized as an extension of Latin America, or what some have named the "occupied territories of the North."

2. I use the dual term "im/migrant" so as to not distinguish between "immigrants" and "migrants." From the standpoint of Mexican Raza, *Mexicanos* are not "immigrants." *Mexicanos* living in the territory known as the United States consider these to be occupied lands appropriated by conquest and deceit on behalf of the U.S. government. *Mexicanos* are not settlers but indigenous to these lands.

3. The Association of Raza Educators (ARE) is a grassroots teacher-led organization. Founded in 1994, the organization has grown, with chapters in Los Angeles, Oakland, Sacramento, and San Diego. During the time of the study, I was in the leadership of the Los Angeles chapter and a member of the statewide leadership body, the State Concilio, which overlooks and coordinates cross-chapter campaigns and the development of the organization across California.

4. Project on Youth and Non-Military Opportunities (YANO) is a 501(c)(3) nonprofit community organization that has had an active presence in the San Diego area, educating the community and students specifically about alternatives to the military. MEChA, a national student organization with chapters on high school and college campuses, stands for Movimiento Estudiantil Chicano de Aztlán, which grew out of the late 1960s Chicano Power Movement in the southwestern United States. The Raza Rights Coalition has a long-standing history in San Diego and is a coalition spearheaded by Unión del Barrio, a revolutionary nationalist organization, perhaps the only organization with such a political line in existence since 1994, with grassroots "bases" in Los Angeles and San Diego.

REFERENCES

Abajian, S. M., and M. Guzman. 2013. Moving beyond slogans: Possibilities for a more connected and humanizing "counter-recruitment" pedagogy in highly militarized urban schools. *Journal of Curriculum Theorizing* 29 (2): 191–205.

Acuña, R. 1988. *Occupied America: a history of Chicanos.* New York: Harper & Row.

Anderson, G. L. 2009. The politics of another side: Truth-in-military-recruiting advocacy in an urban school district. *Educational Policy* 23 (1): 267–291.

ARE. 2010. The Dream Act and the Latino/a legalization pipeline: A nightmare for most undocumented high school students. http://razaeducators.org/archives_pp.html.

Ayers, W. 2006. Hearts and minds: Military recruitment and the high school battlefield. *Phi Delta Kappan* 87 (8): 594–599.

Bartolomé, L. 2004. Critical pedagogy and teacher education: Radicalizing prospective teachers. *Teacher Education Quarterly* 31 (1): 96–122.

Betts, J. R., A. C. Zau, and K. V. Bachofer. 2013. *College readiness as a graduation requirement: An assessment of San Diego's challenges.* San Francisco: Public Policy Institute of California. http://www.ppic.org/content/pubs/report/R_413JBR.pdf.

Boggs, G. L. 2012. *The next American revolution: Sustainable activism for the twenty-first century.* Berkeley: University of California Press.

Buenavista, T. L. 2012. Citizenship at a cost: Undocumented Asian youth perceptions and the militarization of immigration. *AAPI Nexus: Policy, Practice, and Community* 10 (1): 101–124.

Covarrubias, A. 2011. Quantitative intersectionality: A critical race analysis of the Chicana/o educational pipeline. *Journal of Latinos and Education* 10 (2): 86–105.

De Cos, P. 2005. *High school dropouts, enrollment, and graduation rates in California.* California Research Bureau.

de Genova, N. 2007. The production of culprits: From detainability to deportability in the aftermath of "homeland security." *Citizenship Studies* 11 (5): 421–448.

Department of Homeland Security. 2016. FY 2016 ICE immigration removals. https://www.ice.gov/removal-statistics/2016.

Fals-Borda, O. 1985. *Conocimiento y poder popular: Lecciónes con campesinos de Nicaragua, Mexico y Colombia.* Mexico City: Siglo Veintiuno Editores.

Furumoto, R. 2005. No poor child left unrecruited: How NCLB codifies and perpetuates urban school militarism. *Equity and Excellence in Education* 38 (3): 200–210.

Galaviz, B., J. Palafox, E. R. Meiners, and T. Quinn. 2011. The militarization and the privatization of public schools. *Berkeley Review of Education* 2 (1): 27–45.

Garza, I. 2015. Advertising patriotism: The "Yo Soy el Army" campaign and the politics of invisibility for Latina/o youth. *Latino Studies* 13 (2): 245–268.

Gonzales, A. 2014. *Reform without justice: Migrant politics and the homeland security state.* New York: Oxford University Press.

Greene, J. 2001. High school graduation rates in the United States. The Manhattan Institute for Policy Research Civic Report.

Harding, S., and S. Kershner. 2011. Just say no: Organizing against militarism in public schools. *Journal of Sociology and Social Welfare* 38 (2): 79–109.

Hinkson, J. 2015. War culture. *Arena* 135:2–3.

Lawston, J. M., and M. Escobar. 2010. Policing, detention, deportation, and resistance: Situating immigrant justice and carcerality in the twenty-first century. *Social Justice* 36 (2): 1–6.

Morrell, E. 2008. Six summers of YPAR: Learning, action, and change in urban communities. In *Revolutionizing education: Youth participatory action research in motion*, ed. J. Cammarota and M. Fine, 155–184. New York: Routledge.

Noguera, P. A. 2003. Schools, prisons, and social implications of punishment: Rethinking disciplinary practices. *Theory into Practice* 42 (4): 341–350.

Penn, K. R. 2011. A renewed focus on recruitment [Special issue]. *Defense AT&L* 40 (2): 44–45.

Office of the Under Secretary of Defense, Personnel, and Readiness. 2010. *Population representation in the military services: Fiscal year 2010 summary report.* Washington, D.C.: Department of Defense.

Rios, V., and M. G. Galicia. 2013. Smoking guns or smoke and mirrors? Schools and the policing of Latino boys. *Association of Mexican American Educators Journal* 7 (3): 54–66.

Romero, R. C. 2012. Law, social policy, and the Latina/o education pipeline. *CSRC Research Report* 15:1–5.

Saldaña, J. 2012. *The coding manual for qualitative researchers.* Thousand Oaks, Calif.: Sage.

Segal, M. W., and D. R. Segal. 2007. Latinos claim larger share of U.S. military personnel. Population Reference Bureau. http://www.prb.org.

Smith, L. T. 1999. *Decolonizing methodologies: Research and indigenous peoples.* New York: Palgrave.

Spring, J. 2012. *Deculturalization and the struggle for equality: A brief history of the education of dominated cultures in the United States.* Columbus, Ohio: McGraw-Hill.

Tuck, E., J. Allen, M. Bacha, et al. 2008. Par praxes for now and future change: The collective of researchers on educational disappointment and desire. In *Revolutionizing education: Youth participatory action research in motion*, ed. J. Cammarota and M. Fine, 49–83. New York: Routledge.

Zavala, M. 2013a. What do we mean by decolonizing research strategies? Lessons from decolonizing, indigenous research projects in New Zealand and Latin America. *Decolonization: Indigeneity, Education, and Society* 2 (1): 55–71.

———. 2013b. Organizing against the neoliberal privatization of education in South Los Angeles: Reflections on the transformative potential of grassroots research. *Journal of Curriculum Theorizing* 29 (2): 57–71.

———. 2016. Design, participation, and social change: What design in grassroots spaces can teach learning scientists. *Cognition and Instruction* 34 (3): 236–249.

# Schools as Carceral Sites: A Unidirectional War against Girls of Color

*Connie Wun*

Conversations surrounding school discipline and the school-to-prison pipeline (STPP) have largely focused on the ways that schools and their punitive policies have funneled students, mostly Black, Native/Indigenous, and Latinx, into the criminal justice system. Literature from anti-STPP advocates and scholars contend that with harsh school discipline practices and the increase in the presence of school police, students are more likely to be excluded from school, arrested, and/or conditioned for the prison system (Advancement Project 2012; Nocella, Parmar, and Stovall 2014). In recent years, however, there has been an increase in scholarship that argues that schools are not only funneling students into the criminal system but that schools and prisons operate as a nexus—the two working symbiotically to discipline and punish students of color, predominantly Black students (Annamma 2016, 2017; Meiners 2007; Sojoyner 2016; Wun 2016). For Black students in particular, schools are hostile spaces characterized by limited resources, high-stakes testing practices, culturally biased lessons, and repressive policing mechanisms. Extending the literature on school discipline and the school-to-prison pipeline, this chapter identifies ways that schools are characterized by multiple forms of discipline, including formal policies and informal forms of punishment (Wun 2014).

This multilayered construct does more than funnel students into prison or prime them for incarceration. I argue that they are part and parcel of a long-standing anti-Black carceral regime, one characterized by domination and social control over its captive objects (Rodriguez 2006). Language and discourses surrounding the carceral *state* has generally focused on the machinations of prisons or the criminal justice system, including but not limited to policies and procedures. However, by situating schools as an apparatus that enables and is part of the "carceral regime," a term that is sometimes used interchangeably with "prison regime" by scholars including Rodriguez (2006) and Richie (2012), we can better understand the school discipline practices and logics as a part of a larger U.S. culture of carcerality.

This chapter highlights the ways that the school operates as a carceral institution within the U.S. carceral regime.[1] Beyond prisons, "carcerality" encompasses institutions, logics, fantasies, and cultures that systematically enclose upon particular subjects, rendering them fungible objects for surveillance and control. For Rodriguez (2006), "'regime' encompasses discursive and cultural formation, which is extra state." This understanding utilizes "regime" to identify the ways that imprisonment and U.S. domestic war against Black and Latinx communities in general occur beyond state policies and procedures. While most studies on schools and discipline focus on the regulation and surveillance of boys, this chapter examines the experiences that girls of color, particularly Black girls, have with carcerality through school discipline.[2]

Through school architecture (for example, cameras) and discipline policies (for example, school handbooks), all students are subject to constant surveillance and rendered vulnerable to a number of disciplinary possibilities. Yet despite the general susceptibility to scrutiny, Black and Latinx students are far more likely to be punished. These carceral practices and culture often function to enclose upon students, quelling their desires and/or incapacitating their abilities to resist or fight back (Sojoyner 2016, Wun 2016). In Rodriguez's (2006) research on political prisoners, he identifies the ways that the prison regime functions, in part, to incapacitate Black political resistance and resisters. Echoing the findings from other school discipline scholars who center the logics of carcerality and U.S. anti-Blackness, this study finds that there are multiple, sometimes compounding and intersecting methods by which schools, a part of the U.S. carceral regime, incapacitate Black girls and their desires and abilities to resist.

Based on a case study situated at a high school in northern California, findings from this twelve-month qualitative research, which includes interviews with twenty Black and non-Black girls of color, identify schools as multilayered disciplinary landscapes that are undergirded by a logic of carcerality that includes surveillance, criminalization, and punishment—particularly in relationship to Black girls. Initially developed to examine the experiences that girls of color have with school discipline at large, the study found that Black girls (fifteen out of the twenty students interviewed for the project) were more often disciplined and punished than their peers. Centering on the narratives of three Black girls from the study, this chapter focuses on identifying the carcerality of schooling. Drawing from Black feminist scholarship (Richie 2012, Roberts 1997) and critical prison studies literature (Rodriguez 2006, Sojoyner 2013), the study finds that the school's carceral landscape operates as a form of war against its students. More specifically, I consider the ways that school discipline not only incidentally or unfairly targets Black girls but, following the logic of the U.S. carceral regime, also marginalizes and incapacitates them through direct and slow forms of violence.

## School and Prison Literature

### SCHOOL-TO-PRISON-PIPELINE MECHANISMS AND EFFECTS

In 2003, the Civil Rights Project at Harvard University and the Institute on Race and Justice at Northeastern University sponsored a conference to address the "school-to-prison pipeline" (Wald and Losen 2003). Conference participants examined the ways that schools were contributing to the juvenile justice system. The school-to-prison pipeline is defined here:

> The set of policies and practices that make the criminalization and incarceration of children and youth more likely and the attainment of a high-quality education less likely. It is the emphasis of punitive consequences, student exclusion, and justice-system intervention over students' right to an education. (Advancement Project 2011)

These STPP policies are composed of harsh disciplinary practices, including suspensions, expulsions, and arrests. Most of the exclusionary practices, specifically suspensions and arrests, are for nonviolent infractions such as tardiness or drug possession. Mirroring the U.S. pattern of disciplining and punishing communities of color, these exclusionary policies and practices have more often affected students of color, specifically Black youth, than their white peers. According to the Civil Rights Data

Collection (U.S. Department of Education 2014), Black students made up 16 percent of the general student population, yet they constituted 32 to 42 percent of those suspended or expelled. Comparatively, white students represent 51 percent of the student population but make up 31 to 40 percent of suspensions or expulsions.

According to STPP research, students who have been suspended, expelled, or arrested are unable to receive services they may need, including academic support, to navigate and finish school. As students miss class, they progressively fall behind their peers and subsequently drop out or are pushed out of school (Gregory, Cornell, and Fan 2011; Morris 2016). STPP research experts argue that in addition to neglecting students' academic needs, these punitive policies exacerbate discipline problems (Mendez and Knoff 2003; Osher, Bear, and Sprague 2010). Students, feeling targeted or unsupported, are more inclined to become disaffected or distrustful of authority figures. In this sense, the exclusionary policies that disproportionately affect youth of color funnel students away from school and toward the criminal justice system.

Beyond the suspensions and expulsions, the school-to-prison pipeline is also characterized by juvenile arrests. According to the Civil Rights Data Collection (U.S. Department of Education 2014), from 2009 to 2010, more than thirty thousand California students were referred to law enforcement. At least twenty thousand students were arrested or given police tickets for infractions such as truancy violations. In Chicago Public Schools, while Black students make up 42 percent of the student population, they constitute 75 percent of juveniles arrested on school properties in 2011 and 2012 (Merkwae 2015). Students are increasingly arrested for infractions that previously had been deemed issues related to youth development, such as arguing or talking back. As studies have long suggested, Black youth are more likely to be criminalized and punished for behaviors that are otherwise viewed as mistakes when done by white students (Ferguson 2001). In recent years, there has been growing attention to the ways that Black youth, specifically girls, are not only arrested but violently detained by police officers (Smith 2016).

STPP discourse also argues that "school push-out," that is, the pipeline to prison, is characterized by the testing culture of schools. The latter has purportedly encouraged teachers to punish students who do not meet dominant markers of academic success or who may need alternative/additional educational services beyond those offered by their school. According to the Advancement Project (2011), as a result of mandates to evaluate students' test scores, districts, schools, administrators, and teachers are pressured to produce academic results with limited resources and time. This pressure, coupled with the exclusionary policies, has advertently or inadvertently coerced school faculty into creating hostile conditions for one another and their students, subsequently pushing youth who have been rendered low-performing or underachieving students out of school.

## More Than a Pipeline: The School/Prison Nexus

Although STPP researchers have helped highlight the punitive conditions in schools and their potential connections to prisons, the framework has increasingly been challenged (Meiners 2011, Nolan 2011, Sojoyner 2016, Wun 2016). Meiners (2011) expands the STPP framework by examining the symbiotic relationship between schools and prisons. She contends that schools have adopted policing policies that do not only lead students to prison but also create hostile sites of containment. Coupled with harsh disciplinary policies, schools are also characterized by racially biased faculty and contentious relationships between students and staff.

Schools do not only prime students for the criminal justice system; they also employ the prison system's racialized logics of surveillance, criminalization, and exclusionary policies (Giroux 2003, Sojoyner 2013, Wacquant 2001). Importantly, while the suspensions, expulsions, and arrest rates may be high, school discipline is also defined by the school's architectural landscape. The National Board of Education found that, in a study of more than seven hundred school districts across the United States, 39 percent of all urban districts used metal detectors, 75 percent used locker searches, and 65 percent used security personnel (Welsh 2000). In addition to these disciplinary measures, there are police in schools. According to Hirschfield (2008), school police is the fastest growing field of law enforcement. Quoting the Public Agenda report (2004), he adds that across the nation, 67 percent of teachers in predominantly Black and Latino schools have police at their schools. Sixty percent of suburban schoolteachers also report that there are armed police at their schools. Beyond the arrests that may funnel young people into prison or put them in closer proximity to the criminal justice system, the school site is itself a carceral apparatus armed with similar technologies and practices.

The link between schools and the criminal justice system, however, has existed longer than the school-to-prison-pipeline framework has existed. For nearly four decades, school administrators have been authorized to police students on behalf of the criminal justice system. In California, schools began implementing joint programs with the criminal justice system in the early 1970s. In 1973, the California Department of Justice published the first edition of *Law in the School*, a guide intended for teachers, parents, and students:

> While teachers are neither parents nor policemen, they have assumed two duties, which they share in common with parents and policemen. Their first duty is to take affirmative action to see to it that each child is protected from the harm caused by crimes and disciplinary offenses committed by other students, by outsiders, and even by the child himself. Failing this, their second duty is to use disciplinary and if necessary, criminal processes to deal effectively and impartially with misbehavior. (4)

This guide emphasized the responsibilities—and powers—that teachers had to uphold the criminal justice system. Teachers were authorized to implement criminal processes, if necessary, and protect students from crime. More than a decade later in 1984, the state superintendent of public instruction and the state attorney general created the School Law Enforcement Partnership (S/LEP) (California Department of Education 2001, v). This partnership between schools and law enforcement was developed based on the premise that, like police, school authorities were also responsible for "creat[ing] safe and orderly campuses and communities," as required by the State Constitution (Article 2, Section 28). Both of these documents articulated the responsibilities shared between police and school administrators. While STPP researchers have discussed the harsh disciplinary policies and practices, very few have explored the authority that school representatives have to search students, seize their property, or police and monitor them in ways reflective of the U.S. carceral regime.

The anthropologist Damien Sojoyner (2013, 235) argues that these discursive disciplinary practices can be traced back to the 1960s, as a response to Black student politics. In his study of school policing in Los Angeles, he writes:

> While Black communities in Los Angeles conceptualized and used public education as a space to develop alternative models of cultural expression and organizing, city officials, planners, and private capital lobbied for and responded with brute force and policy tactics to undermine liberation movements of Black Angelinos.

Sojoyner argues that schools have historically aimed to contain Black resistance, especially through secondary and higher education. He also argues that schools have not only explicitly criminalized and policed Black students, but have also created an environment in which Black youth are institutionally dispossessed of their culture and politics. Black students are not only denied access to basic resources and culturally responsive education but have historically been criminalized for protesting against these injustices. "Rather than a school to prison pipeline, the structure of public education is just as and maybe even more so culpable in the enclosure of Black freedom, which in turn has informed the development of prisons" (2). While STPP researchers and analysts have helped highlight disturbing connections between schools and prisons, the dichotomization of the two institutions undermines the ways that schools incarcerate youth.

## Theoretical Framework

Through the use of women-of-color feminism, specifically Black feminism, and critical prison studies, this chapter explores Black girls' experiences with schools as carceral spaces. Black feminist scholars and other non-Black feminists of color argue that the experiences and insights of women (and girls) of color have historically been excluded from popular and academic discourses (Hill Collins 2000, James and Sharpley-Whiting 2000). Women-of-color feminism has argued that in order to understand social and institutional inequalities thoroughly, researchers must examine the lives of women (of all ages) who live at the interstices of multiple marginalities (Anzaldúa 1983, Crenshaw 1995, Richie 1996). These multiple marginalities are constitutive of identities and experiences that are based upon race, class, gender, and sexuality. Living at the intersections of these identities includes being subject to multiple forms and layers of violence. Black and other feminist-of-color scholarship theorizes that centering the experiences of women and girls of color enables us to identify and subsequently challenge the intersections of structural, institutional, and interpersonal forms violence that affect the lives of women and girls of color (Crenshaw 1995).

Although most school discipline literature that has focused on boys of color has helped rightfully to frame discipline as a racial inequality, they have only narrowly identified the underlying premise behind discipline disparities. This framework undermines the ways that the intersections of race and gender (among other identifies) complicate experiences with school discipline. Radical Black feminism, in particular, highlights the ways that the state and its institutions (schools, prisons, the foster care system), policies, and practices operate as violent apparatuses that simultaneously fail to provide support for Black and poor non-Black communities of color and perpetually punish them (Crenshaw 2012). In *Arrested Justice*, Richie (2012) writes that state institutions operate symbiotically to criminalize and punish poor women of color and Black women in particular.

Black and non-Black feminism also helps challenge school discipline literature that has relied on a Foucauldian approach (James 1996, Noguera 2003, Wun 2014). In *Discipline and Punish*, Foucault (1977) traced the political history of punishment and disciplinary systems, arguing that "disciplinary power," which in part is characterized by institutions that invoke internalized forms of policing, replaced corporal punishment as a form of state rule and social control. Through panoptic structures such as prisons and schools, individuals learn to internalize dominant norms of "docility" and obedience. In her critique of Foucault, James (1996) argues that *Discipline and Punish* does not account for the ways that Black bodies continue to experience corporal punishment (for example, police violence) and are structurally positioned outside of "normality" (27). Panopticon structures and their disciplinary mechanisms, which produce and reward normal subjects, may demand docility from Black bodies, but the latter are subject to punishment regardless of their ability to internalize dominant standards. She contends that Foucault's theory of *Discipline and Punish* excludes racialized and gendered bodies that permanently occupy the position of the "deviant" subject. James argues that Black bodies are structurally positioned outside of the logic or realm of "normality," thus rendering them perpetually and structurally vulnerable to violence and punishment. This lens enables this study to understand better the girls' experiences with violence and school discipline.

Additionally, this study is informed by critical prison studies, namely from the works of Rodriguez (2006) and Richie (2012), who explore the "prison regime." As noted earlier, the concept of the prison regime recognizes that carcerality or incarceration exists beyond the prison walls. Instead, policing mechanisms and punishment occur at civic and civil levels, through different institutions, cultural practices, and social relationships. Richie (2012) writes about different experiences with policing and punishment against Black women beyond the prison walls. Similarly, Rodriguez's (2006) work on the prison regime helps identify schools as one of a myriad of state institutions undergirded by a logic of carcerality that targets Black bodies for surveillance, criminalization, and punishment.

Rodriguez (2014) also adds that prisons are a form of war that functions to "eviscerate" communities of color, particularly Black people. Put differently, prisons and their attending disciplinary mechanisms operate as state-sanctioned violence. These forms of policing, the study finds, are also performed at school through this multilayered disciplinary structure. Informed by these theories, this chapter focuses on Black girls who have discipline records, both because they have traditionally been marginalized from school discipline literature and because their perspectives may provide nuanced insights into schools as carceral spaces.

## *Methods*

This qualitative study includes in-depth interviews and participant observation conducted at Foundations High School (FHS) in California.[3] During the 2013–2014 school year, the population was 41 percent Asian and Pacific Islander, 32 percent Latino, 7.8 percent white, 9 percent Black, 4 percent Native Hawaiian or Pacific Islander, and less than 1 percent Native American. According to school data, Black students made up 33 percent of all suspensions and 27 percent of expulsions. Latino students accounted for 39 percent of all suspensions and 53 percent of expulsions. White students made up 8 percent of suspensions and 0 percent of expulsions. Asian American students made up 9 percent of suspensions and 0 percent of the expulsions, although Filipinos constituted 7 percent of the suspensions and nearly 7 percent of the expulsions. "Other" students made up 4 percent of suspensions and 13 percent of expulsions.

FHS is among the largest and most diverse high schools in the United States. According to preliminary research conducted in 2012, some of the students travel from major urban areas to attend this school for a "better education." Some of the students purportedly travel for one hour on public transportation to get to school. The school is renowned for its extracurricular activities, exceptional faculty, educational programs, and alumni.

This article focuses on the data collected from participant observation and in-depth interviews of three girls of color who have school discipline records. Using purposive sampling (Patton 1990), this study interviewed twenty girls who had discipline records (suspensions or referrals). One of the school administrators generated a list of names of girls who had discipline records for the second half of the 2012–2013 school year and the first half of the 2013–2014 school year. In 2012, the author conducted a pilot study at the site. As a result, administrators, teachers, and other staff were familiar with the author's presence on campus. The girls who participated in the study self-identified as girls of color with a discipline record, attended the initial recruitment meeting, returned their consent form and parent permission slip, and returned for the interview. This study focuses on three of the twenty girls of color who were interviewed because their narratives were reflective of their peers' experiences. Their ages ranged from fifteen to eighteen years. Each interview lasted between sixty and ninety minutes. The interview protocol focused on how students understood their experiences with school discipline policies. The study was guided by the following questions:

1. What are the types of discipline and punishment that the girls experience at school?
2. Why are they disciplined and punished?
3. What are their responses to school discipline and punishment?

The girls' narratives help identify the disciplinary structure of FHS, including its multiple layers and effects.

## The Violence of a Multilayered School Disciplinary Structure

According to the school discipline records, Black and Latino girls at FHS are more likely to be disciplined than their white and Asian counterparts. In particular, Latinas constitute 37 percent of the population of girls who have discipline records (detention, suspension, or expulsion records). Additionally, Filipino girls make up 12 percent of all girls who have discipline records. Black girls account for 26 percent of the discipline data for girls. Relative to their enrollment, Latinas are overrepresented and Black girls are even more overrepresented in the data.

The girls described that while all students can be subject to school discipline, only some students are subject to perpetual surveillance. In particular, Black girls in the study claimed that they often got into trouble for "defiance" and "disobedience." According to the girls, among a number of consequences, the girls were subject to referrals, suspensions, and arrests. All of these forms of exclusionary practices included surveillance, control, and domination.

### REFERRALS: CONSTANT OBSERVATION AND SCRUTINY

Of the twenty girls interviewed for this study, nineteen of them had been given referrals during their time at FHS. Students who receive referrals are not necessarily excluded from the classroom or school. Instead they are given warnings or lunch or afterschool detentions. When a student has accumulated three of these citations, they will face suspension for up to three days. This graduated process of exclusion provides some insight into students' experiences with mundane rituals of punishment.

Most of the girls who have received referrals recalled that the infractions were often for actions labeled as "defiance," "tardies," "cutting school," and failing to dress for physical education classes. Echoing previous research, the girls recalled getting referrals for behaviors such as "talking back," "getting up to throw away trash," and "not listening to the teacher" (Morris 2016). These infractions were seen as acts that "obstructed the learning environment." According to the girls, very rarely did these referrals positively alter their behaviors; neither did they believe that their actions disrupted the classroom. Instead, the girls often found themselves more upset and contentious after they were threatened with referrals or given them. Based on the girls' narratives, referrals operated as measures that were used to control the girls or to coerce them into submission.

Victoria, a Puerto Rican and Black girl in the ninth grade, shared her experiences with referrals. She contended that Mr. Waters, a white male teacher, constantly policed her actions. Chewing gum, drinking Gatorade, or using ChapStick became punishable offenses.

VICTORIA: He gets mad for everything, like if you're drinking Gatorade he yells, "Put that away!" [I say,] "What do you mean?" "I'm thirsty." You have out ChapStick, he yells, "Put that away!" [I think], "Whatchu mean? You want my lips to be chapped? I'm not gonna be crusty like yours."

C [CONNIE]: What happens when he tells you to put things away?

VICTORIA: I wait 'til I'm done using it [chuckles], then I put it away.

C: What happens after that?

VICTORIA: I get a referral.

These exchanges were common in Mr. Waters's class. While they did not deter her from using things, she was frustrated with Mr. Waters for his incessant attempts to police her behaviors. In addition to the arguments that she was having with other girls over social media and the precarious conditions of her household (where she was living between her mother and father's houses), Mr. Waters's policing affected Victoria's relationship to schooling.

Under the pretense that teachers are required to create effective learning environments, teachers sometimes establish strict rules for their classrooms. However, while studies suggest that students prefer rigid guidelines (Arum 2005), Victoria's narrative indicates that she resisted Mr. Waters's scrutiny. Instead, the more he policed or threatened to punish her, the more Victoria resisted. These microforms of resistance are reminiscent of Sojoyner's (2013) argument, which contends that schools enclose upon Black youth, their culture, and their impulse or needs to resist racialized social control at school. While Victoria's experiences with Mr. Waters can be considered forms of racialized antagonism, Mr. Waters's complaints about her "attitude" or "talking back" are commonly employed against Black girls. As other scholars have studied, girls of color—specifically Black girls—have often been punished for challenging or failing to meet white middle-class norms of femininity (Morris 2007, 2016; Sharma 2009; Winn 2011). Importantly, their actions or behaviors are not necessarily in contradistinction to idealized versions of white middle-class femininity. Rather, as this study suggests, the girls are more likely to be criminalized or punished for behaviors that are typically seen as normal or permissible when done by non-Black peers. Victoria claims that while she is perpetually policed by her teacher, her non-Black classmates are not.

Victoria's resistance and disciplinary experience were not uncommon among the students interviewed. Five other girls share similar stories of feeling as though teachers and administrators were trying to control them. Importantly, Rodriguez (2006) argues that within the context of a U.S. carceral regime, Black and Latinx communities are the main subjects of social control and domination. However, the referrals from Mr. Waters did not alter Victoria's behaviors in his class. She explains, "No one likes him" and that when confronted, students are more inclined to increase their resistance.

While referrals are not commonly studied because of their seemingly benign consequences (for example, detention), these disciplinary actions are the most frequently used forms of policing and surveillance. By narrowly studying disciplinary policies that exclude students from school, the school-to-prison-pipeline literature misses the everyday forms of policing that characterize the girls' experiences. These mundane forms of policing and punishment reveal that schools do not only push students out of school through their disciplinary practices but confine students and punish them within the classroom walls. Although Victoria did not get suspended or expelled, she was under constant surveillance, publicly policed in front of her peers, and then sent to the office for behavioral problems. These forms of policing do not necessarily register as harsh forms of punishment but happen every day to the girls as a condition of their carceral experience. According to the girls, they are regularly reminded that they have limited, if any, control over themselves in school.

## Suspensions: Using the Juridical Language and Logic of Criminality

Girls from this study explained that their suspensions, which included being prohibited from attending school or any school activities, were for
fighting, possession of drugs, or theft. Most of the girls who had been suspended found their experiences to be symptomatic of the school's punitive
culture, one that decenters students' needs and concerns. Findings suggest
that suspensions, like referrals, did not change students' behaviors. In fact,
they often made situations worse for students or increased their distrust
in school staff.

As studies have argued elsewhere, girls of color have layered experiences
with violence inside and outside of school. For example, according to Jones's
(2004) ethnographic study, Black girls are often coerced to protect themselves in their communities, home, and school. With limited protections
as underserved youth, Black girls are vulnerable to situations where they
are inclined to defend themselves physically against different forms of violence, including street harassment. Fighting is also an enactment of their
rage against structural forms of violence such as poverty and its effects on
their single moms or domestic violence in the household (Wun 2016).
Rather than assessing the girls' needs and reasons behind fighting, schools
have more often than not suspended youth for their behaviors. Protection,
unfortunately, is not limited to fighting. In addition to fighting, girls in
this study were also suspended for stealing.

Michaela, a Black girl in the twelfth grade, who also had experiences
with referrals, shared that in addition to having been suspended for fighting, she has also been suspended for selling lunch cards. As a low-income
student, she receives free or reduced lunch cards that enable her to eat lunch
for a reduced fee. Instead of using her cards, she sold them to other classmates. While she did not disclose how much profit she made from this exchange, she shared that when she did not use her cards she sold them to
classmates, usually for two dollars.

MICHAELA: I got suspended for selling lunch cards. I get suspended for
the dumbest reasons. For stealing school property. I got in trouble for
selling it instead of getting lunch with it.

C: How'd they find out?

MICHAELA: Um . . . they said they'd been watching me. They said
students told them. But I think they're lying about that. Nobody's gonna
just tell on me like that for selling lunch cards. But that's what they said . . .

c: For how many days?

MICHAELA: Like three.

According to the school handbook, students are prohibited from selling or "pawning" lunch cards. Lunch cards, the handbook states, are school property. Therefore, students found to be selling the cards are disciplined for theft.

A campus security technician (CST), a white woman, explained that selling lunch cards was equivalent to "stealing the public's money." Her belief was that students sold these cards to generate income for material goods such as shoes and clothing. This perspective and language mirrored that of the "welfare queen" public discourse that has demonized poor Black mothers (Cammett 2015, Cohen 1997). Through the welfare queen discourse, Black women were imagined and framed as undeserving social welfare predators who embezzled public resources and neglected their children's needs. Public officials and policy makers employed these racialized *and* gendered tropes to cut state funding, develop stricter welfare regulations, and criminalize poor families, specifically those of Black women.

The CST's response suggests a similar perspective about students who sell their lunch cards. Importantly, while Michaela dismissed the disciplinary actions as "stupid," she did not disclose the criteria that enabled her to qualify for these subsidized lunches. According to the 2012–2013 "Income Eligibility Guidelines for Free and Reduced-Price Meals or Free Milk in Nutrition Programs," a family of four must have an income of $29,965 or below to qualify for the program (California Department of Education 2013). During the interview, Michaela eventually shared that in addition to the four people that her mother supported, two other family members lived in the two-bedroom apartment. Her mother and her aunt often struggled to provide for a family of six. She also shared that because the apartment was often very crowded and small, she found her solitude in the bathroom; she would occasionally spend hours in the bathtub. Although the description of Michaela's home life is not to provide a reason behind her decisions to sell her lunch cards, it is useful to explore the contexts of her actions. Selling lunch cards was perhaps an option to help alleviate some of her family's financial pressures.

In her seminal work, Richie (1996) discusses incarceration and Black women in Chicago. Her research finds that the women prisoners were often convicted of "crimes of survival," actions that were employed to protect themselves from violence and/or serve the needs of their families. Research on school discipline has often discussed the ways that suspensions and expulsions push youth out of school and into prison. Although important, these studies have also missed opportunities to discuss the ways that schools and prisons share discourses, logics, and practices that demonize and criminalize poor Black women for their strategies for survival.

Importantly, the problem is not only that schools punish students for the ways that they navigate complex environments; it is that schools are also not doing this to white students. In other words, while this study focused on girls of color, specifically Black girls, students often shared that they did not witness school authorities similarly monitoring or punishing their white peers. According to a report published by the African American Policy Forum and the Center for Intersectionality and Social Policy Studies at Columbia Law School (2015), while zero white girls were expelled from school, 90 percent of all girls expelled from New York City schools in 2011–2012 were Black. Although this data focuses on expulsion rates, it demonstrates that Black girls are overrepresented in discipline data. This does not mean that Black girls are committing more infractions (for crimes of survival or otherwise) but that they are getting into trouble more than their classmates.

## Arrests: More Punishment

Kim, Losen, and Hewitt (2010) argue that in school students are governed by both the school system and the criminal justice system. According to FHS's school handbook, infractions such as weapons possession, assault, and theft warrant suspension, possible expulsion, and potential police notification. While most studies that explore the relationship between school and the criminal justice system often focus on the harsh experiences that boys of color have with police officers (Ferguson 2001), this study shows that Black girls are also subject to policing by school authorities and police.

Carla, a Black girl in the tenth grade, shared her experience with getting suspended by school authorities and arrested by police officers on campus. Both institutions, she contended, punished her for an infraction that she did not commit. Since the start of high school, one of her primary goals was to stay out of trouble. Her belief was that teachers and principals should only know her for being a good student. As a result, she did her best to stay "off their radar," which meant completing all of her homework assignments, "keeping to myself," and avoiding "bad crowds." Unfortunately, despite her efforts, Carla had been suspended and arrested, largely for not telling on her peers.

> I was in the locker room and I had seen this girl at the other end. She
> was like going through people's lockers. I had witnessed that she was
> going through people's stuff. I didn't tell her to stop. I said don't touch
> these lockers cuz I know them.

She explained that she did not want to get involved but did want to protect
people she knew and their belongings. As her peer began opening up lock-
ers, Carla would occasionally stop her from taking items that belonged to
her friends. "She had taken an iPhone, a wallet, and I don't know what else.
I had walked out before her and she had walked out after me." Believing
that she had both helped classmates as well as avoided getting into any trouble, she left the locker room.

Following her aim to stay out of trouble, she also chose to keep the
incident to herself and did not report it to school officials. "It wasn't my
business." Staying out of trouble meant abiding by school rules as well as
avoiding potential conflicts with her peers. Despite her carefulness, a couple
of days after the locker room incident, Carla was called into the office about
the theft.

> The campus security came to my class. I thought it was because there
> was a boy who had gotten jumped and they wanted to ask me questions
> about that. And right when I got in [the office], they [the police]
> automatically said I was arrested for taking this, this, this. They read
> me my rights, said I had the right to remain silent. So I stopped talking.
> They asked me questions that I refused to answer . . . they didn't
> handcuff or anything . . . it was just verbal.
>
> [The principal] said they wanted to ask me about what happened on
> Friday in the locker room. I was like okay. He said, "You heard there
> was an iPhone that came up missing?" [I said,] "Yeah, I heard there was
> an iPhone that came up missing." [Then] I stopped talking.

Knowing that she had a "right to remain silent," she did not answer any of
the principal or police officer's questions. She recalled that the police officers, an Asian male and white male, responded to her silence by saying,
"We don't have to deal with your attitude." Carla was transported from
school grounds to a holding cell at the city jail, where the police took her
picture and fingerprinted her.

CARLA: When I refused [to speak], they threatened to take me to
juvenile hall. The white male police officer got mad.

C: How do you know he got mad?

CARLA: He got red. He called my aunt and told her he was going to take me to jail. "We don't have time for this." They took me to jail, took my picture, fingerprints, asked me questions, how tall I was, how old I was, put me in the holding cell until my aunt picked me up.

She was kept in the cell until the evening even though she had not been charged with any crime.

Given that Carla was a witness, had not reported the theft, and failed to cooperate with the police sufficiently, she was referred to a Bay Area–based restorative justice program for counseling services. According to Carla, she did not believe that she needed to participate in the program because she had not committed any crime but decided to accept the "deal" to avoid charges. She was required to check in with the restorative justice counselor for six months. Each week a counselor requested a progress report and meetings with her. While this helped her stay on track, it also served as a form of unsolicited policing. She was being closely monitored for a crime she did not commit. Despite all of her efforts to stay out of trouble, she was still subject to criminalization and punishment.

Studies argue that in the past few decades, behaviors that were once considered minor school infractions are now criminalized and punishable by law (Hirschfield 2008). Additionally, whereas school authorities once bore primary responsibility for managing student behaviors, the criminal justice system is now more actively involved in school discipline policies (Nolan 2011). This layer of punishment includes experiences with getting handcuffed, interrogated by police, and placed in holding cells at the city jail. Studies also show that in recent years, girls are more likely to be criminalized and detained for nonserious cases than boys (Chensey-Lind and Jones 2010). The growing trend toward policing and punishing Black girls in the school system mirrors the experiences of adult Black women. According to the Center for American Progress (2016), Black women are more likely to have been incarcerated than women of any other racial or ethnic group. In comparison to one in 111 white women and one in forty-five Latinas, one in sixteen Black women will have been incarcerated at some point in their lives. Although the advocacy work against the school-to-prison pipeline has gained traction within the past decade, these numbers continue to be underdiscussed or understudied by school officials and youth advocates.[4] They are even less discussed as a characteristic of the U.S. carceral regime. Instead, most discussions surrounding the STPP or "school pushout" have framed the problem as one that is not with schools as a part of the national carceral landscape, which has historically been and is fundamentally anti-Black, but with particular policies, practices, and prison. As Rodriguez (2006) writes, "Brutality, torture, and excess should be understood as an essential element of American statecraft, not its corruption or deviation." Instead, school discipline literature has alluded to contemporary forms of policing as excessive when statistics on Black girls and school discipline (and the criminal justice system) indicate that it is endemic to the schooling experience. This does not mean that all Black girls experience school discipline, but data suggest that it may be that she is an anomaly if she has not.

Girls from the study explained that they had good school records and had no intention of leaving the school system. They were not necessarily being coerced to drop out or felt as though they were being pushed out of school. They understood their experiences at school as a symptom of being a Black female student. A respondent explains, "You're damned if you do, you're damned if you don't." Her sense of entrapment speaks to the confinement of school carcerality. While the girls did not immediately feel at risk of being "funneled" out of school into the criminal justice system, they did feel like the school's criminals.

## The Carcerality of Schools as War

In a public lecture at UC Berkeley in the spring of 2014, ethnic studies scholar Dylan Rodriguez spoke to an undergraduate class about carcerality as a form of war against Black communities and other poor communities of color. This type of war, which claims the lives of more than two million people in the United States, operates as a form of "evisceration." Under the prison regime, imprisoned bodies are made to disappear from their communities (Rodriguez 2006). Incarcerated, these bodies—mostly Black and Latinx—are removed from their families, subject to multiple forms of violence, refused access to proper health care, and denied civic and civil rights. Education scholars such as Saltman (2007) and Nguyen (2015) identify schools and their policing mechanisms as contemporary mechanisms used to train students to become agents of war who are ideologically and materially invested in the U.S. war against terror, but race and critical prison scholars such as Rodriguez (2006) and Sojoyner (2013) argue that schools have long operated as racialized sites of confinement for Black communities. That is, beyond the war on terror, schools in the United States have historically (re)produced logics and mechanisms of carcerality (and violence) that perpetually subject Black bodies to state surveillance and violence. In addition to the ways that school discipline practices may reproduce war logics and agents of war, students from this study highlight the ways that being at school is a form of war, one that aims to confine and dispossess Black kids of their culture, autonomy, and right to resist.

According to the girls' narratives, war through school discipline and the undergirding logics of carcerality position the girls as vulnerable subjects. Through school discipline there is a war against Black youth and Black girls in particular, one that perpetually attempts to control, dominate, criminalize, and punish them. Importantly, the girls' stories demonstrate their determination to resist the carcerality of U.S. schooling. Victoria refuses to surrender her right to use ChapStick or drink Gatorade. Michaela insists on navigating through structural conditions of poverty despite the ways that school discipline policies criminalize her ways of surviving. She also resists by refusing to identify with school discipline. Instead of believing that she did anything wrong by selling lunch cards, she recognizes the policies as "stupid." Similarly, Carla asserts her right to remain silent in the face of the white police officer's anger. Beyond being resilient, the girls' narratives suggest that they are creatively resistant.

As other chapters in this book demonstrate, the logic of war saturates the U.S. schooling system, curricula, and educational policies. This chapter argues that the dominant discourses on school discipline disparities obscure the connection between schools and prisons, both of which target Black communities and subject them to multiple forms of punishment. They are both institutions that uphold and enable a carceral regime that punishes, dominates, and controls its captives. According to Black girls from this study, this occurs, in part, through the school's disciplinary architecture; policies and practices including referrals, suspensions, and arrests; and disciplinary agents. As the girls' stories indicate, when they resist these conditions or act out because of them, they are deemed defiant and subsequently punished. Within this context, this study suggests that the girls' infractions, which are characterized by the school as forms of "defiance," are what Richie (1996) has called "crimes of survival." They are also resistance.

## NOTES

1. A more thorough discussion surrounding the ways that schools as carceral institutions help to enable the U.S. carceral regime is forthcoming.

2. While the study aimed to explore the experiences of all girls of color, findings from the case study school site's data demonstrated that Black girls were disproportionately represented. As a result, this chapter focuses on girls most affected by the school's disciplinary landscape.

3. Foundations High School is a pseudonym. All names have been modified to protect the identity of interviewees.

4. In 2017, I spoke on girls of color, violence, and education at the California Association for African American Superintendents and Administrators. During an important lunch plenary entitled "Mapping the School-to-Prison Pipeline," one of the main speakers highlighted the "disappearance of Black men" through the criminal justice system and discussed the disproportionate rate of school discipline for Black boys but did not mention the overrepresentation of Black girls or women in prisons or discipline data.

## REFERENCES

Advancement Project. 2011. No Child Left Behind catalyzes "school-to-prison pipeline." Washington, D.C. http://www.advancementproject.org/news/entry/press-release-no-child-left-behind-catalyzes-school-to-prison-pipeline.

Anzaldúa, G. E. 1990. *Making face, making soul: Creative and critical perspectives by feminists of color.* San Francisco: Aunt Lute Books.

California Department of Education. 2001. *Safe schools: A planning guide for action.* Sacramento: California Department of Education.

California Department of Education. 2013. *Eligibility scales for 2012–2013.* Sacramento: California Department of Education. http://www.cde.ca.gov/ls/nu/rs/scales1213.asp.

California Department of Justice. 1974. *Law in the school: A guide for California schools, safety personnel, and law enforcement.* Sacramento: California Department of Justice.

Chesney-Lind, M., and N. Jones. 2010. *Fighting for girls: New perspectives on gender and violence.* Albany: SUNY Press.

Crenshaw, K. 1995. *Critical race theory: The key writings that formed the movement.* New York: New Press.

———. 2012. From private violence to mass incarceration: Thinking intersectionally about women, race, and social control. *UCLA Law Review* 59 (6): 1418–1472.

Ferguson, A. 2001. *Bad boys: Public schools in the making of Black masculinity.* Ann Arbor: University of Michigan Press.

Foucault, M. 1977. *Discipline and punish: The birth of the prison.* New York: Vintage.

Giroux, H. 2003. Racial injustice and disposable youth in the age of zero tolerance. *International Journal of Qualitative Studies in Education* 16 (4): 553–565.

Gregory, A., D. Cornell, and X. Fan. 2011. The relationship of school structure and support to suspension rates for black and white high school students. *American Educational Research Journal* 48 (4): 904–934.

Gregory, A., R. J. Skiba, and P. A. Noguera. 2010. The achievement gap and the discipline gap: Two sides of the same coin? *Educational Researcher* 39 (1): 59–68.

Hill Collins, P. 2000. *Black feminist thought: Knowledge, consciousness, and the politics of empowerment*. New York: Routledge.

Hirschfield, P. J. 2008. Preparing for prison? The criminalization of school discipline in the USA. *Theoretical Criminology* 12 (1): 79–101.

James, J. 1996. *Resisting state violence: Radicalism, gender, and race in U.S. culture*. Minneapolis: University of Minnesota Press.

James, J., and T. D. Sharpley-Whiting. 2000. *The Black feminist reader*. New York: Wiley-Blackwell.

Kim, C., D. Losen, and D. Hewitt. 2010. *The school-to-prison pipeline: Structuring legal reform*. New York: NYU Press.

Meiners, E. R. 2011. Ending the school-to-prison pipeline/building abolition futures. *Urban Review* 43 (4): 547–565.

Mendez, L. M. R., and H. M. Knopf. 2003. Who gets suspended from school and why: A demographic analysis of schools and disciplinary infractions in a large school district. *Education and Treatment of Children* 26 (1): 30–51.

Merkwae, A. 2015. Schooling the police: Race, disability, and the conduct of school resource officers. *Michigan Journal of Race and Law* 21:147–181.

Morris, M. W. 2016. *Pushout*. New York: New Press.

Nguyen, N. 2015. Chokepoint: Regulating U.S. student mobility through biometrics. *Political Geography* 46:1–10.

Noguera, P. 2003. Schools, prisons, and social implications of punishment: Rethinking disciplinary practices. *Theory into Practice* 42 (4): 341–350.

Nolan, K. 2011. *Police in the hallways: Discipline in an urban high school*. Minneapolis: University of Minnesota Press.

Richie, B. 1996. *Compelled to crime: The gender entrapment of battered Black women*. New York: Routledge.

———. 2012. *Arrested justice: Black women, violence, and America's prison nation*. New York: NYU Press.

Roberts, D. 1997. *Killing the Black body: Race, reproduction, and the meaning of liberty*. New York: Pantheon.

Rodriguez, D. 2006. *Forced passages: Imprisoned radical intellectuals and the U.S. prison regime*. Minneapolis: University of Minnesota Press.

Saltman, K. J. 2007. *Capitalizing on disaster: Taking and breaking public schools*. Boulder, Colo.: Paradigm.

Smith, A. 2016. #BlackWomenMatter: Neo-capital punishment ideology in the wake of state violence. *Journal of Negro Education* 85 (3): 261–273.

Sojoyner, D. 2013. Black radicals make for bad citizens: Undoing the myth of the school-to-prison pipeline. *Berkeley Review of Education* 4 (2).

———. 2016. *First strike: Educational enclosures in Black Los Angeles.* Minneapolis: University of Minnesota Press.

U.S. Department of Education. 2014. Office of civil rights: Civil rights data collection. Washington, D.C.: Department of Education.

Wacquant, L. 2001. Deadly symbiosis. *Punishment and Society* 3 (1): 95–133.

Wald, J., and D. J. Losen. 2003. Defining and redirecting a school-to-prison pipeline. *New Directions for Youth Development* 99:9–15.

Welsh, W. N. 2000. The effects of school climate on school disorder. *Annals of the American Academy of Political and Social Science* 567 (1): 88–107.

Wun, C. 2014. Unaccounted foundations: Black girls, anti-Black racism, and punishment in schools. *Critical Sociology* 42 (4/5): 737–750.

# Pedagogies of Resistance: Filipina/o "Gestures of Rebellion" against the Inheritance of American Schooling

*Allyson Tintiangco-Cubales and Edward R. Curammeng*

The United States is not at war, the United States *is* war.

—SORA HAN

The relationship between the United States and the Philippines serves as a prime example of how war has shaped and continues to shape the conditions in which we live, garnered through a continuance of militaristic invasion and occupation (Buenavista and Gonzales 2011, Coloma 2009, Kramer 2006). For example, U.S. military tactics used in the Philippines in 1899 mirrors those that the United States is currently engaged in: the Iraq War, the war in Afghanistan, the war in Pakistan, Operation Ocean Shield, and most recently the war on the Islamic State. The historian Reynaldo Ileto (2005, 228) explains, "liberation by the United States, followed by granting its independence in 1946, have made the Philippines the model for Iraq." Notwithstanding these vestiges of war were numerous acts of rebellion and militant resistance (Shaw and Francia 2002). However, the pervasiveness of U.S. imperialism was and continues to be fortified through the institution of education. For Filipinas/os in particular, war is both constitutive of and instructive for what the Philippine historian Renato Constantino refers to as a "mis-education" initiated and maintained through acts of imperialism. Education and war offer insight not easily visible as their meanings shift across time and context.

This chapter draws from anti-imperialist critiques, critical race theory, and ethnic studies to situate Filipina/o Americans and education alongside historical examples of racialization. We expose moments of how Filipina/o Americans have experienced colonial coercion to maintain white supremacy and imperialism but also how they have exerted collective resistance (D. Rodriguez 2010, R. Rodriguez 2009, San Juan 1998). Our first section begins by introducing the (neo)colonial schooling apparatus in relation to the Philippines and the United States. We then turn to what Allyson Tintiangco-Cubales (2013) has termed "Pedagogies of Resistance: The Pillars of Deimperialization," which can be applied to multiple schooling contexts and move us toward a more just postimperial world. We conclude with the ways that Filipina/o American teachers have critically interrupted a bankrupt schooling system through the creation of Pin@y Educational Partnerships (PEP), an innovative ethnic studies educational counterpipeline that has nearly sixty critical educators and serves over three hundred students in San Francisco public schools annually. The teachers' narratives shared here offer insights and applications of pedagogies of resistance.

## The (Neo)Colonial Schooling Apparatus

In order to provide a clear point of departure for considering the salience of war and education in the U.S. context, in what follows we briefly explore the (neo)colonial schooling apparatus—the systemic and deliberate reinforcement of the colonial condition (Tintiangco-Cubales 2011). To underscore the reinforcement of the colonial condition is to attend to the historical moments when education and war intersect. For instance, on July 4, 1901, Independence Day celebrations in the United States commenced while across the Pacific, U.S. military forces in the Philippines were met by calculated resistance movements led by guerrilla fighters. The festivities that year were not aligned with efforts to gain compliance from Filipinas/os for a U.S.-backed governing body (Baldoz 2007, Kramer 2006). Rather, the red-, white-, and blue-strewn parades throughout the country hid a larger public relations strategy. Noam Chomsky (1986) has effectively detailed how the United States' engagement with war is driven by imperialism. He references three key players whose perspectives on war raise contradictions to the seemingly celebratory status posed back in the States. For example, General Jacob Smith commanded his troops to make the island of Samar into a "howling wilderness" and to "kill everyone over the age of ten." Nobel Peace Prize recipient President Theodore Roosevelt claimed that the murder of thousands of Filipinas/os was "for the triumph of civilization over the black chaos of savagery and barbarism." Finally, President Howard Taft remarked that "there never was a war conducted, whether against inferior races or not, in which there were more compassion and more restraint and more generosity." The growing dissatisfaction of many Americans at the U.S/Philippines relationship would arguably lay the foundation for attempts at softening the facade of war.

While the United States was proselytizing "benevolent" compliance in the Philippines, letters sent home by American soldiers fighting in the war there only contradicted what they witnessed of the U.S. occupation. How might this have been achieved—appearing to the public not to be involved in war while simultaneously maintaining and in many ways increasing militarized and political control over the islands? Three weeks after the July 4 festivities, forty-eight American teachers recruited to teach landed in the Philippines. At this moment, the schooling apparatus would gain traction, offering an outlet for U.S. imperial power, assuaging the horrors of war that anti-imperialists and others were sensing. The "great army of instruction," or Thomasites, as they were known, would increase to a thousand in just under a year (Kramer 2006), marking an innovative maneuver in how war is waged. Simply stated, this move rendered schooling a technology of war. The establishment of an American-styled education confirmed what Renato Constantino (1970) remarked: "The most effective means of subjugating a people is to capture their minds." Capture, then, was achieved in schools through multiple means: the mandate of English-only instruction, deference to American customs and values, and the installment of a white teaching force, to name a few.

American imperialism in the Philippines began with war and is sustained through war. War is thus an especially significant relational characteristic for the United States and the Philippines. From the Spanish-American and Philippine-American Wars to World War II and the current "war on terror," the Philippines has been a site of practice, policy, and experiment that has shaped how war is waged globally. Extending the legal scholar Sora Han's (2006) powerful statement that the United States *is* war, we submit that schooling is a battlefield. That is, we call into question what is at stake from the perspective that the United States is rather than is at war. Too often the perception of the United States' involvement with war is downplayed, as evidenced by Taft and Roosevelt. By viewing schooling as a battlefield, we make an intentional interrogation of schooling as a mechanism ensuring the maintenance of American imperialism. In doing so, we put pressure upon the complex relationship between U.S. imperialism, colonialism, and the *(neo)colonial schooling apparatus*—the systemic and deliberate reinforcement of the colonial condition (Tintiangco-Cubales 2011).

Building upon Louis Althusser's (1971) concept of ideological state apparatuses and the school's role in shaping hegemonic ideology, we ask: What is the United States producing through schooling? What "wars" are being waged in classrooms and communities fraught with legacies of empire and cultures of imperialism? Althusser (1971, 155) states:

> It is essential to say that for their part the Ideological State Apparatuses function massively and predominantly by ideology, but they also function secondarily by repression . . . one ideological state apparatus certainly has the dominant role, although hardly anyone lends an ear to its music; it is so silent! This is the School.

If we take seriously Althusser's notion that *the School* itself is at once positioned in a "dominant role" and at best "silent," we may also begin to consider the prevalence of war and the reticence of schooling. This includes the ways in which the (neo)colonial schooling apparatus is part and parcel of the conditions an ideology of war enables.

The (neo)colonial schooling apparatus is easily connected to a wide set of political, social, and historical forces. Vicente Rafael (2000, 21) observes, "The allegory of benevolent assimilation effaces the violence of conquest by construing colonial rule as the most precious gift that 'the most civilized people' can render to those still caught in a barbarous disorder. But instead of returning their love, Filipino 'insurgents' seemed intent on making war." Therefore, the establishment of education (or, rather, the reordering of the schooling system set up earlier by Spanish friars) allowed for the forcible and deliberate change of Filipinas/os' "L's: Life, Liberty, Labor, Language, Land, Legacy, and Love" to ensure Filipinas/os' civility (Tintiangco-Cubales 2007). The historian Dawn Bohulano Mabalon (2013, 32) writes:

> Perhaps more than any other colonial institution, the American educational system transformed the Philippines from a distant, long-neglected Spanish outpost into a full-fledged American colony. So important was "civilization"—and the pacification that Americans hoped would result from it—of the Indigenous population through public education in English that military leaders such as General William Otis established public schools and handpicked textbooks and curricula even as the war continued to rage in 1899.

The relationship between colonialism and schooling for Filipina/o Americans is characterized by the physical and psychological violence caused by the American colonial invasion of the Philippines.

Leny Strobel (2001, 27) explains, "The educational institutions during this period became an instrument for instilling the idea that American ideas, culture, and educational system were superior to the cultural and educational legacies of Spanish colonization and the Indigenous Filipino culture." The installment of colonial education and introduction of Thomasites as both a tactic of and a diversion from war added to the covert nature of American empire-building practices, making them difficult to recognize, a distinguishing characteristic of U.S. imperialism different from previous Western/European empires. U.S. empire, then, is inextricably capitalist and therefore was a manifestation of late capitalism and ultimately embedded in the project of nation building (Campomanes 1999, Coloma 2013b). Moreover, Victor Bascara (2006, 11) elaborates, "Rather than seeing the world as subject to an imperial monarch, American culture imagines itself as a shining beacon of freedom and free trade . . . the course of American empire did indeed proceed, in an effectively less formal way." Bascara's description of the "effectively less formal" process of imperialism practiced by the "unburdened empire" makes clearer how imperial policies operated in ways that allowed for colonialism to wreak the havoc it did. In this way, colonialism then and (neo)colonialism now might be considered tools of imperialism.

The (neo)colonial schooling apparatus is one such tool that remains. For Filipina/o American students in particular, the (neo)colonial schooling apparatus has material effects on their lives. "Invisibility" in history textbooks and sparse culturally relevant curricula (Coloma 2013a; Halagao, Tintiangco-Cubales, and Cordova 2009; Jocson 2008), challenges with access to postsecondary education (Buenavista 2010, Teranishi 2010), and a lack of Filipina/o American professors (Maramba and Nadal 2013) are a few of the many challenges endured. The systemic survival of U.S. imperialism manifests through the deliberate reinforcement of a (neo)colonial condition whose ideologies remain steeped in war. From the historical moments upon which education and war were synonymous to the elusiveness of the (neo)colonial schooling apparatus, what is needed is a way to resist the prevalence of U.S. imperialism in schooling through a process of deimperialization.

## *Pedagogies of Resistance: The Pillars of Deimperialization*

Imperialism did not end, did not suddenly become "past," once decolonization had set in motion the dismantling of the classical empires.

EDWARD SAID

Imperialism has had long-lasting effects on the current generation of Filipinas/os in the United States and has spawned a colonial residue so pervasive that it reproduces itself. As a result, Filipinas/os in diaspora have suffered from a colonial mentality, a psychosocial state of war resulting in a deeply rooted inferiority that has affected them regardless of geography or generation (David 2013, Enriquez 1992, Nadal 2011). The institution of education has an intimate role in the maintenance of colonized consent and "unburdened empire" and is prevalent in the Philippines, the United States, and throughout the globe. Education's neoliberal goals mask imperial ideologies through benevolent "equity" projects such as "eliminating the achievement gap." Such goals are based upon a presumption that students are to blame for their perceived deficiencies, which undermine their learning. Schooling was never designed to disrupt power relations. Rather, as described earlier in this paper, it was meant to reinforce it. Schools continue to operate with imperialist and (neo)colonial structures and practices that breed the repression of colonized peoples, including Filipinas/os.

Conversely, Filipinas/os have survived generations of what the ten-year-old Pinay and PEP student Mahalaya Tintiangco-Cubales (personal communication, June 28, 2014) named as "serial oppression," and they have incited mass movements against the injustice and abusive treachery imposed on them. Tintiangco-Cubales characterizes Filipinas/os' repeated oppressions alongside their resistances. For instance, although corporate history textbooks have centralized the "victors" of wars, resistance has always accompanied imperial legacies and the pandemic of colonial mentality. This resistance has also had long-lasting effects on what it means to be Filipina/o American.

Scholars who focus on Filipina/o American students have tackled the development of decolonization, the process toward become becoming critically conscious, and opportunities to combat colonial mentality. Leny Strobel (2001) was one of the first scholars to centralize the decolonial experiences of Filipinas/os in the United States. She provides a way to understand decolonization through the three main elements of naming, reflecting, and acting. She also delves into the "suturing of split selves" that highlights the painful effects of colonialism on identity while also shedding light on the hopefulness of decolonization. She moves further to describe how decolonization is reproduced through the telling of one's own story because it will inspire others to do the same. Through this type of telling, Roderick Daus-Magbual (2010) encourages us to value the hermeneutic relationship between one's story and one's community's past, that is, how narrative, history, and collective action converge to address past oppressions. Linda M. Pierce (2005, 37) builds on Strobel's work and writes:

> Piecing together the fragments of my own story helped me to understand the narratives of community and nation critical to colonization (and subsequently, decolonization). The politics of my identity are meaningful when understood as belonging to more than just me or my pamilya and extending beyond the life histories of my grandparents and great-grandparents into a colonial history spanning four hundred years.

Patricia Halagao (2010) also extends Strobel's work by exploring the long-lasting effects that decolonization has had on the current generation of Filipina/o American students and teachers and by examining how this can have life-changing effects on their ability to learn more deeply about themselves and participate in activism toward social change.

Alongside the powerful movement for Filipina/o decolonization, ethnic studies, critical race theory, and critical pedagogy have provided roads for Filipinas/os to resist racialization and racism. Daniel Solórzano (1997, 6) provided the five guiding principles for engaging critical race theory (CRT) research in education. These tenets help frame how racist practices and policies serve to subordinate People of Color while reifying white supremacy. The five core tenets that shape the perspectives, research methods, and pedagogy of CRT are the centrality and intersectionality of race and racism, the challenge to dominant ideology, the commitment to social justice, the centrality of experiential knowledge, and the interdisciplinary perspective. Daniel Solórzano and Dolores Delgado Bernal (2001) also developed a widely used framework of "transformational/tive resistance" that highlights resistance and refers to student behavior that illustrates both a critique of oppression and a desire for social justice.

Inspired and highly influenced by the development of CRT and transformative resistance and building on the aforementioned work on decolonization, Tintiangco-Cubales (2013) introduced the "pedagogies of resistance" as a way to guide both individual and collective liberatory action. POR begins by enacting five pillars of deimperialization.

## 1. Critiquing Empire and Its Relationship to White Supremacy, Racism, Patriarchy, and Heteropatriarchy

Pedagogies of resistance start with the principle that historic and current efforts to establish U.S. empire both in North America and throughout the globe have been inextricably connected to the systems, ideologies, policies, and manifestations of white supremacy (Coloma 2013b, Leonardo 2009). Because of imperialism, "race and racism are central, endemic, and permanent and fundamental in defining and explaining how U.S. society functions" (Yosso 2002, 3). Building on Henry Giroux's (1997, 309) call for "a space marked by dialogue and critique in which they [students of color] can engage, challenge, and rearticulate their positions by analyzing the material realities and social relations of racism," this pillar also calls for a space that will connect the material realities and social relations of racism to imperialism. In addition, imperialism becomes the purpose and reason that facilitates the intersections and interdependency between white supremacy and the systems of patriarchy and heteropatriarchy (Crenshaw 1991, Delgado Bernal 1998, Smith 2006). Acts of racism, sexism, and homophobia are manifestations of imperialism and must be resisted when authentically developing a critique of empire, just as the critique of empire and the resistance to imperialism become necessary in the fight against racism and the pursuit of freedom and justice.

## 2. Challenging Imperialist Practices on Institutional, Interpersonal, and Internalized Levels

Imperialism in our everyday practices on the institutional, interpersonal, and internalized levels needs to undergo a deep examination that forces us to hone what Patrick Camangian (2013, 119) names as "ideological literacy." The hegemony of imperialism has become so embedded in our "common sense" that we are often unaware how it has been "constructed, legitimized, and perpetuated to maintain social control through the privileging of more powerful social groups over the voices of those in positions of less power." Understanding imperialist practices as those by which everyone is implicated necessitates the need to acknowledge and think through how our participation may also be complicit in supporting, upholding, and reifying imperialist practices. We often describe our interactions with imperialism as "playing the game," but the danger is when we become so much a part of the game that we justify our dehumanizing acts as acceptable and as the norm. For example, this includes the imperial styles of leadership that have impeded the democratizing of our communities. There is a great need to implement a "Critical Leadership Praxis" that values the nexus between the growth of individual and community capacity (A. Daus-Magbual 2011). The challenge to imperialist practices interrogates how institutions develop structures that imitate imperial hierarchies (Chatterjee and Maira 2014), how we reproduce colonial relationships (Rafael 2000), and how we internalize colonial mentality (David 2011, Leonardo and Matias 2013). The challenge also goes beyond interrogation by shifting the culture of empire to cultivate what Antonio Gramsci and Cornel West have both called "organic intellectuals," to develop counterinstitutional, interpersonal, and internal practices that resist the hegemony of imperialism.

## 3. Centering and Placing a High Value on Indigenous and Historically Marginalized Knowledge

The erasure and demonization of Indigenous and historically marginalized peoples and their intellectual contributions were necessary to the success of colonization and the establishment of empire (Grande 2004, Smith 2006). To deimperialize, we must reclaim the histories, herstories, and ourstories that have been stolen, rebuild the connections that have been destroyed, and place a high value on Indigenous and similarly marginalized knowledges. The unearthing of the soul wounds—historical and intergenerational traumas so named by Duran and colleagues (1998)—of colonialism, racism, and imperialism that have been passed down from generation to generation will lead us to what Linda Tuhiwai Smith (1999) describes as decolonizing methodologies that resist imperialist practices by placing Indigenous and marginalized knowledges at the center of dialogue and teaching. Coloma (2013a, 646) asserts that "their histories and experiences of conquest, genocide, and displacement as well as resistance, resilience, and self-determination are crucial in understanding not just how empire has structured Indigenous lives, communities, cultures, and institutions, but also how Indigenous peoples have navigated within and against it." One must employ this tenet with caution, however. Processes of decolonization and deimperialization run the risk of exerting the same genocidal force upon Indigenous lands, ideas, and ways of life. Therefore, to deimperialize must not recast, appropriate, and perpetuate cultural genocide of the "Filipina/o American condition" (Rodriguez 2010) in one's attempt to learn and honor Indigenous knowledges and cultures.

## 4. Connecting Ourselves to Historical and Contemporary Resistance Movements That Struggle for Social Justice on the Global and Local Levels

Throughout the globe, there has been a long-standing history of resistance movements against imperialism and struggles for social justice (Espiritu 1992; Ho et al. 2000; Omatsu 2003a, 2003b). Locating our pedagogies as part of this legacy is necessary to develop solidarity and create linkages for deep systemic and transformative change (Maira and Shihade 2006, Spade 2011, Viola 2014). Acknowledging the many forms and acts of deimperialization also helps deessentialize activism and create stronger, more sustainable movements. We also need to put into question how we organize our communities for social change and the possibility that our methods and dogmatic tendencies can reassert the very imperialist structures we critique and work against. This by no means is claiming all structures should be denied but rather that the spotlight should be on the purpose of our structural and systematic choices. For example, engaging in critical praxis with our communities is similarly structured to the "scientific method," but the purpose is about a pursuit of social justice (Duncan-Andrade and Morrell 2008, Freire 1970). Connecting ourselves to resistance movements that struggle for social justice on both the global and local level also means that we commit to contribute our various expertise and talents to the development and livelihood of these movements.

## 5. Imagining and Building New Possibilities for Postimperial Life That Promote *Collective* Transformative Resistance, Critical Hope, and Radical Healing

Pedagogies of resistance are ultimately about imagining and building new possibilities for postimperial life that promotes radical healing and hope. A pedagogy of resistance responds to Strobel's (2000, 21) call for reconciliation and healing by "coming full circle, and finding a home and a voice of one's own." This begins with dismantling imperialist practices that get in the way of transformational resistance, which Solórzano and Delgado Bernal (2001, 319) propose "offers the greatest possibility for social change." Pedagogies of resistance build on how Solórzano and Delgado Bernal describe the possibility of individual student transformational resistance by proposing *collective transformative resistance*, where communities act with "both a critique of oppression and a desire for social justice." This is

reminiscent of Frantz Fanon's (1965, 158) push for us as colonized intellectuals to "cross back over the line" and come back to our communities
to engage in a "radical condemnation" of the imperial regime. Pedagogies
of resistance are rooted in *Kapwa*, the Sikoholiyang Pilipino core concept that means that "I am you, and you are me," or a sense of together-
ness and connectedness (Enriquez 1976).

Pedagogies of resistance also need a *collective* critical hope that demands
a committed and active struggle, which is unavoidably protracted, to fight
against what West (2004, 296–297) describes as "wealth inequality, group
xenophobia, and personal despair." This is the hope needed to rebuild our
postimperial lives. This critical hope that Jeffrey Duncan-Andrade (2009)
offers is material, Socratic, audacious, and *must be community responsive and
driven by love.* This will lead to what Shawn Ginwright (2010, 211) describes as "radical healing," a building of the "ecological imagination" and
capacity of a people to "act upon their environment to create the type of
communities in which they want to live." Pedagogies of resistance are
unequivocally committed strengthening the capacity of people to imagine and build postimperial lives that interrogate issues of power to pursue
"the possibility of collective agency and struggle."

## Gestures of Rebellion: Pedagogies of Resistance on the Ground

The pillars of deimperialization as outlined in the previous section come
together to form pedagogies of resistance. As mentioned earlier, resistance
is central to the identities of Filipinas/os in the Philippines, United States,
and global diaspora. Consider the following: The United States *is* war.
Schools are battlefields where war is waged, and the fight is between the
imperial and the colonized, white supremacy and antiracism, and dominance and resistance. These dialectical relationships began with invasion
but were inevitably met with rebellion. As Paulo Freire (2004, 55) reminds
us, "celebrate not the invasion but the rebellion against invasion."

Motivated by the spirit of ethnic studies and radical social justice movements, Filipina/o Americans have "grown their own" critical counter-
spaces, their own "gestures of rebellion" responding to the conditions set
by the (neo)colonial schooling apparatus. As a result, programs such as
Pin@y Educational Partnerships (PEP)—an ethnic studies educational
pipeline—continue to thrive, acting as models for critical deimperial education. By connecting the history of imperial vestiges to the current conditions facing Filipinas/os in U.S. education, we may begin to learn how
these "gestures of rebellion" demonstrate resistance and resilience. Explor-

ing PEP as a case study to elucidate the possibilities of postimperial life, the following section focuses primarily on how PEP implements pedagogies of resistance in its counterspace. We made a deliberate choice to look deeply at PEP's pedagogy as redefined by Tintiangco-Cubales (2010, viii):

> Pedagogy is the art of teaching and learning. Pedagogy is a philosophy of education informed by positionalities, ideologies, and standpoints. It takes into account the critical relationships between the PURPOSE of education, the CONTEXT of education, the CONTENT of what is being taught, and the METHODS of how it is taught. It also includes who is being taught, who is teaching, their relationship to each other, and their relationship to structure and power.

Building on this definition and to center "gestures of rebellion" on the expansion of empire, we look specifically at PEP's collective transformative resistance and its examples of Freire's notion of praxis to develop teachers' "capacity (and their students' capacities) to confront real-world problems that face them and their community" (Duncan-Andrade and Morrell 2008, 25).

To provide evidence of the long-lasting impact of PEP in developing critical educators, we include reflections we have collected from former PEP teachers who are currently classroom teachers. Because we consider them "organic intellectuals," not data subjects, they will be named and cited in this text just as those who are published. To show how PEP's liberatory space directly and indirectly combats schooling as a (neo)colonial apparatus, we intertwine their voices with descriptions of PEP's purpose, context, content, methods, and power.

## PEP's Purpose and Context

As a grassroots ethnic studies pipeline, PEP provides ways for students and teachers to transform the classroom into a "community" in which teachers and students serve one another and work together to respond to broader community issues and systemic problems. PEP's existence in U.S. public schools directly challenges the residue of American imperialism and colonialism while also being responsive to racism and marginalization. The former PEP teacher Evelyn Obamos states, "PEP plays a key role to unveiling these [historical] truths and the way they impact our being." The (neo)colonial schooling apparatus affects Filipinas/os American students in particular and similarly dispossessed communities in general through erasure and dehumanization. As a result, in schools with a significant concentration of Filipina/o Americans, like the schools that PEP serves, students see high rates of "pushout," depression, suicide, economic struggle, and violence in their neighborhoods and homes (Andresen 2013, FCC 2003, SAAY 2004, Tintiangco-Cubales 2013, Wolf 1997). People that view these issues from a deficit framework will blame students, their families, and their culture for their own demise rather than looking more deeply at the systemic reasons that contributed to the hardships. PEP begins with a critique of empire to understand the root causes of these issues, in order to rebuild a space that Mark Aquino, a former PEP teacher and current middle school teacher in San Francisco, describes as one that "helped me narrate my past, present, and my future." This creates more informed, sustainable, and self-determined pathways to hope and has led students, family members, community leaders, and critical educators to push back collectively on the bankrupt inheritance of schooling. In turn, grassroots and innovative solutions such as PEP have disrupted imperialist conditions.

From its birth in 2001, PEP's goals were clearly political: respond to the needs of the students it serves at Balboa High School, PEP's first school site. Along with the social and psychological challenges that Filipina/o American students faced, Filipinas/os did not see themselves in history books or virtually anywhere else in the curriculum. They rarely saw themselves in their teachers, administrators, leaders, or the media. But they could see the hate against Filipinas/os, between Filipinas/os, and within themselves. Angelique Lobo, a former PEP high school teacher and current teaching credential graduate student, describes PEP as a place that "taught me how to confront my oppression and learn how to love self." It was clear that our communities needed this type of radical change. PEP's insurgent act of deliberately placing the work within schools is a gesture of rebellion rather than reform; PEP responded to the specific needs of the community through curricular and spatial interventions not present yet imagined for the students it served. The access to significant populations of Filipina/o students allowed PEP to grow a community of educators, students, and leaders that continually disrupt the (neo)colonial schooling apparatus on a multitude of levels and beyond the scope of PEP.

As the first effort to pursue hope in their community, PEP created a mentorship program at Balboa High School with the modest objective of connecting San Francisco State University students who were taking Asian American studies and ethnic studies courses with high school students who were struggling in school. Although the mentorship proved to be a strong first move, it was not enough. Youth wanted to see themselves in their classes; they wanted to see changes in their school; they wanted to see better lives for themselves and their families and better conditions in their community. Driven by a partnership between students and PEP teachers, PEP taught its first Filipina/o American studies course at Balboa High School in the spring of 2002. More than fifteen years later, the program has expanded into an ethnic studies educational pipeline. Presently, PEP serves students on eight campuses—Balboa High School, Philip and Sala Burton High School, James Denman Middle School, Longfellow Elementary School, City College of San Francisco, Skyline College, University of San Francisco, and San Francisco State University—with more than sixty volunteer teachers and three hundred students from kindergartners to doctoral candidates. Every year, PEP sends hundreds of students to college, graduate school, and credentialing programs. PEP is proud to have graduated a record number of doctorates over the past decade, all of whom are serving our communities in social justice organizations and teaching in schools and colleges across the nation. Over the last fifteen years, twenty-three PEP alumni have entered doctorate programs across disciplines: culture and theory, education, ethnic studies, women's studies, performance studies, psychology, and sociology—ten have graduated, and thirteen are in the process of completing doctoral studies. The multiple fields and careers PEP alumni have pursued include K–12 credentialed teachers, community college instructors, school counselors, social workers, artists, and community organizers. PEP alumni are actively taking what they have learned in PEP into their own classrooms, communities, and responsibilities.

PEP's counterspace provides an opportunity where the pedagogies of resistance can be practiced, honed, and shared beyond the PEP space. Maurus Dumalaog, a former PEP teacher and current ethnic studies and drama teacher in Los Angeles, states:

> PEP is the reason I pursued teaching as my career. This community of educators has helped me define what it means to teach for social justice and the importance of actively addressing issues pertinent to the needs of our students and our schools. PEP has engrained in me a critical ethnic studies lens, which now informs every aspect of my pedagogy. . . . I refused to remain silent.

The community and culturally responsive "training" that one gets in PEP is what Jeffrey Lapitan, a former PEP coordinator and current kindergarten teacher in San Francisco, describes as "different because of the type of ownership one has on their experience of becoming an educator." *Teachers teaching teachers* and *students as teachers* are two fundamental principles of how PEP operates and directly challenges imperialist practices on the institutional, interpersonal, and internalized levels. Verma Zapanta, a former PEP coordinator and current history teacher in Los Angeles, expands on this:

> We learn more from our students than we teach them. We need to learn along with our students and be active participants in their projects and curriculum. We do not empower our students but rather support them in learning how to empower themselves. PEP teaches us how to grow our own and show students that education is accessible and that they have the agency to change the world.

The purpose of PEP goes far beyond the training of teachers; it is about providing opportunities for Filipinas/os and similarly marginalized people to come together to become self-actualized, self-determined, and humanized (A. Daus-Magbual 2011, R. Daus-Magbual 2010). Eunice Mae Lee, a former PEP coordinator and current middle school teacher, supports this by sharing that "PEP has given me a space to grow as a person, as a teacher, as well as a lifelong student." This is both an individual growth process but, as important, it is also collective, in that the purpose is directly related to community responsiveness (Tintiangco-Cubales et al. 2014). Aldrich Sabac, a former PEP elementary/high school teacher and current English teacher at his alma mater in Stockton, states, "PEP has prepared me as a teacher, as a scholar, and most importantly as a servant of my community and my people."

## PEP's Content and Method

PEP's ethnic studies curriculum and pedagogical methods are rooted in the pillars of deimperialization. The content primarily focuses on the marginalized narratives and counternarratives of Filipinas/os in the United States and draws from the history of colonialism and imperialism in the Philippines to ground the current identities of Filipina/o Americans. This in itself combats imperialism. The historian Fred Cordova profoundly states that "Everybody doesn't have to be a hero; everybody doesn't have to be famous. Each person who's Filipino American, to me, is very, very important as a story. . . . Our stories are really in our people. It's not so much in what the achievements are . . . as much as what is the story itself" (personal communication). Delving deeper into the analysis of these narratives with a critique of empire challenges the institutional, interpersonal, and internalized practices that maintain imperialism. Roderick

Daus-Magbual (2010, 126) explains, "The reflection of struggle and survival stories in PEP provides a reading to understand the current manifestation of Filipina/o American identity and the urgency to act."

PEP students from kindergarten through college get exposed to critical analysis and develop a lens that they can use in and outside of the classroom, but ultimately, the content of the PEP curriculum begins with the student and the relationship that teachers have with their students. Maurus Dumalaog, a high school drama and ethnic studies teacher in South Los Angeles, reflects upon how this has influenced who he has become as a teacher:

> In the classroom, I truly feel that PEP has prepared me to be a teacher because I have learned the importance of building meaningful relationships with students. This takes time, patience, hope, and love, but being able to humanize their experiences works wonders, especially in an environment that strongly enforces standards-based learning. PEP has definitely taught me that the student's lived experiences must be the foundation of their learning. I have learned that when students understand how curriculum is relevant to their lives, they are more likely to love learning.

Regardless if students learn about critical moments and movements in Filipina/o American studies, like the farmworker experience or the International Hotel, or if they learn about the impact of colonialism on gender, or if they are learning about the history of Filipinas/os in hip hop, the lessons must be connected to the students' and teachers' experiences for it actually to provide value. Evelyn Obamos, a former PEP teacher, points out:

> PEP has shown me an alternative approach to teaching our students' histories and herstories. PEP has also shown me that this "alternative" for more culturally relevant (responsive) pedagogy should not be an alternative. It should be the main practice.

Along with learning this critical content through community and culturally responsive approaches, PEP's curriculum and practices reflect the effectiveness of deimperializing pedagogy on the development and preparation of community-engaged social justice educators and students. Daisy Lopez, a former PEP coordinator and current elementary school teacher in San Francisco, shares:

> In PEP, community has a wider range, as we consider the classroom, school, and surrounding neighborhood all a part of the community.

With that, the "community of learners" are not confined in the classroom and have opportunities to go out into the community and learn from other educators and practitioners. The students also take what they learned and become the teachers to their own communities.

PEP's implementation of Youth Participatory Action Research (YPAR) and Teacher Participatory Action Research (TPAR) puts into practice the idea that for PEP to be relevant, the methodology must be responsive to the communities' needs. These projects have ranged from studying violence to student "pushout" and has also foregrounded the need to establish ethnic studies as a response to the disengagement of students in schools. Aileen Pagtakhan, a former PEP middle school teacher and current middle school teacher at her alma mater in Union City, expands on this:

> We know what is intrinsically wrong with the system, but sometimes we do not posses the language, tools, or theories to address the injustices. Within PEP, we name the injustices, but we also research the root of the problem to find ways to dismantle/transform/practice it. This is where our hope aspect comes from.

## PEP's *Barangay* Power

> Find your community; if you can't find one, create one.
> JEFFREY LAPITAN, FORMER PEP COORDINATOR AND CURRENT
> KINDERGARTEN TEACHER

Along with the purpose, context, content, and methods, one of the main examples of PEP's evidence of resistance is PEP's deliberate creation of a community, a *barangay*. Literally meaning one of the oldest precolonial watercrafts in the Philippines, the term *barangay* also refers to small political units in the Philippines; in essence, these are the villages and/or communities who work together to achieve their collective goals. Through the creation and establishing of barangays in the classroom, students and teachers work together to do projects, create curriculums, and tackle global, local, and personal problems. Pagtakhan proclaims, "The barangay teaching [pedagogy] prepared me that we do not do this work alone."

PEP aims to provide ways for students and teachers to transform the classroom into a "community" in which they serve one another. Eduardo Daza Taylor, a former PEP teacher, shares:

> PEP has showed me what love and support within a community looks like so that I can bring that same love and hope into the classroom.

That's what is beautiful about what we do in PEP, is that regardless of age, race, ethnicity, gender, sexuality—we are always one. Whether we are talking to our students, mentors, or colleagues, the love and hope remains the same.

PEP's barangay pedagogy begins with humanizing people that are part of your community and encouraging them to become self-determined. Furthermore, Arlene Daus-Magbual (2011, 115) states that teachers' "community action thus becomes an act towards long-term social change and personal transformation." Verma Zapanta, a high school history teacher in South Los Angeles, confides, "I've never had so many people believe that I could make something of myself, and my PEP family always believed in me . . . even when I lost hope in myself." PEP's barangay pedagogy is very much rooted in the belief that *Kapwa*, "I am you, and you are me," is central in our reimagining postimperial life. Similarly, Maurus Dumalaog describes his experience with barangay pedagogy:

PEP has offered me a community that has allowed me to develop my teaching practices, research, and presentation skills with a strong sense of humility from students and teachers both young and old. The process of "becoming" an educator can definitely be overwhelming, but in PEP, I never felt alone because we always functioned as barangays. Therefore, we "hurt" and "heal" together.

As a result of imperialism, communities are often destroyed or erased to ensure no form of rebellion to dominant power. PEP's use of barangay pedagogy at every level, from the students working together in barangays, to the teachers teaching together in barangays, to coordinators and directors working with one another and with the teachers to lead and organize PEP, has been a deliberate gesture of rebellion and one of the major strengths in PEP's resistance. Although it is difficult to maintain such a collective system within schools and institutions that operate with individualistic and hierarchal intentions, PEP's belief is that barangay pedagogy is essential to deimperialization and the imagining and building of new possibilities for postimperial life that promotes collective transformative resistance, critical hope, and radical healing.

## Conclusion

Since we began identifying how PEP enacts pedagogies of resistance and works collectively with students, teachers, and communities toward deimperialization, the necessity for pedagogies of resistance remain. The pedagogies, strategies, and practices outlined in this chapter provide tools for how to envision a liberatory education that can counter an emboldened white supremacy and the proliferation of menacing technologies of empire. This chapter responds to two challenges that education research and practice must face: first, an interrogation of the relationship between imperialism, (neo)colonialism, and war; second, the ways deimperialization and resistance respond to and work toward more just and equitable conditions for students. Informed by anti-imperialist critiques, critical race theory, and ethnic studies, we bring into conversation the ways concerted efforts and collectivized resistance to U.S. imperialism ground our approaches for dismantling the (neo)colonial schooling apparatus. We found that the radical work of critical educators in Pin@y Educational Partnerships (PEP) offers a model for ways critical communities are challenging the pervasiveness of imperialism and responding to the material effects of wars in schooling. As war becomes normalized and the devastation of communities of color in the United States and beyond persists, working toward deimperialization is most urgent. Paulo Freire reminds us, "The future belongs to the Peoples, not to the Empires."

## REFERENCES

Althusser, L. 1971. Ideology and ideological state apparatuses (notes towards an investigation). In *Lenin and philosophy and other essays, 1971–1972*. New York: Monthly Review Press.

Andresen, T. 2013. Knowledge construction, transformative academic knowledge, and Filipino American identity and experience. In *The "other" students: Filipino Americans, education, and power*, ed. D. Maramba and R. Bonus, 65–87. Charlotte, N.C.: Information Age Publishing.

Baldoz, R. 2011. *The third Asiatic invasion: Migration and empire in Filipino America, 1898–1946*. New York: NYU Press.

Bascara, V. 2006. *Model-minority imperialism*. Minneapolis: University of Minnesota Press.

———. 2014. New empire, same old university?: Education in the American tropics after 1898. In *The imperial university: Academic repression and scholarly dissent*, ed. P. Chatterjee and S. Maira, 53–77. Minneapolis: University of Minnesota Press.

Bell, D. 1992. *Faces at the bottom of the well: The permanence of racism*. New York: Basic Books.

Buenavista, T. L. 2010. Issues affecting U.S. Filipino student access to postsecondary education: A critical race theory perspective. *Journal of Education for Students Placed at Risk* 15 (1/2): 114–126.

Buenavista, T. L., and J. B. Gonzales. 2011. DREAMs deterred: Filipino experiences and an antimilitarization critique of the development, relief, and education for Alien Minors Act. *Harvard Journal of Asian American Policy Review* 20:29–39.

Camangian, P. R. 2013. Seeing through lies: Teaching ideological literacy as a corrective lens. *Equity and Excellence in Education* 46 (1): 119–134.

Campomanes, O. V. 1999. 1898 and the nature of the new empire. *Radical History Review* 73:130–146.

Chatterjee, P., and S. Maira, eds. 2014. *The imperial university: Academic repression and scholarly dissent.* Minneapolis: University of Minnesota Press.

Chomsky, N. 1986. Visions of righteousness. *Cultural Critique* 3:10–43.

Coloma, R. S. 2009. "Destiny has thrown the Negro and the Filipino under the tutelage of America": Race and curriculum in the age of empire. *Curriculum Inquiry* 39 (4): 495–519.

———. 2013a. Empire: An analytical category for educational research. *Educational Theory* 63 (6): 639–658.

———. 2013b. Invisible subjects: Filipina/os in secondary history textbooks. In *The "other" students: Filipino Americans, education, and power,* ed. D. Maramba and R. Bonus, 165–183. Charlotte, N.C.: Information Age Publishing.

Constantino, R. 1970. The mis-education of the Filipino. *Journal of Contemporary Asia* 1 (1): 20–36.

Crenshaw, K. 1993. Mapping the margins: Intersectionality, identity politics, and the violence against Women of Color. *Stanford Law Review* 43:1241–1299.

Daus-Magbual, A. 2011. Courageous hope: Critical leadership praxis of Pin@y Educational Partnerships. Ed.D. diss. San Francisco State University.

Daus-Magbual, R. 2010. Political, emotional, and powerful: The transformative influence of Pin@y Educational Partnerships (PEP). Ed.D. diss. University of San Francisco.

David, E. J. R. 2011. *Filipino-American postcolonial psychology: Oppression, colonial mentality, and decolonization.* Bloomington, Ind.: AuthorHouse.

———. 2013. *Brown skin, white minds: Filipino-/American postcolonial psychology.* Charlotte, N.C.: Information Age Publishing.

Delgado, R., and J. Stefancic. 2012. *Critical race theory: An introduction.* New York: NYU Press.

Delgado Bernal, D. 1998. Using a Chicana feminist epistemology in educational research. *Harvard Educational Review* 68 (4): 555–582.

Duncan-Andrade, J. M. 2009. Note to educators: Hope required when growing roses in concrete. *Harvard Educational Review* 79 (2): 181–194.

Duncan-Andrade, J. M., and E. Morrell. 2008. *The art of critical pedagogy: Possibilities from moving from theory to practice in urban schools.* New York: Peter Lang.

Duran, E., B. Duran, M. Y. H. Brave Heart, and S. Y. Horse. 1998. Healing the American Indian soul wound. In *International handbook of multigenerational legacies of trauma,* ed. Y. Danieli, 341–354. New York: Plenum.

Enriquez, V. G. 1976. Sikolohiyang Pilipino: Perspektibo at Direksiyon. In *Ulat ng Unang Pambansang Kumperensiya sa Sikolohiyang Pilipino,* ed. L. F. Antonio et al., 221–243. Quezon City: Pambansang Samahan sa Sikolohiyang Pilipino.

———. 1978. Kapwa: A core concept in Filipino social psychology. *Philippine Social Science and Humanities Review* 42 (14): 100–108.

———. 1992. *From colonial liberation to liberation psychology: The Philippine experience.* Manila: De La Salle University Press.

Espiritu, Y. 1992. *Asian American panethnicity: Bridging institutions and identities.* Philadelphia: Temple University Press.

Fanon, F. 1965. *The wretched of the earth.* Vol. 2. New York: Grove.

Filipina/o Community Center of the Excelsior. 2005. A community needs assessment: An unpublished report on Filipinas/os in the Excelsior District of San Francisco, California.

Francia, L. 2010. *A history of the Philippines: From Indio Bravos to Filipinos.* New York: Overlook.

Freire, P. 1970. *Pedagogy of the oppressed.* New York: Continuum.

———. 2004. *Pedagogy of indignation.* Boulder, Colo.: Paradigm.

Ginwright, S. A. 2010. A radical healing approach for Black young men: A framework for policy and practice. In *Changing places: How communities will improve the health of boys of color,* ed. C. Edley and J. Ruiz de Velasco. Berkeley: Berkeley Law/University of California Press.

Grande, S. 2004. *Red pedagogy: Native American social and political thought.* Lanham, Md.: Rowman & Littlefield.

Halagao, P. E. 2010. Liberating Filipino Americans through decolonizing curriculum. *Race, Ethnicity, and Education* 13 (4): 495–512.

Halagao, P. E., A. Tintiangco-Cubales, and J. M. T. Cordova. 2009. Critical review of K–12 Filipina/o American curriculum. *AAPI Nexus: Asian Americans and Pacific Islanders Policy, Practice, and Community* 7 (1): 1–24.

Giroux, H. 1997. Racial politics and the pedagogy of whiteness. In *Whiteness: A critical reader,* ed. M. Hill, 294–315. New York: NYU Press.

Han, S. Y. 2006. Bonds of representation: Vision, race, and law in post–civil rights America. Ph.D. diss. University of California, Santa Cruz.

Ho, F., C. Antonio, D. Fujino, and S. Yip. 2000. *Legacy to liberation: Politics and culture of revolutionary Asian Pacific America.* San Francisco: AK Press.

Ileto, R. C. 2005. Philippine wars and the politics of memory. *Positions: East Asia Cultures Critique* 13 (1): 215–235.

Jocson, K. M. 2008. Kuwento as multicultural pedagogy in high school ethnic studies. *Pedagogies: An International Journal* 3 (4): 241–253.

Kramer, P. 2006. *The blood of government: Race, empire, the United States, and the Philippines.* Chapel Hill: University of North Carolina Press.

Leonardo, Z. 2009. *Race, whiteness, and education.* New York: Routledge.

Leonardo, Z., and C. Matias. 2013. Betwixt and between colonial and postcolonial mentality: The critical education of Filipino Americans. In *The "other" students: Filipino Americans, education, and power*, D. Maramba and R. Bonus, 1–19. Charlotte, N.C.: Information Age.

Mabalon, D. B. 2013. *Little Manila is in the heart: The making of the Filipina/o American community in Stockton, California.* Durham, N.C.: Duke University Press.

Maira, S., and M. Shihade. 2006. Meeting Asian/Arab American studies: Thinking race, empire, and Zionism in the U.S. *Journal of Asian American Studies* 9 (2): 117–140.

Maramba, D., and K. Nadal. 2013. Exploring the Filipino American faculty pipeline: Implications for higher education and Filipino American college students. In *The "other" students: Filipino Americans, education, and power*, ed. D. Maramba and R. Bonus, 297–308. Charlotte, N.C.: Information Age.

Nadal, K. 2011. *Filipino American psychology: A handbook of theory, research, and clinical practice.* Hoboken, N.J.: John Wiley & Sons.

Obama, B. 2014. Remarks by President Obama and President Benigno Aquino III of the Philippines in joint press conference. Speech presented at Malacañang Palace, Manila, Philippines, April.

Omatsu, G. K. 2003a. The "four prisons" and the movements of liberation: Asian American activism from the 1960s to the 1990s. In *Asian American politics: Law, participation, and policy*, ed. D. T. Nakanishi and J. S. Lai, 135–162. Lanham, Md.: Rowman & Littlefield.

———. 2003b. Freedom schooling: Reconceptualizing Asian American studies for our communities. *Amerasia Journal* 29 (2): 9–34.

Pierce, L. M. 2005. Not just my closet: Exposing familial, cultural, and imperial skeletons. In *Pinay power: Theorizing the Filipina/American experience*, ed. M. de Jesús, 31–44. New York: Routledge.

Rafael, V. 2000. *White love and other events in Filipino history.* Durham, N.C.: Duke University Press.

Rodriguez, D. 2010. *Suspended apocalypse: White supremacy, genocide, and the Filipino condition.* Minneapolis: University of Minnesota Press.

Rodriguez, R. M. 2010. *Migrants for export: How the Philippine state brokers labor to the world.* Minneapolis: University of Minnesota Press.

Said, E. W. 1993. *Culture and imperialism*. New York: Knopf.

San Juan, E., Jr. 1998. *From exile to diaspora: Versions of the Filipino experience in the United States*. Boulder, Colo.: Westview.

———. 2007. *U.S. Imperialism and revolution in the Philippines*. New York: Palgrave Macmillan.

Services and Advocacy for Asian Youth (SAAY) Consortium. 2004. Moving beyond exclusion: Focusing on the needs of Asian/Pacific Islander youth in San Francisco. http://www.policyarchive.org/handle/10207/bitstreams/5970.pdf.

Shaw, A. V., and L. Francia, eds. 2002. *Vestiges of war: The Philippine-American War and the aftermath of an imperial dream, 1899–1999*. New York: NYU Press.

Smith, A. 2006. Heteropatriarchy and the three pillars of white supremacy. In *The Color of Violence: The Incite Anthology*, ed. Incite! Women of Color against Violence, 66–73. Cambridge, Mass.: South End.

Smith, L. T. 1999. *Decolonizing methodologies: Research and Indigenous peoples*. London: Zed.

Solórzano, D. G. 1997. Images and words that wound: Critical race theory, racial stereotyping, and teacher education. *Teacher Education Quarterly* 24:5–19.

Solórzano, D. G., and D. D. Bernal. 2001. Examining transformational resistance through a critical race and LatCrit theory framework Chicana and Chicano students in an urban context. *Urban Education* 36 (3): 308–342.

Solórzano, D. G., and T. Yosso. 2002. A critical race counterstory of race, racism, and affirmative action. *Equity and Excellence in Education* 35 (2): 155–168.

Spade, D. 2011. *Normal life: Administrative violence, critical trans politics, and the limits of law*. Brooklyn, N.Y.: South End.

Strobel, L. M. 2001. *Coming full circle: The process of decolonization among post-1965 Filipino Americans*. Quezon City, Philippines: Giraffe.

Teranishi, R. T. 2002. Asian Pacific Americans and critical race theory: An examination of school racial climate. *Equity and Excellence in Education* 35 (2): 144–154.

Tintiangco-Cubales, A. 2007. *Pin@y educational partnerships: A Filipina/o American studies sourcebook series*. Vol. 1: *Philippine and Filipina/o American history*. Santa Clara, Calif.: Phoenix Publishing House International.

———. 2009. *Pin@y educational partnerships: A Filipina/o American studies sourcebook series*. Vol. 2: *Filipina/o American identities, activism, and service*. Santa Clara, Calif.: Phoenix Publishing House International.

———. 2011. Growing our own hope: Transforming youth to become critical educators in their community. Paper presented at the annual meeting of the American Educational Research Association, New Orleans, La.

———. 2013. Pain + love = growth: What kind of ethnic studies really serves Students of Color? Paper presented at the annual meeting of the American Educational Research Association, San Francisco.

Tintiangco-Cubales, A., P. N. C. Kiang, and S. D. Museus. 2010. Praxis and power in the intersections of education. *AAPI Nexus: Asian Americans and Pacific Islanders Policy, Practice, and Community* 8 (1): v–xviii.

Tintiangco-Cubales, A., R. Kohli, J. Sacramento, et al. 2014. Toward an ethnic studies pedagogy: Implications for K–12 schools from the research. *Urban Review* 47 (1): 104–125.

Tiongson, A. T., Jr. 2006. On Filipinos, Filipino Americans, and U.S. imperialism: Interview with Oscar V. Campomanes. In *Positively no Filipinos allowed: Building communities and discourse*, ed. A. T. Tiongson et al., 26–42. Philadelphia: Temple University Press.

Viola, M. 2014. Toward a Filipino critical pedagogy: Exposure programs to the Philippines and the politicization of Melissa Roxas. *Journal of Asian American Studies* 17 (1): 1–30.

West, C. 2004. The impossible will take a little while. In *The impossible will take a little while: A citizen's guide to hope in a time of fear*, ed. P. Rogat, 293–297. New York: Basic Books.

Wolf, D. L. 1997. Family secrets: Transnational struggles among the children of Filipina/o immigrants. *Sociological Perspectives* 40 (3): 457–483.

# Of Boxes and Pen: Forged and Forging Racial Categories at a Wartime U.S. University

## Maryam S. Griffin

*Maz Jobrani was talking to his high school counselor one day when she delivered some bad news: He was white.*

*At first, he tried to deny it. Jobrani had brown skin, and his parents spoke with a Persian accent. Strangers called him "sheikh" and "towel-head." He was living in the San Francisco Bay area during the Iranian hostage crisis in the early 1980s and would occasionally hear, "Go home, Iranian."*

*But the evidence for his whiteness was plain to see. When Jobrani looked at college applications in his counselor's office, he saw no racial category for Iranians. "That's because you're white," his counselor explained as she instructed him to check the box marked "white."*

*"I told her, 'What do you mean, white? I've been going through all this crap, all this ribbing and teasing for years, and I've been white all this time? You should have told me earlier.'"*

—JOHN BLAKE (2010)

In 2009, a group of Arab, Iranian, and Afghan students at the University of California–Los Angeles began organizing the "IM In Campaign" to assert their critical consciousness of the racial regime that interpellates them. Their efforts aimed to change the way they were formally racially identified on the University of California admissions application as "white," instead demanding the creation of a separate SWANA (Southwest Asian or North African) box. In recognizing their shared social position, the students noted that the "white" box reflected the racial valence of an imperial "Americanness" defined, in part, by their political and cultural exclusion. At the same time, representation within the box schema was understood as necessary to access an alternative notion of Americanness, one characterized by visible multiculturalism. Accordingly, the box schema became a key locus for the students' negotiations of social marginality, liberal multiculturalism, and urgent political solidarities. Furthermore, participation in the campaign allowed the students to build a multiethnic space in which, together, they developed social identities out of their political commitments.

The context in which the IM In Campaign unfolded was defined primarily by the policies, practices, and cultural products of the United States in the era of the "War on Terror" under presidents George W. Bush and Barack Obama. On the one hand, many social institutions rendered people of SWANA descent hypervisible as a looming threat, perpetuating stereotypes of Arabs, Iranians, and Muslims as fanatical, belligerent, uncivilized, misogynistic, deceitful, and menacing (Bayoumi 2008, Jamal and Naber 2008, Love 2009, Maira 2009, Puar and Rai 2002, Tehranian 2010, Volpp 2002). These messages circulated through the media, including wildly popular TV shows (*24*, *NCIS*, *Homeland*), films (*Zero Dark Thirty*, *Argo*, *The Kingdom*), and flamboyant talk show personalities (Bill Maher, Glenn Beck, Bill O'Reilly, etc.). They also inflected the statements of public officials across the political spectrum (Kumar 2012, 59), from First Lady Laura Bush's famous 2001 speech justifying the military invasion of Afghanistan as "a fight for the rights and dignity of women" to presidential hopeful Hillary Clinton's 2016 debate remarks in which she reduced all Muslim Americans to "our eyes and ears on our front lines [of Homeland Security]."[1]

While pernicious stereotypes of SWANA and Muslim people became hypervisible during this period, the actual experiences and struggles of these communities remained far less so. Two interrelated dynamics produced this invisibility, particularly during the Bush II and Obama years. The first was a cultural espousal of colorblindness (or "postracialism," the slightly modified version that emerged under Obama; see Haney-López 2010). As others have argued, colorblindness does little to address injustice substantively; rather, it focuses on the appearance of racist intent and rejects overt discussions of race (Crenshaw 1998, Gotanda 1991). It prioritizes the rhetorical presentation of race neutrality and wrongly qualifies the appearance of such neutrality as a valid defense against charges of racism (Peery 2011). The hegemony of colorblindness made it difficult for any communities of color to express their grievances without contravening implied imperatives to avoid any mentions of race. This was particularly true for SWANA people trying to testify to their experiences with racism by harnessing existing racial discourses and schemas.

In addition to the hurdles imposed by colorblindness and multiculturalism, another dynamic also reproduced SWANA invisibility. Despite their demonization in the realms of culture and politics, U.S. Americans of Southwest Asian or North African heritage have not been consistently, officially recognized as belonging to a nonwhite racial group. According to a racial classificatory regime that was informed by historical immigration restrictions, court cases, and shifting U.S. Census categories, Arabs and Iranians have been legally labeled "white" in the United States since 1915 and have been joined in the "white" box by people of other Middle Eastern and South Asian ancestry over the course of the intervening century (Aidi 2014, Gualtieri 2009, Tehranian 2008).

As a result of both colorblindness and the prevailing U.S. racial schema, then, SWANA Americans occupy a peculiar position as nominally included but substantively excluded from whiteness. This dissonance exacerbates the representation gap, creating a condition in which social problems experienced by SWANA people, for example, racial discrimination and underrepresentation, cannot be redressed. The Arab American activist Ray Hanania articulates this logic simply: "How can we be discriminated against when we're white?" (Aidi 2014, 170). The lived experiences of many SWANA people in the United States attest to the inaccuracy of the white label. For example, the Jobrani interview used as this chapter's epigraph exposes the absurdity of official, nominal whiteness during a time when Iranian and other SWANA Americans were targeted not only by bigoted "ribbing and teasing" from suspicious neighbors but also by coercive state policies of documentation, detention, and deportation. These policies have enjoyed a resurgence in the decade and a half since the terrorist attacks of 9/11 (Cainkar 2009, Cole and Lobel 2009, Hassan 2002).

The contradictions between SWANA Americans' lived experiences and their official racial whiteness have motivated activists to attempt to revise the racial categories of the U.S. Census (Love 2009; Samhan 1987, 1999). The U.S. War on Terror brought these contradictions to the fore, causing SWANA Americans to feel dislocated from the representational regime that disciplines social understandings of race. In turn, these contradictions opened up space for SWANA political organizing to expose the limitations of prevailing notions of race as a mask for power relations and at the same time to participate directly in their remaking. In advance of the 2010 U.S. Census, national campaigns emerged to urge Arab and Iranian Americans to "Check It Right," that is, mark the "other race" box instead of "white" (Blake 2010). This activism was met with ambivalence across various SWANA communities, who raised concerns that formal nonwhite identification would make government surveillance, suspicion, and harassment easier (Aidi 2014). Still, recent reports indicate that the U.S. Census Bureau is seriously considering adding a "Middle Eastern or North African" racial category to the 2020 Census, among other changes (Chow 2016, Cohn 2015).

I have bracketed the period from 2001 to 2016 for discussion to distinguish it expressly from the developments that have followed. I do not mean to draw a stark line between 2016 and 2017, as of course the "War on Terror" has not ended, but rather to mark the culmination of a gradual process. During this period, a national anxiety emerged out of the contradictory combination of two fears in the United States: the fear (and hatred) of Middle Easterners and Muslims and the simultaneous fear of appearing racist (under the hegemony of colorblindness). This anxiety found its fullest expression in the ascent of Donald Trump to popular political figure and ultimately to the U.S. presidency. Trump's ascendance was predicated not only on popular promises to register all existing Muslims in the country and ban any new ones from coming in; it was also based on his widely celebrated refusal to capitulate to so-called political correctness, choosing instead to "tell it like it is." In other words, whatever continuities might exist between Obama's and Trump's "War on Terror"–related military and immigration policies, the apparently fragile hegemony of liberal colorblindness has been thrown into crisis in the transition. Perversely, these recent developments might make it easier for SWANA Americans to achieve official nonwhite status while simultaneously making such a status more dangerous and less desirable. As such, the research presented in this chapter must be considered within the specific cultural and political context in which the IM In Campaign occurred (2009–2013).

In this chapter, I analyze a portion of interview data I gathered over the course of six months from 2009 to 2010 and follow-up research I conducted sporadically from 2010 to 2013. During the initial data-gathering period, I conducted semistructured, one-on-one interviews with ten students who were involved in or supportive of the IM In Campaign at UCLA. As an Arab American graduate student at the time and UCLA alumna, I engaged in participant observation at four organizers' meetings that were generally attended by six to eight students and attended the meeting of the Arab student group when the initiative was originally introduced to the membership, which twenty students attended. With their permission, I also interacted informally with my interview participants via social media. Between 2010 and 2013, I arranged follow-up conversations with one of the main organizers, Ghassan, who updated me as the campaign spread to UC Berkeley and other UC campuses before finally achieving success at the system-wide level in 2013.

My analysis proceeds by highlighting four of the themes that emerged during my interactions with the student organizers and supporters of the campaign. First, I introduce the IM In Campaign, describe its various activities and phases, and discuss its motivation to address the status of SWANA students as an "invisible minority." I then present the students' explanations of their categorical exclusion from racial whiteness and the connection between their nonwhiteness and hostile U.S. foreign policy in the SWANA regions. Next, I trace the conversations and debates involved in crafting the specific SWANA box schema that the students ultimately requested. In the fourth section, I discuss the way that "Americanness" is coded by a particular brand of multiculturalism that presently excludes, or at best ignores, SWANA people. It is this multicultural dimension of "Americanness" that opens up space for the students' bid for inclusion. Finally, I offer brief suggestions as to how the complex insights of the student organizers might guide university educators who work with student activists during wartime.

By organizing directly to address the contradictions of the racial regime, the SWANA students exposed the forgeries used to categorize them while simultaneously forging their own representation in the same schema. Their organizing offers two important insights into the way war provides the setting for a partial unmasking of racial regimes. First, the context of the wartime university, which reflects grave transnational social processes in a microcosm manageable to students, opens up a unique opportunity both to expose the contradictions of the prevailing racial regime and to forge alternative racial formations in the gap. This is a particularly invaluable chance for educators to tap into their students' already fluid understandings of race to illuminate even more nuance and complexity, grounded in the concrete consequences of racialization around the globe. Furthermore, the student organizers featured in this research explicitly articulated the intertwining of foreign policy and domestic racial formations, highlighting the fundamentally global nature of the U.S. racial regime. In other words, the wartime context not only opens up space for sophisticated education about race but also demands that such education grapple with the global dimensions of racial projects. Taken together, these two insights indicate the simultaneous inadequacy and relevance of contemporary racial categorization schemas and the challenges facing students and educators who must engage them.

## *The IM In Campaign*

In 2009, a group of UCLA student organizers launched the IM In Campaign to advocate for the addition of an ethnicity box labeled "Southwest

Asian and North African" (SWANA) on the University of California admissions application. The students involved in the campaign represented Arab, Iranian, Afghan, Armenian, and Assyrian ethnicities and Druze, Baha'i, Christian, Shi'a, and Sunni Muslim religious identities. Spearheaded by the leaders of the Iranian Student Group, the Arab Student Group, and the United Afghan Club, the campaign contested the invisibility of SWANA-American experiences of subordination and struggles for justice.

The IM In Campaign sought specifically to alter the portion of the UC admissions application that requests racial and ethnic data for statistical use. After completing the application, each prospective student is prompted to fill out an anonymous demographic survey that includes two questions about their race or ethnicity.[2] The first of these questions is generated by the U.S. Department of Education, the second by the University of California. The UC question presents a more complex schema than the federal one, whose specifics are beyond the scope of this essay but are included in Appendix A. In 2010, the UC question presented a core of umbrella racial groups, each followed by a list of subcategories that track national or ethnic divisions: "African American/Black," "American Indian/Alaskan Native," "Asian/Asian American," "Hispanic/Latino," "Pacific Islander," and "White/Caucasian." This schema is reproduced in full in Appendix B. The White/Caucasian umbrella category included the subgroups "European/European descent," "Middle Eastern/Middle Eastern descent," "North African," and "other white/Caucasian, please specify." The IM In Campaign's schema devised a "Southwest Asian and North African" (SWANA) box for "Middle Eastern/Middle Eastern descent" and "North African" students to select instead of "White/Caucasian." The SWANA umbrella category would then be followed by thirty-four subcategories—Afghan, Algerian, Armenian, Assyrian/Chaldean, Azerbaijani, Bahraini, Berber, Circassian, Djiboutian, Egyptian, Emirati, Georgian, Iranian, Iraqi, Israeli, Jordanian, Kurdish, Kuwaiti, Lebanese, Libyan, Mauritanian, Moroccan, Omani, Palestinian, Qatari, Saudi Arabian, Somali, Sudanese, Syrian, Tunisian, Turkish, Yemeni, Other North African, and Other Southwest Asian. Appendix C presents the SWANA box as eventually adopted by the UC Office of the President and as it appeared on the 2016 UC application form.

Beginning in 2009, the student-led campaign focused on developing the specifics of the SWANA box schema and on gaining support from students whom the box would affect, other allies, and the UCLA student body. The campaign proceeded in several phases. First, the aforementioned identity-based organizations introduced the idea of the box and the importance of this alternative representation to their memberships separately and also held cross-organizational forums. Members from the different organizations who were particularly interested in working on the campaign began to meet to discuss the specifics—what box schema to propose, why it was important, how to conduct outreach to their memberships, and how to convince the UC administration.

Once the organizers had met and developed the representational schema of their choice, it was presented to the student government on campus, while the campaign organizers made efforts to involve analogous identity groups at other UC campuses. Eventually, the UCLA student government passed the resolution. Meanwhile, the idea gained support at UC Berkeley after one of the UCLA student leaders made concerted outreach efforts. By April 2013, student governments at five of the UC campuses—Irvine, Davis, Los Angeles, Berkeley, and San Diego—had voted to support a separate SWANA box on the UC admissions application. In late May 2013, a representative of the UC Office of the President announced that the SWANA schema would be adopted on the admissions application, beginning with the 2013–2014 admissions cycle (Hafner 2013).

The "IM" in the name of the original campaign was an acronym for "Invisible Minority." This particular name seems to have been a fleeting creation of the early 2009–2010 UCLA organizers; it did not last very long or spread beyond the campus. For example, once the initiative reached Berkeley, its name appears to have become simply the "SWANA Campaign" (Yoder 2013). I use IM In here for ease of reference because it was the name the organizers were using at the time that I conducted my fieldwork. Moreover, the word choice "invisible minority" is interesting in its own right and key in understanding one of the central motivating factors of the student organizers: to claim visibility on their own terms.

The students who supported the addition of the SWANA box believed that their lived experiences of marginalization would be validated through official recognition as nonwhite. Furthermore, during the course of their campaign, the students articulated a nonwhite identity that they saw as conditioning the possibility for American cultural citizenship. As formally "white," many students felt that their specific experiences of discrimination were rendered invisible, making it difficult to assess the scope of the problem or demand redress. As stated in a UCLA student government resolution supporting the campaign: "Because of the lack of representation in the United States, the Middle Eastern community has formed into an 'invisible' minority, or a minority group that faces issues similar to other minority groups (such as a lack of access to resources and low socio-economic status) but does not receive recognition as such" (El-Farra et al. 2012). For this reason, the SWANA student organizers believed that their absorption into the U.S. racial landscape could only be accomplished through their categorization as nonwhite and specifically as SWANA.

The crux of the IM In Campaign can be understood as a creative and critical intervention into the current U.S. "racial regime," or the prevailing organization and representation of racial power. In writing about the creation of Black stereotypes in theater and film from the sixteenth to the mid–twentieth centuries, Cedric Robinson (2007) deployed the concept of "forgeries" to explain the functioning of racial regimes. The forgery is found in the way that power hierarchies masquerade as natural facts under a cloak of racial essentialism. Race appears to be fundamentally biological and culturally unchanging, composed of categories rooted in fixed corporeal realities and historical lineages. As a result, racial regimes characterize the misery of social hierarchy as the inevitable consequence of natural, historical constellations. The forgery, then, is a convenient disciplinary tool to diffuse opposition to power hierarchies because it is difficult to resist something that presents itself as natural. This leads Robinson to warn that "racial regimes are unrelentingly hostile to their exhibition" (xii). The exposure of contradictions, contrivances, and deficiencies within racial regimes amounts to a powerful step toward their undoing because it reveals that racial hierarchies are not a natural fact but rather a cynical fabrication created to organize the very social dynamics it presents as natural and inevitable.

The students of the IM In Campaign identified the forgeries of the prevailing racial regime of the time, seizing upon its internal contradictions to expose the underlying power relations it attempted to mask. Yet this unmasking was only partial, as the organizers chose to "play along," proposing their own forged category as a way to remedy the contradiction and benefit from the (reorganized) regime itself. Their approach and success demonstrate the limitations and enduring relevance of racial representational regimes as the raw material for exposure and engagement of racialized power dynamics at a wartime public university. By authoring the terms of their own racial recognition, the student organizers refuted the naturalizing myth that race is essential and transhistorical while simultaneously using the vocabulary of race to claim belonging in the current racial regime.

## A Forgery Exposed

In the organizing meetings I attended and interviews I conducted, the student participants of the IM In Campaign routinely asserted their non-white identification. Rima, a twenty-two-year-old Muslim woman who emigrated to the United States from Iraq when she was four years old, insisted that she was nonwhite because she had not lived "the life of a white person in this country." She prioritized racial justice and antiwar activism in her description of her extracurricular involvement. When asked to clarify her statement that "obviously our experiences are different than the experiences of the average Caucasian child in America," Rima highlighted the racism that she experienced as an Arab American and outsider within the American racial regime:

> Well I think we have to face things like racism more than they do. Like being judged by how you look or where you come from or where your parents come from, the fact that they're immigrants, the fact that . . . your grandparents were immigrants and might not be citizens. We get judged for that kind of stuff. But the average Caucasian kid doesn't because their parents have been here or their families have been here for hundreds of years. So our experience is different than theirs.

The experience of racism to which Rima alluded is tied to a state of national nonbelonging, an exclusion from the hegemonic conception of "Americanness" that is defined by racial whiteness.

The co-constitution of whiteness and Americanness produces the American nation as a bastion of whiteness (Horsman 1981), and this dynamic manifests especially in times of war (De Genova 2006). George Lipsitz (2006, 72) argues that war-related racisms, which characterize as racially inferior each new "enemy" group on whom the United States wages war, "depend upon the assumption that true cultural franchise and full citizenship require a white identity." The anti-Indian, anti-Black, anti-Latino, anti-Asian, and anti–Middle Eastern racisms generated by continental expansion and overseas conflicts together intensify the identity between Americanness and whiteness in wartime. These processes, in turn, shape the cultural dimensions of national belonging, which are always inflected by race, national origin, gender, class, and religion (Maira 2009, 80). Lisa Parks (2005, 5) explains that cultural citizenship also communicates behavioral expectations that are different across groups defined by social markers, such as race and gender. In other words, the cultural dimensions of citizenship define and restrict the ways that people of color engage with and experience the power of the state. Against this backdrop, the IM In Campaign sought a kind of inclusion into cultural citizenship based on their exclusion from American whiteness.

## NONWHITENESS AND POLITICAL ACTIVITY

In explaining their exclusion from whiteness, the SWANA students corroborated these repressive dynamics, citing restrictions they have experienced from full participation in politics and in particular from exercising a right to political dissent on issues of American foreign policy. One dimension of this experience of exclusion revolves around the silencing, misrepresentation, or stigmatization of political positions that are sympathetic to Arab and Muslim causes. Many of my respondents characterized pro-Palestinian and antiwar positions as central to their identities. Rima linked her political commitments to her family background and influence:

> I think if I were white, I probably wouldn't be involved in this because I don't feel like I'd have a personal stake. . . . I wouldn't come from a family that . . . always talked about these things—the U.S. in Iraq, Israel and Palestine. So I've grown up with this awareness of the government and the bad things it can do.

Many of the students I interviewed were aware that specifically pro-Palestinian activism or the mere expression of pro-Palestinian sympathies stigmatized them. Because U.S. public discourse about the Palestinian liberation struggle is so restricted, the students understood that their pro-Palestinian politics were considered unpopular or even dangerous by the mainstream.[3] Therefore, an intrinsic part of their political selves, which they explicitly tied to their heritage, excluded them from the prevailing notion of acceptable American civic participation.

At the time of our first interview, Ghassan was completing his second month at UCLA, after transferring from a community college in the San Francisco area. His brother Ayman was one of the original organizers of the IM In Campaign, and Ghassan eventually took the lead after Ayman graduated. Ghassan and his family emigrated from Syria when he was twenty months old, but he still feels a strong connection to Arab culture and politics, which he credited to his close family relationship and his involvement with an Arabic-language school in the Bay Area as a child. He and his brother also proudly identified themselves as the descendants of a famous anticolonial Syrian revolutionary of the early twentieth century.

Ghassan identified a racially specific form of political repression as characteristic of the Arab American experience—that being Arab and openly pro-Palestinian may be met with police harassment—by relating the experiences of friends in the Bay Area:

> I . . . have friends in low-income areas, like the Mission district, who have been racially profiled. They were decked out in Falasteen [Palestine] gear, their Falasteen hats, and their *hattas* [also known as *keffiyas*, the black-and-white scarf worn by the famed Palestinian leader Yasser Arafat]. A few of them were just walking down the street and the cops asked, "Hey, can we search your bag, can we search your backpack?" I'm sure it's because these articles of clothing make you stand out, who you are.

He described other instances of unjust police treatment that he attributed to anti-Arab racism:

> There was an incident . . . at one of the Gaza protests. A few of the kids were taunted by Israel supporters . . . the kids are hotheads so they kind of responded, got in each other's faces, and the Israel supporter pulled out pepper spray and sprayed them in the eye. . . . The police came, jumped on the Arab kids, arrested them, had their boots basically on their faces. . . . The Israel supporters were standing ten yards away just . . . laughing. . . . And my friend was like, "What the hell did we do? We didn't do anything! The guy sprayed us, he taunted us, he cussed us, he said racial slurs and things like that." And my friend was like, "Can I have your badge number?" To the cop, and he was like, "Shut the fuck up, you guys are all going to get what you deserve." And then you know they ended up going to jail and they wanted to charge them with domestic terrorism. [chuckle] They got out of it, so that's why I can laugh. But at the time we were like, that's ridiculous, domestic terrorism! One of the kids was about to cry because he had gotten accepted to a university . . . and if they didn't drop the charges, they'd revoke his admission.

Ghassan made clear that his friend's vulnerabilities were mediated by his middle-class status; his primary concern was whether his college admission would be revoked. This stands in contrast to the vulnerabilities of people belonging to more precarious social classes, who might fear a long-term prison sentence, loss of livelihood, deportation, or other forms of social dispossession. Ghassan continued by reflecting on the intersectionality of class and race that conditioned his and his friends' varying susceptibilities to police harassment:

> Most of the stuff I've heard has to do with maybe the lower-income
> Arabs. . . . My mom's a dentist and my dad is a manager, a supervisor at
> a factory, so we're well-off. So I don't know if that comes down to
> whether it's more of a class issue than a race issue. But a lot of stuff
> that I've heard is from Arab friends who live in "ghetto" areas. . . .
> But then again coming back to the situations that happened, like I'm
> telling you the ones with the *hattas* and the Falasteen hats, getting
> stopped by the cops for no apparent reason walking down the street in
> broad daylight, that makes me think, no, that's because they're Arab.

While acknowledging that the class privilege and economic assimilation available to some Arab Americans acts to buffer them from the sharpest experiences of structural racism, Ghassan insisted that even his middle-class friends have encountered racial discrimination "because they're Arab." Ghassan, whose social and political engagement with other racially marginalized people contributed to his race consciousness, understood police hostility to Arabs as an entrenchment of the division between Arabness and whiteness. Not all Americans are protected from police abuse, but white Americans enjoy a default innocence that his Arab friends were not afforded.

## The Shortcomings of the Racial Schema

While some of the students characterized their formal white status as a mistake that could be corrected with the addition of an appropriate racial box, others indicated that their miscategorization evinced a deeper deficiency of the prevailing racial schema. One of the campaign's lead organizers, Shadi, a Muslim Iranian American, was born and raised in Chicago and prides herself on her ability to embrace both her Iranian and American identities successfully. She noted how "arbitrary" and ill-fitting the notion of whiteness is when it purports to include people of distinct social experiences:

> Yeah, okay, somebody will tell you that geographically our ancestors
> are all Caucasian, but nobody really cares about that now. That's not
> really a representation of what's real. So like if Caucasian is what they
> like to label all of these different people who they are saying are from
> this different geographical region, that's fine. You can label it that for
> historical and ancestral reasons if that's what you like. But I don't
> really think that does anything for us, especially in the case of "white."
> If we're looking at white, Black, and Hispanic, I mean, Black and
> Hispanic are still more appropriate labels in terms of race and are

more relevant in daily life. White is just like an arbitrary, like, hunking all these people together who really have nothing in common.

When asked how she would racially identify, Shadi responded:

> Well, I mean, if . . . we have the four choices, Asian, white, Black, and Mexican, then, like, I guess technically, racially I'm white. But that again comes down to, can I say I'm Iranian racially because is that a correct technical term? I keep bringing this up in the meetings like, is it okay that we're raising these? These are all ethnicities! What about race here? But if that's the technical term of white, then, hey, yeah, I'm white. But that doesn't really tell you anything.

She further explained that, in fact, one of the reasons she became interested in the addition of a separate SWANA box in the first place was to rectify the misapplication of a white label that denied her lived experiences as culturally, politically, and socially distinct from white people.

Hanan, an eighteen-year-old Muslim woman who was born in Yemen and moved with her family to California when she was three years old, became frustrated trying to describe what race and ethnicity meant to her:

> Yeah, I guess just race seems so simple, like it should be something really simple. Like it should be your skin color or it should be whatever. Even though that's the thing with the Middle East, we're so different. There's so many light and like blue eyes and blond hair, and so many dark and dark hair and stuff. I don't even know. We shouldn't even have these words such as race and ethnicity. You can't really, it's really hard with us. Because if you're going to go, at least ethnicity-wise, yeah, we're all similar based, not ethnicity-wise but like cultural I guess we're all similar. But when it comes to skin color, we're all different, so I don't really know what category they would do.

In her answer, Hanan exposed the forgeries of the racial regime—the false notion that common racial categories are somehow coherent, consistent, and complete. It was precisely in recognizing the regime's deficiencies that the student organizers opened up space to propose their own box as an effective supplement.

## Forging SWANA

In addition to opting out of the white box, the UCLA students also forged an alternative racial category. They undertook this intervention knowing that the racial regime represented by the existing categories was so internally contradictory that it was itself a fraud—"a makeshift patchwork masquerading as memory and the immutable" that is not actually either (Robinson 2007, xxii). The proposed SWANA box was indeed a forgery of a racial category—an imitation of existing cultural currency paired with a claim of its authenticity. But it was a forgery intended for a counterfeit bank, a demand to transact within a flawed representational schema that nonetheless conditions campus life and politics. The students indicated that achieving recognition within that framework was necessary to make their social experiences intelligible on campus and would lead to an accrual of supportive research and resources.

The backdrop of the War on Terror not only opened up the opportunity for the students to expose the weaknesses of the existing racial representational regime. It also influenced the criteria they considered in forging their alternative SWANA category. Finding oneself in the United States as a result of imperial projects, including war and conquest, produces a racialized nonwhite subjectivity characterized by an elision of national origin and cultural, religious, and linguistic distinctions. The UCLA students engaged this elision, which is typical of racial projects in the United States, as a political and historical reality. Despite this cultural and religious diversity, they recognized that they share common experiences of political marginality in the United States that demand a common representation on the UC application. Ayman, who emigrated from Syria when he was three years old and who retains a deep connection to the country's culture, history, and politics, described the way that U.S. foreign policy conflates the many groups in the SWANA region, in terms of both representation and treatment.

> In foreign policy, they do group these people together . . . I think war does that in the sense that it's unjust. . . . We're all kind of suffering together here, and . . . our people over there are suffering for the same reasons. Iraqis and Afghans are both being killed and their societies are destroyed because of wars brought on by the United States.

He described the decision to include a diversity of groups in the proposed SWANA box as a diasporic opportunity. He noted that the campaign's panethnic approach was meaningful because of the conflation of diverse identities into a monolithic racial "Other" that is typical of the U.S. racial imaginary.

> In the American society perspective, it's one of those, finding the closest people to you. Where an Algerian might not be considered my brother in Syria, but when I'm in the United States, he's an Arab, he

speaks Arabic. Even though I don't always understand what he's saying, he's still Arab. It's kind of like picking and choosing the closest among all these strangers. In America, it's totally different. You'd never get away with this in any Arab country—"Hey, let's bubble in Arab as our ethnicity." It's just the specific society that we live in allows for this to happen, where it can't happen anywhere else.

He continued to explain that, in particular, September 11, 2001, and the ensuing wars in Afghanistan and Iraq produced this conflation as a matter of racial common sense. He argued that the SWANA category, then, is an accurate reflection of the social processes already grouping them together.

That's what's drawn the most distinct line, that the post-9/11 world has drawn a circle around our groups. I feel like if you take a poll and . . . did it by name, like, "Which one of these peoples go together?" I think that's what it would be grouped as. We'd all be grouped together. It's almost like, well you guys grouped us together, you might as well give us this bubble.

Hanan expressed a similar belief that Western foreign policy in the Middle East unites SWANA people:

Even like Turkey, which is more Europeanized, has the same point of view as like Jordan or Saudi Arabia. . . . We're all going through the struggle of European influence in the Middle East. For example, the war in Iraq, Israel's war with Lebanon, the occupation in Palestine. A lot of that region is going through problems and . . . that's something that also unifies us because even when I'm talking to . . . my Palestinian friends, I understand where she's coming from, [which] . . . makes them really similar to each other in a way.

Through the shared experience of being subjected to cross-cultural elision and to more materially violent forms of colonial domination, the students found common ground on which to build the panethnic SWANA category.

The UCLA student campaign emerges in response to the eliding process of racialization without completely adopting its terms. They rejected, for example, the more commonly used term "Middle Eastern." Ayman explained that the term "Middle East" is an inaccurate label that views the region from the perspective of Europe. He pointed out that the concept is still contingent on Western imperial projects: "Now people believe the

Middle East includes Afghanistan and Iran because of the U.S.'s involvement there."

Eventually the students selected "Southwest Asian/North African," a label that paralleled the existing racial groups whose perimeters are geographically defined. During one campaign meeting, the option of a set of boxes defined by religious affiliations ("Muslim," "Baha'i," etc.) was proposed. The students roundly rejected this idea because it would establish an exceptional position for their newly formed group—a feature not included under any other racial category—and would thus undermine their assertion that they share common status with other people of color.

Indeed, the IM In Campaign students were highly influenced by the existing representation models of other communities of color. Shadi explained to me that the idea for the SWANA box was derived from a previous campaign carried out by the Asian Pacific Coalition. In 2005, the "Count Me In Campaign" successfully lobbied the UC to expand the list of represented ethnic and national identities subsumed within the Asian/ Asian American category and to create a separate racial category for Pacific Islanders. The IM In campaign organizers identified "Count Me In" as their model because it was successful in adding a new box to the UC application. Count Me In, however, was different from IM In in an important way: the former mobilized to differentiate national and ethnic identities within an already established, nonwhite racial identity, "Asian/Asian American." Nonetheless, the SWANA students expressed a desire to propose their box in as similar terms as possible to other racial groups, especially to those represented by the Count Me In Campaign.

The choice to default to the contours of the existing schema reflected a desire to construct the group's self-identity in a way that would render it contextually intelligible. Yen Le Espiritu (1992, 10) explains that this is a typical characteristic of panethnic movements: "To interact meaningfully with those in the larger society, individuals have to identify themselves in terms intelligible to outsiders." Forging new identities in the extant panethnic mold is beneficial and, at times, required for groups who seek access to political systems. Standing in a broad coalition, the IM In Campaign subverted the invisibility, or racial namelessness, that they identified as an integral component of their social marginalization. The box, with its many meanings, became "a medium of imagination by which . . . [they author] their sense of self" (Espiritu 1992, 11) by rendering themselves visible as nonwhite in the University of California admissions process.

## The Box and Its Benefits

While an exclusion from Americanness engendered an experience of nonwhiteness for my research participants, they conceived of formal recognition of nonwhiteness as a way to access some of the democratic promises of Americanness. Nonwhiteness generates an exclusion from cultural citizenship, yet formal recognition of that exclusion serves as a form of alternative inclusion. And social integration into the racial hierarchy, even if not into mainstream "whiteness," comprises a powerful form of naturalization. Devon Carbado (2005) defines racial naturalization as "a social process that produces American racial identities . . . [and] a broader social practice wherein all of us are Americanized and made socially intelligible via racial categorization" (633, 637). Carbado describes an ascriptive racialization process that involves legal and cultural mechanisms. For Southwest Asian and North African students, this process is internally inconsistent between simultaneous, contradictory ascriptions of formal whiteness and of racialized marginalization. Thus the SWANA students at UCLA made an intervention to render themselves racially legible in a coherent way.

The box schema that the students demanded was an avenue by which to recover rights, recognition, and resources. The SWANA students claimed a right to be counted and monitored for achievement gaps, but the misclassification of Middle Easterners as white was inhibiting the collection of community-specific diagnostic data. Ghassan queried, "If we don't have statistics, how do we even know if we are underrepresented?" The box was seen as a tool by which SWANA students can assess their community's circumstances on campus. They also believed that demographic data gathering would enable access to university resources that are dedicated to helping historically marginalized students of color succeed at the university level. Rima, who had recently begun the master's program in education at UCLA, explained:

> Arabs in general face a lot of issues in higher education, and it hasn't been tackled at all because there's no data, it's hard to find data. . . .
> Whereas if you had a computer system that just said, "So many Arabs applied to UCLA and so many got in, and this is why their GPA scores are low." Or "We only had such a small number of Arab Americans apply to UCLA out of how many are in LA. So we need to target more." We just don't have it because it doesn't exist.

For Rima and for others, the box was seen as enabling the provision of support to SWANA students. This was a particularly salient feature of the box for the student leaders of the IM In Campaign who planned to use the data to reach out and recruit identified students. Their belief in the political power of official recognition as nonwhite echoes the motivations of national SWANA American activists, like the seasoned organizer Helen Hatab Samhan, who explains, "We have to get counted. Race and ethnic data is [*sic*] used to enforce civil rights law" (Aidi 2014, 161).

But the students' motivations were not entirely utilitarian. In some ways, the students seemed to prioritize the exposure of the racial regime's contradictions and demands for their resolution. Ghassan insisted that, while statistics are important, "the main thing is to get the hell out of the white box." Like him, other students also emphasized official acknowledgment of their treatment in society and at the university as an important consequence of the box. Ayman echoed Ghassan's position that the central issue is that the students feel misrepresented by nominal inclusion under the "white" category. Shadi explained that "Society doesn't see us as white. So I don't understand why we have to be categorized as white. . . . Because it's not really reflecting how society views us." The classification of SWANA as white contradicts their social experiences; their racial namelessness makes those experiences invisible.

The students demanded inclusion into a substantive notion of cultural citizenship through their assertion of official, categorical nonwhiteness. Their demands operated in an open political terrain, and the formulation of these demands had multiple implications. On the one hand, they appealed to an alternative narrative of Americanness—that of liberal multiculturalism, which absorbs the representation of diversity into its image for the purposes of individualized gain. Lisa Lowe (1996, 30) argues that the adoption of a post–civil rights era national image of "multiculturalism" created a symbolic realm in which to alleviate the material limitations of the liberal state. This multiculturalism subverted the movement's claims for substantive equality by offering instead the representational integration of diverse groups "as *cultural* equivalents abstracted from the histories of racial inequality unresolved in the economic and political domains." Shadi made reference to this paradigm as she compared the IM In Campaign to its UC predecessor, the Count Me In Campaign: "There was this shift where now ethnicities and cultures, [do] not necessarily want to have a separation, but there's like this individualism . . . on the rise. Everybody wants to be labeled appropriately. The [Asian Americans] felt that, and we feel that." The pervasion of multiculturalism puts pressure on unrepresented groups to carve out their place.

Yet minority identification holds potential for resisting the racial regime that makes the category intelligible. At the same time as they navigated the seduction of multiculturalism, the students' rejection of legally ascribed whiteness evinced solidarity with a long civil rights tradition that envisions full participation in society for all people. Their emphases on interethnic solidarities transcended the realm of strategy and manifested as grounded commitments to social justice. For example, by virtue of the fact that the box had to be collectively demanded, it represented a means for mobilizing coalitions. Laleh, a UCLA alumna of mixed Iranian and Swiss heritage, explained that she urged Shadi to launch the campaign because she felt that the SWANA community needed to come together in the same way that other racial groups on campus had done. The box, in its capacity to represent the shared identity of multiple ethnic groups, required interethnic coalition building and active recognition of common subjectivities. "The problem with Middle Easterners is that we all do our own thing and don't stick together," she lamented. She illustrated her point with a story about an Iranian religious leader in Southern California who was indicted by federal authorities on a number of bogus charges related to terrorism, embargo violation, and immigration fraud. After a long and traumatic confinement, the religious leader was cleared of the political charges and was released to his family to await trial on immigration charges. Laleh emphasized the Iranian community's failure to band together in defense of the religious leader. She pointed out that were the Middle Eastern community, including Arabs and Iranians, to unite around these types of issues, it could bring significant political pressure to bear on the federal government. The box and the campaign it necessitated provided an opportunity to develop a community consciousness toward this and related ends.

## Conclusion

The contemporary racial crisis in the United States provides the context in which conflicting racial ideologies are challenged by groups such as the IM In Campaign. The crisis is characterized by the achievement of progress in the formal and symbolic realms of racialism and the simultaneous deepening of racialized structural disparities (Winant 2006, 995–996). While, on the one hand, formal colorblindness emerged as the prevailing racial ideology (even if now embattled), on the other, racialism remains a salient conduit of social control and common sense. Racist nativism shapes the omnipresent immigration debate, including the new presidential administration's various proposals to ban and wall out anyone perceived not to be "American," with its implication of whiteness. In addition, racial tropes are mobilized, for example, to justify the mass incarceration of African Americans, Latinxs, and indigenous people or to gain popular support for military aggressions abroad. Formal colorblindness desperately performs damage control, coding racialized dynamics in seemingly neutral economic, ideological, and cultural terms. The disparate impact of these racial regimes cannot be ignored, however, especially not by those they oppress. And so race remains salient not only to forces of social control but also to people who organize against and around it.

In California, the passage of Proposition 209 purportedly institutionalized formal colorblindness by prohibiting the explicit consideration of race in public university admissions. In fact, since its passage, racial inequality in admissions has skyrocketed in the state's largest and most prestigious public university system, the University of California (see Pusser 2001, Robinson et al. 2003, Santos et al. 2010).[4] The UC also continues to collect data about its applicants through a question about each applicant's race and ethnicity. Within that schema, the IM In Campaign rejected the mask of whiteness that had rendered their racialized subordination invisible. They may not have had the direct means to challenge successfully the legal and cultural aggressions perpetrated against them and their communities domestically and abroad. But their demand for recognition, through the box, of the diverse communities that are conflated by raced national power is itself a form of resistance: to reject invisibility, to name subordination, and to forge new identities within *and* against the prevailing racial regime.

The sophisticated conversations of the IM In Campaign's student organizers and supporters offer productive insights for university educators. U.S. war-making abroad reverberates in the domestic racial regime, and this dynamic, in turn, necessarily influences the way students understand race, racism, and racial identity. Teachers may find that this creates a uniquely open terrain in which to add nuance and depth to their students' already complex notions of race. One of the ways this opportunity might be used is in the popular lesson about race as a social construction, which is sometimes demonstrated by locating the source of these constructions in historical institutions that may seem distant from the students. The successes of the IM In Campaign and other organizations like it suggest that university students can play an active role in shaping the project of racial formation, which is always already dynamic despite racial mythologies claiming the contrary. Moreover, as the SWANA students were themselves aware, the incompleteness of racial regimes and the existence of spaces for intervention do not necessarily suggest that race is a capricious and cruel fantasy with no real meaning. Indeed, some teachers may worry that lessons about race as a social construction could lead to students dismissing racism as the result of race consciousness, believing instead that the fiction of race should be ignored rather than engaged. Instead, the IM In Campaign organizers repeatedly demonstrated quite the opposite; especially in the context of global war-making, university students are quite adept at holding together the two seemingly dissonant parts of social constructivism—that race is an ongoing, human-made, flawed process but that its parameters and meanings hold very real consequences for everyone and thus must be seriously engaged.

Educators may also learn from the SWANA students' specific understandings of race and racial identity as a global phenomenon. Some teachers may quite reasonably worry that to involve the international dimensions of race would risk an imperialist imposition of the United States' racial schema onto the rest of the world. The IM In Campaign students, instead, exhibited an awareness that their racialization is contextually contingent—for example, many of them would point out that, while in the United States they are treated as Arab or Iranian or Afghan rather than white, back in the country of their or their parents' births, they would be categorically identified as American. Yet at the same time, their U.S.-specific racial identity was deeply informed by political and economic events abroad. In light of their keen analyses, there is no longer room for U.S. educators to focus narrowly on the racial dynamics that happen within the arbitrary boundaries of the U.S. state; they instead should exercise great diligence in learning the enduring influences of international dynamics on domestic racial projects.

Last, the rich conversations of the IM In Campaign leaders and supporters remind educators and social analysts of all stripes not to dismiss students' bids for visibility and representation as simply hollow attempts to opt into the cynical, superficial multiculturalism that has sought to subvert the powerful legacy of the civil rights era. Undoubtedly, this atmosphere affects student organizing at the university, but it does not constitute its limit. Instead, we may look to the SWANA students as working within this context to forge cross-ethnic and racial connections and solidarities in order to *revive* the civil rights legacy. In other words, student organizers who engage with the racial order of liberal multiculturalism, which has undermined the political power of aggrieved communities by promoting individualism, may do so with a playful, revolutionary spirit—deliberately but critically joining in racial construction—in ways that seek to empower those same communities by bringing them together.

APPENDICES

**Appendix A:** The U.S. Department of Education "ethnicity" question as it appeared on the University of California Application for Undergraduate Admission in 2010. This question appeared unchanged on the 2015 application.

---

### Select Ethnicity (for US Dept of Education)

The University is required by the U.S. Department of Education to ask you to answer the following two questions.

Do you consider yourself Hispanic or Latino?
Includes persons of Cuban, Mexican, Puerto Rican, South or Central American or other Spanish culture or origin
○ Yes
○ No

Which of the following groups best describes your racial background? Check as many categories as may apply.
☐ African American or Black
☐ American Indian or Alaskan Native
☐ Asian
☐ Pacific Islander or Native Hawaiian
☐ White

---

**Appendix B:** The University of California "ethnicity" question as it appeared on the University of California Application for Undergraduate Admission in 2010.

---

### Select Ethnicity (for UC)

For University of California purposes, to help us understand the diverse racial and ethnic backgrounds of our students, which of the following groups best describes your background? Check as many categories as may apply.

**African American / Black**
☐ African American
☐ African
☐ Caribbean
☐ Other African American / Black

If other, please specify _____

**American Indian / Alaskan Native**
☐ ⓘ American Indian / Alaskan Native
Specify tribal affiliation _____

**Hispanic / Latino**
☐ Cuban / Cuban American
☐ Latin American / Latino
☐ Mexican / Mexican American / Chicano
☐ Puerto Rican
☐ Other Hispanic, Latin American or of Spanish origin
If other, please specify _____

---

(Continued on the next page)

*Maryam S. Griffin*

Appendix B, continued:

**Pacific Islander**
- ☐ Fijian
- ☐ Guamanian/Chamorro
- ☐ Hawaiian
- ☐ Samoan
- ☐ Tongan
- ☐ Other Pacific Islander

If other, please specify _____

**Asian / Asian American**
- ☐ Asian Indian
- ☐ Bangladeshi
- ☐ Cambodian
- ☐ Chinese / Chinese American (except Taiwanese)
- ☐ Filipino / Filipino American
- ☐ Hmong
- ☐ Indonesian
- ☐ Japanese / Japanese American
- ☐ Korean / Korean American
- ☐ Laotian
- ☐ Malaysian
- ☐ Pakistani
- ☐ Sri Lankan
- ☐ Taiwanese / Taiwanese American
- ☐ Thai
- ☐ Vietnamese / Vietnamese American
- ☐ Other Asian (not including Middle Eastern)

If other, please specify _____

**White/Caucasian**
- ☐ European / European descent
- ☐ Middle Eastern / Middle Eastern descent
- ☐ North African
- ☐ Other White / Caucasian

If other, please specify _____

**Appendix C:** The SWANA Box as it appeared on the University of California Application for Undergraduate Admission in 2016, after the success of the IM In Campaign.

## Southwest Asian and North African

- [ ] Afghan
- [ ] Algerian
- [ ] Armenian
- [ ] Assyrian/Chaldean
- [ ] Azerbaijani
- [ ] Bahraini
- [ ] Berber
- [ ] Circassian
- [ ] Djiboutian
- [ ] Egyptian
- [ ] Emirati
- [ ] Georgian
- [ ] Iranian
- [ ] Iraqi
- [ ] Israeli
- [ ] Jordanian
- [ ] Other North African
- [ ] Other Southwest Asian

- [ ] Kurdish
- [ ] Kuwaiti
- [ ] Lebanese
- [ ] Libyan
- [ ] Mauritanian
- [ ] Moroccan
- [ ] Omani
- [ ] Palestinian
- [ ] Qatari
- [ ] Saudi Arabian
- [ ] Somali
- [ ] Sudanese
- [ ] Syrian
- [ ] Tunisian
- [ ] Turkish
- [ ] Yemeni

NOTES

1. This statement was made during the second preelection presidential debate, on October 9, 2016. Clinton went on to say, "I've heard how important it is for [Muslims] to feel that they are wanted and included and part of our country, part of our homeland security, and that's what I want to see." Despite disavowing her opponent Donald Trump's anti-Muslim rhetoric, Clinton reinforced the notion that American Muslims must first and foremost be understood as potential terrorists or terrorist-adjacent. For a thorough treatment of the similarities and differences between liberal and conservative Islamophobia, see Kumar (2012).

2. These questions appeared on the UC application while I was conducting my research and writing up my findings in 2009–2010, and their inclusion was confirmed again in 2015.

3. There are myriad examples of people who have been censured for advocating justice for Palestinians at U.S. universities. Some of the more recent, high-profile academic cases include Steven Salaita's dismissal from the University of Illinois after using Twitter to criticize Israel's 2014 siege

on Gaza and the 2011 prosecution of students at UC-Irvine and UC-Riverside for interrupting a speech by the Israeli ambassador Michael Oren. Others' ordeals are chronicled in various texts (see, for example, Abraham 2014, Chatterjee and Maira 2014, Palestine Legal and Center for Constitutional Rights 2015, Robinson and Griffin 2017).

4. These are not unconnected phenomena, as the directive to ignore race can create prejudices against applicants of color whose personal statements and letters of recommendation may necessarily reflect the racially inflected realities of their lives (Carbado and Harris 2008).

### REFERENCES

Abraham, M. 2014. *Out of bounds: Academic freedom and the question of Palestine.* New York: Bloomsbury Academic.

Aidi, H. D. 2014. *Rebel music: Race, empire, and the new Muslim youth culture.* New York: Vintage.

Bayoumi, M. 2008. *How does it feel to be a problem?* London: Penguin.

Blake, J. 2010. Arab- and Persian-American campaign: "Check It Right" on census. *CNN.com*, April 1.

Cainkar, L. 2009. *Homeland insecurity: The Arab American and Muslim American experience after 9/11.* New York: Russell Sage Foundation.

Carbado, D. W. 2005. Racial naturalization. *American Quarterly* 57 (3): 633–658.

Carbado, D. W., and C. I. Harris. 2008. The new racial preferences. *California Law Review* 96 (5): 1139–1214.

Chatterjee, P., and S. Maira, eds. 2014. *The imperial university: Academic repression and scholarly dissent.* Minneapolis: University of Minnesota Press.

Chow, K. 2016. New U.S. census category proposed for people of Middle Eastern, North African descent. *All Things Considered*, October 25. http://www.npr.org/2016/10/25/499343633/new-u-s-census-category-proposed-for-middle-eastern-people.

Cohn, D. 2015. Census considers new approach to asking about race—by not using the term at all. Washington, D.C.: Pew Research Center. http://www.pewresearch.org/fact-tank/2015/06/18/census-considers-new-approach-to-asking-about-race-by-not-using-the-term-at-all/.

Cole, D., and J. Lobel. 2009. *Less safe, less free: Why America is losing the War on Terror.* New York: New Press.

Crenshaw, K. W. 1998. Race, reform, and retrenchment: Transformation and legitimation in antidiscrimination law. *Harvard Law Review* 101:1331–1387.

De Genova, N. 2006. *Racial transformations: Latinos and Asians remaking the United States.* Durham, N.C.: Duke University Press.

El-Farra, L., A. Hasnain, and T. Mason. 2012. A resolution in support of the creation of a Southwest Asian and North African checkbox on the University of California Application. https://www.usac.ucla.edu/ documents/resolutions/UCLA%20SWANA%20Resolution.pdf.

Espiritu, Y. L. 1992. *Asian American panethnicity: Bridging institutions and identities*. Philadelphia: Temple University Press.

Gotanda, N. 1991. A critique of "Our constitution is color-blind." *Stanford Law Review* 44 (1): 1–68.

Gualtieri, S. 2009. *Between Arab and White: Race and ethnicity in the early Syrian American diaspora*. Berkeley: University of California Press.

Hafner, K. 2013. Ethnic category for Southwest Asian and North African students to debut in 2013–2014 UC undergraduate application. *Daily Bruin*, May 17.

Haney-López, I. F. 2010. Is the post in postracial the blind in colorblind? *Cardozo Law Review* 32:807–831.

Hassan, S. D. 2002. Arabs, race, and the post–September 11 national security state. *Middle East Report* 224.

Horsman, R. 1981. *Race and manifest destiny: Origins of American racial Anglo-Saxonism*. Cambridge, Mass.: Harvard University Press.

Jamal A., and N. Naber. 2008. *Race and Arab Americans before and after 9/11: From invisible citizens to visible subjects*. Syracuse, N.Y.: Syracuse University Press.

Kumar, D. 2012. *Islamophobia and the politics of empire*. Chicago: Haymarket.

Lipsitz, G. 2006. *The possessive investment in whiteness: How white people profit from identity politics*. Philadelphia: Temple University Press.

Love, E. 2009. Confronting Islamophobia in the United States: Framing civil rights activism among Middle Eastern Americans. *Patterns of Prejudice* 43 (3/4): 401–425.

Lowe, L. 1996. *Immigrant acts: On Asian American cultural politics*. Durham, N.C.: Duke University Press.

Maira, S. 2009. *Missing: Youth, citizenship, and empire after 9/11*. Durham, N.C.: Duke University Press.

Omi, M., and H. Winant. 1994. *Racial formation in the United States: From the 1960s to the 1990s*. 2nd ed. New York: Routledge.

Palestine Legal and Center for Constitutional Rights. 2015. The Palestine exception to free speech: A movement under attack in the U.S. https:// ccrjustice.org/sites/default/files/attach/2015/09/Palestine%20Exception%20Report%20Final.pdf.

Park, L. 2005. *Consuming citizenship: Children of Asian immigrant entrepreneurs*. Palo Alto, Calif.: Stanford University Press.

Patterson, O. 1982. *Slavery and social death: A comparative study*. Cambridge, Mass.: Harvard University Press.

Peery, D. 2011. The colorblind ideal in a race-conscious reality: The case for a new legal ideal for race relations. *Northwestern Journal of Law and Social Policy* 6 (2): 473–495.

Pew Research Center. 2015. Religious projection table. http://www .pewforum.org/2015/04/02/religious-projection-table/2010/percent/ North_America/.

Puar, J. K., and A. S. Rai. 2002. Monster, terrorist, fag: The War on Terrorism and the production of docile patriots. *Social Text* 20 (3): 117–148.

Pusser, B. 2001. The contemporary politics of access police: California after Proposition 209. In *The states and public education policy: Affordability, access, and accountability*, ed. D. E. Heller, 121–152. Baltimore, Md.: Johns Hopkins University Press.

Robinson, C. 2007. *Forgeries of memory and meaning: Blacks and the regimes of race in American theater and film before World War II*. Durham: University of North Carolina Press.

Robinson, N., K. Caspary, V. Santelices, et al. 2003. *Undergraduate access to the University of California after the elimination of race-conscious policies*. Oakland: University of California, Office of the President.

Robinson, W. I., and M. S. Griffin. 2017. *We will not be silenced: The academic repression of Israel's critics*. Chico, Calif.: AK Press.

Samhan, H. H. 1987. Politics and exclusion: The Arab American experience. *Journal of Palestine Studies* 16 (2): 11–28.

———. 1999. Not quite white: Race classification and the Arab-American experience. In *Arabs in America: Building a new future*, ed. M. W. Suleiman. Philadelphia: Temple University Press.

Santos, J. L., N. L. Cabrera, and K. J. Fosnacht. 2010. Is "race-neutral" really race-neutral? Disparate impact towards underrepresented minorities in post-2009 UC systems admissions. *Journal of Higher Education* 81 (6): 675–701.

Tehranian, J. 2008. *Whitewashed: America's invisible Middle Eastern minority*. New York: NYU Press.

Volpp, L. 2002. The citizen and the terrorist. *UCLA Law Review* 49:1575–1600.

Winant, H. 2006. Race and racism: Toward a global future. *Ethnic and Racial Studies* 29 (5): 986–1003.

Yoder, C. 2013. UC to include Southwest Asian, North African category on next year's undergraduate application. *Daily Californian*, May 27. http:// www.dailycal.org/2013/05/27/uc-to-introduce-new-category-for-southwest -asian-and-north-african-students-in-2013-2014-undergraduate -application/.

# War and Occupation

*Dolores Calderón*

The outcomes of war and education are varied and have long-lasting effects. In the context of the United States, one normally does not consider that the nation's founding had to do with ongoing wars and a resulting occupation (at least from the perspective of Indigenous peoples and Mexican settlers in what is now the contemporary U.S. Southwest). With regards to education, the outcome of such histories results in an education model that has its foundations in the inherent violence of wars and their aftermath. In this chapter, I explore the larger scope of what it means to consider education through occupation, centering on a borderlands context. I ask, how do colonial societies construct and maintain educational models and practices that make invisible occupation models of education? Situating occupation, I hope to show, brings together sometimes disparate approaches in ways that reveal the totalizing violence of occupation and its manifestation in schools.

Geographically and spatially, borders include Mexico/United States, United States/Canada, and Tribal homelands/United States. These bordered contexts are unique as the diversity of locations they represent, but they are also similar in a fundamental way: The realities of the colonial project(s) continue to play out in the violence typical of these border towns/ crossings. (A note of caution: Duane Champagne [1996] reminds us that the resiliency and agency of Indigenous peoples, indeed the strategies we employ to maintain our cultures, are often overlooked by theories that center on colonial dominance.) People who reside at these borders are differentially situated, from citizenship status (tribal, nation-state, undocumented) to one's relationship with Indigeneity (immigrant or American Indian/ Alaska Native). While these binaries are offered as provocative starting points, positionalities overlap, shift, and change over time. Most Americans I meet, however, are ignorant of lives lived on the border, a type of epistemology of ignorance (Calderón 2009; Tuana 2004, 2006).

When we, border dwellers, tell our stories, we are at times met with incredulity. Oftentimes our stories are filtered through the dominant singular lens of U.S. settler colonialism, which shapes attitudes and ideas about the Mexico/U.S. border. Moreover, the notion of borders has been, at times, abstracted beyond the original intent of the work of scholars such as Anzaldúa. In this chapter, my intimacy with the border and indigeneity allows me to claim space in theories of the border/borderlands important to the way I think about educational projects.

For this reason, I am having a difficult time approaching the question of war and education without also naming the concurrent project of occupation, the forceful and violent taking of lands. Occupation is a product, a component, of war, and across the border I am witness to the genocidal emptying of towns for a "new" occupation of empire. Thus it is through the idea of occupation that I hope to explore the impact of this vast question. To reach an analysis of what war and education, or education as occupation, looks like, I must first struggle to articulate the war(s) that inform that goal. Without understanding the context for what I broadly mean by war, I cannot contextualize how I conceive of occupation and, specifically, of education as occupation. Here I engage examples of education as occupation that have been shaped by the clashing of colonial projects along the borders of cultures and places.

## *Methodologies: Territorializing the Narrative*

I am writing this paper from a crossroads, a place where nation-states meet, creating what Gloria Anzaldúa (1987) described as *una herida abierta*, an open wound: the border of the United States and Mexico. It is also a place where multiple cultures and peoples meet: Indigenous, settlers, arrivants (Byrd 2011), and those forcefully brought. It is a valley crossed by a once vibrant river (Rio Grande/*Rio Bravo*), surrounded by several mountain ranges, which made this a natural crossing point. It continues to be a place of crossings: where people come and go; where transnational capital loses its transnational label, becoming landed, emplaced; where drugs are smuggled from the Mexican side into the United States; and where histories and stories and bodies elide the notion of nations divided by borders. It is also a place that refuses to surrender its relationship to its originary peoples, and although surnames that can be traced to the initial Entradas by the Spanish in the 1500s are commonplace, they did not deterritorialize the Indigenous presence. I am located in El Paso, Texas, in the Lower Valley, less than a mile from the Rio Grande. This place, I believe, is emblematic of war and of occupation.

My familial, ancestral legacy is woven into the legacies of Indigenous sovereignties and bordered lives and is caught up and shaped by the historical regional histories of Spanish, then Mexican, then Anglo occupations of New Mexico and Texas. The genesis of war in this place—territorial acquisitions, natural resource expropriation, and dispossession of peoples—has been ongoing since the Spanish Entradas in the 1500s, the first entry of the Spanish conquistadores into the lands we now refer to as the Southwest. The outcome of these wars of conquest has been an occupation that has resulted in the ongoing "settling" of territories, first by the Spanish, then the Mexicans, then the Anglos; the ongoing expropriation of resources (both labor and land); and the continued dispossessions of people and ecologies. Yet this place is also an embodiment of survivance, the resistance and survival of people in the face of oppression (Vizenor 1994, 2008), indeed, occupation.

For this reason, I rely on the framework of coloniality to center the project of multiple colonialisms in general (Grosfuguel 2007, Lugones 2008, Mignolo 2000, Quijano 2000) and in education specifically (Bang et al. 2014; Calderón 2008, 2014; Patel 2014; Sintos Coloma 2012; Tuck and Yang 2012, 2014). Coloniality refers to the manner in which modern systems of colonialism operate epistemically, economically, ontologically, politically, and spatially (Grosfuguel 2007, Lugones 2008, Mignolo 2000, Quijano 2000). In order to decolonize, we need first to provide a context for the particular colonial project(s) we are responding to. In the United States, we need to attend to settler colonialism, yet the idea of the United States as a settler nation, or even the idea of colonialism in general, is little explored in educational research (Coloma, Means, and Kim 2009). Even less explored is the manner in which multiple colonialisms manifest or transit, in this case, along the border. I maintain that this work is key in order to cultivate holistic (Cajete 1994, Pewewardy 2002) educational ideas and practices that can speak to the complex needs of Indigenous peoples and/ or border communities in ways that truly make space for decolonizing approaches in education. In this sense, the guiding framework helps me excavate and make clear the transit of colonialisms (Byrd 2011).

## The Border /*La Frontera*

In the truest sense of the territorialization of narratives, I am writing this from place, from land. Certainly, my cell phone reception serves as a metaphor of this place, at times picking up the local Mexican cellular coverage. When I do have my U.S. carrier coverage, it is a measly one bar and at times reads no service. Indeed, my cell phone coverage is an apt metaphor for the politics and economic policies in place along these borderlands: They are intimately woven together, yet power is only available for the few. It is also an apt metaphor for the ideological currents of the current moment invested in the logics of anti-Blackness, Indigenous appropriations, and the exclusion of undesired immigrant populations. These logics, representative of the settler colonial logics of U.S. imperialism (Feldman 2015, Salaita 2006, Smith 2012, Tuck and Yang 2012, Wolfe 2006), however, are not sufficient for the borderlands. It is here where the project of coloniality, in conversation with critical Indigenous studies, comparative ethnic studies, border studies, and a land-based approach, offers me tools with which to think through the differing colonialist project that implicates a different set of logics that continues to operate and bleed through to the U.S. side and immigrate with the peoples indoctrinated within these processes (Grosfuguel 2007, Lugones 2008).

Here, I draw from the unique community land-based knowledge I possess, which is informed by a politics of borders and Indigenous projects of self-determination that I am in the constant process of engaging with and learning from. I am a product of the Spanish Entradas, a historical colonial project that plays out to this day. I am a daughter of the Indigenous story (Tigua) and the complicated and messy story of Mexican settlers and arrivants. I am also a beneficiary of U.S. citizenship, where documents can mean life or death.

Therefore, considering war and education from this location *me impulsa*, moves me, to think critically through how multiple colonial projects and histories demand I approach the question I explore here: What does it mean to think of education as an ongoing legacy of war? In thinking through this question, it is hard for me to separate the *acontecimientos* from one side of the river to the other. The day-to-day lives from the Mexican side, though shaped by a different politics, are not contained from the U.S. side. I also cannot divorce myself from the ongoing violence of the "other side," the narco-state violence that has seen Juarez and the surrounding areas caught up in what many describe as a war, though of late, the violence has reportedly diminished. I am also compelled, from this location, to center those narratives, those voices and bodies that are erased and unseen: those disappeared, whether figuratively like the Black body, or physically, like the women of Juarez in this location of the borderlands.

Methodologically, I return to the cell phone as tool and metaphor in intimate relationship to land. As a tool, the cell phone—via a very slow connection—is currently allowing me to connect to social media in order to read critical perspectives on the Charleston terrorist massacre of nine African Americans at Emanuel Church by a white supremacist intent on starting a race war. The cell phone also connects me to local social media, which reminds me of the ongoing violence just on the other side of the border in Mexico. Yet the cell phone, indeed, the social media I navigate, is largely silent on the specificities of the violence I saw reported on the Mexican news that we pick up on this side of the border—a mirror of the way those away from borders conceive of politics, society, and economics. The television, like the cell phone, is also silent about the landed voices of my family and friends, which speak of tales of violence *and* resistance, the voices that whisper the stories of how entire families were massacred, disappeared, how mothers and fathers and sisters and cousins fled to the United States seeking political asylum, knowing that they would be the next victims after their sons and daughters. The cell phone offers me agony, anger, and pain.

## LANDED KNOWLEDGES

However, the place I am writing this from—home—is also offering me, is giving me, sustenance. With limited access to the Internet and situated in a different relational positionality, I listen and talk and visit and drive through this place I call home: a sort of landed knowledge characterized by the community I live in. In writing this, I am forced to hear my own self truly and the voices of those around me to contemplate this question. I believe this approach is generative, though not definitive. Make no mistake, though, the landed voices offer me hope and resistance: they point me to pictures and words that document these stories, stories I understand I must disseminate. The voices remind me that we have persevered in this desert, in part since time immemorial, and they remind me of the transitive nature of war and occupation.

Thus, in this chapter I use an assemblage of these stories (Facebook statuses; personal ruminations; the voices of Mexican political asylees and human rights activists gathered in the powerful graphic novel *La Lucha: The Story of Lucha Castro and Human Rights in Mexico*, drawn and written by Jon Sack; and the landed voices of my community) to shape a narrative of war that will make clear the reality of education as a project of occupation. These voices, though they might at first appear disparate, are all tied together by land and, in particular, the borderland context from which they emanate. It is highly exploratory, and I hope that this creative endeavor will lead to generative points of departure that can offer concrete ways my research can work against the mechanisms of education as occupation.

In the following section, I look at how specific descriptors of wars targeting specific populations, shaped by particular colonialist logics and territorial projects, result in types of educational policies reflective of the notion of occupation. In some cases (as with Blacks and, arguably, Indigenous peoples), the war(s) is part of the same project yet deployed in different ways and producing, at times, distinct structural adaptations and narratives on behalf of the settler colonial project. In other cases, the war(s) is not perceived to be connected to U.S. domestic issues, such as the narco-state-sponsored wars against Mexican populations (in this case along the Mexico/U.S. border). However, using a territorializing approach in both instances allows me, on the one hand, to demonstrate how anti-Blackness is a product of occupation. On the other hand, I show how multiple colonialisms interact at the border, which reminds us that colonialism(s) cannot be neatly articulated and resisted; this is the lived reality of people who inhabit the geographic borders of the El Paso/Juarez area.

### War(s) and Borders: The Permanence of Violence in the (Settler/Post/Neo/Late) Colonial Nation

Scholars from settler colonial studies and critical Indigenous studies often speak of the dominant logics that order racism and power in the United States. Such logics are perceived as a triad between the logics of exploitation or slaveability, the logics of extermination or Indigenous dispossession, and the logics of appropriation or settler territorialization (Smith 2012, Tuck and Yang 2012, Wolfe 2006). One can add a fourth logic: the logics of exclusion that largely frame groups such as Asians and Muslims as perpetual foreigners or, in the case of Mexicans, peoples that must be excluded from settler identity (Smith 2012). Black and Indigenous critical thinkers are certainly asking whether this triadic understanding reduces more complex onto-epistemological questions in ways that perhaps are not sufficient to account for Blackness, immigrants, and refugees. Here I also ask whether settler colonial studies does an adequate job of accounting for the overlapping colonial projects and the resulting web of bordered lives that reflect back identities and sovereignties unintelligible to the U.S. gaze. Perhaps it does not, nor am I suggesting it should, as there are other areas of inquiry that can be read together with settler colonial studies to arrive at a *seeing* that is more nuanced but that certainly takes more work.

How might different areas of inquiry allow us to understand what Mignolo (2000) names the "colonial difference"? Certainly, the work of Jodi Byrd—an important contributor to critical Indigenous studies, in conversation with scholars such as Steven Salaita, whose work bridges Indigenous studies, settler colonialism, and critical Muslim studies—offers theoretical insights that are useful in beginning to understand why such approaches are necessary to understand this difference, indeed recognize it. It is also worth looking at the work of Black critical thinkers that argue that Blackness is unintelligible to settler colonial studies in the United States (Sexton 2016) and the responses of Indigenous scholars and other Black studies scholars (Barker 2017, Day 2015, Medak-Saltzman 2015). Indeed, there are existing explorations in education through comparative ethnic studies approaches that use settler colonialism to understand aspects of the Black experience structured through dispossession (Paperson 2014), but here I focus on how understanding settler colonialism through the lens of occupation might help us weave the story of these dislocated, unintelligible sites of contestation and rupture.

## White Supremacy, War, and Blackness

Hence, I briefly examine how notions of Blackness can be read alongside some of the questions I pose regarding war and occupation. I focus on occupation rather than settling because the former emphasizes the ongoing violent, dispossesive nature of such a process, a process that is not static but rather that remakes itself to maintain a territorialization requiring ongoing dispossession. By foregrounding occupation, I consider how the multiple colonialisms that operate in places might overlap and inform power and identity. I ask us to think about education through this lens. Recently, the work of Michael Dumas in education seeks to engage Black critical thought in ways that sharpen critiques on liberal multiculturalism in education through an Afropessimist approach. Correspondingly, I look to those works, and in particular how Black radical thought is engaging with settler colonial and Indigenous theorizing of colonialism, to arrive at a place that acknowledges that occupation is not only about Indigenous dispossession but also about Black suffering, particularly in schools, which is a mainstay of the afterlife of slavery (Dumas 2014, 2016; Hartman 1997).

Recent critiques argue that in some settler colonial theorizing, Blackness is too easily distilled to labor (King 2014, Sexton 2016). For instance, in some theorizing around settler colonialism and its dominant logics (slave/native/settler or slaveability/anti-Black racism/genocide and Orientalism), Blackness is theorized around the logic of slaveability or exploitation (Smith 2010, Wolfe 2006). For example, Wolfe explains that for African Americans, the one-drop rule characterized people as enslaveable, property, and rendered their relationship to the state and to white supremacy in the United States as one of chattel (see also Alexander 2012, Paperson 2014, Robinson 1983). However, if one examines how current modes of Blackness operate in the United States, Black bodies are not valued for their exploitability in relationship to labor but rather for their ontological necessity to whiteness (Wilderson 2010). By drawing from Wilderson, moreover, King (2014) argues that such a simple reduction of Blackness to labor, a reduction common in the theorizations of Blackness and slaveability, means that Black subjects are capable of "interpellating themselves within settler colonial relations," which "reduces Blackness to a mere tool of settlement rather than a constitutive element of settler colonialism's conceptual order."

In other words, a binary positioning of slaveability against colonialism misses the more complex ways slavery and Indigenous dispossession interacted and coinformed each other and continue to exist today (Hartman 1997, Leroy 2016). Leroy (2016, 1) elaborates: "The projects of slavery and colonialism have never been concerned with which came first, or which is more elemental—they have in fact thrived on the slippages and ambiguities of their relationship to one another." Leroy, who draws from Day (2016), offers a useful dialectical approach to slavery and colonialism, one that represents a constructive way to think about occupation and what that means today. Leroy clarifies that "for all their differences, settler colonialism and slavery are violent justifications for extermination—of bodies, of sovereignty, of self-possession. Suspending claims to exceptionalism allows us to see how such forms of extermination blend into one another." Additionally, if occupation born from this dialectic means to seize or take possession of a place, then the dialectic of colonialism and slavery are also about empire beyond nation-state borders:

> The United States has exported the dual logic of colonialism and racism through its own imperial ventures as well as through its political and cultural relationships to other settler states. This export process has been crucial to the overlapping influence of ideas about settlement and Blackness *even in* colonial situations that may lack a clear indigenous population or a history of slavery, as is the case in twentieth- and twenty-first-century U.S. expansion into the Pacific and Middle East. (Leroy 2016, 1)

The terrain of occupation shifts, the context within which it is created remains, and its manifestations in educational projects abroad are familiar. For instance, Coloma (2009, 496–497) argues that in places like the Philippines, U.S. imperialism and its attendant formations around colonialism and race shaped the schooling programs imposed on Filipinos, arguing that "the schooling for African Americans became the prevailing racial template for the colonial pedagogy of Filipino/as." It also compels us to think of places where empire carves borders.

One only has to look at day-to-day manifestations of occupation in the United States to see occupation in action. Anti-Blackness functions to reify settler identity, which at its core is about settler futurity, the discursive, ideological, and structural moves settlers make to protect settler spaces, indeed settler nativeness (Tuck and Yang 2012), which are constantly being negotiated and violently performed:

> "These white folks, they think the world belongs to them," Grandma told me 12 hours after Susie Jackson, Ethel Lance, Clementa Pinckney, Tywanza Sanders, Cynthia Hurd, Sharonda Coleman-Singleton, Depyane Middleton Doctor, Daniel Simmons and Myra Thompson were murdered in a black Charleston church by a cowardly white American thug. "White folks been misusing us since I been in this world, if you wanna know the truth, Kie. If you expect any thing more after all they done, you the world's biggest fool." (Laymon 2015)

Here, Kiese Laymon's narrative, a response to the terrorist massacre of nine African Americans in Charleston, North Carolina, moves my thinking within the U.S. settler colonial context, pushing me to link settler identity and war. His grandmother lays out the terrain of our expectations vis-à-vis white people and white supremacy. It also reminds me of Barker's (2016) challenge to us that "we need to be careful about grouping all racial, ethnic, diaspora, and immigrant communities in with settlers and pitting them and their presumably shared struggles for civil rights against Indigenous sovereignty and territorial claims." For me, a generative starting point is therefore occupation.

In essence, settler subjectivities are about learning and maintaining occupation. The white supremacist terrorist Dylann Roof's own words accusing Blacks of "taking over the country" are a chilling testament to the specificity of white nationalism as inherently one of occupation, an occupation that has to account for perceived threats. Indeed, one only needs to look at Donald Trump's diatribes against Mexicans to understand how reliably unstable occupation subjectivities are: They stand in permanent fear of their destabilization by Blacks, Latinos, Asians, Muslims, American Indians, etc. Afropessimism has mapped out this ideological and bodily taxonomy of the settler in opposition to Blackness (King 2013; Wynters 1995, 2003). Indeed, for Blackness, Indigeneity, and other dispossessions to be understood dialectically, land and bodies must both be the sites of our spacialized investigations within an occupation framework (King 2013, Solis 2013).

Returning to the importance of multiple colonialisms in place, land (and the interactions of peoples, bodies, and the nonhuman) becomes an important component for thinking around the specificities of occupation subjectivities. Thus, I argue we must disentangle the messy ways that, for example, in the Southwest of the United States Blackness and white supremacy formulated in the Anglo expansion in North America is different than the caste system used in parts of the Southwest and Mexico. Specifically, the way territory, or land, and citizenship is imagined and operationalized in such contexts differs as well. This originary colonial difference (Mignolo 2000) does not disappear once the U.S. settler state occupied the lands we now refer to as the Southwest; rather, it complicates how we must conceive of occupation identities that overlap and intersect. Such an entanglement, or border thinking, is precisely the type of thinking needed when we consider places like the border because it embodies and marks such types of distinctions. If Blackness is an ontological marker inherent to white settler colonial identity, and if spatial expansion and thus settler occupation relies on Black death and inhumanity, then Black death—both the threat and reality of it—is central and constitutive to occupation in settler contexts. Hence, we can understand the administration of such death as constitutive, indeed inherent, in settler colonial contexts: Death is a foundational aspect of occupation.

## WHEN THE BORDER WALL LOOKS LIKE IT'S FROM JURASSIC PARK

Driving on the border highway, exiting to my mom's house, I am confronted with the Border Wall, which looks like one of those large fences from the Jurassic Park films made to contain and keep out vicious dinosaurs. I know who the undesirables are in this case. Looking across the border to the other side, I breathe in a colonial project in action: The smell of the *aguas negras*, untreated sewer water, from the other side of the river wafts over, pulled into the house by our swamp cooler. The pungent smell reminds me that a thin red line of economic and political policy allows me to sit in one of the safest cities in the United States while just on the other side sits Juarez, formerly one of the most violent (Sack 2015, 5). But that thin red line that announces the limits of safety also announces the privileges we obtain as citizens and residents of empire, closer to the belly of the beast, the heart of global capital. Nevertheless, we are affected by the violent and ongoing economic and political policies of a narco-state. We know the dead. We grieve them, tied by blood, connected by family, connected by old histories of geography and place: The thin red line becomes emplaced and the river a concrete culvert separating the United States from Mexico.

Photo courtesy of Dolores Calderón

One might say that along the border you have parallel yet intimate wars, experienced differentially depending on location but experienced nevertheless. Indeed, in war there are those that are at the front lines, those that are in danger but far enough from the war zone that their lives are lived uneasily but with some semblance of safety—and those from whom war marches, who live their lives from the comfort of empire: a thin red line.

I remember seeing a post on Facebook from *El Diario de Juarez* that a child was killed at a party in Juarez. I clicked on the link, and the name of the boy's school on the U.S. side caught my attention. This was the school two of my sisters taught at. I texted them the name of the child and asked if they knew him. I really did not think much of texting them in what was the middle of the school day for them, thinking that they already knew about this and that they would not check my text until after school, anyway. But that was not the case. One of my sisters saw my text and started crying. Her students wanted to know what was wrong. Though she did not tell them, she asked another teacher if she had heard about this young child's death. That teacher also did not know and was likewise devastated. Word got to the principal, and he was angry that word was spreading at the school. He called my other sister in and asked her if she had been telling other teachers about the student's death. She broke down crying. She had not seen my text. This young child was one of her students. His seat had sat empty. Now she knew why. He was shot in the back at a party—another victim of the war that rages just on the other side of the river.

As Alma, a human rights activist in Juarez states: "We are in the middle of a 'war,' which is a war but isn't. We don't know what the warzones are or who the enemy is . . . so in general there's a feeling of insecurity and fear that has changed daily life for men and women in Chihuahua" (Sack 2015, 30). Across the border is a war to cleanse the populations in these hamlets. The reasons given, whispered, are multiple: to make the lands available for commercial development for the new Tornillo-Guadalupe international bridge that will cross at this place and to exploit the natural resources rumored to be abundant in the area. Here, capital is reterritorializing, disappearing, dispossessing, and exterminating people—like it has before—for the purposes of empire. War is occupation, and occupation comes at the cost of someone.

But for my family, for my community, the story of the young boy is not the beginning nor the end of such stories, for in the Juarez Valley, a series of agricultural villages across the border near Juarez, the violence was worse than that of the purported deadliest city in Mexico (del Bosque 2012). In this desert there were and are new occupations, different occupations that

do not value the lives of those dispossessed: a different colonialist enterprise I have yet to find an adequate label for. I believe this is challenging
because the neat categories offered, such as settler, post, or neo, are all aspects of the hybrid colonial project that functions plurally in a Mexico
that has struggled since its inception as a nation with the challenge of plu-
rality and place (Joseph and Nugent 1994).

Occupations shift, but the violence inherent in this process of the colonialisms in place does not. Saul Reyes Salazar, an activist from Guadalupe,
Chihuahua, explains:

> One thing we have to have clear is that when the army came [to the
> Juarez Valley] and the war on drugs started, the traffickers fled. Who
> is left then, in the town? Those who did not have the financial means
> to escape and those, who, like my family said, "Why am I going to
> leave? I don't owe anybody anything." The war on drugs served as a
> smokescreen to eliminate opponent and other critical voices . . . voices
> that make the government uncomfortable: journalists, human rights
> defenders and political leaders.
>
> Guadalupe is one of the places that has been hit the hardest by the
> violence. There are more than triple the number of deaths per capita
> than Ciudad Juarez . . . a fact recognized by the UN. Only about
> 25 percent of the population remains. You also have more than 100
> houses that have been burn down and many more destroyed by
> vandalism . . . Guadalupe is practically a ruin . . . I believe that for all
> these dead there will never be justice . . . no one will be detained . . .
> no one jailed . . . no one condemned . . .
>
> (SACK 2015, 81–82)

Saul's testimony speaks to the reality of lives on the border. He notes that
some fled (some into the United States, where his remaining family eventually received political asylum). Guadalupe is important to me. My great-
grandparents are from there, my grandfather born there, my father born
there, though before this my family hailed from Ysleta and Socorro in
Texas. In this brief history of me, the transit of empire, of occupation, is
made manifest.

While there is tragedy and suffering in this narrative of violence, there
is also resistance, one that the landed knowledge that guides this delibera-
tive essay reminds me must also be voiced. I only have to look within my
own family to bear witness to a tremendous capacity for survivance: from
an immigration attorney who takes on Mexicans fleeing state-sponsored
violence in Mexico pro bono; to the women who have been for seven years

now, month in, month out, collecting food and other items to send to the besieged people of an ancestral town on the other side of the river; to the teachers who teach in the public school system and in a school within walking distance of the Rio Grande and are caught up in the neoliberalization of schools in the United States, which cares little for the complex, bordered lives of its students that live out the violence of occupation.

Indeed, territoriality, as I stated above, must also account for what Jodi Byrd refers to as the transit of empire. Though she speaks of the Indian as the elusive ghostlike figure in the context of U.S. empire, her idea of transit of empire allows me also to consider the glimpses that the refugee, the asylee, the immigrant, or the undocumented offer into the transit of empire as a movement emplaced, as a trajectory of ideologies and practices across time *and* space. Without a doubt, these narratives also allow me to consider the transit of war, of occupation in relation to Blackness. This offers me the opportunity to explore nuanced and spacialized research questions and projects that take seriously the particularities of colonialities. While I can put these ideas into conversation with notions of race and power, I must always endeavor to root these ideas in the complicated transits that produce and situate them.

## *Looking Beyond These Borders and Lands*

In conclusion, these borderlands help concretize what coloniality theories hint at: that the colonial project(s) is manifested most concretely as a continued occupation. This is why occupation, though it has gone through different iterations, continues to reproduce itself. It is colonialism in transit, extracting tribute, whether in the form of labor, natural resources, or lives. To be sure, the modern nation-state produced by modern European colonialism is, after all, about occupation. Is this a reflection of what some refer to as the state of permanent war in the current mode of global capital? Looking toward another border, toward another settler project, might illuminate some of these answers and signal another type of potentiality that, like Blackness, figures into our accounting of occupation: Israel and Palestine. According to Feldman (2015), who argues that the Israeli-Palestinian conflict has fundamentally shaped the idea and practice around racism in the United States, "the analytic of permanent war," which was originally framed by the "anticolonial writers and activists" of the late 1960s and early 1970s of "Africa, Latin America and South Asia, and the extensive effects of the declared 1967 and 1973 wars between Arab states and Israel . . . framed the violence of racism in American life as animated by a seemingly permanent war-making structure" (5). For Feldman, the naturalization of the Israeli-Palestinian conflict is representative of how this permanent war-making structure operates.

In other words, racism relies on the creation and maintenance of a perceived threat to fuel the ideological and structural manifestations of white supremacy, in the United States, for instance, this is something made concrete by the words of the white supremacist terrorist that executed nine Black lives, Trump's calls to build a wall along the U.S./Mexico border, and the terror of ICE raids on immigrant communities. Feldman explains: "To grasp and make critical the systemic contours of racism was to understand the long-standing racialized practices of threat-production adhering in the enduring violence of white supremacy and settler sovereignty" (5). The transit of occupation ideologies and practices maintains a permanent threat that has become a key ideological tool used to drive policy and practice, something that we see schools do through zero-tolerance policies (Unzueta 2014), for example. Returning to the place from where I speak—the border—I can also observe how in Mexico, religion, politics, and popular media play primary roles, as used by the state, to instill a sense of a different type of threat production, perhaps better understood as the permanence of violence. For some (Lomnitz 2005), the centrality of death in the Mexican imaginary, generated by a structural governance that employs killing, is representative of the administration of death by the Mexican state.

Consequently, in Mexico, death operates as an important ideological and discursive product that is administered to inform political and social life. Yet the actuality of death (premature or premeditated death facilitated by the state) is enacted in gross disproportion in the margins of Mexican society. The irony is that the margin *is* most of Mexico. Like the majority of the world's countries, whose economies serve empire, Mexico's people are disposable within the framework of global capital that searches for cheap labor, then moves on to the next exploitable site. In Mexico, the state has dealt with a populace perceived as entirely expendable. This has fomented a state in which social and real death permeates its legal, political, and social institutions. Moreover, in Mexico, the state uses the Narco arm of the state to reconsolidate power. For instance, in the period of the supposed war against the Narcos in Mexico from 2006 to 2012, sixty thousand were killed in Mexico. In Juarez alone, it is estimated that over ten thousand were killed during this period (Booth 2012). Yet just southeast of Juarez in

El Valle de Juarez, "By 2009, the valley, with a population of 20,000, had a shocking murder rate of 1,600 per 100,000 inhabitants—six times higher than its neighboring 'deadliest city in the world'" (del Bosque 2012). In Mexico and along the border there is an explicit governmentality that allows such death to occur. This is, I argue, the governmentality that awaits us in the United States, a logical structuring of occupation rendered more visible by the current Republican administration.

To inhabit the space of the occupiers, to be complicit in the project of occupation, requires an investment with such logics and or ideologies that sustain occupation. That does not mean, however, that one becomes an occupier; rather, one becomes entangled with the political, institutional, and ideological mechanisms that maintain occupation. This is also predicated on the existing colonial contexts upon which occupation exists, and in some places, there are different occupying regimes layered on one another (for example, Hispanos in the Southwest). Blackness, like Indigeneity, represents the underside or dialectical element of occupation in a settler society, where territory is read as both body and land.

Therefore, going forward as educational researchers, keeping in mind war as occupation, here are some suggestions to consider:

> Because occupation is transient, we have to attend to colonial-blind ideologies in schooling (Calderón, 2014) and colonial aphasia writ large (Stoler 2011);
>
> Epistemologically, we must attend to how epistemologies of ignorance might preclude engagement with occupation ideologies and practices in education;
>
> Theoretically, methodologically, and concretely, we must territorialize our approaches;
>
> We must remain vigilant to the way settlement as occupation influences us;
>
> We must ask how the borders we encounter—the real borders of peoples (Indigenous, settler, arrivant)—shape our practice; and
>
> We must ask how borders reshape, keep, protect, and maintain occupation education.

My hope is that the preliminary exploration offered here presents a timely entry into the growing area of decolonial studies in education. Moreover, this discussion reminds us that as we speak of decolonizing work, we must remain attendant to the inherent land-based components of this work (Tuck and Yang 2012). In other words, to decolonize affirms a radical (or not-so-radical, depending on your position) understanding of education as a mechanism of occupation that in turn implies an ongoing "war" with populations that do not facilitate the continued occupation of territory, what Tuck and Yang (2012) refer to as "settler futurity." We cannot continue to ignore the injustice of occupation in our moral obligation to create pedagogical spaces of hope and humanity that are derived from the material realities of occupation.

In conclusion, I offer the testimony of one of the many dispossessed, Saul Reyes:

> But some day I'll go back [to Guadalupe] and erect a great monument that says in waging war Calderon [former president of Mexico] supported the deaths of all these people. And all the names will be there . . . so the memory of those who died stays with us forever because these were human lives. (Sack 2015, 83).

Dead but not forgotten. I keep my dead with me. The dead keep me, through land, to place and memory. Though wars and occupations persist, our collective memory and resistance is greater.

### REFERENCES

Alexander, M. 2012. *The new Jim Crow: Mass incarceration in the age of colorblindness*. New York: The New Press.

Anzaldúa, G. 1987. *Borderlands: La frontera*. Vol. 3. San Francisco: Aunt Lute.

Bang, M., L. Curley, A. Kessel, et al. 2014. Muskrat theories, tobacco in the streets, and living Chicago as Indigenous lands. *Environmental Education Research* 20:37–55.

Barker, J. 2016. *The analytic constraints of settler colonialism*. Paper presented at the annual meeting of the American Studies Association, November 17–20, Denver, Colo.

Byrd, J. A. 2011. *The transit of empire: Indigenous critiques of colonialism*. Minneapolis: University of Minnesota Press.

Cajete, G. 1994. *Look to the mountain: An ecology of Indigenous education*. Durango, Colo.: Kivaki.

Calderón, D. 2008. Indigenous metaphysics: Challenging Western knowledge organization in social studies curriculum. Ph.D. diss. University of California, Los Angeles.

———. 2014. Speaking back to Manifest Destinies: A land-based approach to critical curriculum inquiry. *Environmental Education Research* 20 (1): 24–36.

Coloma, R. S. 2009. "Destiny has thrown the Negro and the Filipino under the tutelage of America": Race and curriculum in the age of empire. *Curriculum Inquiry* 39 (4): 495–519.

———. 2013. Empire: An analytical category for educational research. *Educational Theory* 63 (6): 639–658.

Coloma, R. S., A. Means, and A. Kim. 2009. Palimpsest histories and catachrestic interventions. *Counterpoints* 369:3–22.

Day, I. 2015. Being or nothingness: Indigeneity, antiblackness, and settler colonial critique. *Critical Ethnic Studies* 1 (2): 102–121.

Del Bosque, M. 2012. "The Deadliest Place in Mexico. Who's Killing the People of the Juarez Valley?" *Texas Observer* 104, no. 3.

Dumas, M. J. 2014. "Losing an arm": Schooling as a site of Black suffering. *Race Ethnicity and Education* 17 (1): 1–29.

———. 2016. Against the dark: Antiblackness in education policy and discourse. *Theory into Practice* 55 (1): 11–19.

Feldman, K. P. 2015. *A Shadow over Palestine: The Imperial Life of Race in America*. Minneapolis: University of Minnesota Press.

Grosfuguel, R. 2007. The epistemic decolonial turn: Beyond political-economy paradigms. *Cultural Studies* 21:211–223.

Hartman, S. V. 1997. *Scenes of subjection: Terror, slavery, and self-making in nineteenth-century America*. New York: Oxford University Press.

Joseph, G. M., and D. Nugent. 1994. *Everyday forms of state formation: Revolution and the negotiation of rule in modern Mexico*. Durham, N.C.: Duke University Press.

King, T. L. 2013. *In the clearing: Black female bodies, space, and settler colonial landscapes*. Ph.D. diss. University of Maryland, College Park.

———. 2014. "Labor's aphasia": Toward antiblackness as constitutive to settler colonialism. *Decolonization: Indigeneity, Education & Society*.

Laymon, K. 2015. Black churches taught us to forgive white people. We learned to shame ourselves. *Guardian*, June 23. https://www.theguardian.com/commentisfree/2015/jun/23/black-churchesforgive-white-people-shame.

Leroy, J. 2016. Black history in occupied territory: On the entanglements of slavery and settler colonialism. *Theory & Event* 19 (4).

Lomnitz, C. 2005. *Death and the idea of Mexico*. New York: Zone.

Lugones, M. 2008. The coloniality of gender. *Worlds and Knowledges Otherwise* 2:1–17.

Medak-Saltzman, D. 2015. Empire's haunted logics: Comparative colonialisms and the challenges of incorporating indigeneity. *Critical Ethnic Studies* 1 (2): 11–32.

Mignolo, W. D. 2000. *Local histories/global designs: Coloniality, subaltern knowledges, and border thinking.* Princeton, N.J.: Princeton University Press.

Paperson, L. 2014. A ghetto land pedagogy: An antidote for settler environmentalism. *Environmental Education Research* 20 (1): 115–130.

Pewewardy, C. 2002. Learning styles of American Indian/Alaska Native students: A review of the literature and implications for practice. *Journal of American Indian Education* 41:22–56.

Quijano, A. 2000. Coloniality of power, Eurocentrism, and Latin America. *Nepantla: Views from the South* 1:533–580.

Robinson, C. J. 1983. *Black Marxism: The making of the Black radical tradition.* Chapel Hill: University of North Carolina Press.

Sack, J. 2015. *La lucha: The story of Lucha Castro and human rights in Mexico.* New York: Verso.

Sexton, J. 2016. The vel of slavery: Tracking the figure of the unsovereign. *Critical Sociology* 42 (4/5): 583–597.

Smith, A. 2012. Indigeneity, settler colonialism, white supremacy. In *Racial formation in the twenty-first century*, 66–90. Berkeley: University of California Press.

Solis, S. 2013. *Essay on feminist discourse on land and body.* Unpublished manuscript. University of Utah, Salt Lake City.

Stoler, A. L. 2011. Colonial aphasia: Race and disabled histories in France. *Public Culture* 23 (1): 121–156.

Tuana, N. 2004. Coming to understand: Orgasm and the epistemology of ignorance. *Hypatia* 19 (1): 194–232.

———. 2006. The speculum of ignorance: The women's health movement and epistemologies of ignorance. *Hypatia* 21 (3): 1–19.

Tuck, E., and K. W. Yang. 2012. Decolonization is not a metaphor. *Decolonization: Indigeneity, Education, and Society* 1 (1): 1–40.

———. 2014. R-words: Refusing research. In *Humanizing research: Decolonizing qualitative inquiry with youth and communities*, ed. D. Paris and M. T. Winn, 223–248. Thousand Oaks, Calif.: Sage.

Unzueta, R. 2014. Dissertation proposal: Carceral schooling. University of Utah, Salt Lake City.

Vizenor, G. R. 1994. *Manifest manners: Postindian warriors of survivance.* Lincoln: University of Nebraska Press.

———. 2008. *Survivance: Narratives of native presence.* Lincoln: University of Nebraska Press.

Wilderson, F. B., III. 2010. *Red, white, and black: Cinema and the structure of U.S. antagonisms.* Durham, N.C.: Duke University Press.

Wolfe, P. 2006. Settler colonialism and the elimination of the native. *Journal of Genocide Research* 8 (4): 387–409.

Wynter, Sylvia. 1995. 1492: A new world view. In *Race, discourse, and the origin of the Americas: A new world view*, ed. V. Lawrence Hyatt and R. Nettleford. Washington: Smithsonian Institute Press.

———. 2003. "Unsettling the coloniality of being/power/truth/freedom: Towards the human, after man, its overrepresentation—An argument." *CR: The new centennial review* 3 (3): 257–337.

This work would not have been possible without the support and feedback from Dolores Calderón, Ryan Gildersleeve, Dimpal Jain, Maria Ledesma, and David Stovall. They helped shape our ideas and the direction of this project from the outset.

We also express sincere gratitude to the chapter authors, Suzie Abajian, Yousef K. Baker, Dolores Calderón, Edward R. Curammeng, Chandni Desai, Maryam S. Griffin, Heather Horsley, Clayton Pierce, David Stovall, Allyson Tintiangco-Cubales, Sepehr Vakil, Shirin Vossoughi, Connie Wun, and Miguel Zavala—many of whom could have published their pieces in other forums but understood the spirit of this project and so graciously contributed.

We are grateful to our editor, Richard Morrison, at Fordham University Press, who saw the promise of this project years ago and helped shepherd it to completion. His guidance for two novice editors was immeasurable.

We are deeply indebted to Jordan Beltran Gonzales, for his amazing conceptual and technical editing. His work, which does not show up in the authors' credits, was not only significant but central to this project and much of our writing. His work clarifies, sharpens, and strengthens the ideas throughout the book.

We also thank our friends and families, who have sacrificed time with us as we labored on this project. Curating this volume truly was a project of our passion. We are honored to have participated with such community-oriented, radical, and dedicated scholars in the creation of this text.

DR. SUZIE ABAJIAN is Assistant NTT Professor at Occidental College, Los Angeles, California. Dr. Abajian is a community organizer, serves on the steering committee of the Ethnic Studies Now Coalition, was involved in the successful campaign to implement an ethnic studies graduation requirement in the Los Angeles Unified School District, and in 2015 was elected to her local school board.

DR. ARSHAD I. ALI is Assistant Professor of Educational Research at George Washington University. Dr. Ali is an interdisciplinary scholar who studies youth culture, race, identity, and political engagement in the lives of young people. He has published numerous research articles on Muslim youth identities and politics. The fundamental question he is concerned with is how young people from historically marginalized communities come to make sense of urban life in the U.S., and how they find meaning in their lives through understanding the manifestations of political and cultural ideologies in daily action.

DR. YOUSEF K. BAKER is Assistant Professor of International Studies at California State University, Long Beach. His work focuses on theories of globalization and development, social movements, nationalism, and questions of race and migration, with a specialization in contemporary Middle East and North Africa.

DR. TRACY LACHICA BUENAVISTA is Professor of Asian American Studies at California State University, Northridge (CSUN), and co–principal investigator of the CSUN Dreamers, Resources, Empowerment, Advocacy, and Mentorship (DREAM) Center. Dr. Buenavista has published articles on U.S. Pilipinx college access and retention, undocumented Asian student experiences, and the militarization of immigration reform.

DR. DOLORES CALDERÓN is Associate Professor at the Fairhaven College of Interdisciplinary Studies at Western Washington University. She was born and raised in the Lower Valley of El Paso, Texas, where her family

(Mexican and Tigua) has lived since the time of the Pueblo Revolt. Her research focuses on Indigenous education, culturally relevant/multicultural education, Chicana(o)/Indigenous student success, critical race theories, and multiple colonialism.

Dr. Edward R. Curammeng is Assistant Professor in the Teacher Education Division at California State University, Dominguez Hills. His research examines the relationship between ethnic studies and education in shaping the experiences of students and teachers of color. He received a PhD in education at the University of California, Los Angeles, and an MA in Asian American studies from San Francisco State University, where he taught with Pin@y Educational Partnerships (PEP). He is also a member of the People's Education Movement.

Dr. Chandni Desai is Assistant Professor at the University of Toronto. Her research focuses on the radical tradition of Palestinian resistance culture in the Palestinian liberation struggle. Her areas of interest include social movements, art and activism, decolonization, critical race theory, anticolonial feminism, and anticolonial/postcolonial theory.

Dr. Maryam S. Griffin is Assistant Professor in the School of Interdisciplinary Arts and Sciences at the University of Washington, Bothell. Her research areas include movement and mobility studies, people power and resistance, the racialization of Middle Easterners in the United States, critical race theory, sociology of the Middle East, and sociology of law.

Dr. Heather L. Horsley is Assistant Professor of Literacy, Early, Bilingual, and Special Education at California State University, Fresno. Her research agenda is concerned with analyzing urban school reform initiatives and in-school programs that school reform leaders publicly justify as programs of opportunity, to understand if the goals function as intended from the perspective of those most affected by such programs.

Dr. Clayton Pierce is Assistant Professor at the Fairhaven College of Interdisciplinary Studies at Western Washington University. He is the co-editor of two volumes of the collected papers of Herbert Marcuse, *Philosophy, Psychoanalysis, and Emancipation* and *Marxism, Revolution, and Utopia*, and the author of *Education in the Age of Biocapitalism*. Pierce's most recent research, which appears in the *American Educational Research Journal*, focuses on W. E. B. Du Bois's work on caste education in the United States

Dr. David Stovall is Professor of Educational Policy Studies and African American Studies at the University of Illinois at Chicago. Using critical race theory, sociology, and critical policy analysis, his research engages the intersection of race, place, and school. He is the author of several articles and books, including *Born Out of Struggle: Critical Race Theory, School Creation, and the Politics of Interruption.*

DR. ALLYSON TINTIANGCO-CUBALES is Professor of Asian American Studies at San Francisco State University's College of Ethnic Studies and an affiliated faculty member in the Educational Leadership program. She is the founding director of Pin@y Educational Partnerships (PEP) and cofounder and codirector of Teaching Excellence Network (TEN) and Community Responsive Education (CRE). She has authored several books and numerous articles focusing on the development of ethnic studies curriculums and community responsive pedagogy.

DR. SEPEHR VAKIL is Assistant Professor of STEM Education and Associate Director of Equity and Inclusion in the Center for STEM Education at the University of Texas at Austin. Dr. Vakil's teaching and research are informed by sociocultural, cultural-historical, and critical theories of learning, practice, and pedagogy, and his work centers primarily on the cultural and political dimensions of STEM education, with a disciplinary focus in computer science and engineering.

DR. SHIRIN VOSSOUGHI is Assistant Professor of Learning Sciences at Northwestern University's School of Education and Social Policy, where she draws on ethnographic methods to study the social, cultural, historical, and political dimensions of learning. Bringing together cultural-historical approaches to learning, interaction analysis, and theories of embodiment, Vossoughi seeks to integrate macropolitical concerns (the roots of educational inequity, transnational migration, neoliberalism) with detailed studies of educational settings that imagine and inhabit alternative social and intellectual relations.

DR. CONNIE WUN is the founder and director of Transformative Research: An Institute for Research and Social Transformation. Her areas of expertise include community-driven research, violence against girls and women of color, and school discipline and punishment. She has written extensively in academic journals and the popular press about intersectional violence against women and girls of color as well as about schools as sites of anti-Black violence.

DR. MIGUEL ZAVALA is Associate Professor in the Attallah College of Educational Studies at Chapman University and teaches in the Integrated

Educational Studies and Master of Arts in Curriculum and Instruction (MACI) programs. His research interests include ethnic studies, decolonizing pedagogies, and grassroots organizing. Over the last fifteen years he has been involved in grassroots organizing and the Paulo Freire Democratic Project.